MELISSA BROWN

Number 1 FLINT HILL

Published in Australia by Overarch Publishing
mulysa.online
First published in Australia in 2020

Cover design: Nathan Thomas
Typesetting: WorkingType Studio

Disclaimer: This is a work of fiction. Names and characters are purely the imagination of the author. Any resemblance to actual persons, living or dead is purely coincidental. Some institutions, towns and historical places mentioned within the work are real and reveal a true depiction of life in colonial Victoria.

National Library of Australia Cataloguing-in-Publication Entry:
Creator: Brown, Melissa, author

NATIONAL LIBRARY OF AUSTRALIA
A catalogue record for this work is available from the National Library of Australia

Title: *Number 1 Flint Hill*
ISBN: 978-0-6488807-0-7 (paperback)
ISBN: 978-0-6488807-1-4 (ePub)

For Tander — for without whom
this story would have not come to light

Acknowledgements:

To my editor Dr Sharon Dean who gifted me her belief that this story needed to be shared.

Cover Design by Nathan Thomas who nailed the brief, capturing the soul of the story with just one image.

Chapter 1

His cheekbone hurt as his spectacle frame dug into his skin, but still he pushed his face against the timber. As only one of his eyes could garner a view through the peephole, it was his hope that his distorted vision was dealing him a cruel deception. He squinted so he could hone in on the tiny form. She faced the door and was unaware of being spied on. With her head drawn down to her chest and her body slumped against the wall, she looked like a child.

He stepped away and pulled his spectacles from his face. Shaking his head as he placed them in his pocket, he drew a deep breath into his nostrils. Disbelief took hold. Could he have come to the wrong cell after all? He looked at the number. This was the cell recorded on the ledger.

He leaned onto the door once more and allowed the timber to absorb his body weight. It would not do for him to let his frustration and confusion best him at this present moment. He took another deep breath and readjusted his eye to the peephole. A second look did not dull his senses. He shook his head back and forth in disgust. To see any human being in this situation was disturbing enough, but to know it was *her*, was just too painful to acknowledge.

Her limbs protruded from a filthy smock. She was so covered in dirt it was difficult to see where the fabric ceased and her skin began. Although transfixed by the confronting image before him, he forced himself to move forward with his plan. While the disturbed sounds of deranged inmates filtered from the locked cells and through the dark hallway, he had to make very little sound. The nurse on duty could appear at any moment and he did not want to call attention to unusual sounds rising from the unlocking of a cell door.

He adjusted his stance ever so slightly so he could slip the key into the padlock. Hearing the click of the barrel, he slid the shank from the metal coupling and placed the padlock in his pocket. He grasped the bolt and slowly released it from its sheath. The sound it made was loud to his own ears and he lifted his shoulders in reaction. He looked to his right, where darkness enveloped the end of the ward. Now looking to the left, he could see nothing more than the stairs leading upward with brick walls on either side. That narrow opening was the only exit for which he could make his escape with her.

He peered back through the peephole, waiting for the sound of the door to force a response from her. She neither looked toward, nor acknowledged his presence in any way. As he stepped over the threshold, cold air raced up his trouser leg. He shuddered. Again, he doubted his choice of cell as he took slow steady steps toward her. Dropping to his knees, he placed his face close to hers. He looked at her, really looked at her, and his inspection produced the answer. He had chosen the correct cell but felt no satisfaction in this triumph. Terror took hold of him and he held his breath. How could she have become *this?*

Her hair hung in thin strands that stuck against the hollow of her cheeks. The beautiful, smooth skin he had once kissed with tenderness was now filthy and rough. He halted the intake of air through his nostrils, taking haphazard breaths via his mouth to stave the stench exuding from her. He had considered this moment many times, but he had never anticipated the dismal condition in which he would find her. The disgust keened through him as he wondered if, since being locked away, she had even once been bathed, given a clean nightgown or had her hair brushed.

From the corner of his eye he saw a rat scamper along the wall, undoubtedly in search of food, or more likely, escape. This rodent was wasting his short life, he thought. There was neither a crumb for him to feast on nor a drop of water to be found. The creature could spend hours scouring the abysmal seven-by-eleven-foot cell but would find no joy.

His pity turned to anger. Inhaling then expelling a gust of breath from his mouth, he cast a clear eye over her deranged body and wrestled with the reality of his decision. He would follow through with his plan to secure her release from this hellhole.

Gathering her in his arms, he walked to the open door. As he checked the corridor in both directions, he heard a nurse's voice in the cell opposite. The door was closed but the sound of two women caught in an argument was prevalent. With the keening sounds of other inmates careening around him, he pulled the door closed and dropped her to her feet. He held her with one hand whilst grappling to pull the door closed behind him. Her knees gave way as he grunted to keep hold of her. The sound of the bolt sliding back into the locked position made a hiss. He grimaced. Looking to the door opposite, he prayed it would not swing open at this very moment to expose him with his quarry.

He reached into his pocket and retrieved the padlock. Swivelling the shank around and threading it back through the coupling, he snapped it back into place. Propping her wrist up over his shoulder, he reached awkwardly around the back of his neck to grasp it. The befouled smock was bunching at her hip as he gripped her close to his side. He propelled her forward to the end of the hallway where the width of the stairs looked set to thwart his mission. Keeping her at his side, he hoisted her off her feet. The walls dragged at them as though trying to halt her departure. He struggled against them, winning the battle, as he pulled her up and onto each tread. She was weightless but her frailty was of concern. The curves that had once defined her body had succumbed to the deprivations of a ruinous diet. Only those the devil possessed could render the useless want or need for food to nurture or assist in survival of the soul. He now doubted that he had intimately known this woman at all. He could not recognise one nuance of the beauty he had vowed to love, honour and protect.

As a young corporal, he had sensed his life was set out before him. This feeling had compounded after he had met her, with the thought of creating a family and a life with a good woman cementing his future. He would have never envisaged the events that would lead them here to this remarkable end.

He pushed these thoughts clear and turned his mind to the task ahead. The administration area was close. It was here that he was at greatest risk of being caught. Matron's office and the door to the main entrance both lay ahead of him. He eyed the heavy panelled door, willing it to stay closed. He would not consider such an obvious escape route and turned instead to his immediate left, racing along as her body bobbed and her head lolled forward.

The luggage store was only halfway along the corridor. He forgot momentarily that she could not hold her own weight and loosened his grip on her. She began to flop forward. He quickly steadied her and propped her against the wall. Each time he released the slightest pressure in his grasp, her body would fold or slip downward. Eventually, he pushed the length of his body against her, pinning her to the wall so he could free his hands. He scrounged in his pocket and found the key. Securing it between his fingers, he shoved it into the padlock and cursed as it resisted his haphazard attempt to turn it.

'Come on, come on,' he said, with desperation, feeding his fear they would be seen. Finally, the padlock relented. He pushed the door open and could barely retain his grasp of her as her body slid down the wall.

'I got ye,' he said, grabbing her beneath the armpits. Surely it would be easier to lift rather than drag her? He stepped carefully through the open door, checking he would not trip on anything beyond its threshold. Once inside, he noticed a chair and lowered her into it. He then pushed the door closed behind him with the heel of his boot. He knew the room would be cast into darkness. He felt his way along the interior wall until he found the gas lantern housed on a nail. He pushed the glass upward and struck a match to the wick. A brilliant flame appeared and suddenly the corner of the room was cast in light.

Looking down at her, he cocked his head to the side to view her face. The light danced across her hollow cheekbones. She stared ahead, oblivious to the change from dark to light. She was totally unaware of him at all. Her eyes flickered slightly then closed. He held his breath. While her movements were slow, he could feel that there was still some life in her. The skin of her eyelids danced a few moments before opening once more. She looked up at him and while her vacant stare did not connect with his, he was startled by the unexpectedness of it.

He whispered in desperation, 'Are you still in there, Audrey?'

There was nothing to be gained by his question. She was no longer that pretty young thing he met only two years earlier. He closed his eyes to halt the pain but the memory of their first meeting skittered through his conscience.

Corporal Michael McGowan had been summoned to visit Colonel Price. As a young corporal who had his sights set on a higher rank, he could not rebuff the invitation to his superior's hometown of Ararat. As he gathered his duffel from the rack above his seat and the train pulled to a stop, the sound of the brakes and the hiss of steam reminded him of home. England was so far away in distance but never too far from his memory. He missed the insular surrounds of towns that were located close together.

Australia had proven nothing like home in that regard. Here, it took hours of travel to traverse the countryside and arrive at your destination. The climate was much unlike England also. Though the winters were not dissimilar, the summers were protracted and soul destroying. He was thankful for his current posting on the coast. At the least the beach with its cool breezes allowed some reprieve from the harsh temperatures.

Pushing his arm into the sleeve of his jacket, Michael cursed the heat once more. Ignoring the stifling discomfort, he pushed the buttons through the holes and tugged the garment downward. He had travelled all the way from Queenscliff and the relentless hours of transit had taken their toll on his appearance. Peering at his reflection in the train window, he decided a visit to the barber was of paramount importance.

He welcomed the silence whilst the barber shaved him. It was only after the man had removed the heated towel from the young corporal's face that he posed a question to him. 'What brings you here to our fine town …' the barber hesitated as he craned his neck to look toward the coat stand, where he caught sight of the insignia on the arm of Michael's jacket, '… Corporal?'

'I'm here to visit with Colonel Price.' Michael replied, watching the barber's reflection in the mirror. He had gathered the clippers in his hand and was lining them steady above Michael's ear. As he leaned low to see precisely where he was to trim he said, 'Ah, an excellent man. Well respected, too.'

'So I have heard,' Michael said, tilting his head to the side to allow the barber a better vantage point.

'Is this your first visit to Ararat?'

'Yes, a short visit I am afraid. I need to get back to my post.'

'Well, I hope you decide to return for some leisure if time permits you.'

As Michael exited the barber's premises, he glanced along the street. The Shire Hall Hotel's beckoning door was only a few feet away. His hankering for a drink was strong, but he would visit the establishment after his meeting with the Colonel. He did not want the smell of liquor on his breath. That would only serve to jeopardise the man's opinion of him.

A young lady walked towards him. She was a pretty thing. Normally, when confronted by a woman's handsome appearance, he would exuberantly voice his delight. However, in this instance, he was reminded that a small town such as Ararat would have word swirling that he had shown disrespect to one of its fine women. Her gown covered her figure in a way that was appropriate for her age and social standing. Nonetheless, whilst he knew it to be wrong he could not help but cast his eyes over her entire form. Following the line from her shoulder to her shoes and back upward again, his gaze stopped at her face and his stomach quivered momentarily, for she was returning his attentions. Her eyes too, moved slowly from his face to his collar and then touched on every button of his jacket before travelling down the line of his trousers to settle on his boots.

The cheeky minx, he thought, as he waited for her gaze to wander back up to his face. He arched one eyebrow as their eyes finally met and held. Had her mouth not turned up in a grin at that moment, he would have braced himself for an expression of disdain. After all, it was as though she had just been a lamb coveted by a wolf of lascivious hunger. He had not seen such beauty since leaving London. Until now, he had not realised how wealthy this district had become courtesy of those who had made the most of the gold that had been pulled from the ground. It showed promise that families in the district could afford their young charges an excellent education and in turn, good grooming.

He had heard that the town of Ararat did not have as much to offer as Ballarat and other districts — although one prized characteristic both places shared was the proliferation of establishments where booze and loose women were plentiful. Michael anticipated a visit to one of these hotels for a few ales and, in turn, an introduction to a category of significantly less fair women. For tonight, at least, a lower standard of female company would suffice. He could invite the vision of the young lady into his bed while pleasuring himself between the legs of a whore.

It had been so long since he had felt a woman's touch. Since the voyage from England, Fort Queenscliff had demanded his full attention, and in being away from home he had adapted to many changes. This newfound place, which the enemy would infiltrate should he and his fellow army men not fortify and protect it, was rugged. The vast coastline of Australia was beautiful but ferocious. If there was one thing of which he could be assured, it was that the feel of a woman and the things she could deliver were the same everywhere.

Pondering this thought, he arrived at the Colonel's home, which was not far from the centre of town. He had taken the time to walk and clear his mind to ready himself for the hopeful news about a higher rank and a new posting.

As he approached the home, he admired its wide verandas and the welcoming steps that invited one up to a large front door. The path leading him there was bordered on both sides with perfectly trimmed hedges. Tiny flowers poked their heads from beneath the hedges as though coming out from hiding to welcome him. He stomped his boots on the steps to shake off any dust that had collected on the soles. He did not want to leave any trace of dirt on Mrs Price's carpets. He would be the shame of the regiment.

He expected a maid to greet him and was caught off guard when the Colonel himself opened the door.

'Come in, come in, Corporal McGowan,' the Colonel ushered.

Michael stepped over the threshold and followed the Colonel down the hallway and into his office.

'Sit, sit.' The Colonel pointed to the chair with its back to the door as he walked around to the opposing side of his desk. He sat down and leaned back in his chair. 'How was the journey from Queenscliff?'

'Fine thank you, sir. Long.' He smiled as he looked up at the bookshelf to his left.

'To be sure. It has been some time since I made these sorts of transits myself. I prefer to be home for longer periods than away these days.'

Michael shifted his attention from the books back to the Colonel. 'You have a lovely home, sir. There would be little reason to want to turn from its comfort.'

'Well, I am not the young man I once was. I had much to prove and plenty of time to fulfil everything asked and expected of me. Now it is time for new appointments to be made.'

'You provided service beyond expectation, sir. I have heard the stories about you. Your ability to rally troops and to turn situations to your favour is well known, and something not achievable through luck. You are a tangible ally and respected by all who have served beneath you.'

The Colonel waved his hand dismissively. 'I earned my rank and due to this I now am in the position to gather the best in the regiment and disperse them to the most vulnerable fortifications.'

'I do know this, sir. I assume that is why I was summoned?'

'Yes. I decided to meet with you personally. I have a dedicated post that needs a particular type of soldier and you come highly recommended.'

'Well sir, I am flattered.' Michael adjusted his position on the seat and placed his flattened palm to the front of his jacket.

'Do not be. Not yet. The post is an attractive acquisition due to the importance of its location, however it is a tough assignment for that very reason. I feel you are the perfect choice for this outfit. You have proven your worth at Fort Queenscliff and you are definitely past the point of outgrowing your rank there.'

Michael was in no doubt that there could be any harsher post in Australia. 'With respect sir, considering the winds that blow across the bay to Fort Queenscliff, I cannot see how any placement could be more severe. The weather that crosses the ocean during the winter months is unrelenting, and the northerly winds in the summer are gruelling.'

'Let me assure you, the post I'm suggesting has a similar climate but is far enough away from Fort Queenscliff to give you a much needed challenge. The workload will disallow any thoughts of the weather that will roll around with the seasons.'

Michael stared at the Colonel, awaiting further information.

'From Fort Queenscliff, do you look across the rip from time to time, Corporal?'

'Ahhh.' Michael narrowed his eyes. 'Point Nepean.'

'Correct, and I have …' the Colonel ceased talking and turned his head at a slight angle.

Michael could hear clipped footfalls coming from beyond the office door.

'Audrey, is that you?' the Colonel hollered.

The door opened and Michael slowly alighted from his seat. The gorgeous creature he had encountered after his trip to the barber's shop stood in the doorway.

'Hi, Daddy,' she grinned and looked toward Michael.

'This is Corporal Michael McGowan. And this … is my daughter Audrey.'

Their eyes met for the second time that day.

'It is a pleasure.' Michael held out his hand as Audrey placed hers delicately in his grasp.

'That it is,' she held her perfect smile in place. 'I do believe I saw you in town today, Corporal.' Her eyes danced with mischief.

It was no secret the flirtation was acknowledged by both parties.

He would not allow her to best him at this moment however.

'No, I believe I have never seen you before. After all, I would remember such an encounter.'

Her smile faltered momentarily. 'It could have been another officer. After all, you all look much the same in uniform.' Her eyes twinkled in triumph as she bested him after all. She turned to walk from the room.

'Did you leave your mother in town?' The Colonel spoke to her back.

'Yes, she was taking far too long with the parish committee so I walked home. She has the carriage.'

Michael grinned at her gumption. She was a spoilt, flighty thing and he had not finished with her quite yet. Before she shut the door he turned his full attention toward it and away from her father's gaze. It would not do for the Colonel to know he had the man's daughter steadfast in his sights. However, he would make her aware she was his for the taking. As he knew she would, Audrey looked at him before pulling the door closed. He winked at her and pursed his lips to send her a kiss through the air, across the arc between them.

He watched her eyes widen slightly with the unexpected shock of his audacity.

If he was not mistaken he heard the distinct sound of a giggle as the door closed and the Colonel resumed his conversation.

'So your transfer to Point Nepean will be swift. It is a vast stretch of coastline much harsher than what you are used to. I believe you will prove to be the correct fit for the area. I have your orders here.' He handed the paper across his desk.

Michael folded the document and placed it in his breast pocket. 'I will look over this later this evening. For now I will bid you farewell and thank you for the opportunity.'

He encountered Mrs Price as he stepped out onto the veranda.

'Corporal McGowan! I am glad I caught you.'

Michael gathered Mrs Price's outstretched hand and

shook it lightly. 'Mrs Price, I too am glad to have made your acquaintance. You have a lovely home.'

'I have just come from the church,' she announced. 'The ladies of the parish will be throwing a celebration for you on Sunday. To be held directly after mass has concluded.'

And a lovely daughter, he thought to himself. He could hardly hear Mrs Price as the dialogue in his mind and the vision of the lovely Audrey Price danced among his thoughts.

'I will wait with anticipation until then,' he said as he departed the veranda and pulled the gate closed behind him.

Glancing back, he could not help the feeling of disappointment that Audrey had not come to bid him farewell. Maybe his overstep of all things proper had turned her attention away from him. Michael would seek out Miss Audrey Price tomorrow and feign an apology for his behaviour.

Stepping out onto the road he reached up to grab a handful of leaves from one of the trees lining the roadside. After tearing them apart, he scattered them in a trail behind him as he considered his new post. He needed a drink and set his direction towards town and the Shire Hall Hotel in particular.

As he passed a huge oak at the end of the road something moved in his periphery. A flutter of fabric caught his eye. Someone was leaning against the trunk of the tree. She pushed away from the huge trunk and stood in his path.

'Ah, I wondered where you had gotten to,' he said, feeling relieved.

'I did not care to speak with you with my father scrutinising my every word.'

'Does he know you are here, with me?'

'The question should be: Does my father know you dared

to blow me a kiss as though I were a woman of the most common variety?'

Michael was taken aback by Audrey's bold accusation and liked the lift of her chin as she challenged him.

'Do you mean to frighten me, Audrey? Will you tell your father I dared flirt with you in such close proximity?' As he spoke he took slow steps toward her. 'Did you not appreciate my attention? If not, say so now and I will direct no further signs of affection your way. This is my promise.'

He liked her. He had told her as much now. This would be the moment to gauge her reaction. He was now so close to her that he could see her pupils dilating. He watched with satisfaction as they expanded to the point where they obscured the blue of her eyes.

'You better tell me what attention you desire, if any at all,' he threatened with a mild smirk on his lips.

'Very well then,' she stared up at him, still in full possession of the assertive demeanour he was finding so alluring. He could not help his reaction. In battle he had shown more restraint. She had reached into his soul with her haughty defiance and brazen attitude, and he meant to seduce her. He knew they were alone, but even if someone had been present to witness their encounter, he would not have cared.

Michael reached an arm out to Audrey — pausing only momentarily to examine her expression, for he was confident there would be no sign of fear or repugnance on her face — and gathered her to him. As anticipated, her lips parted slightly and her gaze dropped down to his mouth.

'Just as I thought,' he whispered as he pulled away. Her look of disappointment made his heart quicken. He wanted to retake her in his arms and plunder her mouth but could not. Not here. She deserved all the respect that was her right as a lady of high social bearing. But now, at least, he had confirmation of her true feelings; his affection would be reciprocated. He could set his sights on making Audrey his — in every way.

He stepped away from her. 'I believe your mother, not to mention your father, may be looking for you. It will not bode well for either of us to be caught here, alone.'

She hid her disappointment well as she began to walk backwards from him but did not take her eyes from his. He stood rooted to the spot and watched her until she had no choice but to turn away from him as she reached the gate to her house at the end of the street.

Later that evening, hours after Audrey had captured his soul with the depth of her stare, Michael found that he was still dwelling on the bold nature of their meeting at three separate times over the day. He began to consider the prospect of asking the Colonel for the hand of his daughter in marriage. His rank would be set to rise over the years and he hoped this would reinforce his standing as a great match for Audrey, who also had much to offer him as a prospective wife. Their life would be far from dull. All he had witnessed today proved she had some spunk about her.

Chapter 2

Looking into her eyes, Michael tried to capture the tiniest vestige of the girl he once knew. The eyes that had been the most alluring blue were now pools of deep and lifeless black. His gaze dropped to Audrey's mouth. That bold mouth that could deliver untold flirtatious words and kisses that sent his head into a spin was now incapable of speech.

The seconds ticked by as he watched her with intent, awaiting something. She did not blink and seemed to look right through him to the opposing wall. Clamping his mouth shut, he tore his eyes from her. He feared he would disappear within the depths of her lifeless stare and become trapped inside her hell. 'The devil has done this to you,' he hissed, 'and damn you for allowing him to do so.'

Forgiveness was impossible. Michael could never make peace with the sin Audrey had committed. He understood the devil's work and knew all too well how much might and control he yielded over his subjects. His wife had caught the devil's attention somehow. His power had made her do an unfathomable thing, and now her mind and soul were ruined. She had become a vessel to do his bad deeds, and now that those deeds had been accomplished, she was devoid of spirit, unable to communicate and incapable of standing of her own accord.

Michael looked down at Audrey and found himself staring at the top of her head. Her chin was lowered to her chest and her shoulders curved forwards. 'I cannot, nor will I, turn back. I am afraid this day has become inevitable,' he said.

Lifting the gas lantern from the nail on the wall, he dangled it in front of the shelves so he could scan the lines of luggage. A curse left his lips for having failed to anticipate the sheer abundance of suitcases and duffel bags. After all, he was well aware of the large number of inmates housed here at the asylum. How on earth would he find her belongings? 'God damn this place to hell,' he cursed through gritted teeth. How he wished that before today he had made a more concerted effort to identify all the things that could waylay his plan.

At least he had factored in the date of Lady Montague's Christmas Party, which was held on the first Sunday of December each year. That was today. Right now the doctors were attending the party, filling their bellies with food and liquor, smoking cigars and enlightening the crowd with their highbrow opinions. He should know. He was once among those revellers.

Due to the absence of doctors in the wards, the celebration allowed the Sunday staff to relax somewhat. Very few would be doing rounds, if they did their rounds at all.

He allowed himself a moment or two of fervent day dreaming, imagining the excitement at the party when the distinguished guests heard the staggering news of what he was about to do. While the town's respected upper echelons had decided to spend the day enjoying themselves among their wealthy friends and peers, the filth that surrounded this place would wind itself in and around their consciences forevermore.

It would seem Ararat Lunatic Asylum was an island, protected by the walls that surrounded her. Looked upon as an untouchable force, she stood on the highest hill with her huge expanse of whitewashed walls suggesting the opulence of a castle, a building more suited to the European countryside than the tiny town of Ararat. This left her at odds with one's sensibilities. For although she appeared majestic from the outside, the townsfolk considered her to be a foreboding place one would only enter voluntarily if seeking employment. Otherwise, she threatened to swallow any person who had had the misfortunate to experience a spate of regretful luck with their health.

Only two doctors' signatures were required to seal an inmate's fate. For anyone ending up on the wrong side of a locked cell door, the outside world would be lost forever.

When Audrey was incarcerated to the asylum, her father, the Colonel, had immediately cut Michael off. This brutal act transformed Michael's initial feelings of worry and concern into a fierce and burning anger, an anger that motivated him to seek employment at the asylum in an effort to get closer to her.

But he had been forced to take certain measures in the process. Even though he retained his christian name, for instance, he felt compelled to drastically alter his appearance. He could not risk being recognised.

Many townsfolk who knew him worked at the institution,

and to complicate matters, the superintendent Dr Charles Lawler had once been a close friend. The pair had met around the same time Michael had first encountered this once beautiful creature, and had quickly become trusted confidants. Back then, who would have thought their lives would ultimately become entangled in such a manner? After all, Charles was the reason the woman seated on the chair before him, saturated in her own urine and faecal matter, was being kept imprisoned under a cloak of secrecy.

Whilst Michael held immense anger at those making decisions on Audrey's behalf, he conceded that the blame for her predicament could not be laid solely on Charles. After all, it was no secret his former friend's behaviour was bound by the influence of her family, the same family that had welcomed he himself into their world, before having Audrey committed, and then spurning him.

At first, all changes to Michael's outer bearing were intentional. He donned spectacles. He also stopped shaving and allowed his hair to grow; small acts of neglect that quickly distanced him from the clean-cut appearance formerly associated with his military persona. As intended, he landed a job as an asylum orderly, and from that point the changes in his appearance occurred as a matter of process. His facial hair grew to the point where a full beard and moustache now covered his chin, upper lip and jawline. Long hair disguised other defining features, while lack of sleep and an abundance of worry etched deep lines into his forehead. His cheeks became ruddy courtesy of the copious amounts of whisky he consumed each night.

After only a few months of working at the asylum, Michael

resembled a man at least ten years older. To reinforce this deception, he lowered the pitch of his voice while at work. His speech took on a colourless and stern quality, to the point where no one who had known him previously would have recognised his gravelly intonations.

Suffice it to say he had thoroughly transformed himself into an entirely different man to the one Audrey had married, and that after inserting himself here at the asylum he had simply been biding his time, getting ready to pounce — all along appearing to be just another orderly, invisible, dressed in white. Much like a ghost. By assimilating, he had been able to carry out his duties, establishing a pretence that he was neither significantly aware of the ward in question nor the woman housed there. There was little to no risk anybody would single him out for attention.

However, his plan to get closer to Audrey had taken a spin of an unexpected kind when he had finally gained sufficient proximity to learn of her psychiatric treatment, or rather a lack thereof, and he now fully intended to not only liberate Audrey from her predicament, but also to pull down from their righteous thrones the superintendent of Ararat Lunatic Asylum and all those who dared to call themselves medical practitioners.

'Aha,' he whispered as he raised his fist in a gesture of triumph before grasping the handles of one particular case. It was the gilded letters on the expensive leather bag that had aided him in the end. Her luggage was of superior quality compared with the other bags and cases.

A.P.

Touching the letters with his fingers, he was reminded of those first days after their marriage, when they had ended their 'bridal tour' with his move to Point Nepean. The copious amounts of baggage she had required to move all her things across the countryside were laughable. He would tease her no end with regard to this, pointing out the duress the additional weight was putting the horses under as they traversed the roads to get them to their destination. This would mark the beginning of his post at Point Nepean and their new life on the Mornington Peninsula as husband and wife. Back then, he never would have imagined their lives would turn out this way.

Dumping the case onto the floor, Michael unfastened its buckles before pulling out the neatly folded gown, which unfurled before his eyes. Letting it fall onto the open case, he turned to Audrey and grasped her hands, pulling her to her feet. A slow gurgling sound became a hum. He eyed her with shrewd apprehension. She was humming the tune of the 'British Grenadiers', and it sent his heart racing.

Bending over her with abrupt movements, he wrapped his arm around her waist, steadying her as best he could. He tugged the putrid smock up past her waist. 'Raise your arms,' he whispered. She looked like an innocent child as she lifted her arms above her head. He angled the fabric this way and that, before pulling it over her head then tossing it into the suitcase.

Holding her steady with one hand he bent down and picked up the gown and watched a million dust particles swarm around it. The expensive fabric was a cruel reminder of the life from not too long ago, yet a life that was lost forever.

Throwing the garment this way and that until the wide neckline surfaced, he threw the bulk of the gown over her head.

For a time Audrey's humming was lost within the heavy material, but once her face had cleared the fabric, the sound ceased. She blinked her eyes and stared at him. He could swear that her head moved back ever so slightly as a slither of recognition dawned on her features. Could it be possible that the feel of velvet on her skin had broken through her psychosis? Michael was hopeful, as his hands stilled and he stared at her. 'Audrey?' he questioned.

The silence between them was sliced open as the sound of her humming resumed. The damn tune continued to reverberate from her chest, up and out into the open space between them. He shook his head and cursed under his breath. 'That damned tune will haunt my dreams,' he muttered. The last time he had heard it was at the celebration the Colonel had hosted for his newest recruit taking a post at Point Nepean. It was this meeting that would bind her to him forever.

He watched her alight from the carriage. She smoothed her gown, pinched her cheeks and bit down on her lower lip. No doubt, it was a remedy her mother had taught her. To look one's best a spot of colour on the cheeks and reddened lips were imperative to capture a suitor's attention. He knew it to be true.

Although she had a bonnet fixed atop her head she placed her hand up to her brow in order to shield the glare from the sun as it bounced off the pristine render of the Shire Hall. Her mother grasped her and spoke in her ear.

As she was hurried toward the front doors he left his

vantage point at the window and began to move toward the entrance. The sound of The British Grenadiers bellowed forth as he watched the doorman push the doors open, then relieve her of her gloves and hat. She craned her neck as she entered the Main Hall. He made sure he was the first person in her sights. He had dressed in full uniform with his sword strapped securely at his waist. Her chest rose and fell visibly at the very sight of him. He was staring directly at her. He smiled and made his way toward her.

'Hello, Audrey. That is your name, correct?'

'Oh you toy with my confidence. You know my name.'

'Audrey!' her mother scolded.

Audrey lowered her gaze and whispered, 'Well, it is true.'

Michael laughed. 'Forgive me, Mrs Price. I am merely teasing your daughter.'

'It takes a true gentleman to admit such boldness,' Mrs Price conceded, although in a clipped tone.

'I think you could make up for your impertinence by fetching me a drink,' Audrey ordered with a smirk on her lips.

'I will do just that. Will you accompany me to the beverage table?'

'I would love to.' She placed her hand on the inside of his elbow and allowed him to lead her through the room. 'I am not that thirsty,' she added in a whisper thrillingly close to his shoulder.

He looked down at her by his side. 'Was this a ploy to get away from your mother? Was I part of your plan?'

She looked up at him. 'Merely a ploy for me to ask why you seek to tease me so.'

'I think it is you that teases me in more ways than you

know.' His face remained passive as the intensity of his eyes penetrated her gaze, making her heart quicken.

He wanted her to realize that this was not a mere flirtation, it was a seduction. As they strolled through the room, he was steering her towards an external door that led to the rear garden. He grasped her hand and stepped through the doorway, pulling her along behind him. He looked back to see if any eyes were on them, but the room was full of people already engaged in discussion or greeting friends.

Michael led her to a bench seat that was cast in shade. 'Would you like to sit down?' he said as he drew her hand from his elbow and held onto it.

'Yes, I would,' she said, pulling her skirt away from her legs and spreading it out so it would not crumple. He remained standing with his back to the doors they had just exited.

'I want you to look at me and nowhere else,' he said casually. 'I want you to look at me in a way that suggests we are simply discussing the weather or our surrounds.'

Audrey stared at him with wide eyes, nodding like a ninny. He was commanding her attention and she seemed lost for words, unable to defy him.

'You are the most beautiful creature I have ever seen, Miss Audrey Price, and I intend to make you mine as soon as I possibly can. In a few weeks I will be deployed to Point Nepean, so it will not do for me to dally on this matter. I know I seem to make this sound like a barter for property but I want to lay claim to you forever — both in my life and in my bed.'

Her mouth opened then closed once more. He would hazard a guess that this was the first time in her life she'd been astonished into silence? As much as his hope was for her to jump up from the bench and into his arms he knew she could not. The windows allowed anybody within the hall a view of their behaviour. She could ill afford to bring shame to her father, or — God forbid — her mother. It was improper, of course, for such a new acquaintance to be speaking to her so boldly, but he could tell she was exhilarated that the two flirtations she had hitherto shared with Michael McGowan had led to this moment — a moment in which he was expressing his clear and fully defined intention to *possess* her.

'I take it that your silence means you have no objection to the situation as it stands?' He looked down at her with grim determination.

She nodded. She remained at an utter loss for words.

'Now, if you will, I wish to return you to the room full of guests. But soon, I will pick you up in my arms, carry you away and sate myself with your lascivious body and what it has to offer.'

Tears glistened in her eyes. He held his hand out to lead her back inside, and when she alighted the bench she seemed to float up towards his touch.

Throughout the afternoon, they shared smiles across the room. When there was nobody watching, he winked at her. As she was preparing to leave the celebration, she blew him a kiss while her father's back was turned.

He followed close behind her as she prepared to board the carriage with her mother.

Michael walked the path from the hall in the company of her father. 'Ah Colonel, I would like to visit with you this week, if it suits?'

'Absolutely, Corporal. Any day that does not fall midweek is suitable.'

Michael then looked towards the carriage and touched his fingers to the brim of his hat. 'To the fair Price women, I bid you a good afternoon.'

Audrey leaned from the window as the carriage pulled away from the gravel dip. 'I did not catch your name, soldier!' she yelled.

'Audrey!' he heard her mother gasp as he lowered his head to hide his smile.

His nerves were bristling as the haunting tune continued to arc between them.

Frustrated that the memory of it was so far from his reach, as was she, he diverted his anger towards those who had allowed her to sink further into hell. He gripped her left hand and pushed it into a sleeve. It slipped through easily. Once he had made sure both arms were adjusted comfortably inside the garment, he held her against his chest and reached easily round the back of the gown to fasten only a few buttons. He could feel her back vibrating beneath his hands as the incessant humming continued. His back teeth were clenched so tight that his jaw was beginning to ache.

The gown draped and sagged round her body. Seeing the heavy velvet against her skin, he felt the memories tease at him like a cruel joke. His heart thudded in his chest as he stilled and looked at her. The humming became haphazard, conveying no particular tune, setting his nerves further on edge. He ground his teeth and forced out, 'The devil lives within.'

He didn't look at her after that. Could not. Instead, he

steered her in front of him toward the door and gave a quick check right and left before crossing the threshold. Holding her with one arm, he slipped the padlock shank back into place and gave it a quick push with his palm until it snapped locked again. He wanted to leave as many unanswered questions as possible. For the doctors and Audrey's family, today would remain a mystery. Maybe it would set their minds at ease to some extent, knowing she had escaped and was no longer trapped in the devil's grasp?

However, he could not let them rest too easy. He had to show them there was a person committing atrocities in here that they could neither control nor understand. To the staff and inmates, there would be fear unimagined. The event would trigger no end of gossip. This would impel Constable Bryant to race up the hill to investigate. He would demand answers as his job required. He would question the doctors and their practices. Then surely this would uncover the medicinal disharmony that existed beneath the asylum's veneer.

Michael was angry with the establishment for keeping her locked away in these conditions, and incensed by the way her family had abandoned her in this place. The bitterness he felt at losing someone he once loved would stay with him forever but he would never again need to worry about her welfare.

He looked ahead at the darkened hallway. Every ward and doorway throughout the place was familiar to him, and yet suddenly this hallway seemed to extend further than ever before. While it had taken him a short time to make his way to the refractory ward below, he was now encumbered by the drag of this lifeless form in her heavy gown. With each step he felt his heartbeat quicken. The elaborate dress would draw unwanted attention to them — although perhaps not as much as the filthy smock she had been wearing earlier. Besides, the heavy gown helped confine the stench emanating from her body.

Voices rang out behind him, and he turned to see two inmates ambling along, lost in conversation.

One looked at him and pointed a finger. 'What you doin' there?' Her voice bounced along the hallway. He was thankful they were far enough away that he would be able to slip around a corner.

Hoisting Audrey up in his arms he yelled over his shoulder, 'She is not well, a visitor!' and bolted toward a door at the end of the corridor before either of them had a chance to catch up to him.

His heart was beating as he rushed along. 'Not long now,' he whispered to Audrey, whose body moved haphazardly, jolted by his footsteps. It was paramount he get her to the belltower before they were seen by anybody else. As he rounded the last corner of the women's ward, he strategised the last piece of the puzzle. He had to make his way from this building to the belltower.

He pushed the door open and was blinded by the intense brightness of the morning. As expected, the normally busy courtyard was empty, and he could hear the distant strangled voices of the inmates singing hymns. He carefully placed Audrey back down and steadied her before grasping her elbow and leading her from the doorway out into the daylight. She smarted at the sharp light, which made him realise how much the previous few months of light deprivation had affected her.

He hadn't anticipated this, and the best he could do in the moment was to shield her eyes with one hand and pull her closer to his side as he rushed forward.

He looked to the covered veranda on his left then followed the line of the building connected to it. He did the same to his right. There was nobody to be seen in the immediate area. He hesitated for a moment longer. He stared at the door just sixty feet ahead of him.

It may have been a thousand feet away at this pace. Whilst the belltower was the smallest building in the asylum and had its own door at the base, it was connected to the ballroom. The grandeur of these particular buildings were not lost, as not only were they adoringly embraced by the symmetry of the wings of the main building but they were at the centre of the asylum. Like the jewel in a crown the ballroom was adorned with a beautiful interior while the belltower overlooked the entire asylum and grounds like a protective overseer.

Michael was thankful that the sound of Sunday morning mass was being conducted in the ballroom. The undulating voices bounced from the massive interior and out into the morning's sunlight. He did not want to spend any time pondering the confines of the ballroom but rather, reset his sights on the grand belltower. He looked up at its high spire that haughtily looked over its subjects below and harrumphed. 'You will have a shameful secret to keep after today,' he said under his breath. With his sights set intently on the door, he set his course toward it.

Each step felt slower than the previous as the cumbersome subject in his grasp became harder to handle. He looked over his shoulder numerous times expecting to see somebody in pursuit. If the lady in the hall had raised the alarm he would be caught. But really, he need not despair. He imagined an inmate prattling on about seeing a lady in a fancy gown racing through the hall with an orderly. Nobody would believe her for a moment.

Without letting Audrey free from his grasp, he placed the key in the padlock and unlatched the door, but when he attempted to push it open, it would not budge. He glanced upward. 'Lord, give me strength.' A stubborn door would not see him abandon his plan. He placed his boot up and waited a few seconds until he heard a crescendo of voices. At that moment, he kicked the door as near to the doorjamb as he could. He did not want to damage it for fear he would be unable to close it again, thus drawing attention to his actions before sufficient time had elapsed. The door opened and the sound of it scraping against the ground was so loud that his shoulders automatically lifted towards his ears. His paranoia was besting him at present.

Consciously relaxing his own shoulders, he now grasped Audrey's and steered her inside the small square confines of the tower's ground floor. He looked up the staircase. It hugged each interior wall and was so high that he wondered how he would climb the nine separate flights. He took a deep breath. There was only one way. Hoisting Audrey further into his arms, he strode up the stairs taking two at a time until he found himself at the top gasping for breath. He was no longer a fit young soldier. Over the previous few months he had regularly drunk himself into an unseemly state and had eaten so poorly that he had put on many pounds. His heartbeat was a testament to this.

The rope for the bell was wrapped loosely around the banister. Holding Audrey around the waist, he untied it swiftly, creating a noose that he then slipped over her head. 'I did love you,' he whispered. Then, closing his eyes, he lifted her over the side of the bannister and let her go. 'God forgive me,' he said aloud.

His words were drowned out by one solid ding from the bell's clapper. He should have made haste but knew the sound of the voices reaching up to their saviour would block out the solitary sound. Now, he felt calm. It was done. His eyes were dry. He could not cry for her. That time had passed.

As he circled the swinging body on his descent from the tower, he did not look at it. Nonetheless, he was aware of it dangling lifelessly, slowly twisting on the end of the rope. Once he had departed the belltower and pulled the door closed behind him, he did not look back until he had retraced his steps through the door leading into the main building.

The worst he could hope for was that the keeper of the bell would find the grisly scene in the morning. The best would be for her to be discovered missing from her cell long before the day was over.

Each week the bell, like those trapped within the asylum, was given one day of rest. Unlike the churches in the district that would, in fact, toll on Sundays, the bell high up on the hill in the Ararat Lunatic Asylum was given a day of reprieve. The other six days of the week the bell worked on the hour, every hour of the day, to alert staff and inmates to breakfast, lunch, dinner, the beginning of the work day and the downing of tools at the day's end. Today, however, the single and solid clang of the bell would have gone unheard with the sound of the congregation bleating the good Lord's word. Michael would not allow himself to ponder that one solid clang as the rope snapped her neck, snuffing her life out in one single beat. He supposed he had given her over fully to the devil now. She would be welcomed through the gates of hell.

He walked across the courtyard, ducking between the covered verandas as sunshine pooled in the exposed areas left untouched by the shadow of the three-storey main building. After crossing the divide between the wards, he entered the men's ward and locked the door behind him. He then resumed his rounds. If anyone queried him on his whereabouts over the preceding hour, he would attest that he had been right here all morning.

Chapter 3

'Nurse!' the kitchen hand yelled down the hall.

Trinny, the nurse on duty, looked up from the ledger she was hurrying to complete. Her morning had been arduous. The women under her care had been particularly frenzied and noisy. Something had had them riled. Although one could not tell most times what set their hysterics to rise. Martha, the oldest woman in the ward, who was suffering from consumption, needed a transfer to the hospital cottage. Unfortunately, Sunday was not the day to arrange such a thing. Trinny had been waylaid for hours tending to the poor woman. Amid her symptoms, it was the incessant coughing that would bring fresh blood drizzling from her lips.

Trinny looked at the kitchen hand. 'What, what is it?' Her frustration becoming prevalent at the inmate that had been assigned kitchen duty.

'Sally Smith is not in her cell,' she said casually. 'Has she finally made it to the morgue?' The kitchen hand had just come from the cell of the woman in question, and was holding a tray bearing a tin cup of cold tea and a small piece of bread. There was no accompanying plate.

'It cannot be possible,' Trinny muttered as she looked down at the ledger, checking for a report of removal from any of the cells. There was no such entry from the night nurse. And besides, she herself had been on duty yesterday and knew Sally Smith was in her cell during that time. She raced to the kitchen hand's side.

'She was in there at the beginning of my shift,' Trinny said adamantly, even as she began doubting whether she had in fact seen Sally Smith on her initial round. Then, with horror, she recalled the racket that had caused her to overlook the entire row of even-numbered cell doors that morning, including Sally's.

Trinny raced down the hall with the kitchen hand at her heels and peered through the peephole. 'Was the bolt across when you arrived at the door?'

'Yep.'

'Was it locked?'

'Yep.'

Trinny continued to stare into the empty cell. 'I do not understand where she could be. Did you collect the master key from its usual place?'

'Got it 'ere.' The young woman balanced the tray in one hand and held the key up for Trinny to see.

'Can you open it up, then?' Trinny said with mild irritation. The kitchen hand also being an inmate was making the situation far more difficult to deal with. Her snide remarks and less than polished behaviour were making Trinny grapple with her own patience levels at present.

As the kitchen hand placed the tray on the floor and grasped the padlock between her fingers, she said, 'Should have known she was not in there. I can smell her long before I arrive at the door.' The kitchen hand looked as though her mouth held a morsel of rotten food.

Trinny did not appreciate her subordinate's snide remark. At present her mortification over her own neglectful behaviour was causing her angst. She could not gather her senses with the kitchen hand staring at her, as though looking for answers that she simply did not possess.

The kitchen hand slid the bolt across and pushed the door open. Trinny stepped over the threshold and looked around the cell as though Sally Smith could be hiding in a corner. She took a deep breath and ran her hands down her uniform nervously.

'Thank you. Now could you please resume your meal delivery? I need to seek help.'

She raced past the kitchen hand, who was yet to move. The woman stared after Trinny as she gathered the tray from the floor and let out a huff.

'Well, get on with it!' Trinny yelled over her shoulder as she ran back down the hall, her mind in a whirl. How could Sally Smith have escaped? Not only was the woman incapable of moving, the door to her cell had been locked! The kitchen hand had said as much, and she was an inmate who was never backward whilst stating the truth. After all, she hadn't held back about Sally Smith being filthy and unkempt, though she was incapable of washing or doing anything for herself. The heavy-handed orderlies would strip her, toss her into a bath and hold her under until she was some semblance of clean, but that process never happened as often as it should — perhaps because Sally Smith's screams never ceased to have a ripple effect on the other poor souls in the refractory ward. She would holler and thrash around in the water as though it were the flames of hell licking at her body.

Trinny rushed up the staircase to the administration area and yelled more loudly than was acceptable. 'Matron!'

'What is it?' Matron scolded as she appeared in the doorway to her office.

'The inmate from cell six is missing.'

Matron paused for a moment. 'Sally Smith? You must be mistaken.' Her throat moved up and down as she swallowed uncomfortably.

'Unfortunately, I am not. The kitchen hand delivering the meals discovered her absence. Has she been taken to the hospital cottage by any chance? Maybe her transferral was not put into the ledger overnight.'

'I have not heard of any such thing.' The matron retreated into her office, where she ran her fingers down a log sheet.

'Her name is not here. She has not been removed for any reason. How long has she been unaccounted for?' The matron's cheeks flushed crimson.

'I could not say. As you will see from my time sheet, I resumed duty at six this morning and I am ashamed to admit I did not check her cell.'

Matron frowned. 'You are to check each cell at the beginning of your round. You know this.'

'Yes Matron, I do, but Martha Jones in the cell opposite is so unwell. I am afraid I was caught checking the odd numbered cells and could not see my way clear to …'

Matron held up her hand. 'Enough.' She scribbled a note, folded it and placed it into an envelope, which she then sealed.

'Take this to the gatehouse. Tell Mr Gibbs this is to be delivered to Doctor Lawler promptly. Tell him that Doctor Lawler can be located at the home of Lady Montague.'

'Yes, Matron.' Trinny turned toward the large entry door.

Matron let out a huge breath before saying, 'His celebration will come to an abrupt end, I am afraid.'

Trinny wrenched the massive front door closed behind her and sprinted along the flat entry to the driveway before slowing her pace as it dipped downward. The building that sat on the asylum's perimeter held her attention.

'Mr Gibbs! Mr Gibbs!' she called. The side door opened and the lined face of a surly man looked toward her. The gatehouse was the first bastion of the asylum where every visitor, staff member and inmate passed on entry and exit respectively. Mr Gibbs knew everybody who crossed in either direction. If Sally Smith had attempted to pass him today he would have recalled it, and if he had seen her and had been suspicious of her passage, he definitely would have raised an alarm.

'Mr Gibbs, you need to deliver this letter post haste to Doctor Lawler. He is at Lady Montague's home.'

Trinny watched him move with the grace and speed of a baby elephant and wondered what the words 'post haste' meant to this man. After untethering his horse and hitching her to a wagon, he meandered back to the side door from where he had alighted and reached back inside to pull his hat from a hook. Shoving it on his head he re-buttoned his coat and held his hand out for the note.

'Matron did say it was urgent.'

'Yeah, I heard ya,' he said as he scrunched the envelope and shoved it in his trouser pocket. With one foot on the buckboard he teetered between the bluestone step and the wagon. After rocking back and forth trying to gain momentum, he groaned as he eventually made it up onto the seat.

He slapped the reins and gave a shout to his horse. Trinny watched the wagon roll and sway slowly away from her.

She mumbled, 'Would have been far quicker to walk to the Montague home myself.'

There would not be enough time left in her shift to painstakingly watch the wagon pass over the railway tracks and turn out onto the road.

She hurried back up the driveway. With her heart heaving in her chest, she dropped the heavy knocker on the front door and waited for Matron to open it.

'Is he on his way?' Matron asked as she held the door open for Trinny to re-enter.

'Yes, but I dare say we begin our own search. He could take a while.'

'Very well, you make your way back to the refractory ward and help with the search. I have sent other staff to assist, although I am not holding any hope she is still down there.'

Trinny sent a prayer that she would hear the cries of joy that the inmate had been discovered. As she took the last step into the refractory ward she realised that Sally Smith had not been found. Every cell was being scrutinised, with more than one nurse or orderly attending each inmate.

She joined the search, trying hard to concentrate on the task at hand. She worried over when she would be called upon and questioned as to why she had failed to notice the missing inmate. After all, it had taken a kitchen hand delivering meals to discover the missing inmate.

Mr Gibbs yanked the reins, pulling the wagon to a halt outside the stables at the Montague home.

'Stay,' he ordered the horse as he walked towards the front steps of the nearby home, where he handed the note to the doorman. The man disappeared inside as Mr Gibbs retreated back down the stairs from the veranda and paced the driveway that ran the length of the home. He rolled a cigarette while he waited and took slow steps. Lighting it, he inhaled deeply. His pacing followed the line of the garden bed that held him a discreet distance from the home, making sure he was not privy to its graces. The lamps were ablaze in every room, casting golden pools of light upon the guests as they enjoyed the finest beverages, food and cigars.

Mr Gibbs harrumphed. 'Fancy havin' the lights ablaze in the daytime.'

He looked sideways into each window, perusing the huge dining table set for so many guests to enjoy. 'Wouldn' mind a leg o' turkey,' he said with chagrin.

He watched a group of men gathered in the drawing room, pool cues in hand with cigar smoke slowly circling them like tiny grey ghosts. He saw the butler hand the note to Doctor Lawler, whose lips pursed as though he was drawing once again on his cigar. Doctor Lawler then walked over to his colleague Doctor Simon Rushby and whispered close to his ear, before disappearing through the interior door.

Gibbs' body creaked and groaned as he attempted to make it back to the wagon.

Just as he had perched himself in the seat the doctor appeared on the front veranda, wrenching his coat up his arm and pulling his hat on his head, yelling to Gibbs as he ran toward the wagon, 'Well, get going then! There is no time to waste!' The doctor then climbed up onto the seat beside Gibbs.

Gibbs urged the horse on as she galloped along the side road before turning onto the main street of Ararat, which merged with the road leading away from the town. The wagon began to slow as the driveway to the asylum steepened. Breaking the silence for the first time, Doctor Lawler yelled in frustration, 'For God's sake, man. Could you hurry this animal up? Let me off!' He then lurched from the wagon and sprinted the rest of the way. He banged the knocker at the asylum's entrance numerous times, and when Matron opened it for him he walked straight past her as she attempted to greet him.

He raced toward the staircase and ran his hands along both sides of each wall as he skittered down each step until he stopped at the bottom and stared down the length of the ward. The refractory ward was heaving with mewing sounds and terrified screams. The disregard of normal routine had turned the normal chaos of the ward into anarchy. The ward had been searched numerous times and was now abandoned with the exception of one orderly.

Only one door stood ajar. Cell six. He walked inside and looked down at the straw mattress and canvas blanket. He let out a gust of breath. 'Well then, let me see if we can uncover your whereabouts, Miss Audrey,' he whispered to the empty cell.

Once back out in the hallway he looked both ways before quickly making his way back up the stairs. 'Alert me if anything is discovered,' he shouted to the orderly below.

Doctor Lawler walked the length of the hallway leading away from the administration area. He could not allow an oversight to hinder her discovery. His responsibility to take control of the situation started now. He flung the door open and stepped out into the courtyard.

Orderlies, nursing staff and some of the more mentally intact inmates were rushing past, disappearing around corners, opening doors and calling for Sally. Doctor Lawler pulled out his watch and stared down at it. It was five to three. He released a huge breath. Where could she be? Anger broke through his normally calm façade as he bellowed across the landscape, 'No inmate will be put to bed, nor a single staff member allowed to leave, until she is found!' In the frenzy that followed, everyone's brisk walking turned to a chaotic run. The staff would now have to contend with inmates forced from their normal routines; surely this disruption would turn the place into further havoc for all.

Doctor Lawler rushed back to the door leading into the main building and then raced down the hallway until he was once again at the front door and administration area.

'Matron!'

'Yes, doctor.' Matron came bolting through her office door.

'My office, now.'

He ascended the staircase with her close behind him and held the door open for her. It deftly slammed once she was inside. She winced as the reverberating sound hurt her ears.

'What in blazes is going on? Where is she?' Doctor Lawler banged his palms on his desk as he faced her.

'I do not know, Doctor. All I can tell you is the nurse in charge of the refractory ward was caught up with another situation, and had not realised that the inmate in cell six was missing.'

'We both know who the woman is and it is vital she be found and returned to her cell before I have to alert the Colonel.' Doctor Lawler whispered even though they were alone.

'I understand, Doctor.'

Matron was almost through the door when Doctor Lawler said, 'No matter what happens, do not let it be known that she is anybody other than Sally Smith. Do you understand?'

'Yes, Doctor.' As the door closed he uttered, 'Just where in hell's name are you, Mrs McGowan?'

Doctor Lawler presided over the search of the entire women's ward. He had confirmed reports that the graveyard, garden beds and all airing courts had been checked. Each row of the vineyard and vegetable garden had been scoured. The kitchen, laundry, pigpen and milking area had been explored. She had simply disappeared.

He ordered that the refractory ward be searched again. Cells were unlocked, checked thoroughly and relocked once more.

Doctor Lawler sent a dozen orderlies to walk the entire base of the ha-ha wall that surrounded the perimeter of the asylum. While anyone on the outside of the institution could climb up and perch on the wall that stood at a height of around three foot, the inside was vastly different. The grounds contoured from a vantage point that allowed you to look out across the landscape beyond, but then sloped downward to the base of a flat wall that was sixteen foot high therefore ensuring inmates could gain no foothold nor climb. He was well aware that the trench running along the wall's base could easily hide someone, which is why the orderlies were now out searching the perimeter.

Doctor Lawler was confident that a woman would not be sufficiently able bodied to scour the wall. However, with current circumstances revealing no sign of the missing inmate, he needed to be assured there was no place left unsearched. Back in his office, staring out of the window that overlooked the countryside below, he placed his forehead against the glass to gain support for his throbbing head. The afternoon sun dipped beyond the horizon just as any hope of finding her wavered. 'Where in God's name are you?'

He thought of all the places that had been checked but suspected there was something he was missing. What was eluding his attention? 'The men's ward.' The glass fogged as the statement left his lips.

It would not seem a feasible pursuit, but out of desperation he now considered any place not yet searched. As he left his office he became angry at this oversight. There was no way Audrey could have escaped her cell alone. He should have thought of every alternative, including the possibility that somebody in the asylum had assisted her. That included staff from all areas and the slim chance that an inmate had infiltrated the refractory ward with a stolen key. It was plausible with the hours that had passed that his search would be futile but he was desperate to see an end to this saga. He stalked to the end of the corridor, unlocked a door that led straight into the men's ward and called to an orderly in the distance.

'You there.' Catching the man's attention he waved impatiently for him to approach.

The man limped toward him. Doctor Lawler looked down at his watch. He did not have time for this. The man before him looked more like an inmate than an orderly.

The time it took for him to approach had Charles clenching his teeth. Time was roaring past as dusk approached and yet every moment, every second slithered by as he waited for some truth to be uncovered.

'I take it you are aware there is an inmate missing?' he questioned tersely as the man finally stopped before him.

'That we are, sir. Every cell has been searched and there's nothing amiss.' His words slurred and were in line with his walking pace.

Charles overlooked the man's speech impediment. He needed information regardless of how long it took to acquire it. 'Have all the men been accounted for in each ward?

'Yes, I believe so. And nobody seems to be acting excessively untoward, despite the current upheaval, sir. We have no reason to think a female inmate is in the vicinity of the men's ward.'

'I see and what is your name?'

'Michael, sir.'

Doctor Lawler looked beyond Michael's shoulder. There were a number of orderlies milling around the nurses' station midway between him and the corner of the wing.

He yelled, 'Search this ward again. Now!'

'Yes, sir,' came a rushed response from the men.

Charles turned and stepped back through the door. Michael smiled as the door thudded closed. 'She ain't here, sir,' he whispered.

Confident in his dramatically altered appearance, Michael

did not worry that anyone would recognise him. Also, the militia had taught him many things. Of upmost importance was the strategy of keeping a lie as close to the truth as possible. This would assure you the upper hand. Use every morsel of information to your advantage in an effort to elude your enemy.

Michael turned and walked back through the ward. He smiled when he thought of the ruse he had created. When seeking a job in the facility to get closer to Audrey, he had been grateful it was Matron who had interviewed him for the position of orderly. Had Doctor Lawler been across from him at that early stage he would surely have been recognised. He had acquired the limp and slurred speech after he began his employ in the asylum. After all, if a man with a limp and speech impediment had asked for a job he would have been refused and possibly thrown in a cell for his mental inability to function.

There were far too many judgements placed on those who had even the slightest imperfections to their characters. The poor were the most vulnerable, and the rich controlled everything in this town, including the asylum on the hill. His lovely wife had been part of the respectable establishment but that had not prevented the demons from stealing her mind and soul. Her mother and father had dealt with this theft as only those in the upper classes do. They had hidden her illness; in turn shutting her away and then lying to their friends about her whereabouts. As far as everybody was concerned she was still living the life of a military wife at Point Nepean or some exotic place abroad. He dared allow himself the memory of the life to which he and Audrey were once privy. It was ripped from him the moment she had fallen ill.

Michael strode into the cottage. 'Audrey, I have returned!' He had been on manoeuvres for nearly a fortnight and was excited to see his wife and daughter. The cottages at Point Nepean were allocated to officers and their families. They were spacious and more comfortable than the single officers' quarters. Michael yelled down the hall and looked into the sitting room. Audrey was not there. As it was a lovely day with a light breeze whispering across the heads, she may have taken Charlotte for a walk. He had less than two hours to see his girls before he was required to leave again for a further three or four days. He passed the bedroom door but took steps backward when he noted the bedspread askew.

'Are you unwell?' he asked as he found Audrey lying beneath the covers. She did not answer. He walked around to the side of the bed. 'Are you angry with me for being away so long?' Her eyes were open as she continued to stare at the wall. 'Are you having some difficulty today?' he asked. After only a few seconds he felt a sinking dread. The situation looked worrisome.

He called for the maid. She rushed to the doorway.

'How long has she been unwell?'

'She has not moved from her bed these last three days.'

'What about Charlotte? Has she seen to her?'

'No, sir. I have looked after everything on her behalf.' The maid tried to keep her terse reply light but it did not work.

'Did you call for the doctor?'

'I did but he has been called across to Queenscliff, sir. An epidemic has broken out, apparently.'

'Dammit. I did know that.' Michael placed his fist to his lips.

Michael left the cottage and walked the short distance to the residence of the Commander in Charge. Hot wind whipped round him, running through the tea trees dotted around the cottages. He ran his hand down his face as the Commander opened the door to him.

'My wife is ill at present, sir,' he said.

'What is wrong?'

'She will not leave her bed but does not seem to have symptoms pertaining to cold or influenza. When will the doctor return?'

The Commander in Charge pushed his glasses up onto the bridge of his nose. 'He is days away at present but if it is bed rest she needs she is better left here than be dragged miles to the city to see another physician.'

On Michael's return to the cottage the maid met him at the door. She was in a state of emotional turmoil. 'She climbed out of bed, sir.'

'Where is she then?' he asked.

'She has been outside looking across the bay since you left. I could not get her to come inside. I have been desperate for you to return.'

Michael raced from the cottage and looked across the expanse of grass. It fell away to the small sandy beach, where they had often enjoyed sun-filled days wandering through the shallow waters. Now, in the darkness, he watched his wife's back as she stared across the bay.

She held their baby in her arms. 'Audrey!' He yelled so loud that his throat hurt.

She did not turn but stepped further into the water, swinging the baby she was carrying to and fro.

He screamed her name over and over. As he ran, he felt the distance swallow him. He would not make it in time to stop her. Before he could reach her she threw the baby into the water. Small waves lapped at her nightgown.

'What have you done?' he yelled as he ran past her and lunged toward the baby swaddled in the blanket. Grappling to right the child, he looked down at the sopping wet blanket wrapped securely around one of Charlotte's dolls.

He heaved a sigh and dropped it again. Lifting Audrey from the water, he could not believe how frail she had become. How had he not noticed it?

Before he placed Audrey back into bed, the maid bathed her and changed her into a fresh nightgown. As the evening progressed she began to wail.

'Has she been doing this the last few evenings?' he asked, perplexed.

'I am afraid so. It sounds like the cries of a wounded soul, sir.'

'I thank you for caring for my wife. It cannot have been easy,' he said with seriousness.

'I did as best I could sir,' she said.

'Take the evening for yourself. I will look after her until morning.'

'Oh sir, I hoped she would come good these past few days but she seems to be getting worse.' Her statement frightened him. After all, the maid would know. His observations over the last few hours were frightening and to have his fears confirmed was difficult to deal with.

He held their baby in his arms and sat beside Audrey through the night, listening to sounds that were inhuman.

He hoped that Charlotte's presence would evoke something, anything from his wife. Charlotte's cries for food went unnoticed and if he was not mistaken Audrey's wailing continued to grow louder over the child's cries. In the early hours of dawn he made a difficult decision. He would send her home to her mother and father, wait for his replacement and then follow.

Since he had been away for the past fortnight it did not seem that she had contracted a curable illness, but rather, that her mind had been cursed. He had watched her change after the birth of their daughter but had put this down to motherhood and the life that it forged moving forth. The maid had confirmed with her observations that things were spiralling downward. The course of action he had decided on would be for the best, and clearly the most helpful way to see this illness diminish, thus bringing his Audrey back to him. He believed the familiar practitioners and surrounds of home would help to heal her. Besides, Doctor Lawler was a trusted and respected friend whose medical expertise would surely help him arrange for the best doctors to care for her. Michael felt hopeful.

Placing Audrey in the carriage, he stared at the woman who was now a shell of her former self. She had not spoken a word since his return. There was nothing of the woman he had married in her demeanour anymore. A wet nurse held their daughter in her arms. She would ensure the connecting train, and then carriage, would see Audrey safely home to her family in Ararat.

Kissing his wife goodbye, he could only hope and pray that when he saw her in the coming weeks she would be back to the woman he knew. He touched Charlotte's tiny hand and kissed her on the forehead. 'I love you,' he whispered to his daughter before closing the carriage door and sending them on their way.

He had not begun his own journey to Ararat when he received a telegram from the Colonel.

SITUATION DIRE STOP DOCTOR LAWLER TAKEN CHARGE STOP DELAY JOURNEY STOP CP

The telegram was written in such a way that anyone else reading it would not discern the reality behind the words. There was no mistaking the succinct message that only he would understand. That Doctor Lawler had taken matters into hand could only mean he had Audrey in his care in the asylum. There was no mistaking this. It would seem his precious wife was lost. She had slipped beyond the realm of normality by the time he returned to their cottage to find her cocooned in her bed. The telegram was their bid to allay him from contacting Audrey, but if they thought they could keep him from his precious Charlotte they were mistaken.

Audrey had been placed in the asylum in Charles' care. How dare they turn her over to Charles? How dare he take her in? Why had Charles not conferred with him on the matter? He could not believe that so few words would unravel his life in one swoop. He reread them over and over, hoping he had misinterpreted their meaning, but there was nothing to be gained.

Audrey's family had cast him away so easily. Had they been angry that he had tried to return her to them for a cure without his accompaniment?

Be damned. He could not ignore orders from a superior. His father-in-law was a force that he could not reckon with but how he longed to see his wife. They had become a family and now he felt he had lost everything.

After the telegram's arrival, he became less inclined to care about the militia and more interested in the contents of a whiskey bottle.

He was expected back at his post at dawn seven days after the dire news had been delivered but could not rise from his drunken haze. A soldier knocked at his door with a command that he turn out at the south barracks within the hour. He pushed the soldier from his doorstep and slammed the door closed. This action set in motion a downward spiral that would soon end his military career. He did not care to listen or take command any longer. He had lost everything held dear to him. That afternoon he was ordered by the Commander in Charge to visit him at his quarters. As a further act of defiance he waited until the hour was late, pulling on his coat and leaving it unbuttoned, and sliding his feet into his shoes but leaving his laces untied. He pounded on the door of the commander's cottage. The maid showed him to the study.

'You wanted to see me?' Michael said.

'Good Lord, man.' The commander looked him over. 'You look as though you have just landed at the point on a ship that has been at sea for months.'

Michael knew the reason he had been called here. He was to be relieved of duty. With his experience in the militia he knew the look a commanding officer bestowed on a soldier that was a loss to him now.

Michael did not care to respond with talk of his appearance or his present situation.

'What do you want, Commander?'

'Be very careful, Corporal McGowan. I would not appear too indignant if I were you.'

'If I may be blunt with you sir, I no longer care for the rules or regulations of my superiors.'

The commander ignored the statement. 'I know a beaten man when I see one and you corporal will not find your saviour in the bottom of a whiskey bottle. I am aware you received some devastating news.'

Michael nodded once while retaining eye contact.

'I have discussed the situation at length with Colonel Price, if you must know.'

'And what did he communicate to you?'

'That he considers it is best for all parties that we find you another post. A fresh start so you can get along with your life.'

'Is that a fact? And where would I be going, sir?'

'Tasmania. There are varied established posts there. You could settle into something and take some time to forget all the happenings of late.'

Michael's immediate anger was difficult to mask. Forget all the happenings of late? This should have come as no surprise to him. The military was proving as cold and unfeeling as the rip he looked across day after day between the heads. That he was being discarded from his post for the comfort and security of everyone else was no surprise.

'The Colonel has expressed that you cease any communication with him. As you will understand, it is his wish to keep this situation cloaked in secrecy. It is best for all concerned.'

Michael bit back the words he wanted to say. It was not best for him, but suited everyone else it would seem. He would not allow them to get away with that so easily. Their lies and deceit would be revealed but he needed to withdraw from the sham the militia had placed before him. His father-in-law along with the high-ranking officials he had in his favour made him ill.

'Very well then, sir. If you think it best.' He would not reveal any intention that he was considering opposing orders.

'All the necessary plans are in place and you are to make your way to Melbourne tomorrow.'

'Well then, it has all been laid before me,' Michael said as he stood. 'I bid you farewell then, sir.'

He left the commander's cottage and walked toward his own. The sound of the water lapping onto the sand stopped him. The last time he had been here he had watched his damaged wife wade into the water with her nightgown on. He should not have sent her back to her parents. If only he could see her, he could aid her recovery. He was sure of this. He had to help her and he had to reunite her with their baby girl. He sat on the beach while contemplating what to do. The summer breeze had cooled after the sun had dipped away and the sand was cold on his backside. He knew his decision before he had pondered it. He must leave the militia and bid Point Nepean goodbye. According to his superiors, he was set to take up his new appointment in Tasmania. Tomorrow would cement his plans.

The following morning Michael was escorted on horseback to the gates of Point Nepean by one of his officers. 'I regret your leaving us, sir,' the young soldier said.

'You do not need me to show you the way. You hold promise without my command,' he said as he swung his leg over the saddle and dropped to the ground.

'Your carriage will be along shortly to escort you to Melbourne. I will wait with you, sir.'

Michael began to pull his belongings from the saddle. 'I thank you for the escort but I will be happy to wait for my connecting transportation alone.'

He turned away and threw his duffel bag over his shoulder, mumbling as he walked from the gates and the young soldier, 'I need nothing more from the militia. I bid you good riddance.'

He looked toward the rutted road ahead and took quick steps, determined to get away from Point Nepean as quickly as he could. He would be arrested for desertion if caught. The road inclined for miles then pitched downward, then rose up once more, then declined again. His pace slowed and he chastised his pride that had caused him to refuse the comfort of a carriage. This frustrated him as darkness pressed in and he was in desperate need of liquor. His boots pinched his sweating feet. His shirt collar began to chafe his neck. The uniform he had worn with pride now annoyed him immensely. At the first sign of civilization he would rid himself of it and purchase new clothing, but not before he had a bottle in his grasp.

With many miles until the next hotel and the possibility of a drink, he was getting weary. In the early hours of the morning he was forced to stop and sleep. The dense bush allowed him some protection and he thanked the summer season for a mild night.

The sound of gulls woke him. He sat up and felt the

muscles in his back and shoulders resist his movements. Once his body had succumbed to sleep it became obvious that his exhaustion had allowed the discomfort of gravel and rocks to dig into his skin. He moved his head from side to side and wrapped his hand over the top of his shoulder in a bid to massage the aches away.

He stared out over a bluff and could see across the bay. He traced its arc all the way to the Port of Melbourne. The road before him fell away and flattened out and was lost as the end of the peninsula curved away in the distance. He had travelled further than he realised with the darkness hiding the view of the easy route. If he followed it for at least seventy miles he would find Melbourne town. It would take him days but this would give him time. A course of action needed to be well thought out. Would he ignore the Colonel's order and demand the release of his wife, or would he have a better chance to re-enter Ararat as a stranger?

Michael decided he would walk, even to the point of exhaustion, until a pub came into view. He would stop and drink himself numb then stumble to the nearby scrub and tea trees and sleep off his drunken disgrace. The sea air and harsh sun burnt his hands and face as he traversed the coastline and drew closer to Melbourne. Pubs became plentiful and as the population increased, so too did the prospect of suitable clothing and further obscurity.

By the time the city streets came into view he felt no consolation from the long walk. He could not forget her, as the militia and her parents had expected him to, and he could not forgive the devil that had taken his wife. How could her mother and father forbid him from seeing his family? He had entrusted her to them and they had neglected to care and protect her. He bought a train ticket and departed Spencer Street Station bound for Ballarat. With pubs aplenty in the inland city, he spent the next week falling across every bar disallowing his head to clear.

He began the fifty-five-mile walk from Ballarat to Ararat on a Sunday afternoon. As the pub on the outskirts of town shut its doors he tucked a bottle of brandy beneath his arm and headed west. Taking deep swigs from the bottle he walked into the darkness and awoke in a ditch on the side of the road.

He could blame the brandy for making his head heavy but the dark cloud of anger had settled in his mind. Everybody who had wronged him would pay attention. He would rescue his wife and daughter and take them far away from here.

It was dusk as the unfamiliar road gave away its location as the expanse of white buildings turned almost grey against the sky. It dominated his attention. He stopped and looked up at it for the longest time and felt his anger leap. He yelled, 'I will rescue you, my girl.' His voice was whipped away and lost to the wind, just as she had been. He bowed his head and trudged on.

He was glad it was dark as the shopfronts came into view. Should he happen across anybody familiar in town he worried he would be recognised. This could not help his plan as the Colonel would know by now he had defied orders and would possibly be on the lookout for his return. Until he could figure out his plan fully, word could not get out that he had returned. He walked past the barbershop window and looked at his reflection with the gaslight casting one side of his face aglow. He was nothing more than a dishevelled vagrant with a scruffy beard and filthy hair that hung over his eyes and collar.

Michael rented a room at the Shire Hall Hotel. Tomorrow he would purchase clean clothes and new boots. He bathed but did not shave. He shook out his clothes and wiped his boots with a wet cloth.

He threw his duffel into the corner and locked the door behind him as the bar beckoned with the promise of dulling the pain of the past weeks.

'New in town?' the publican asked.

Michael kept his gaze on the bar and was surprised that he had not been recognised. He had been in here a number of times over the few weeks when he had first visited Ararat. It was a short while ago when he was courting Audrey and setting the impression upon his soon to be father-in-law.

'Just lookin' for work,' he answered as he paid for a bottle of whiskey and took a glass from the publican.

He found a table in the corner and set the bottle he had bought on it and filled his glass over and over. Of the few patrons that came into the establishment, nobody approached him. He gave off a terrifying look of brooding anger that would deter anyone's attention — whether of a friendly or threatening nature. He drank until he could not stand unaided.

Light spilled through the small window into his room and burned his eyelids. He did not recall making his way to his room or how he had managed to find his way clear to close the door behind him.

He walked through town and became bold as he passed

some once familiar faces. Nobody gave him a second glance. After purchasing some new clothes and a pair of glasses he took the time to walk to the base of Flint Hill and calm his thumping heart. After ascending the steep driveway and signing the register for Mr Gibbs at the gatehouse, he could feel his heart pummelling inside his chest due to the exertion of the situation, both in a physical and mental sense. Before his nerves bested him, he knocked on the door.

Matron invited him inside and he was offered a job within the hour. It would seem the military had given him the ability to gain the confidence of the Matron. Whilst she may have deemed his appearance unruly, she judged him strong enough in physical as well as mental disposition to work in the asylum as an orderly. He started immediately and easily blended in.

The number of staff working in that horrible place was staggering. The inmates were in wretched condition. He found the place simply awful. Watching the conditions the inmates endured was only bearable due to his capacity to drink, in turn making him somewhat numb. He had never asked about Audrey's whereabouts. He did not dare but his agitation grew when he considered Charlotte was being kept from her mother whilst she was locked away in here and her father had been pushed from her life. It plagued him that things had spiralled away so quickly and with little to no control on his part.

It was prevalent that the doctors and staff were ill equipped to look after these poor souls, with cures not working as expected. He had been unable to find Audrey's location. Her name did not appear on any ledger and he had checked them all. Either she was no longer in here or had been moved to another asylum. He doubted this possibility. The doctors in here were well known to the Price family and it would be in the interest of all concerned to keep her close in the case that she would improve.

He looked through the ledger that held the dates of inmates' admissions and discovered that there was only three the day preceding the telegram. One was a male and there were two women within two days of one another. Ruth Oxford and Sally Smith had both been signed in by Doctor Lawler, the superintendent. Her name had been changed. That made him more angered at her parents. He would ensure that everyone was held accountable for this. The torment of learning she had been hidden away in here under the guise of another name made things much worse. This was all he could stand. Night after night in his drunken state, whether he lay in bed at the hotel or paced the wards while on duty, he planned and thought of nothing else but freeing his Audrey from this hell-hole and rescuing his daughter from her grandparents' care.

Chapter 4

Doctor Lawler walked from the connecting door of the men's ward. The women's ward was quiet with locked doors lining both sides of the corridor. This level held the less disruptive cases within the asylum. With the setting sun each day a change occurred with the inmates. They became noisy as dusk threatened. A nurse passed and she did not lift her eyes to look at him; instead, she quickened her step. It was a wise move on her behalf. He was angry.

As he began unlocking successive cell doors and peering into the interior of each small space, Doctor Lawler acknowledged only those inmates who spoke to him while ignoring any who were asleep or happy in their own silence. He swung each door open and walked to the next, leaving all open behind him. It would serve the staff well to have more inmates to put to bed once this ordeal was over.

As he reached the banister of the staircase he looked back to see the inmates wandering from their rooms. Some were dancing in jubilation. Others were walking from their cells in confusion. Walking down the staircase to his office, he could hear squeals rising from the freed inmates. He closed the door, leaned back against it and emptied his lungs in a gust of breath. What to do next? Running a hand down his face he whispered in exasperation, 'Somebody must have seen something.'

He unlocked a cabinet, flung the door open and pulled a bottle of brandy from the shelf. He pulled the cork and swigged from the open neck of the bottle as he began to pace the floor talking between mouthfuls. 'The Colonel will have me tossed from this facility when he hears of this. My professional name will be worthless after this fiasco has become news.' He was babbling, allowing his fear to spring forth.

'Think, Charles, think,' he intoned as he gently knocked his open palm against his forehead. Talking out into the open to nobody at all allowed him to process the situation in the hope that a clue he had missed would arise. 'She was removed from her locked cell and it was relocked. She has to be somewhere obscure. Where? There is no place that has gone unchecked. So that leaves what? She could not scale the damned wall. That would be impossible. Somebody removed her from that cell. That leaves only one other scenario. She has been removed from the asylum altogether?'

It was fast becoming apparent to him that he was wasting time locked away in his office with no answers to be found. Considering she had not been seen since the evening before, could the night staff hold any answers? He would summon them. The nurse had failed to check the even numbered cells at the beginning of her shift so she would be unable to tell whether Audrey had been in there or not. It would not take long to learn the whereabouts of the individual staff member on duty in the refractory ward last evening, and it was all he could think to do at present. Leaving his office, he slammed the door closed behind him.

As his hand clutched the banister he stopped mid tread on the staircase.

'Celia,' he whispered. It was a revelation. She had not been in her bed when he had risen this morning, and he had not asked her where she had been when they had sat in silence across the breakfast table from one another. Their conversations had been very terse of late. His wife had some explaining to do.

Charles yelled out to the nearest nurse, 'You, down there!' His yelling commanded more than one staff member's attention.

'Me?' The nurse put her hand up to her neck, her eyes widening in fear.

'Yes, you. Come here,' he said in frustration. 'And be swift about it.'

The nurse scurried forwards and curtsied in front of him.

'That is not necessary.'

'My apologies, Doctor,' she said, as a red hue began to rise from her neck up to her face.

'What's your name, then?' he asked brusquely.

'It's Trinny,' she answered, dropping her eyes to the floor.

'Ah, the one who neglected to note our missing inmate?'

'I am, sir.' She began to sob.

'Now is not the time for nonsense,' Charles interjected. 'I need you to do something for me.'

'Yes, sir.'

'I need you to fetch my wife. We live in the superintendent's lodgings. Do you know where that is?'

'Yes, sir. I do,' Trinny said, blinking back tears.

'Go then. Run as fast as you can and tell her to return with you right away. It is of the upmost importance. Do you understand?'

'Yes. Yes, I do.' Trinny turned from him and rushed down the corridor.

'Wait, one more thing,' he barked as she stopped abruptly and turned back toward him. 'Answer me this.'

'Yes, sir.'

'Are you certain the door to our missing inmate's room was locked when she was discovered missing?'

'The kitchen hand said the door was locked and the cell was empty.'

'I would wring your neck if I knew it would help the present situation.'

'I am sincerely sorry, sir,' Trinny said as she wrung her hands in front of her.

'There is no time for any of this, however. Please fetch my wife right away.' He turned his back and walked away.

Trinny took a deep breath and wiped the tears from her eyes and cheeks over and over. Once out in the courtyard, she took a deep breath and walked quickly past the dairy, feeling some ease as she escaped the pressure from within the interior. Since beginning work here mere weeks ago, she had seen Mrs Lawler on occasion visiting the female inmates. The nurses she had befriended thus far held Doctor Lawler's wife in high esteem. One in particular, Jillian, had taken a real shine to Mrs Lawler and had promised Trinny she would offer an introduction the very next time she visited. This afternoon's circumstance was certainly not what she had imagined would be her first introduction to the superintendent's wife. After today, there may never be a chance to meet Mrs Lawler as she feared her future employment at the asylum was unassured.

If not for the tumultuous events within the asylum tonight, Trinny would have been skipping towards the superintendent's lodge. Instead, she walked briskly past the massive vegetable garden and open paddocks. As she approached the lodge she could see the housemaid gathering washing from the line.

Is Mrs Lawler at home?' Trinny questioned before putting her hand to the gate.

'Yes, she is. Who are you?'

'Could you tell her Doctor Lawler sent me?'

'Didn't answer my question. Who are ya?'

'Oh, my name is Trinny. I am a nurse from the asylum. It is urgent that I see her.'

The nursemaid hoisted the full basket to her hip. 'Wait at the front door.'

Trinny had hardly taken the first step to the veranda when she heard voices.

'To whom are you talking?'

'Some nurse from the asylum, ma'am.'

The door swung open and Celia looked at Trinny.

'What are you doing here? It is almost dark? What has happened?' Celia's tone was sharp.

Trinny curtsied. 'I have been sent by Doctor Lawler to fetch you.' She was so taken by the beauty of Mrs Lawler that she blurted the statement out before showing her respect by introducing herself. Mrs Lawler had wide blue eyes that showed concern but shone bright, and their effect against her blonde hair was startling. She wore a beautiful dress that cinched in at her small waist. Trinny stared up at her from the middle step of the veranda and could not find her voice for a moment.

'Has something happened to him?' Celia asked. Charles had left Lady Montague's party with such haste. She knew he had been summoned to the asylum urgently. Something dire had happened.

It was no surprise he had not told her he was leaving. Once upon a time he would have, but things had been difficult between them of late. She worried for him and the constant pressure he was under. While she could be blamed for a good deal of it she could not go on should anything happen to him.

Trinny whispered harshly, 'Sally Smith is missing from her cell.'

Celia frowned. 'Who?'

'Nobody knows where she is.'

Celia's anxiety over her husband's wellbeing dissipated as quickly as it had surfaced. Her features hardened as she surmised the real reason behind the order for her to make haste to the asylum.

'And Doctor Lawler sent you to fetch me? Why on earth?' She reached inside the door and gathered her hat and coat.

'Yes, he told me to bring you to the facility right away. He is very angered by the disappearance of the inmate.'

Jamming her hat down on her head and pushing her arms into the coat sleeves, Celia pulled the door behind her and yelled out to the housemaid, 'I'll be back for supper, Lydia.'

At the asylum, Charles was waiting in the courtyard and promptly dismissed Trinny as she walked towards him with Celia.

The cool air that fell upon the evening was not a flicker on the chill of the meeting of husband and wife. Though Trinny knew neither of them well due to their higher social standing, she saw no difference between people's emotions no matter their pecking order in society.

Charles watched Trinny retreat enough into the distance before turning his gaze to his wife and staring down at her.

Celia huffed, 'I will not have you look at me as though I am guilty of a crime.'

'A crime? Who said anything about a crime? It seems to me that you have stuck your nose into business that is not yours to own, and now we have a woman missing who has supposedly not set foot outside her cell and yet is nowhere to be found.'

Celia looked at him with indignation. 'It would seem that the problem is in the very words you say.'

'And what is that?'

'That your patient has seen neither daylight nor fresh air in the year since she arrived. The very fact that you are calling upon me to assist you, can only mean you are suffering discomfort, Charles.' Hearing his name drop from her lips with disdain caught him off guard momentarily, and he tried to refocus as his wife continued with her observations.

'Why else would you call upon your lowly wife to help find an inmate from within the many nooks and crannies of this godforsaken hellhole? An inmate, nonetheless, I would not know if I fell over her.'

Charles ground his teeth. 'Oh to the contrary, my darling wife. You are well acquainted with this inmate.' He leaned in so close to prevent anyone passing by from hearing his words. 'It is the elusive Audrey McGowan we seek and if I gain so much as a sniff that you know of her whereabouts, I will personally put you over my knee and give you a hiding of the kind that you have never experienced before.'

Celia sucked in her breath. The immediate shock she displayed proved to Charles that she did not know anything of Audrey's disappearance.

Celia felt tears forming. She would not let him see her cry. That, in itself, was heartbreaking. In the early days of their courtship and marriage, she had never withheld her emotions from Charles, and her marriage was set to unravel if she did not make amends with him. She loved him dearly but was still so angry with him for his actions over these past weeks. If she had been able to foresee her life on arriving in Ararat two years earlier would she change anything? No, she would not, but it was important she assist in any way to uncover Audrey's whereabouts.

She took a deep breath to stave off the emotion brewing inside her, squared her shoulders and said, 'What can I do?'

Charles watched her intently. 'Where do you think she could have got to? Did she say anything to you when you discovered her?

'When I discovered her locked in that cell in the refractory ward?' she harrumphed. 'Charles, she was incapable of saying a word. She is so damaged and emaciated I would hardly think her capable of escape unencumbered.'

Charles leant in and whispered, 'That is why I thought you may know of something of her disappearance. It would seem that since you became involved with her she has now gone missing. Every time you place yourself in the midst of these women, things unravel. I have asked you many times to stay away from my work here and you feel it is your god given right to poke around and preach of my shortcomings. Well, it stops after tonight. Do you hear me? No more.'

Celia looked up at her husband and the disdain with which he stared back signalled the gravity of the situation. He was very angry with her. Her only hope of proving to him that she held worth in the asylum would begin if she uncovered Audrey.

'Were you here in the early hours this morning?' Charles asked.

Celia bit her lip and did not answer.

'You were not in your room before breakfast.'

She was surprised by the question. He had sought her this morning. That he had looked in on her showed he cared for her more than she thought was possible at present. They had quarrelled so much in the past weeks that Charles had neither touched her nor sought her for anything.

It would anger Charles further if she answered his question but she could not lie. 'I was here.'

Charles closed his eyes and sucked in a huge breath. 'Did you have anything at all to do with this situation?'

She opened her mouth to speak but he placed his hand up to halt her. 'And let me just say that if you do not tell me the absolute truth I will lose what morsel of trust I have in you, which is but a slither at present.'

'I had nothing to do with her disappearance. I would not dare to jeopardise your career or another person's life. I cannot see why you would think me so deceitful.'

'I do not think I know you any longer. You have shown my career little respect, and the lives of others only concern you when you believe they will benefit directly from your decisions. For the moment, though, I do not need you to talk your way around this situation. I need you to search more than I require your honesty, so if you would assist in any way, that is all I require. She may be more receptive to seeing you if you should happen upon her.'

'Very well, then.' Celia turned away from him and walked through the courtyard to find Trinny waiting for her. Celia was so rattled by Charles' low opinion of her and the harsh way he had spoken that she took a few moments to collect her thoughts.

'Where should we begin, or rather, which places have not been checked as yet?' she asked the young nurse.

'I am quite unsure as I have been in numerous places since the chaos ensued.'

'Very well then, why don't we head in this direction?' Celia pointed a finger ahead of her as they set forth.

While it was the beginnings of summer, a sunny day with a clear sky still allowed the chill of the evening to press down on them. Celia pulled her coat closer around her not only in a bid to block the fresh night air, but also in some small attempt to hold herself together.

'Where are you?' she whispered to the darkness. Looking across at an airing court, an open round space protected by a shingled roof, she saw a lone figure seated on a bench. Her heart soared.

'Who is there?' she asked excitedly.

'Miss Celia, is that you?'

'Oh Marjorie, it is you,' Celia said, trying to force some eagerness into her voice.

Marjorie flapped her hands, beckoning Celia closer.

Celia leaned in close to the woman. 'What is it, Marjorie? Do you have something to tell me?'

Marjorie giggled. She placed her index finger up to her lips. 'Shhhhhh.'

Celia smiled. 'I will not tell them you are here.'

Trinny was standing behind Celia. 'Mrs Lawler. I do think it best if we return her to her ward.'

'No,' Celia said as she straightened. 'We do not possess the time to return her to the ward. Besides, she loves being outside. Rightly, she despises being locked away, just as you and I would.' Celia stared at Trinny in defiance, almost daring the nurse to argue the point.

Trinny lowered her eyes and stepped away. 'Very well, then,' she said quietly.

Celia squeezed Marjorie's shoulder and turned to follow Trinny.

They walked side by side in silence until Trinny said, 'I can see why the women speak so lovingly of you, Mrs Lawler.'

'I am their advocate, that is all.' Celia was on the precipice of tears. Torn by her undying need to help these women and the sad fact she would be cut off from them.

'Why don't we move forth to the perimeter wall?' Celia said as she pointed ahead.

As soon as the ground began to slope away to the base of the wall, they adjusted their footing and walked sideways.

Trinny made it to the base of the wall first. Bracing her hands against the smooth render, she looked up at the sheer height of the structure and without turning to Celia said, 'I'm afraid I will lose my job here.'

'And why would you think that?'

'Because I was the nurse in charge of the refractory ward today and I neglected to note that Sally Smith was missing.'

Celia closed her eyes. How she wished they could call Sally Smith by her true name. 'Well, I am certain that once we find her and the situation is rectified you will be able to explain your case as to why she was overlooked.'

'I am also fearful they may think I had something to do with her being released from her cell. After all, the person who let her out had to be somebody with a key, and I was the nurse charged with her care this morning.'

'I doubt they would point a finger at you. After all, if you had released her, you would be missing also, would you not?'

'That is a point, I suppose. Although a skeleton key can open most every lock in this place.'

'Did you have anything to do with Sally Smith? Is that why Doctor Lawler summoned you?'

'Yes, I have been privy to the refractory on occasion and have worked with the women there.'

As the lie left Celia's lips she closed her eyes and took a deep breath. The memory of the day she met Audrey made her want to sob out loud but she held it within. The meeting had coincided with the very first time she had met Charles.

Celia gazed at the high ceiling, in awe of the square coloured glass panel at its centre. The room was the most beautiful one she had ever seen. The walls were decorated with elaborate paintings framed with ornate carved timber. Patterned plaster cornices decorated with flowers caught her attention. Her surrounds were something to behold.

The lamps placed at intervals around the home gave it an alluring light. The heat from the day was dissipating as dusk fell, and whilst the windows had been left open for the heat to ooze from its interior, the room, now full of people, was making it rather stifling.

'It is a lovely room, is it not?' The comment came from a woman standing nearby, and drew Celia's attention back to the crowd of people milling around inside.

Celia addressed the stranger, 'Why, it is.'

'I'm Audrey.' The young woman held her gloved hand forward.

'I'm ...'

'I know. You are Celia, Lady Montague's niece. I have heard all about you.'

'Oh,' was all Celia could respond. It seemed her reputation preceded her, making her feel at a distinct disadvantage. While everyone seemed to know who she was, she in fact knew nobody.

'After all, this party is being held in your honour.' The young woman smiled warmly.

'I arrived last night and was told there would be a huge gathering this evening,' Celia said. 'I am quite bewildered at the number of people in attendance.'

'Lady Montague was thrilled to have you visit for the very first time; she just had to proclaim it.'

'Considering I arrived only last night I fear I am not acquainted with anybody as yet. I spent most of the day in bed recovering from my journey. I would have welcomed some time to settle and explore before my aunt thrust me into such a glaring spotlight.' Celia looked around her and flushed as smiles were cast her way.

'Do not worry.' Audrey touched her arm. 'There will be plenty of time for you to discover the grandeur of your aunt's home and the surrounding district.'

The first Celia had seen of the countryside was the view from her bedroom window only this afternoon. She decided to take a quick stroll but was taken over by the maid who had been installed at her beck and call to primp, preen and dress her for the evening.

'So you live by the seaside, your aunt tells me,' Audrey said.

'Yes, yes I do,' Celia answered. 'I live with my father and sister.'

'It must be lovely living by the sea?'

'Oh, it is. However, I will admit one thing; the countryside is thrilling to me. I hope to share my education with my sister upon my return.'

'There you are, dearest.' A young man approached in military uniform and grasped Audrey's gloved hand.

Celia watched the interlude with interest, noting that the man's greeting brought a flush to the cheeks of her new acquaintance.

Audrey's eyes widened. 'Why, hello dearest. Michael, this is Celia Loddon.'

'Ah, Lady Montague's niece. We have heard so much about you,' he answered, grasping her hand in a warm gesture. 'It is a pleasure to meet you, Celia. How was your trip across the countryside?'

'It was quite fast by train but the carriage ride from the station was somewhat rickety in the dark. I am happy to be here at last.'

'Celia was just telling me she resides by the sea. Do you

think we could plan a move closer to those parts?' she gazed at Michael, her eyes wide in anticipation of his answer.

'If all goes to plan that is precisely where I will be stationed and you will be right by my side. That is if your father gives us his blessing.' Michael grinned at both women in turn.

Audrey giggled. 'I do not think there is any risk he will say no. Daddy has already sent word that he endorses your move to the lovely Point Nepean.'

'Let us not bore our new friend with such matters, my darling.' He then leant in low and whispered. 'I am going to ask him now, out on the terrace.'

Audrey clapped her hands together like a small child. 'Yes, I was hoping it would be tonight!'

Michael winked at her and she smiled. Celia was in awe of the exchange. She felt her heart beat wildly in her chest. It would be untoward of her to seek confirmation of what was obviously a marriage proposal in the making.

Fortunately Audrey leaned in to validate her suspicions. 'He is asking Daddy if he can have my hand.'

Celia grinned at her. 'That is glorious news and I have only just met you.'

'Quickly, people are staring at us.' Audrey giggled as she slid her arm inside Celia's. 'Let us take a walk out in the garden. That way we can gaze across to the terrace and see what is happening.'

'Let's!' Celia replied as she allowed herself to be swept along with the excitement. The two young women made their way through the crowd, making slow progress as guests stopped them at intervals, seeking introductions.

Once outside, they walked directly across the lawn. The

night was now dark, and light extended from the windows, as well as from the terrace doors, which had been thrown open so guests could spill outside.

The new friends soon learnt that their birthdays were exactly four months apart. They held similar interests, including a fondness for literature of the unusual kind, and both despised needlework, which as accomplished ladies they were expected to enjoy.

An elaborate bench seat was aptly placed beneath the canopy of a magnificent willow tree. It was the perfect place from which to spy through the slim curtain of leaves, allowing them privacy. The prying eyes of those searching out the guest of honour were blind, as the two girls had disappeared beyond the curtain of darkness the willow allowed.

'Alone at last.' Celia let out a breath as she pulled her gloves from her fingers then ripped them from her hands. 'I despise these things. They are so tedious,' she said, fanning them back and forth across her face.

Audrey's backside hovered over the bench as she found herself caught between finding reprieve for her aching feet and assuaging her curiosity over the moment presenting itself on the terrace.

'I think I can see Daddy talking to a group of men. Oh, I am so excited.'

'I can only dream that someday it will be my turn to marry,' Celia said wistfully.

'You will get the opportunity, I am sure,' Audrey responded, all the while staring toward the terrace. 'Is there anybody courting you at home?'

'Absolutely nobody. Our town is so small and my father

is the reverend, which hardly bodes well for the young local men to come knocking.'

'What about your mother? What happened to her?'

'She died when I was twelve and my sister was eight. I was left to look after things while my father kept the local clergy afloat.'

Audrey laughed. 'In a seaside town keeping afloat must be quite an interesting challenge.' And then, noticing what was happening on the terrace, she squealed, 'Michael is talking to Daddy! He is there! He is there!'

Both girls leapt to the edge of the canopy, keeping within the overhang of the tree's outer branches. Excitement and anticipation arced between them.

Celia could see Michael in close liaison with an older man dressed in full military uniform. 'Your father looks foreboding,' she whispered to Audrey.

'Everyone calls him *The Colonel*. However, he's a pushover when it comes to his only daughter. He has no choice but to approve of Michael. He introduced us.'

Silence fell between them as they observed a conversation that could only be imagined from their position so far afield. Guests approached the two men and it seemed Michael would not gain an opportunity to direct his question. Finally, the Colonel reached an arm out and gripped Michael's hand in his own. He then slapped him on the shoulder numerous times.

'Come along then!' Audrey grabbed Celia's hand and pulled her along. Celia was trying to wrench her gloves onto her clammy hands as they neared the front door. Audrey walked inside to gasps and applause. The Colonel was in the midst of a crowd gathered in the main lounge. 'There she is,' his voice boomed.

'Audrey, come here! Michael! Where are you?' The crowd laughed as guests pushed the young couple forward. Celia enjoyed having the focus being removed from her.

'Three cheers for the soon to be Mr and Mrs Michael McGowan!' the Colonel's voice boomed.

Cheers erupted throughout the room. Celia eventually made her way through the throng to wish Audrey and Michael all the luck in the world.

Audrey clutched Celia's hand and said, 'You must stay for the wedding. You must!'

'I hope to,' Celia said, before mouthing, 'We will talk again soon!' as the waiting crowd pushed in on them, everyone wanting to add their congratulations.

Lady Montague approached Celia. 'Well, my darling niece. It has been an exciting party, don't you think?' she looked down at the young woman with mirth. 'One can only hope that very soon we will have some news of our own to share with our neighbours.'

Celia looked at her aunt. 'I am in high doubt of that, Aunty,' she said as she took a glass of punch from the tray a member of the wait staff held out to her.

With the glass in one hand and her aunt's arm sufficiently seated in the crook of her elbow, Celia took a stroll throughout the room.

'That is Mrs Price, Audrey's proud mother,' Lady Montague explained. 'Over there is Councillor Sherwood, and that fine looking gentlemen he speaks to is the good Doctor Lawler. He has just returned from Ballarat where he worked in the vicinity of the waning goldfields.'

'I beg your pardon Aunty, where did you say he had been?'

Celia put the punch glass to her lips and took a large sip. As her gaze fell upon the doctor, her mouth suddenly turned dry and her ears filled with the thudding of her heart. And just at that moment, as though feeling her eyes lingering on him, the young doctor turned in her direction and offered a slight bow of his head.

Celia felt her face flush as she stared at him. He was the most handsome man she had ever seen. To be a practitioner was to be held in high esteem. Add to this excellent social standing, a handsome face and bold manner ... and well, it would be an understatement to say Celia found herself staring at Doctor Lawler in awe.

He began to cross the floor towards her but was stopped by a guest who had been identified to her as Mrs Stokes.

Celia heard the high-pitched sound of Mrs Stokes halting his course. 'Doctor Lawler! Why, we are so blessed to have you amongst us once more! When do you begin your work on the poor unhinged folk at the asylum on Flint Hill?'

'Mrs Stokes, I am so grateful to be back, hopefully for good. I start there in a week's time. Now, if you will excuse me, I seek an introduction with Lady Montague's niece.'

Doctor Lawler looked away from Mrs Stokes and smiled at Celia as he approached. She was well aware her stupefied gaze made her look like an imbecile but she could not change the look on her face, just as she could not halt the racing beat of her heart. She was under no illusion that he could see signs of her heart's excitement pulsing through her bodice.

Mrs Stokes was still talking to his back. 'Well, do not let me stop you then, Doctor. Press on.'

Doctor Lawler's gaze returned to Mrs Stokes for a mere

moment before swinging back around to Celia. He had the bluest eyes she had ever seen. His intense gaze pressed into the very depths of her soul.

Doctor Lawler politely switched his gaze to Celia's aunt as he extended his hand to hers and held it in his grasp. 'Lady Montague, I do thank you for inviting me along. Forgive me for being unable to accept until my arrival today.'

'That is satisfactory, Doctor Lawler. I am so glad you were able to make it. Besides, no advanced notice was needed. This … is my niece.'

'Miss Celia Loddon. Yes, I am aware she is the reason for the party. Such a worthy cause.' He looked down at her through his eyelashes as he lowered his body to kiss the back of her gloved hand.

Celia's voice faltered as she said, 'I arrived only last night, not long before you, it would seem.'

He did not take his eyes from her as she stared at him, waiting for him to say something, anything. Finally, he said. 'We may have been on the same train. I am sure I would have recalled seeing you if we had passed in the aisle.' His eyes danced with mischief. Celia felt her cheeks begin to burn.

He coughed into his closed fist. 'Do you think I could steal your niece away for some refreshment? My throat is rather dry.' He held his arm out towards her and she placed her hand on the inside of his elbow, allowing him to lead her away from her aunt.

'Excuse us,' he said as Lady Montague beamed after them.

'Of course,' she replied.

Celia gulped her fruit punch so she could place the empty glass on a tray that swung past her. Faces swirled in front of her as guests approached to be introduced. Words of praise and welcome to the doctor were also spoken in passing, and it was not long before the heat in the room pressed in on Celia and she felt she would swoon. While she knew she was in the best company with a doctor close to her side, she was also terrified of the risk of bringing unwanted attention to herself.

'Could we please sit? I fear I am becoming overwhelmed at present.'

'Absolutely.' Doctor Lawler gestured to an unoccupied window seat. 'This way. I will get you some tea with sugar to give you some strength.'

'That would be wonderful.' Celia welcomed a few moments to catch her breath, away from the many guests demanding an introduction. More distressing was the close proximity of the doctor with his handsome face and attentiveness. The thought of gathering her wits while awaiting the refreshment of a sweet drink would settle her nerves twofold.

She smoothed her skirts out as another guest approached. The young man introduced himself as Jack Harding, and explained his father's longstanding friendship with her aunt. He had hardly completed his statement when an arm stretched between. Held aloft for her to take was a saucer with a teacup balanced perfectly on it.

Celia drew a breath as she gripped the saucer and tried her best to stop it from rattling. She placed the cup to her lips and felt the heat of the tea, which was sweetened to perfection, run down her throat.

'I'm Charles Lawler.' He placed his hand out to Jack and Celia could not help but feel the tension in his voice that suggested to the new arrival that Celia was being well looked after by a suitor.

Jack excused himself with a promise to call on her in the coming days.

'Charles.'

'Yes.'

'That is your name?'

'That it is.'

'I had not been privy to it before now.'

'Well, I would like you to use it from now on. I like the way it sounds coming from your lips.' He stared at her mouth for a long moment. Nervously, she looked at his eyes as he continued to stare back at her. She desperately tried to turn his attention from her. She had never been shown this sort of consideration and it frightened and elated her all at once.

'I do long to stroll in the garden in the daylight,' she said finally. 'My aunt has a lovely garden.'

He sat beside her and leaned in close to her ear.

'The loveliest sight is indoors today.' He said.

Celia looked down at her lap and tried her best to stop the cup from jangling against its saucer.

'You are not used to such focussed attention are you?'

Keeping her eyes cast downward, she quietly answered. 'No, I am not.'

'Well, I must say that you are a welcome surprise. I know your aunt is a spirited woman of the community but it would seem she is turning her hand to matchmaking.'

Celia's eyes swung up to meet his gaze and the curve of his lips, and his grin held her captive.

Celia did not believe her aunt to be so resourceful as to deliver this handsome man to her in the hope he would make her his wife. She did not believe herself to be so beautiful and worthy of such attentions.

She decided the excitement of the evening and its events were hallucinogenic. In order to anchor her feelings in reality, she positioned the back of her hand to her forehead.

'It is rather warm in here,' Charles commented, staring intently at her. His gaze missed nothing and did not waver, and while she could not brazenly stare back, she was able to observe all too clearly the feeling he stirred within. He was monopolising her, holding her in his grip like a hound on a hunt when it fixed its gaze on a fox.

'Yes, it is,' Celia said, 'and these gloves hold me captive.' As well as you, she thought to herself.

'Would it not be rather freeing to rip them from your hands?' Charles said. I would happily do it for you if such an action were not considered untoward.'

Celia looked at him as his bold attentiveness shocked her.

There was an unmistakable look in his eyes that suggested he intended to take much more than her gloves from her, given the chance. He cleared his throat and decidedly changed the subject. 'Pray tell, young Celia. Have you travelled any further than Ararat?'

'No, this is my first time in this part of the country. Actually, it is my first time away from my father and my dear sister.'

'Really, and what do you make of the country so far?'

'I have seen it from my upstairs window this afternoon and it looks quite lovely. I was in the garden before and the breeze does seem to hold more humidity here.'

'Indeed. I hazard a guess that it is much drier inland than the bay side.'

Celia nodded politely, allowing her gaze to sweep to and fro — from his face to the surrounding room — like a pendulum on a clock. She could neither stare straight at him nor tear her eyes away for any length of time. Mesmerised by his blue eyes, dark lashes and dark hair, she knew his heritage was likely to be Irish. For seconds at a time, she dared to stare into his eyes. She could feel herself falling into their depths like a stone sinking to the floor of the bay.

'Speaking of dry. It does remind me.' Charles rubbed his chin in thought. 'Would you like to accompany me to the Barnard's next Sunday? I speak of this as Mr Barnard supplies muslin to the hospital and has hardly a sense of humour about him, however, he hosts a cricket match annually. It raises a charitable sum for the less fortunate. It so happens this event is next weekend and I would be much obliged to have you accompany me.'

'If my aunt expresses her support, I would be happy to.'

'Oh, I will be sure to seek her approval.' Charles gathered the cup and saucer from Celia's grasp and placed it beside her. He held her gloved hand as he spoke. 'You will not be lonely. I believe you have met the acquaintance of Audrey Price. She keeps things lively each year at the match. But for now, I will leave you. It was most pleasant to have met you and until next Sunday, I will think of you in the grim heat of a summer spent away from the bay.' Once again, Charles leant close to her ear and whispered, 'I am hopeful I will show you a pleasant day.'

His words resonated long into the evening, and she was still holding them close to her heart as the last of the guests bid her farewell. She hardly listened to their questions and conversations as she allowed herself to dwell on the encounter with Doctor Lawler. The words he had spoken filled her being — body and soul — and she could not wait for the calendar to swing around to Sunday. Her aunt had smiled at her as the last of the carriages pulled from the drive.

'Doctor Lawler is fetching, isn't he?' she said over her shoulder.

'He seems quite amiable,' Celia answered evenly, all the while wanting to jump up and down like an excited child.

Chapter 5

Celia was shaken into the present as the nook of two walls halted her search. Looking behind to where she had been and unable to focus, she swiped at her eyes to remove the tears that formed there. Catching herself beneath Trinny's gaze, she swiped more violently.

'Are you all right, Mrs Lawler?'

'Yes, yes I am. I am just so very worried about Sally.' To divulge the reason for her tears was beyond comprehension, therefore, she wound the truth of her worry into a lie.

The memory from two years ago had shaken her more than she cared to ponder. It had been the beginning of a life she could have never imagined and the final vestige of her innocence. From the moment she became acquainted with Audrey, then meeting Charles, her world had sprung open. Romance. Love. Animosity. Cruelty. She could have never imagined that the skylarking young woman she had once been, with not a care in the world, had become a headstrong belligerent creature.

Like this wall, her ideals were now impenetrable. She had seen things in this place that most from beyond these walls would not comprehend. The cost to her sensibilities had been calamitous. Her future looked bleak at best. She wanted to drop to her knees and give up. The excitement she once felt when her assistance was required now lay lifeless in the wake of her tattered dreams.

Celia sent a silent prayer for Audrey to appear. She remembered her dear friend and could not believe her once happy life, full of travel and fun, had become a ruse. Celia had absolutely no idea how long Audrey had been locked inside the asylum and it was quite obvious Michael had allowed such a thing to take place. No doubt, he had found it easy to forget her and move forth with his career. By now he would have a new wife, with whom he would have created a new family.

Celia groaned at these thoughts that flooded her mind. Audrey and Michael had started a family. Was Charlotte oblivious to any memory of her true mother? One could only hope that such a thing could not happen. How had Audrey's situation taken such an abysmal turn? What had happened for her to end up at this place high on the hill? Just how had she sought to escape?

Celia wrung her hands. 'Think, think!' she said aloud as Trinny looked on in disbelief.

'Do you need me to fetch Doctor Lawler for you?' the nurse fretted.

Celia shook her head. 'No. I am fine. Let us move forth.' The last thing she needed was Charles admonishing her. Could she have foreseen a time she would not want her husband beside her? She found it almost impossible to accept that the two most wondrous people she had ever met were lost to her now.

After the excitement of her welcome party, Celia could think of nothing more than the impending weekend. She was wishing the days away and by the middle of the week, time was moving so slowly Celia thought she would burst. The sun was oppressive, deeming it almost impossible to leave the house by the afternoon. She walked each morning and waited for the sun to create a burning sensation through her bonnet before seeking reprieve on the bench seat beneath her favourite willow tree.

On this particular day, her attempt to lose herself in a book was futile. She caught herself reading the same paragraphs numerous times, and simply could not concentrate on anything without the vision of Charles Lawler entering her mind time and again. Although suddenly she was now finding it difficult to recall his features and began worrying he was a figment of her imagination.

A carriage rounded the top of the drive and halted at the steps. Was it Charles? Oh, how she hoped so! She craned her neck to see who was alighting. Mrs Price stepped from the carriage followed by Audrey. Celia sprang to her feet, clutched her book to her chest and sprinted across the lawn, almost toppling when her skirts caught around her legs.

Mrs Price looked down her nose as the two girls fell into one another and laughed like infants.

'Young women of social standing do not run and fall all over one another whilst they are greeting.'

'No one is here as witness, Mother,' Audrey commented.

Celia gathered Audrey's hand in her own and said, 'Come, let us sit beneath our tree and talk.' They swung their hands back and forth as they crossed the lawn and sought escape from the sun as it beat down on them.

Audrey sprawled on the ground beneath the willow and stared up through the canopy of leaves.

'I cannot believe I am getting married.'

'It must be so exciting.' Celia plopped down beside her and with arms outspread breathed a sigh. 'Have you set the date?'

'Oh yes, and I cannot wait. It is going to be announced in *The Advertiser* this coming Friday, and the date is exactly one month away.' Audrey pushed herself up onto her elbows and looked at Celia. 'You will stay, won't you?'

'I dare say I will be here for the month at least. I have no pressing desire to leave.'

'Would you like to come along to the cricket match this Sunday? Michael and I can collect you, if you would like.'

Tiny flutters filled Celia's insides. 'Thank you, that is very kind, but Doctor Lawler has asked me to accompany him.'

A huge grin spread across Audrey's face. 'Really? The handsome Doctor Lawler has a companion for the cricket game!'

'Stop it.' Celia giggled. 'That is highly inappropriate to speak in such a way.'

'So, are you saying you do not find him handsome?'

Celia stared into the distance. 'I am afraid I find him truly lovely and it frightens me if I am honest.'

'Oh, do not be frightened of him. If he has asked you to accompany him to the cricket match surely he must think you lovely also.'

'He did stare at me in the most peculiar manner. It made me all warm inside.'

Audrey laughed. 'I know exactly what you mean, and it is

that look that tells a woman she has the means to cast her spell over a man.'

'Oh, do not be absurd.' Celia threw her hands down in her lap.

'If you do not believe me, try a few of my assured tricks and I guarantee he will be driven mad with desire for you.'

Celia looked mortified. 'I cannot lure a man. I am not experienced in any of these matters.'

'Oh, it is simple enough. You can touch him for a moment longer than is acceptable or hold onto his arm and squeeze it lightly to gain his attention. The best and most fool proof way I have found is to stare at him as though he is the yummiest cream cake you have ever seen.'

'Do those things really work?' Celia asked in surprise.

'Absolutely. These are only a few of my learned secrets. Try these things on Sunday and you will have Charles Lawler begging for your hand in marriage.'

Celia smiled and stared heavenward. 'I could only hope for such a thing.'

'Well, he has been a promising bachelor for many years now. Maybe he will meet his match at the cricket match.' Audrey burst into laughter. Celia flopped back onto the grass and joined her, her body shaking heartily.

The day of the cricket match finally arrived. A carriage slowly ambled along the drive. Celia watched its progress from her bedroom window. Taking deep breaths and pushing her forehead against the window, she audibly squeaked as it rolled to a halt at the steps below and Charles alighted.

Moving her weight from one foot to the other, she remained in her bedroom until the maid tapped at her door.

She wished to rush down the staircase but took each step delicately as only a lady ought.

'Why, you look alluring,' Charles said as he took her hand and led her to the door.

'Well thank you, Doctor,' she said, blushing beneath the gaze of those penetrating blue eyes. It had taken her three dress changes until she was satisfied with the powder blue dress adorned with a deep blue satin belt tied tightly around her waist. The neckline was the lowest of all her gowns and showed just enough of her bosom to remain respectable.

'Remember to address me as Charles.' He said as his eyes wandered the length of her, stopping momentarily on her bosom before quickly slipping upward to her face.

'Silly me, I forgot.' She blushed profusely as he helped her into the carriage. She would put some of Audrey's advice into play before the day was over.

He had introduced her to the couple accompanying them. 'This is Doctor and Mrs Rushby. They live on the property adjoining your aunt's, and I offered to collect them along the way.'

Mrs Rushby held her hand out to Celia and shook it eloquently. 'It is a pleasure to meet you, my dear. Apologies we could not attend your arrival party last week. It was the talk of the town. We were held over in Ballarat.'

'I see,' was all Celia could offer as Doctor Rushby's abrupt conversation filled the carriage.

'Charles, I have pressing matters you need to attend to first thing tomorrow,' he gushed.

'Absolutely. As soon as I set foot inside the place I will listen with intent.'

'Indeed. There are all sorts of hoops the government is hell bent on having us jumping through and I am not liking the turn events are taking.'

Charles sat forward in his seat. 'I am happy to have grievances aired tomorrow but today let us enjoy the game and give these lovely ladies our full attention.'

Doctor Rushby harrumphed and turned his attention to the window. Mrs Rushby fanned her face, and Charles winked at Celia, who smiled profusely.

Charles gathered Celia's hand as she stepped from the carriage. He found them a shaded area beneath a tree and was holding Celia's full attention with stories of the goldfields when he was called upon to bowl. 'I have paid ten pounds for this privilege,' he told Celia, while holding her gloved hand and grinning. 'Be sure to watch closely, my dear. I will be sorely showing off for you.'

Celia giggled. 'I will not dare look away,' she said as she smiled at him flirtatiously. She had never been as carefree with a gentleman before and it warmed her to know she had the power to do so. Charles looked her over, and noticing her bravado touched her cheek lightly with his index finger. Tossing the ball in small arcs over his head he sauntered toward the pitch and handed his hat to the umpire. He looked her way before taking a run up and bowling aggressively.

Celia stepped from the shade to observe Charles. Shielding her eyes from the sun she momentarily lost sight of the ball as it flew down the pitch. The batsman swung and missed, and the ball sent the bales flying through the air. The crowd cheered triumphantly. Charles completed the over, and then graciously accepted his hat back from the umpire before returning to Celia.

'That was most impressive, Doctor … I mean Charles.' She reached out and squeezed his arm, grinning at him as though he were the tastiest treat she had ever seen. She saw the same look cross his features that she had told Audrey of. His face moved closer to hers and his eyes showed a hunger she could not mistake for anything other than desire.

He had managed to create a need within her, one she could neither control nor ignore. Young women of her standing did not allow such feelings to exist. It was rather dangerous to let one's emotions rule one's heart. At one stage, Doctor Rushby came to stand beside them, trying his best to monopolise Charles and seeming most unimpressed when Charles gently excused himself to take a stroll with Celia around the perimeter of the oval.

'What do you think of the day?' he asked as she stared at the play.

'I am most impressed at the generosity of these people.'

'Do you think you could see yourself among them?'

'But I am,' she smiled at him.

'That is not what I mean.'

'What *do* you mean?' Her response emerged from a dry mouth. She could hardly believe the direction the conversation was taking.

'What I am eluding to is, well, could you see yourself living here and being part of this community?'

'Are you asking an open question? Like a hypothetical?'

'Maybe,' he laughed, and they continued to walk along in silence. She was surprised he could not hear her thundering heart and sense her disappointment at his non-committed response.

Taking a glass of lemonade from the long trestle table set up for refreshments, Celia gulped it down. The heat of the day was pressing down on her and the sugar was a welcome relief for her headache. After a moment, she was relieved to catch sight of Audrey and Michael in the crowd, and greeted Audrey fondly but in a much more socially acceptable manner than the pair had demonstrated earlier in the week. The friends took a seat beneath a sheet of calico that had been tied between two trees. They watched the remainder of the match, with Audrey chattering incessantly about her wedding preparations until suddenly the young women noticed that the cricket pitch had emptied and the sun had begun to disappear behind the trees in the distance.

'Where are Doctor and Mrs Rushby?' Celia asked as Charles held the carriage door open for her and helped her inside.

'They took their leave hours ago. Now, I promised to have you safely home before supper so best we get going,' he said as he slammed the carriage door.

Before Celia had a moment to ponder the lack of a chaperone, the carriage was away. Looking at Charles sitting opposite her with a smug grin on his lips, she wondered whether he had planned this all along.

'Did you have a pleasant day?' he asked as the carriage sidled along the drive and out onto the road.

'I did,' she said quietly as she met his gaze and then just as quickly broke it by looking out of the window.

'Audrey was in all her glory showing off her newly engaged hand,' Charles commented.

'Her ring was very lovely and most unusual.'

'Michael was telling me it is a precious stone from Queensland, an opal.'

'Well, it was very beautiful with those emerald hues. It quite reminded me of a peacock's feather.'

'Michael made mention that Audrey likes you very much,' Charles stated.

Celia swallowed under his gaze. 'I like her very much also. Actually, she has invited me to dine with her on Wednesday.'

'It will be nice for you to have some female company your own age while you are visiting.'

Celia felt a fierce heat wash over her as she fanned her face.

'Are you all right?'

'Yes, I am fine. It is very warm in here,' Celia said, discovering that continuing to force air into her face with her gloved hand was proving futile.

'Take those off. Surely, if you are feeling clammy your hands would do to be free of them.'

'It would be rather inappropriate.' Celia felt a wash of heat run through her body once more. She was apt at dealing with manners and civilities but she had never been alone in a gentleman's company. To expose hands or any other amounts of skin was unheard of.

'Actually, if I could be so bold as to ask you to remove your shoes.'

'I beg your pardon!' she shrieked.

'It will certainly cool your body down far quicker than anything else you might try.' He grinned and looked absolutely unabashed. The look he gave her all but tore the rest of her heart wide open to him.

'I feel I am in the best position to give you medical advice.'

Catching her in a weak moment, he crossed the carriage and sat so closely beside her she felt she would swoon.

He bent over her and pushed her petticoats from her ankles and took hold of her right foot ever so gently and lifted it to his lap.

She could not be comforted in the knowledge that her thighs were spread wide apart into a most unladylike position. She quickly propped her other foot beside the raised one.

'I ... I do feel this is most untoward.'

'It is neither inappropriate nor wrong. If you are not aware by now of my intention to see much more of you than your bare feet and ankles, now is the time to accept it. So, before you pass out and need me to unbutton your dress also, I would suggest you allow me to remove your shoes, thus saving yourself further discomfort on more than one level.'

Within moments he was kneading her stockinged feet. The delicious sensation of the cool air and his wonderful touch caused a warm curling sensation to drift throughout her body. She could not hide her pleasure as she placed her head against the seat and watched his profile. He was staring most lovingly at both her feet, now held fast within his grasp.

'How does that feel?'

'Wonderful,' she whispered.

'Are you feeling cooler?"

'In some ways.'

'Ah, am I giving you cause to like the feeling more than you would otherwise allow?'

'That, I believe you are.'

His advances were giving way to some confidence on

her part. That which was deemed to be inappropriate in an unmarried man's company, somehow felt so right.

His hands wandered their way up her slender calves as she felt heat wash over her again and her breath caught in her throat. She watched him slowly pull her skirts down over her calves and place her shoes back on her feet, and then he surprised her by swiftly pulling her onto his lap. She gasped as she placed her hands up to his chest to steady herself. His hand found her waist and the other trailed down her cheek, tilting her chin as his mouth found hers and she fell further into his allure.

Celia's senses were in turmoil. His lips felt incredibly soft upon her mouth. His hands caressed her and the gentleness made her want it to never end. Yet her mind screamed that his was most unladylike and could ruin her reputation and chances of marriage forevermore. She could neither tear her lips from his and nor did she want to. If she did not end her days being Mrs Charles Lawler then she would not find love or happiness anyplace else.

With her desire being fanned like flames in a forest fire, she grew bold. Her hands began to move slowly over his vest and when she found no way to touch his skin directly, she moved her hands up through his hair. She heard him hiss ever so slightly as his tongue slowly made its way into her mouth. The invasion was effervescent and she found herself whimpering with the need of wanting more. A spiralling sensation curled around her and held her vice-like in its grip. It was an odd feeling. One she had never considered possible.

Charles ripped his mouth from hers and threw her aside as the carriage door opened. The pair had been so lost in their tryst that they had not noticed the carriage draw to a halt. Being caught in this situation would prove simply dire. The driver stood back from the door as Charles alighted and placed his hand out for Celia to alight also. Her head was spinning from the feelings and emotions he had triggered in her. She was almost leaning on him as he accompanied her up the steps to the front veranda.

The housekeeper opened the door. 'Lady Montague is waiting for you in the dining room, Miss Celia.'

'Thank you, Greta.' Celia licked her lips and smoothed her skirt down.

Charles took Celia's arm and placed it over the crook of his elbow. As they entered the dining room, Lady Montague looked up from her soup.

'I would normally scold such tardiness but it seems on this occasion I will yield. Doctor Lawler, I trust you had a lovely day with my niece.'

'That I did, Lady Montague.' Charles held a chair out for Celia, which she all but fell onto.

As he pushed it in for her he stilled and said, 'I am afraid to say I took a few small liberties that I should have resisted.'

Celia, thankful she was already seated, felt her stomach drop to her feet; the same feet that had been so lovingly adored only minutes earlier and now felt like cement in her shoes. She almost fell from the chair as she turned to look up at him. He was grinning down at her.

'Oh Celia, do not be so stunned. I am not about to have you cast from the family. To the contrary! I am hoping your aunt will send word to your father. I would like to ask for your hand if he agrees.'

Lady Montague slowly rose from her chair. 'Bramwell! Bramwell!' she yelled as she raced from the room.

'Oh dear, I didn't expect that sort of reaction.' He came around to the side of her chair and smiled lovingly into her face.

Dropping down on one knee, he gathered her hand in his. 'After only two meetings I have fallen in love with you, Celia. Would you do me the honour of becoming my wife?'

'I would love nothing more,' she whispered as she stared at him. He was the most handsome man she had seen or would ever see again, and she would be his wife. Neither had she dreamed nor dared to think of such a thing.

Lady Montague re-entered the dining room talking over her shoulder.

'Bramwell is here. He will ensure a prompt message makes its way to the reverend for his blessing. This is absolutely astounding news,' she said, clapping her hands sharply.

Chapter 6

The search had continued for hours. The exhaustion of all confined within the asylum was apparent as feet began to drag and the frenzy from the initial search was now lost within the impeding dusk.

'Doctor! Doctor!' an orderly yelled as he raced past Celia and Trinny before disappearing behind a door. The women picked up their skirts and ran in the same direction. Then they too flung the door open and rushed inside the administration building.

The ruckus inside was deafening as the attendant yelled over and over for Doctor Lawler. His yelling seemed to bring everybody running from all directions as it became clear that Sally Smith had been found.

Celia reached the top of the staircase and saw Charles standing on the threshold of his office door. The orderly was gasping for breath as he pointed his finger away from Charles while offering an explanation. Celia should have been close enough to hear what the orderly was saying but the overall noise level in the asylum was drowning out his words. Celia watched Charles' face first express relief, which immediately gave way to pain and anger.

'Everybody, be quiet!' he yelled. Immediate quiet ensued, enabling Celia to hear the desperate question Charles then directed to the orderly.

'Where did you say you discovered her?'

'In the belltower, sir. It is grim indeed.'

Charles called over his shoulder to the orderly as he pushed past the posse crowding around. 'You, come with me.'

He stopped at Celia. Gripping the tops of her arms, he turned her toward him, looked squarely into her face and said, 'You need to see this.'

Celia wanted to shake herself from his hold and run in the opposite direction. 'No, I fear what I may see.'

'It is much too late for that, I am afraid. You want to meddle in my work here. I will allow you full exposure for the very last time.'

Celia looked at him and sensed this was likely to be the beginning of the final moments of her marriage also. 'I am regretting some of my meddling now. Truly I am, Charles.'

He grimaced. 'Let me give you this as a parting gift to your meddling ways, then. You are through here, Mrs Lawler.'

The mean slant in his tone shifted her sincere remorse to anger. She pulled herself from his hold, took a large gulp of air and said. 'Lead the way, then. If you must punish me, get it over with.'

'After you.' Charles held the door open for Celia. She stepped from the confines of the administration building and stood aside. Charles walked ahead of her, taking the short way across the lawn to the ballroom and tower. Celia used this time to suck in huge amounts of fresh air in preparation for whatever she was about to witness. She looked up at the belltower then at Charles' back. The ballroom door was not locked so they stepped directly inside, but the inner door leading to the belltower had a secured padlock fastening it. Charles stood back and waited for the orderly to unlock it. Charles stepped forward and entered as the orderly and other staff who had gathered around stood back.

Everyone looked at Celia. The collective expression on their faces was one of pity. She realised they knew what she was going to see. She stayed behind Charles and observed him look upward. His shoulders sagged. She took another deep breath and stepped past the onlookers. Joining Charles inside the base of the tower, she too looked up.

The staircase turned on itself, over and upward, making a square one could stare into with angles and lines confusing the senses. However, one could not ignore the grubby feet that dangled overhead as belonging to Audrey McGowan. The beautiful velvet gown she wore seemed to make a mockery of the scene. Her filthy hair hung around her face as saliva dripped onto the floor at their feet.

Celia cast her eyes downwards to avoid the image only to see instead a pool of liquid, the stench of which filled her nostrils. Audrey's bodily fluids had left her when her neck had snapped. The rope that looped around her neck had made her face bloated and blue. The other end was tied steadfast to the top floor balustrade to ensure maximum tension after her flight had ended. The bell directly above was held fast at an angle with the clapper resting on its inner wall.

'Get her down.' Charles' tone was restrained. Two orderlies stepped forward and began the arduous journey up each flight of stairs. They stopped momentarily to pull the body into the stairwell then made their way to the very top to loosen the knotted rope. They neither harried nor rushed, as it would appear there was no urgency now.

Celia dared to look up once more and viewed a now empty space although the image she had witnessed would remain entrenched in her mind forever.

Charles' face came into view as he stared down at her with a look of disdain. 'Satisfied?' he ground out before taking to the staircase.

Celia bolted from the scene and ran through the darkness, her vision blurred by the tears that stung her eyes as she crossed between the vegetable garden and vineyard, stumbling and righting herself as her ankles kinked and rolled along the uneven ground.

She arrived at the house and was greeted by Lydia, her housemaid. 'Are you all right, Mrs Lawler?' she said, aghast.

Celia flung her hand up. She did not want to answer any questions. She looked dishevelled and her nerves felt raw. 'I am fine. Leave me, please.'

Celia shut her bedroom door and wrenched her arms from her coat sleeves. She ripped her gloves from her hands and tore her hat from her head and threw it aside. Dropping onto the bed she put her hands up to her face and sobbed. Hours later she finally succumbed to sleep as the everyday activities of the house settled around her.

Charles had not returned. She imagined him holed up in his office. There was no doubt he would be stifled by his responsibilities. The constable would be summoned as well as the undertaker. The image of Audrey on the table in the morgue further wracked Celia's nerves. Colonel and Mrs

Price would be saddened at this turn of events. The situation was sad from all perspectives. Charles would be busy clearing up this mess amid the mystery of how Audrey had met her demise. There was only one thing of which Celia was assured. On his long list of things to unshackle was the wayward wife for whom he had lost all respect.

The tap on the door jarred Charles from his thoughts.

'Enter,' he said abruptly.

The orderly opened the door only halfway and leaned inside the office.

'Mrs Lawler is safely home, sir.'

'Thank you.'

As the door closed, Charles leaned back in his chair and placed his closed fists over his eyes. He felt sick at the events that had transpired. He had neglected Audrey. This event would cause his demise. The guilt that pushed in on him threatened to railroad his investigation. He needed to focus and ponder one question. Who had done such a ghastly thing?

There were many factors that had him stumped, but the one thing that made him most vexed was the gown. It made a statement all its own. It would seem the perpetrator had gone to great lengths to plan the scenario, making sure to incorporate a particularly noteworthy detail.

Charles decided not to summon Constable Bryant tonight. He needed time to clear his thoughts and make precise judgements. It was imperative that the news of Sally Smith's demise be kept within the asylum for the moment. To reveal her identity would raise many questions and bring Colonel and Mrs Price into the fray. This was to be avoided. In order to announce beyond the walls of the asylum that Sally Smith was the woman who had been hanged in murderous circumstances, he would first need to prepare documents that substantiated her existence in the first place. He could not wrap his mind around that predicament at present, so Constable Bryant would be informed once he had his house in order, so to speak.

Could his reluctance to call on the constable have everything to do with protecting himself, the Prices and the island that was the asylum? Yes, it could. Doctor Rushby had always maintained the utmost discretion in the goings on within the asylum's walls. It was easy for him to protect the secret and himself if he said nothing more on it. He would investigate it himself, starting with a meticulous search of the bell tower and its surrounds.

He cast his mind back to the scene that had unfolded tonight, recalling the look of shock on Celia's face when she had seen such a ghastly sight. Her expression would haunt him as much as the scene itself. He was angry with himself for losing his temper and forcing her to witness such a shocking thing. While he was incensed at her behaviour, he knew he loved her more than life itself. Currently, however, he sought some distance from her. The need to shake her tempted him each time she disobeyed him. She had proven to be a strong woman but her strength was quickly unravelling his resolve as a husband and respected doctor in the community.

From the moment he had caught sight of her at the party at her aunt's home he had wanted to possess her heart and soul, and he had. That very night, after he had found the strength to leave her, he had tested his attraction to the bewitching aura she exuded, but to no avail. He found himself lost to every other woman from that moment.

Charles strode to the carriage and let out a huge breath as he pulled himself up inside. 'Driver! Shire Hall Hotel.' The afternoon at Lady Montague's home had delivered him far more than he could have envisaged, and now he needed a stiff drink — or rather, a few.

'Yes, sir. Getup!' the driver yelled as the carriage lurched forward.

Charles needed alcohol, as well as a release from the alluring graces of Celia Loddon. She had disarmed him without realising it. The young woman was positively oozing grace and charm despite her childlike appearance. Her skin was as pale and smooth as marble. The masses of blonde hair cascading around her shoulders set his mind wandering. He could do nothing more than imagine it tumbling over his chest as she kissed her way down his body.

From the moment he stepped inside Lady Montague's, he had fought against the devious thoughts that flittered through his mind after his gaze instantly fell upon Celia. Those thoughts and the feelings that ensued were positively delicious. He considered her body writhing beneath his while he possessed her, pushing her into a mattress and conquering her womanhood. Those huge blue eyes that nervously darted from him to any place else revealed her true feelings. She was attracted to him and he knew it. But his behaviour was unwarranted. He should not have whispered sensuous messages in her ear with wanton promises of seeking her out for future pleasure. He had not been able to help himself.

Watching her from across the room as vast numbers of people made her acquaintance had made him want to save her but he had enjoyed watching her expression so immensely that he had held back. When she had disappeared with the young Audrey Price he had quietly listened to polite conversation while shrewdly looking for her. His relief when she had reappeared with her new friend to hear the announcement of Audrey and Michael's engagement had filled him with a sense of relief. The room brimmed with excitement as he kept an eye on her. All the while, he had steered many a young man astray and chatted about all manner of boring subjects just to keep them from meeting her. Coming between her and Jack with the hot cup of tea had been a rude course of action, but had secured his intention of seeking a solo audience with Celia.

If he didn't find some release from his desire for Celia, the wait for the following Sunday and the cricket game would send him to the grave.

'Here we are then, sir,' the driver shouted as Charles pushed open the door and stepped from the carriage onto the bluestone step, ducked under the covered veranda and into the dimly lit hotel. Within moments, he caught sight of a woman wearing heavy make up, a skirt hitched up to show too much calf, and a bustier two sizes too small for her heaving bosom. He walked quickly to the bar and ordered a shot of whiskey.

'Doctor Lawler. Long time. How was Ballarat?' the publican said, shaking Charles' hand.

Before answering, Charles threw the whiskey back and felt

its heat run down his throat, race to his chest, and finally fill his stomach.

'Spirited, to say the least,' he answered as his gaze moved to the woman staring at him.

The publican looked between Charles and the woman as she pushed her arms together to expose her cleavage. 'Been a long few months on the goldfields, I take it?' He raised his brow.

'That it has. That it has,' Charles said as he stood and winked at the woman who all but knocked over a table of patrons in her haste to join him.

'Betsy.'

'Beg your pardon?' He leaned in to hear her.

Her breasts pushed into his arm as she stood on tiptoe and said, 'Betsy. My name.'

'Well Betsy, what can you do for me?'

'Anything you like, handsome.' She grabbed his hand and led him down a passage where the doors mirrored one another on both sides. She unlocked a door and pushed it open. Charles followed her inside and began to untie his cravat while he looked her over.

Betsy propped one foot up on a stool in a flirtatious manner and then, pulling her skirt up past her knee and over the top of her thigh, began to roll her stocking down. While her intention was obvious Charles did not possess the patience or time to have his senses aroused.

'Taking too long to build my suspense, dear,' he said as he descended on her and threw her onto the bed.

She giggled but the sound died on her lips when he shoved her skirt up to her waist and plunged his fingers into her. She began to moan immediately. Charles knew he had not yet begun to arouse her, aware that this type of woman honed her skill to get the show underway and over with as quickly as possible. They wanted to be paid so they could just as quickly move onto their next customer. He was no barbarian and he was in sore need of release but he hoped to have her somewhat ready to receive him.

'You are the most handsome one I've ever had,' she breathed between sighs.

'Oh sweetheart, I bet you say that to all the men.' He did not smile.

For the next hour he plied her with his touch and pounded into her with as much ferocity as he dared but he could not find any solace in her arms. She touched him all over and tried all her tricks. The warmth of her mouth did not escape any part of him but to no avail. He could not find the desired release. Every ounce of him was bewitched by the demure graces of one Miss Celia Loddon.

Betsy looked disappointed when he kissed her hand and bade her farewell, leaving her a few pounds on the side dresser in her room.

Celia's face swam in his vision as he departed the room. The guilt of his actions held him captive. He would never find solace or release in another's arms again. His experience with women as a doctor held him in good stead to know how they ticked inside and out, and yet he was lost like a foolish schoolboy after one meeting with the woman he knew was destined to become his wife.

Leaving the hotel, he stared across the street at the grand columns of the Shire Hall and the lush lawns that surrounded it, and felt the shift of his new life coming into existence. He had no sooner accepted the new position of superintendent at the asylum than he had unwittingly met his soon-to be-wife. Doctor Charles Lawler was on his way to being a husband. Celia Loddon would be a loving wife who would give in to his every whim, he was sure. She would fit the bill perfectly. A good doctor's wife who would be respected in social circles and support his career. She was exactly what he needed. By the conclusion of this weekend's cricket match he was certain there would be another engagement announcement in the district.

Chapter 7

Charles woke with his cheek pressed into the surface of his desk. The events of the previous day slammed through his mind like some garish nightmare. He winced as the vision of Audrey hanging overhead made his stomach roil. This, teamed with the reek of stale brandy filling his nostrils, did not assist his present state of dishevelment. Swiping dribble from the side of his face, he lurched to his feet and pulled on his overcoat to cover his unkempt appearance.

While Charles briefly considered stopping in at his residence to change, he decided he could not face Celia at this point, so he left the asylum by way of the front door and set off down the driveway. It would benefit him to walk into town, helping him to clear his mind before he delivered the grim news.

Dawn had just broken through the darkness and the streets were empty. As he walked, he turned the previous day's events over and over in his mind. By the time he reached the Price home he concluded that he would stop in on Constable Bryant on his way back to the asylum. A heinous crime had been committed and he would be out of his depth trying to find the perpetrator. He could manipulate patient records to reflect Sally Smith's identity and her ailment. It would be the only way to assure the protection of the Prices and to allow all knowledge of the overall deceit to rest solely with staff.

He knocked at the door a dozen times before the sound of footsteps could be heard. The maid greeted Charles. 'I need to see the Colonel immediately,' he said as she stepped aside for him to enter.

'I'm afraid he is still asleep, sir,' she whispered.

'Well, you will have to wake him. It is urgent,' Charles snapped at her.

It would seem that the Colonel did not appreciate being wrenched from sleep following the celebrations of the previous day. He ushered Charles into his study. Rounding the desk, he looked in no mood for the unannounced visit.

Charles pushed his hand through his hair as the maid delivered a tray of tea to the room. 'That will be all,' the Colonel said, dismissing her quickly.

At the door, the maid passed Mrs Price, who was pulling her morning jacket around her body and fastening the belt. 'Hello, Doctor Lawler,' she said, reaching for the teapot.

'Dare I say you look as though you have hardly slept?' the Colonel asked Charles as he watched his wife pour three cups of tea. 'What has happened?'

Mrs Price handed Charles the first cup, and he looked down at the mist swirling from it before answering, 'It is about Audrey.'

'Has she become more unwell?' Mrs Price's voice held angst.

The Colonel said, 'She is already unwell, dear. I doubt

Charles would visit this early simply to announce a further decline in her health.'

Charles acknowledged the Colonel's statement with the shake of his head. 'I am afraid you are right, Colonel. The news I bring is dire. Audrey is no longer with us.'

Mrs Price mashed her fist into her lips and steadied herself against the desk. The Colonel took the teacup from her hand before she dropped it. Charles spared the couple any further detail, as he feared that if Mrs Price knew the full truth she would succumb to heart failure mere hours after her daughter's demise.

The Colonel waited for his wife's hysteria to abate but it seemed it would not end for some time. Charles took the situation in hand and dispatched her to her bedroom, where he promised to fetch her something to calm her nerves.

He spent the next hour discussing the scenario of the previous day's events, finding that the Colonel's questions far outweighed his capacity to answer them. During the process, he was surprised the Colonel showed him more mercy than he felt he deserved.

'Charles,' the Colonel said, patting his shoulder roughly, 'she is at peace now from the Devil who took her over. I thank you for all you have done.'

Charles heaved a breath. 'I feel your suffering has abated but it still does not answer the question as to who has committed this crime. I will leave you and seek advice from the constable on the matter.'

The Colonel's hand rested on Charles' back as he waited for the younger man to finish talking, before calmly announcing, 'Leave the authorities out of this.'

'I beg your pardon, sir?' Charles looked confused. 'It seems that somebody in the sanctum of the asylum is a murderer. I think we need to foster the attitude that we intend to find this perpetrator.'

'Whilst it is unfortunate, we can only be of the impression that the poor souls in the place are much better off if they are done away with.'

Charles stood there aghast. He did not have a response to such a callous statement. 'But it is my ...'

The Colonel drew Charles nearer to him. 'Let me be clear on this, Charles. In no uncertain terms can you create a fictitious character like Sally Smith and hope it does not come to light at some point that this Sally Smith is not who you say she is. It is too risky, I am afraid. Should a story like this capture the attention of *The Advertiser* — or, God forbid, *The Argus* — and that is likely, how are we to prevent anyone from uncovering the truth? If it were ever discovered that Audrey McGowan is the murdered inmate ... well, there would be a price to pay for all of us. I am sure you do not want this inconvenient situation ruining careers, do you?'

'Now, neither my wife, nor I, want to hear any more about this. We will end up being the gossip of this town. Mrs Price would not survive the anguish of having such a story surface, knowing full well who the victim really is.'

'I understand your concerns, Colonel, but I have a responsibility, an oath I have undertaken as superintendent.'

The Colonel stared at Charles as the obviousness of his dilemma sat heavy in the room. 'Charles, I have entrusted you with the care of our daughter and you delivered well on your promise to keep this secret. Do not jeopardise your relationship with me, or with the other doctors, whom we hold in good stead. There is to be no further discussion on the matter. Do you understand?'

Charles understood the field of play he had stepped into. His reputation — together with the reputations of all those in the asylum — would unravel if he were to take the course to which he had been alluding. He knew he was in the midst of defeat.

'I do understand, Colonel.'

It would seem the decision had been made. Charles would have to rely on the possibility that the truth would be uncovered without the assistance of the constable. He would still do his own investigating in the hope something would turn up.

'Very well, Colonel. I will leave you now. I will send some laudanum along for Mrs Price within the hour.'

'Thank you, Doctor Lawler.'

The Colonel walked Charles to the end of the hall. At the front door he put his hand on Charles' shoulder. 'Mrs Price and I will discuss the best way to move forward with this situation. We will need to think of a plausible story as to how such a tragedy has befallen our daughter and granddaughter. I will send word to you as to how we will proceed.'

'As you wish, Colonel,' Charles answered. 'There is no rush. A few days to gather your thoughts on how to move forth is acceptable.'

As he left the Price home he did not envy them the lies that would have to be upheld to keep this situation at rest.

As he walked through the back roads so he could dodge anyone desiring a conversation, Charles admonished himself for his decision to hide the truth about Audrey in the first instance. Now he was left with a huge problem and no real way of seeking the help required to solve it. He was angry at himself for being railroaded from the beginning. He made it out of town without seeing anybody he knew. As the asylum came into view, he looked up at the expanse of cream coloured buildings.

If he thought back to his first days there, when he held high hopes for the lost souls he was determined to treat, he realised he had never truly played the role of superintendent. If he had shown more strength back then, perhaps he could have avoided this type of tragic outcome. He had accepted Audrey entering the asylum under a guise and now, in order to protect everyone privy to the circumstances, his hands were tied.

Also, the risk to his reputation was twofold. If he had refused the colonel's wish to keep this a secret he would find himself cast from the district. If the constable found that such a heinous crime had been committed and not reported, he would be hauled from his position as superintendent and would never work as a practitioner again. The government would see to that.

Again and again, he felt he had been cornered whenever an ultimate sign of authority had been required. Other men seemed to pull the strings. It was clear that Doctor Rushby held court over the asylum. If Charles himself was ostensibly in the highest vestige of charge, now the Colonel was brow-beating him into keeping the latest tragedy a secret from the community, which meant that he himself in turn would have to muzzle the asylum staff accordingly. He sighed. He would charge Matron with the responsibility to tell the staff they were to remain silent on the matter. The threat of loss of employment was normally all that was required to gain the desired effect.

His feeling was to single-handedly pursue the truth of what had transpired, a course of action that would have to begin with him pulling rank on Doctor Rushby. He should have known this time would come. From their very first encounter, when he had crossed the threshold of the asylum, he should have opened his eyes wider.

'Here it is, Doctor.' Matron maintained her hold on the handle as she swung the door open. 'This is your office.'

Charles stepped over the threshold and immediately hung his hat and coat on the stand in the corner. Light from a slender arched window was spilling onto a large desk, which he walked behind. He ran his hand along the timber top and grinned slightly.

'May I say it is about time we had a superintendent in our midst. Doctor Rushby has been plagued with so many cases of illness among the inmates he rarely leaves the asylum.'

Charles found this to be quite a surprising statement.

'Are you serious, Matron?' he questioned.

'I am, Doctor Lawler. Not only does he have to attempt cures but he is in constant attendance at the hospital cottage treating all forms of wounds the inmates inflict on themselves and others.'

'Well then, I hope my being here will alleviate Doctor Rushby's workload from now on. As a matter of fact I think I will begin my morning with a visit to the hospital cottage. That would be the best starting point, I imagine.'

'Definitely, Doctor. The women in the hospital cottage ward have some disturbing injuries that could improve with your swift attention.'

'Would you accompany me to the hospital cottage? I believe you could acquaint me, in any way you see fit, with the souls who reside there and their recoveries.'

Charles had learned quickly in his time as a practicing doctor and surgeon that the support of staff was paramount. His educator, Doctor Grimsby, had given him this advice. 'Make them feel worthwhile and they will make it worth your while.' Now, as he stood before Matron, seeking her advice and council, he felt he already had her confidence.

'That will be my pleasure, Doctor.'

As they left the confines of his office and took the staircase to the lower level, Matron acquainted Charles with the general surrounds.

'It is quite easy to familiarise oneself with the layout,' she said. 'To the left of where we stand are the men's wards and to the right are the women's. The lower levels are the refractory wards. This level is for the more demure cases, and the layout is mirrored over every level, with the only difference being the intensity of security measures and the relative freedom accorded to inmates. Some wards have locked doors twenty three hours of the day whilst other wards have open doors the whole day through.'

'May I have access to keys for these locked doors?'

'Why yes. I will give you a skeleton key upon our return to the administration office.'

'Could it be today? I wish to visit the refractory ward next.'

'As you wish, Doctor.'

Charles walked the hall with Matron and could not halt his anticipation of the satisfaction he would feel in restoring order to the lives of the men and women in the entire place. The hospital cottage and refractory wards seemed the two places most of his attention were required.

The hospital cottage was separated from the main building and looked pleasant enough upon his approach. Its welcoming pathway to the covered veranda seemed misplaced compared with the monstrous building behind him.

As Matron closed the door behind him the diminished natural light made the entryway feel cooler than he expected.

'We separate the women according to their situations. At present we have four women with consumption. They are in the room to your left. In the room to your right we have those who have been harmed by their own hand or others.'

Charles walked between each ward. The bruising and abrasions inflicted on one woman in particular piqued his senses. Her jaw was dislocated. A bandage spanned the circumference of her face and her eyes were severely bruised. It was obvious the sockets were shattered. Charles had seen men inflict this sort of injury on one another during fistfights.

'Who did this to her?' he asked Matron.

'Another inmate.'

'Who?'

'I don't know, Doctor. All I can tell you is that she was found in the stairwell three mornings ago.'

'Is it possible she has had contact with someone from the men's ward?'

'No, Doctor. There is never any contact between the men and women. Never.'

'What about male staff? Has there been any contact?' he asked with apprehension. The prospect of dealing with violent staff and the onset of an investigation on his first day was daunting, to say the least.

'The ward in which this woman resides requires very little oversight, therefore it is staffed entirely by female nurses.'

Charles remained perplexed by some of the cases he was treating but none plagued him like the mystery of the battered woman. As his first weeks slipped away Charles revisited the hospital cottage daily. While some patients had made it back to their wards in far better health after having been there, two of the women with consumption had succumbed to the disease and were now buried in graves beyond the fence line of the asylum.

Meanwhile, Charles quizzed the woman who had been assaulted time and again, asking her to enlighten him on what had happened to her. She was non responsive, only looking away from his inquisitive gaze when he spoke to her. She was no older than twenty years and barely able to utter a sound with her mouth clamped shut by the bandages holding her chin fastened. One afternoon Charles resorted to giving her a piece of chalk and small blackboard, but she dropped the chalk from her fingers and rolled her head sideways. One thing that concerned him was the swelling of her abdomen. She looked bloated and he feared that his suspicions would lead to more questions that were beyond answers. He sought Matron's assistance to give the young woman a thorough examination. His notion was confirmed. It was revealed she was with child.

This immediately set his teeth on edge and sent his mind into a spin. Upon studying the woman's medical record and admission form, he discovered she had been in the asylum nearing six months. Charles deduced her impregnation had occurred four months previously. Somebody was responsible and they were within the confines of the place.

'You must tell me who did this to you,' he implored the girl, but to no avail. She would neither look at him nor utter a single word.

He could not give up the search for the truth but was at a loss as to which direction to take. He questioned Matron extensively on the women's work roster and any means by which the woman could have gained access to the men's ward. It was a mystery. She worked in the kitchen. There was no crossover between male and female inmates in this area. He quizzed the gatekeeper with regard to all deliveries to the asylum. Again, there was no incidence of contact between the female patients and any male. Delivery staff only traversed as far as the storage areas where the male wards were situated, leaving Charles in no doubt that the culprit had to be an orderly.

Doctor Rushby tapped at his office door. 'Can I see you, Charles?' he said. Without awaiting an answer, he sat down in the chair opposite Charles' desk.

Charles had not yet looked up from his paperwork. 'Yes of course, Doctor Rushby. Sit, sit,' he said whilst realising Doctor Rushby had already taken the liberty of doing so.

Doctor Rushby looked over the rim of his glasses and down his bulbous nose at Charles.

'What warrants this visit?' Charles asked. He was not impressed with the scrutiny Doctor Rushby was exuding at present. His dark eyes were narrowed in slits and his chest and stomach were moving in rapid succession as he looked to be rather excited at the prospect of an argument. His large build gave away just how compromised his own health was at present.

'I wanted to have a chat about the scouting you have been doing with regards to the women in the hospital ward.'

'And that chat would entail?' Charles' brow furrowed. He was perplexed at the timing of this conversation. If Doctor Rushby had any information with regard to the women, or rather a particular woman in the hospital cottage, it would have assisted him to have known before so much time had passed.

'These women are mischievous and senile. They suffer from hysterics and do not possess the brain matter to know who they are most days. They can manipulate a situation to bend to their own whim and I believe, judging from the information Matron has bestowed on me, these women are already fallen before they arrive here. It is of no concern to us if staff or inmates service or assist their disposition. After all, what else do they have, Charles?'

Charles did not have a response to this proclamation but rather, found himself tripping over his words. 'So let me … let me … see … if I understand … '

Doctor Rushby held his hand up and halted Charles mid garble.

'I am saying exactly what you hear and just understood. Leave some things be and all will turn out well. We do not want any outside authorities adding to the comings and goings on in here.' With that said he stood and left Charles' office.

Charles remained in his seat and stared at the closed door for the longest time. He decided he would not let these things slide. He was the person supposed to stand between these women and the risk of any untold abuse by the staff responsible for their welfare.

Having made his decision to act, he visited the hospital cottage the following morning. His steadfast resolve turned to shock when he found the young woman's bed empty. 'Where is she?' he asked the nurse on duty.

'She was transferred to Yarra Bend this morning. Doctor Rushby thought it best. It was obvious there had been a breach of security between the men's and women's wards.'

In disarray over Doctor Rushby's instruction to send the woman all the way to an asylum in Melbourne, Charles questioned the nurse. 'Why did he not want to seek the truth from her to halt the breach? The crime will be repeated if we cannot find out where and how it occurred.' Reminding himself of the inferiority of the nurse's position, he quickly righted himself. 'Very well, then.'

Charles was angered that his authority had been undermined. He intended to take the matter up with Doctor Rushby, but for the moment, he needed to keep a level mindset. It did not matter that the woman had been transferred. Hopefully the transfer would keep her safe but it did not alter the fact she had been seriously abused. The largest concern to him was the timing of numerous violations inflicted on the woman. Days ago she was beaten, and a pregnancy had occurred months ago. The abuses were far too unsettling to ignore. How many times had a male found a way to be alone with her and commit these torturous actions?

Chapter 8

Ribbons unfurled from the bough of a huge oak tree. Eleanor Price thrust her head to and fro in an effort to evade the tickling fingers of bright orange and red. Her head was still lolling from side to side as she woke from her dream, her mind clearing just enough for her to recall why she was feeling such a heavy pulsing from within, a pulsing that felt as though it were pushing her eyes against her brain.

Audrey was dead. The truth of the moment dawned on her amid a haze. She was going to be ill. She flung herself from the bed and skun her knees on the floorboards as she made a dive for the chamber pot. It would seem the laudanum had taken effect and allowed her to sleep off the shock of the news. Unfortunately, its side effects negated its purpose, pulling her recklessly from sleep so she could empty her stomach.

She pulled out a handkerchief that she had tucked in the sleeve of her nightgown. Wiping the corners of her mouth, she whispered, 'My Audrey is dead,' before clutching it to her forehead and closing her eyes. Her only child had perished. Images of her daughter as a happy young woman flooded her memory. Yes, Audrey had married, thus adding a son-in-law to their family. It was after the birth of their child that things spiralled downward. Now, Eleanor Price had nothing left. She blamed the baby for having the devil's curse, which caused her daughter to fall under an evil spell. She had heard of such things happening but never dreamt it would shatter her own kin.

With difficulty, Eleanor lifted herself up and onto the bed where she fell back onto the pillows. Taking deep breaths and wiping her brow, her thoughts returned to the time where the gravity of the situation had landed solely on her shoulders.

The Colonel met her in the parlour. He was looking rather shaken.

'I have just received word from Michael.'

'Is everything all right with the baby?' Eleanor said with panic edging into her voice.

'The baby is fine. It would seem the problem is with Audrey.'

'What has happened? Is she unwell?'

'I do not know much. Only that Michael is most concerned. He said she has been acting rather strangely in recent days.'

'What nonsense. What on earth could that mean?'

'He was not overtly direct in the telegram I received, but he has grave concerns, and is sending her back with Charlotte accompanied by a woman in his employ.'

'When are they to return?'

'I have reason to believe they are on their way as we speak.'

Eleanor drew in a sharp breath. 'Heaven and earth. They were only here but a few weeks back. I am not practically ready to have them back so soon. What is he thinking?'

She called for the housemaid who appeared at the door

within moments. 'Ready a room for Audrey and the baby. They will be arriving shortly.'

'Yes, Mrs Price. This very minute,' the maid said, and then hurried away.

Eleanor turned her attention back to her husband. 'I cannot believe Michael is incapable of looking after Audrey if she is ill. It is preposterous that he send her all the way here. The journey alone will push her health beyond resolve.'

The Colonel looked at her. 'Do not begin to anticipate what she is ailing with. Michael would not have sent her unless it was absolutely necessary. I think we must brace ourselves for some difficult nursing of her if she is making this journey back.'

The following evening, as dark descended, a carriage drew to a halt outside their home. Eleanor was gazing out the window and quickly gathered her shawl around her shoulders before leaving the house and hurrying down the path.

The woman accompanying Audrey alighted the carriage with the baby in her arms. Eleanor reached out to take her granddaughter from the woman. 'Hello, my little darling,' she said as she looked down into the cherubic face of Charlotte. But when she lifted her gaze to see Audrey standing before her, she almost dropped the infant.

Audrey's stare was vacant. She did not greet her mother as she would have done in normal circumstances. Her head was not covered with a hat, her hands were not adorned with gloves, and her plain frock was fit only for chores. Her feet were devoid of shoes and her figure looked emaciated.

Suddenly, the Colonel appeared at Eleanor's shoulder. 'Let's move inside, shall we?'

She felt her husband's hands gently grasp her shoulders

and turn her toward the house. Without his assistance, would she have been able to move her feet?

Once inside the house, Eleanor turned to her daughter's travelling companion and demanded, 'What has happened to her?'

'I know very few details, Mrs Price. I was only called to assist with the baby one week ago.'

'What is your name, then?' the Colonel asked.

'Maggie.'

The Colonel held her hand in his grasp. 'Well then, Maggie, we are indebted to you for accompanying our daughter. There is no doubt she is in need of your assistance.'

Audrey sat on a chair with her knees pulled in toward her chest. Her arms securely fastened around her legs. She stared out the window into the darkness and neither spoke nor moved.

The Colonel stalked past them and announced, 'I'm going to fetch Doctor Rushby.'

Eleanor approached Audrey with Charlotte safely encased in her arms. The baby began to grizzle, sensing the nearness of her mother.

'Audrey,' Eleanor whispered. 'Do you want to feed your baby?'

Audrey turned to look at Charlotte as the baby cried for her attention. She cast her eyes for the smallest moment on the infant then turned her attention back to the window as though repelled by the child.

It was in that moment Eleanor looked at Charlotte in a different light. Could the baby be the devil incarnate? Could this infant have caused Audrey's illness?

'I have been feeding her,' Maggie said from the doorway.

'My goodness. It makes one wonder whether Michael has been doing right by my daughter,' Eleanor said with disgust. 'A wet nurse? Michael hired a wet nurse to feed my granddaughter? I need to know just what has been going on the last few months since this infant entered the world!' After all, Eleanor had not been given even the slightest notion that her daughter had fallen ill.

Maggie remained quiet. She was at a loss as to how to respond to Eleanor's questions. She was also unaware of the timeline since Audrey had become ill. After all, she had only been employed to feed the baby.

The room was beginning to become more chaotic as Charlotte's wailing reached a pitch that could not be ignored. Eleanor shoved Charlotte in Maggie's arms.

'You can use the nursery. It is set up through here.' She walked ahead of Maggie and showed her into the guest room turned nursery.

As Eleanor closed the door, giving Maggie privacy, she shut her eyes and whispered. 'If there was ever a time I needed you, Lord, it is now.'

Reaching the doorway of the now-empty sitting room, her voice escaped her in a shrill cry. 'Audrey? Audrey? Where are you?'

The kerosene lantern that cast light as far as the table did not extend to the chair but Eleanor was nonetheless aware it was empty.

She dashed from room to room searching for Audrey. The ongoing silence did not surprise her, as Audrey had not yet uttered one word.

Once it was clear Audrey was nowhere to be found, Eleanor descended the back stairs to the yard. The last thing she required was for the neighbours to come running, so she carried out her search quietly. Rounding the front of the house, she was met with nothing more than the sound of crickets in the garden and the thudding of her heartbeat in her ears. She hissed Audrey's name.

Hurrying down the drive and peering over the front gate, she could see a carriage in the distance. It was motionless.

'Oh no,' she pressed her fist to her lips. As her legs propelled her forward toward the carriage, her mind warred with itself. She would much rather turn around and run away from the fact that her daughter was not the person she once knew. What if Audrey had fallen and been caught under the carriage? But as she bridged the distance she was soon sighing with relief, for the Colonel had Audrey in his grasp and was attempting to push her up into the carriage with the assistance of Doctor Rushby.

'Thank goodness,' Eleanor breathed.

'I will see you at home, Eleanor,' the Colonel said between gritted teeth.

Eleanor, ashamed she had allowed Audrey to waltz straight out the door, simply nodded and slunk back to the house. Any number of mishaps could have befallen her daughter. Most horrifying to her mind was the thought of the neighbours discovering her. Such an outcome would become the gossip of the district.

Doctor Rushby assisted Audrey into the house. 'Which room am I settling her into?' he asked.

'In here,' Eleanor said as she raced ahead to turn down the

bedclothes. It was all she could to show her remorse. In doing so she scattered the dolls and cushions haphazardly across the room. Audrey had occupied this bedroom since she was a girl. Eleanor now watched her daughter with intense scrutiny. How she hoped to see some recognition of the room on the young woman's face. But alas, there was nothing to be observed. Doctor Rushby slowly released her from his grasp and lowered her onto the pillow. After checking Audrey over, he left the room with a look of grim resolve.

Eleanor and the Colonel were waiting for him in the drawing room.

'How is she?' Eleanor was wringing her hands with worry.

'It would appear she is very ill since giving birth. I would go as far to say that the devil has taken a hold of her,' Doctor Rushby said.

Eleanor burst into tears. 'Oh my goodness. What are we to do?'

The Colonel stepped forward. 'What would you suggest, Doctor Rushby?'

'May I speak with you alone?'

The Colonel ushered him toward his study. Once the men had closed the door, Eleanor could hear only their muffled voices, and found herself sobbing uncontrollably alone. She remained in the sitting room, surrounded by closed doors. A stranger was coddling and feeding her grandchild in the nursery, her daughter was locked away in her bedroom and her husband had shut her off from the discussions and any pending decision that was to be made. Was Audrey to be hauled off to the asylum? The thought pained Eleanor with such intensity she almost swooned. What would she tell her friends? She would be so ashamed that this had happened to her family.

Screams suddenly erupted from Audrey's room. Eleanor jumped in fright. The study door swung open and Doctor Rushby raced to the bedroom door and flung it open. The Colonel was close behind him and as Eleanor reached Audrey's room she heard Doctor Rushby order, 'Close the door!'

Again, she was shut out of proceedings, which rendered her unable to offer any assistance to her daughter. It was some time before the door opened again, and when it finally did the Colonel came directly to the sitting room. Eleanor looked at him with pleading eyes and concern weighed on her features.

'Doctor Rushby has given her something to help her sleep,' the Colonel said.

Eleanor did not know what to say. She had so many questions but knew the answers she sought would not be forthcoming.

The Colonel sensed her confusion. 'Doctor Rushby will remain here until he is assured she is in a relaxed state.' Silence ensued between them until the Colonel quietly stood and returned to Audrey's room.

The next time Eleanor was aware of her husband's presence he was speaking to her in a stern voice. 'Have you checked on our other guest?' His words startled her and she woke with a jolt. She must have fallen asleep after the Colonel had left to assist with Audrey.

'No, no I have not checked on the baby. I will do so now.' Eleanor stood and put her hand on the edge of the daybed. She looked defeated as she stared at her husband. 'I cannot believe this is happening. What are Doctor Rushby's thoughts on a treatment? Maybe the familiarity of home will help her cure.'

The Colonel looked at his wife with hope. 'I feel the only possibility is prayer at this stage — for a miracle. Doctor Rushby has seen many cases like this before. He did say that whilst we can be hopeful, he has not seen too many women return to their former health. He has recommended we keep Charlotte with us. Meanwhile, he has offered to preside over Audrey's care at the asylum.'

Eleanor felt her chest tighten. She clutched at the edge of the upholstery in an effort to control her emotions. While the thought of Audrey being taken to the asylum made her feel ill, she could not hide the fact that her fear of caring for Audrey would harbour its own difficulties. How would she and the Colonel explain Charlotte's appearance? They would have to make up a believable tale to cover Audrey's whereabouts, all the while ensuring her placement in the asylum was kept a secret.

'No, I want to keep her here with us for the moment until I can figure myself out. We will also keep Maggie here. Tomorrow, you will send word into town so Doctor Rushby can confirm that I am unwell and that nobody is to visit until further notice. In the meantime, he can tell anyone who may have seen him visit with us tonight that it was me he was calling on.' With that said, Eleanor pursed her lips to herald that the end of the matter was nigh.

The Colonel looked ruefully at his wife. 'Whatever you wish, my dear. But let me implore you, that if things do not change or if, regretfully, they worsen, you will allow Doctor Rushby to take over our daughter's care.'

Eleanor nodded once and left the sitting room to check on Charlotte and Maggie.

But several days heaved past, and although Audrey's situation did not worsen, it certainly did not improve. Each day brought the same routine behaviour. On waking each morning, Audrey would appear confused by her childhood environment before gradually settling down to staring at the walls within her room, or out the window if she sat in the chair provided. She was little trouble and never spoke.

The nights were the most difficult. As dusk approached Audrey would become agitated and eventually begin to scream in outbursts that would set Eleanor's teeth to grinding. She would scratch and fight the Colonel in his attempts to subdue her. He was the only one with strength enough to control her. Lacing her lukewarm tea with the medicine that Doctor Rushby had delivered, he would then bide his time until the remedy eventually sent her to sleep.

Since Audrey's arrival Eleanor had relieved the housemaid from her duties. She did not wish any gossip about her home life seeping into the community. This left her to undertake the preparation of meals and the running of the entire household. By the week's end, she was overcome with exhaustion, and if she had harboured any intention of attending church, doubted she would have been able to rise from her bed. Fortunately, the widely circulated fiction about her ill health spared her the interminable guilt of having to personally lie about her absence to the minister and individual friends.

Donning her bravest exterior, Eleanor watched her daughter's mental health unravel time and again. Maggie was taking constant care of Charlotte and it mostly seemed the baby was not her grandchild at all but rather a guest staying with them. Eleanor felt less and less inclined to touch Charlotte or cuddle her, which was something for which she had previously pined. She felt a disdain begin to grow.

A week passed and Eleanor was encumbered with an increasing desperation to see a change. Nothing, however, was progressing as she had hoped. One cold afternoon, hidden between the house and the clotheslines so her neighbours could not see her, she found herself tussling with soaking wet bed sheets and cursing her current lack of domestic help. The sagging clotheslines were succumbing to the weight of the sheets and threatening to allow them to swing across the ground as the wind blew them dry.

She had not been strong enough to turn the handle on the wringer and had given up on doing it. Her dress was wet as were her shoes. She pushed her hair from her face in frustration and reached into the basket for the remainder of the washing. A cloth nappy was among the napery. She flung it back into the basket. She could not hang it up for fear a neighbour would observe it. It would cause the kind of gossip she did not care to instigate. Her daughter was causing her all sort of bother and that baby was going to be a huge burden before long.

Approaching the stage at which her supposed illness should have passed, Eleanor feared the neighbours would soon be calling on her, and she did not know how she would face them. She was fast losing perspective on how to deal with the situation in which she found herself. The Colonel had only spoken the evening before about the impending decision to turn Audrey over to the asylum. It was looking inevitable, but what kind of lie could she come up with to cover the fact that Audrey was not able to look after her baby? Charlotte was the seemingly innocent one at present but Eleanor now believed the child was completely to blame for this whole mess.

An idea formed in her mind. Amid the anger and loss she felt, it seemed to be the only way to deal with the situation. It was the only way she could make this right.

Returning the wash basket to the laundry, Eleanor looked up at the baby bath that hung beside the door. She had been bathed in it as a babe, as had Audrey. Lifting it from the hook, she staggered backward, countering the weight of the heavy steel.

Returning to the house, she tried to set it down quietly on the kitchen table. Eleanor then placed the kettle upon the stove to heat some water. Whilst it warmed, she crept to the hallway and placed her ear to the door of the bedroom.

Charlotte had been unsettled overnight. As a result, Maggie was lying down napping while the baby had an afternoon sleep. Once she was assured there was no movement in the bedroom, Eleanor filled the bath with the warm water from the kettle, and then crept into the nursery. Gathering the sleeping baby in her arms, she made sure she did not wake the nanny.

Back in the kitchen, she undressed her granddaughter and placed her into the water, pushing her firmly beneath the surface. Tiny bubbles escaped the baby's mouth. Her little arms and legs began thrashing around. Soon, both bubbles and thrashing subsided.

Eleanor stepped away from the baby bath and rushed to Audrey's bedroom. Pushing the door open, she saw that the once beautiful young woman was sound asleep, all sunken cheekbones and pale skin. After approaching the bed, she gently shook Audrey's shoulder to wake her. Then, taking her hands, she pulled her from the bed. Placing a blanket across her shoulders and with tears in her eyes, Eleanor led her to the kitchen.

'You see, my darling? I have made it right. Everything is going to be fine now. The devil has been vanquished from your life.' Eleanor looked at the vacant stare her daughter cast into the tub. Nothing had changed.

Eleanor became more anxious as she shook Audrey's hands in the hope of agitating her back to normalcy. 'You shall be the girl I knew once more. Please tell me my Audrey will come back to me. Please!' she screeched.

Eleanor's screams woke Maggie, who followed the noise directly to the kitchen, where she found the two women standing over the bath.

Sensing Maggie's approach, Eleanor began screaming directly at Audrey, 'What have you done?'

All three women stared down at the lifeless body beneath the water.

Maggie quickly dragged the tiny baby from the bath in a rush that sent a surge of water sailing over the tub and onto their shoes.

A slow wail escaped Audrey. It rose until it was a high-pitched scream. She began to flail her arms around as though trying to grasp reality. With a backward thrust of her hand she knocked her mother over and then dived on top of her. She wrapped her hands around her mother's throat and screamed into her face as it began to lose colour.

A moment later the world turned black for Mrs Eleanor Price.

When she came round all was quiet and she was in her bedroom with Doctor Lawler standing over her.

'How are you feeling, Mrs Price?'

'I do not know. I ... I ... must have passed out.' She looked past Charles and noted it was dark outside.

'What is the time?' She attempted to sit up.

'No, you just lie back and rest, Mrs Price. You are in shock. I have administered something to help you relax.'

'Why? What has happened?'

'There has been some excitement, it would seem. The Colonel would like to sit with you for now. I will alert him to your awakened state.'

Eleanor's heartbeat quickened. She felt compelled to clutch at Doctor Lawler and confess, but fear held her back. It was a fear of her husband's wrath and the possibility that he would cast her from his life. He would never understand why she had done such a thing. So she stayed silent and allowed Doctor Lawler to retreat. While she waited for her husband to appear, she watched the lamplight dance across the walls. Surely the shadows cast by the flickering flames would haunt her dreams.

There was a tap on the door. Eleanor looked around to see the Colonel standing on the threshold with a look of dread draped across his features. He walked in and sat down on the chair beside the bed and grasped her hand. 'Eleanor, my dear. I have some very devastating news.'

Eleanor looked perplexed. 'Doctor Lawler said there was some excitement. What has happened?'

'It would seem our daughter has committed the most evil of acts.'

'What, what has she done?' Eleanor did her best to sound desperate for the answer.

'She has drowned our beautiful granddaughter and sent her to heaven.' His voice broke on the final word as he began to sob. He laid his forehead on their clasped hands. Eleanor broke into her own resounding voice of despair.

'Where is she?' she sobbed as she tried to sit up.

'No, do not attempt to leave this bed. You are far too weak. Doctor Rushby has taken her beneath the cover of darkness to the asylum.'

'What if our friends hear of this? What will they say? We will be shamed forevermore.'

'I have taken steps to prevent that. You need not worry about things from now on. It will be best if you stay in bed and rest, allowing the bruises on your neck to fade.'

Eleanor touched her fingers to her neck. She winced as a dull pain reminded her of what had befallen her.

'I'm afraid you were going to be next if Maggie had not managed to rescue you from her murderous hold.' The Colonel's sorrow turned to anger. He stood and looked down at his wife. 'I am sorry she has caused us such heartache. I will send word to Michael in the coming days and alert him to what has happened. I will give him orders to keep well away. That will make it easier to maintain the pretence that they are living the high life on a soldier's salary at the Peninsula.'

'What are we to do about Charlotte?' Eleanor placed her fingers to her lips as though it was all too much to bear.

'Doctor Rushby has used his position as a practitioner to

commission the undertaker. He will ensure Charlotte's identity is kept hidden. We will have her placed in an unmarked grave at the cemetery.'

Eleanor released a slow breath. Knowing Doctor Rushby would deal with the situation discreetly gave her confidence that, in time, everything would turn out well. Doctor Rushby was a trusted friend who would ensure that Audrey's true identity be kept a secret at the asylum — a feat no doubt easily accomplished considering the young woman would be locked away and forgotten among the hundreds of other cursed souls imprisoned there. Both her daughter and granddaughter were lost to her forever.

By the time Eleanor was able to leave her bed, her bruising and headaches had subsided, and she duly noted all traces of Audrey's recent visit had disappeared. She sat at the breakfast table and looked at the Colonel. Raising her teacup from its saucer she asked, 'Where did you put her belongings?'

Her name would not be spoken between them again, as it had not been since the Colonel had discovered the mortal sin his daughter had committed against their granddaughter. He talked around mouthfuls of porridge.

'I sent everything off with Maggie. I paid her handsomely for her silence on the matter.'

Eleanor scalded her mouth on her tea. 'Those gowns cost a minor fortune, and those hats! How could you?'

'Well, it would not seem that she will not have any use for them, and neither will we. We were not about to send her off with a trunk full of gowns. Doctor Rushby is keeping her hidden up at the asylum and Maggie has assured me she will be discreet with regard to the events that have unravelled.

She assisted me with her removal from the house, and was most gracious in the face of what occurred. Giving her the gowns was the least I could do under the circumstances, do you not think?'

'I suppose.'

'Maggie did dress her up in the best gown among her belongings. She found a pair of gloves and a hat and sent her off in the carriage with her suitcase as though she were going on holiday.'

The Colonel looked down at his breakfast and shook his head. 'I cannot believe what became of her. I just cannot believe it.'

Eleanor stared at her husband and chose her words carefully. 'Some things are beyond one's control.' She gently placed the teacup back onto the saucer and looked up at her husband. 'And we had to make a decision based on the only thing we could control.'

The Colonel looked at her and shook his head in remorse. 'What would I do without your strength and courage?' he said.

Eleanor took a small bite of toast and sipped her tea. It was all she could do to stave the guilt that rose within her and threatened to burst forth from her lips if she did not keep them busy. She almost gasped out loud as the image of her tiny granddaughter lying lifelessly in the water arose in her memory. At least she was free of the constant fear of the risk that Audrey would be recognised in the asylum, an outcome that would be nothing short of disastrous for them. The Colonel's position and her respectable standing in the community looked to remain intact, thank goodness.

Chapter 9

The shard of daylight streamed through the open curtains, awakening Celia. Her eyes stung as she attempted to open them. She blinked a few times to free them from the dry heat and pain that settled there. The endless stream of tears and fitful night's sleep she had endured all added to her discomfort. She had awoken over and over throughout the course of the night as the image of Audrey's bloated and blue face slammed into her memory time and again.

Charles had relished watching her distress and no doubt welcomed her taking flight from the belltower as confirmation she would not interfere any further.

Her stomach pained her and her head hurt. She placed her hands on either side of her temples in a bid to push the pain away. Raising herself into a sitting position, she sat on the edge of the bed. As her feet felt the floor she swayed and gripped the edge of the mattress to steady herself.

Her body ached from holding herself so rigidly. She was wound so tight that had she been a spring, she would have snapped. As she passed the door to Charles' room she bobbed low to peek through the keyhole. It was no surprise the bed was vacant and the coverlet undisturbed.

When she stood upright the world spun. She steadied herself against the wall and once the world stopped spinning, made her way to the kitchen. Lydia was not there, which seemed unusual at this hour, but she was thankful. She lit the stove and placed the kettle on the plate. Her stomach churned, reminding her that she had not eaten since lunchtime at her aunt's home the day before. She cut a slice of bread and lathered it with strawberry jam only to find it sat like a stone in her mouth. Sitting with her teacup poised in her hands, she sipped the hot liquid slowly in an effort to assist the bread's passage down her throat. But the process was made more difficult by the sobs she could not hold back. Tears ran down her face as she mourned her friend. Who had done such a thing to Audrey?

An image of Audrey's dead face seared into her mind's eye once more. It was so horrifying; she feared she would never be free from the macabre image. Would it ever leave her? The last time she had witnessed Audrey alive she had been covered in filth and was a mere shard of the young carefree spirit Celia had come to cherish. Lack of sleep had rendered her senses raw. Images of her dear friend at different stages of her life warred with one another. As though conjuring some ghastly pantomime, she would recall a happy memory only to have the death mask of her friend arise in her mind. This caused her to crash back to the horrific realisation that Audrey was gone forever, and in such ghastly circumstances. Had Audrey been afraid as she fell to her death, or was she beyond any degree of rational understanding by that stage?

Celia's heart hurt for the loss of all they had shared. The pair had vowed to be lifelong friends. After the announcement of Audrey's engagement to Michael it was confirmed that he was being posted to the Peninsula. While the excitement of impending womanhood and becoming cherished wives was afoot, they had kept in touch via letters after Audrey had married and moved away. It was only when Audrey became a mother that the letters stopped, and Celia had made the assumption that caring for a little one while dealing with the demands of being an officer's wife had rendered her friend far too busy to write.

Now, sitting in the kitchen all alone, Celia placed her hand to her throat as she finally managed to swallow a hard wad of bread. Instantly, she felt a strong pain in her chest. Continuing to sip her tea, she grimaced at the difficulty her body was having absorbing even the lightest form of sustenance.

She had forged a bond with Audrey of a kind she had not shared with anyone up until that point. Audrey had been unafraid and adventurous. She had taught Celia the courage and strength to match Charles in terms of self-confidence as their courtship unfolded. The memories of the time she and Audrey had shared were cherished now and that is all they ever would be: precious recollections. She would not make another new memory with Audrey.

The aroma of the tea struck Celia as a reminder of one day in particular that she had shared with her beloved friend, when it had seemed as though their lives were destined to move in exact unison as they laughed and loved and shared mischief. She looked down at her teacup and stared into the amber liquid. A single teardrop plopped into the cup causing the hot liquid to ripple outward. As it hit the cup's inside edge it halted as though it had never existed. Would her memories of Audrey end in the same manner? She willed herself to remember Audrey in happier times.

Bramwell had delivered the invitation to the breakfast table. Lady Montague peered at the note then flipped it closed. 'It would seem we have been invited to Miss Mable's Tearoom for a meeting of some sort.'

'What kind of meeting?' Celia looked perplexed.

'The invitation does not precisely state the topic of conversation though considering it is signed by Mrs Rushby, I imagine it will have all to do with the big house on the hill.'

Celia wondered how she would contain herself. The announcement of her engagement had been postponed until her father had sent return word. She was to become Doctor Charles Lawler's wife. She squealed inside her mind each time she thought of her engagement, and feared she would blurt out her secret news to all within earshot.

'We will aim to arrive at the tearoom late morning so please finish your breakfast and run upstairs. Dress in a gown suitable for a luncheon and meet me at the carriage on the quarter hour.'

Celia left her seat and began hurrying from the room, but skittered to a halt as her aunt placed her hand up.

'Refrain from any mention of the proposal.'

'Yes, Aunty,' Celia smiled as she walked quickly from the room.

An hour later Celia alighted the carriage and was very impressed at the throng of women already inside Miss

Mable's Tearoom. Audrey waved wildly at her from the table against the window.

'Here!' Audrey patted the empty seat beside her. 'Did you hear what happened at the asylum?'

'What?' Celia asked in surprise.

'There was a fire last night. It destroyed the sewing room. Apparently word has spread that the entire contents of the room have been destroyed. Sewing machines, fabric and all the cottons have been lost.'

'That is terrible. Was anybody hurt?' Celia asked.

'No. The fire happened overnight, I believe. I am sure Charles will enlighten you with all the details when he calls on you next.' Audrey grinned.

Celia's face flushed. 'Maybe we will discuss the fire if he calls on me this evening.'

Audrey leaned in and whispered. 'Very soon it would seem he will be the first person you see in the morning and the last at night.'

'Oh Audrey, stop it!' Celia giggled, all the while pining to tell her friend that the very scenario she was describing would indeed be the truth.

Miss Mable approached them with a plate of scones. As she placed them in the centre of the table she announced, 'Tea service will resume shortly.'

Lady Montague commented on the sad situation at the asylum. 'No doubt the room will be rebuilt in the short term but I have heard that fabric and machines will be a long way off replacement.'

The chatter stopped abruptly as Mrs Rushby's voice resounded across the room. 'I called on you for this meeting for good reason. As you are all aware, the sewing room was destroyed last night up at the lunatic asylum. My husband tells me everything was destroyed. We need to band together and make haste to assist in replacement of the haberdashery that was lost. We need volunteers to visit the asylum and meet with the women to assure them that help is at hand. Is there anybody here who would like to offer support to those who are now at a loss, to aid their recovery? Anybody who can hand embroider or crochet is called upon to assist in any way that she is able.'

'I will go!' Celia's hand shot up as all eyes cast toward her.

Lady Montague drew in a sharp breath and placed her hand up to draw Celia's downward. 'I think we will allow somebody else to volunteer their service.'

Celia looked at her aunt with confusion. 'I would like to assist. I am quite accomplished at all the exploits required. It is the least I can do. And besides, I am sure Charles will think it a splendid idea.'

Lady Montague whispered, 'Until your father has been alerted to your impending marriage we cannot disclose it here, so please stop speaking.'

'I realise this and I am quite capable of holding onto my virtue in this circumstance,' Celia whispered.

Lady Montague halted the conversation, aware all eyes were upon them. Good judgement was something at the top of everybody's agenda in these situations. She did not want to cause a scene in the company of the most renowned women in the district.

Pasting a grin on her lips she looked around the room at prying eyes and announced, 'I agree. It would be of great assistance if you could administer your exceptional sewing skills for those less fortunate.'

'Fabulous!' Mrs Rushby clapped her hands together. 'Would anybody else like to ...'

Audrey leaned against Celia and whispered. 'You will do almost anything to get close to your doctor.'

Celia forced herself to ignore her friend's comment, as she did not want to draw further attention to their table. It took great strength not to grasp Audrey in her arms and hug her in excitement.

'Lady Montague,' Audrey suddenly said, clasping Celia's hand in hers, 'whilst you and my mother finish your tea, may I take a stroll through town with Celia?'

Lady Montague stared from Celia to Audrey and said in a clipped tone. 'I am not sure we have time for that.' Her eyes held with Celia's in an unspoken expression that she did not trust her niece to keep her secret if left alone with Audrey.

Audrey drew her up from her seat and pulled her hand over the crook of Celia's elbow. 'Please, Lady Montague! I will not waylay her for long and I would love to show her the fabric I have decided on for my wedding gown.'

Celia chimed in, 'And I can seek out some fabric to begin the classes for the women in the asylum!' By this stage, she and Audrey were almost at the door and hardly waited for Lady Montague's answer as they pulled it open and rushed out.

They giggled and bustled down the street at breakneck speed to ward off an expected halt by Lady Montague or Mrs Price.

The haberdashery store window was stacked with lace and

fabrics draped across dressmaker's busts. Audrey gave the window a fleeting glance before continuing along the street.

'Why, aren't we meant to be heading inside?' Celia questioned.

'Later. I have something to show you first.'

'My aunt will be looking for me very soon.'

Audrey flipped her hand outward. 'She will be talking with those women for an eternity, leaving us time to do as we please. I would like to sit with you and talk of all things marital. We need to be alone.'

Audrey held fast to Celia's arm, which remained fastened over her own, and led her to a bench seat situated within the gardens of the Shire Hall. The ornate white building with its gothic columns was a sight to behold and its pristine white exterior looked out of place against the timber buildings that lined the opposing side of the street. Celia stared out over the streetscape, where she was catching the attention of more than one gentleman out walking or riding.

'Audrey, I must tell you some grand news but you must swear to me you will not tell a soul.'

'I will promise, if you will also!' Audrey grinned as she pulled a magazine from her bag.

'Does it have your bridal gown inside?' Celia asked.

Audrey put her hand over her mouth to stifle a giggle. 'Not exactly,' she countered as she opened the book to expose a magazine hidden inside. She stared at Celia's profile and waited for her reaction.

Celia could not tear her gaze from the page. She drew in a breath at the pure blasphemy of it. 'What if somebody approaches us? What will we say?' Celia looked coy as she stared back at the street at the passers-by.

'Easy, we will just close it over. See?' Audrey flipped the pages and voila the magazine once more embodied the idea of social acceptability in the form of a book.

Celia slowly reopened the book and flipped to a magazine page that had initially caught her attention.

The article was both fascinating and scintillating. It stated, "The wiles of a woman could allure her husband to never seek the services of another." Celia devoured the article, which explained that a wife "must take action, just as she looks after the duties in the home." Her eyes widened as she continued reading. "She can be assured he will not wander from the marital bed if she appears in control. Women are learning the skills from their counterparts in brothels in France and confining them to their own boudoirs."

Celia placed her fingers up to her lips and bit on the fabric of her glove as she continued to read.

Audrey let out little giggles every few moments as she peered at the photographs of entwined bodies demonstrating the methodology described in the accompanying article.

Celia was now reading aloud in an excited albeit hushed tone, 'It has long been the duty of a woman of the night to fulfil the whims of a married man when his wife cannot go beyond the accepted expectations of the marital bed. Well, it is long overdue that the chore and monotony of these women be alleviated by the one person more suitably qualified to fulfil the role.'

The article had been written by 'anonymous' and while Celia knew she should not be reading such things, she could not take her eyes from the words on the page.

The article explained things about men she neither knew

nor should know — revealing, for example, that the male appendage could be stimulated via the mouth. It was quite a shocking thought to entertain but she felt a slight thrill when she looked at the illustration. She wondered if Charles would enjoy such a thing? If it was something he would like, she could perform the action for him, and if he delighted in it, she need never be concerned that he would stray from their marital bed.

'Where did you get this?' she whispered to Audrey.

'One of my amazing friends has just returned from London, where she stumbled upon it in a bookstore. She even went as far as to sew it into the lining of her travelling trunk so her mother would not seize it. She said she has committed it to memory and we should do the same before passing it along to our fellow sisters.'

Celia held onto Audrey's hand. 'Now, there is something I must tell you.'

'I do hope it is that you plan to woo Charles with the suggestions within the pages we just perused?' she said giggling.

Celia nodded her head vigorously. 'I dare say I will keep my husband satisfied in our marital bed long after we are wed.'

Audrey screamed and gathered her up in her arms. They jumped from the bench scrunching the magazine within their entwined hands and squealed. Celia could not help but feel a tinge of fear that should her aunt witness such a spectacle, she would be in no doubt Celia had shared her secret news.

'I am so excited for you, Celia,' Audrey gushed. 'We will be lifelong friends and will raise babies over the coming years. Oh and we can spend summers together on the Peninsula.'

Lady Montague's carriage drew to a halt at the haberdashery store just as Celia and Audrey had entered its doorway. When the older woman joined them inside, both girls behaved as though they had been in the store for quite some time. Audrey piled three bolts of fabrics across the arm of the store owner and said, 'May I show my friend the fabrics I have chosen for my dress, please?'

He smiled at her. 'Well of course, Miss Audrey.' He carried the selections to a bench in the middle of the store, grabbed the end of one length of fabric and pulled it until it unravelled a few feet.

'It is the most expensive fabric they have in the store.' Audrey leaned closer to Celia so she could whisper in her ear. 'It is the finest silk and comes from Japan. Who would have ever thought there could ever be such an exotic fabric in our town?'

Celia ran her fingers along the fabric and looked at Audrey. 'It is very beautiful.'

'It is indeed,' the man said.

'Celia, you need to consider your purchases,' Lady Montague stated. 'We need to take our leave.'

'Yes, Aunty,' Celia said, before turning to the man. 'Could I see your needlepoint colours, please?'

'Most certainly.' The storeowner hurried to a tall set of drawers. 'Each drawer holds a number of colours in a range of hues'.

Celia chose sixty-seven separate coloured wads, twenty-five feet of calico and thirty-four tapestry frames. She then arranged for them to be delivered directly to the asylum the following day, thus ensuring her supplies would be ready for her first visit. It was a starting point. Once she had met the women and had calculated how many would be regularly in attendance at needlepoint sessions, she could organise more supplies as needed.

Celia felt such excitement as she raced up to her room upon her arrival back to her aunt's house. She had much to look forward to in the life that lay ahead of her.

As the afternoon slipped away, her head was brimming with her newfound knowledge. She considered discussing with Charles all she had learnt, but soon thought better of it. What a surprise he would have when they were married and she could show off her newfound education to him in their bedroom.

Her stomach flip-flopped with the anticipation of such things — and on top of all the news of the day, she felt thrilled by the knowledge that she now had the opportunity to assist Charles at the asylum and help the poor unfortunates who were housed there. Her life would be so exciting.

Chapter 10

Celia sat reading that morning's copy of *The Ararat Advertiser,* feeling incensed at the report. Only two days had passed since her precious friend had met her grim end, and now news of the tragic death of a mother and child was sweeping through the district. It had taken the Price's only two days to set a story — albeit an elaborate one — in motion to announce their daughter and granddaughter's demise. Nonetheless, the funeral for Audrey and her daughter Charlotte were scheduled for later that week.

According to the newspaper article, a fire had swept through the young mother's home on the Peninsula while she and her daughter slept. The pair had perished in the tenacious blaze that engulfed the cottage. A service and burial would be held for them at Holy Trinity Church in Ararat this coming Friday on the ten o' clock, followed by a prayer vigil at the Price home for all the women from the district. The men of the district, meanwhile, would gather at a local hotel to hold their own vigil.

Celia could not have been more on edge. In the days before the funeral, she did not know whether to look forward to, or to dread, the opportunity the service would provide to spend some time with Charles, even if that time would be spent in silence. Her greatest fear was that he would fail to sit beside her in the pew, signalling for certain the end of their marriage. This made her nervous. If she had to endure this sort of treatment in front of their friends and her aunt it would bring shame on her. She did not know what kind of behaviour to expect from her husband today. She had neither seen nor spoken to him since the tragic events of the previous Sunday evening.

Ever since that fateful night, she had stayed home waiting in vain for a chance to talk with him about the incident. Only on one brief occasion had she left the house, and that was to visit her aunt. Lady Montague had been so distressed on hearing the reported news that she had sent her maid with a note requesting that Celia call on her at her earliest convenience.

'I cannot believe this calamity has befallen poor Eleanor!' Lady Montague stated the moment Celia entered the drawing room.

Celia chose her words with care. 'It is very sad indeed.' Her eyes were sore and swollen from the tears she had cried. Looking drawn and gaunt, she was aware that for all outward appearances it would appear that she was struggling with the sudden news of the tragedy and crying fresh tears.

'There has been too much tragic news of late,' Lady Montague remarked. 'First, there was that despicable event at the asylum over the weekend, and now the Prices are ferrying the charred remains of their beloved daughter and granddaughter home to bury them. I cannot bear it.' Lady Montague shook her head in defeat.

Celia gulped at the statement. If her aunt only knew the link between the two events, it would seem too absurd for belief.

'It is very sad indeed,' Celia said again. The news of Audrey and Charlotte's deaths at their residence on the Peninsula had overshadowed the gossip that had begun about the suspicious disappearance of an inmate who had been found hanging in the belltower in the asylum. This had worked in the Price's favour. All that was required now was a sombre service and burial and, like the bodies of their daughter and granddaughter, their secret would be buried for good.

'Where is her husband? There was no news of him. I wonder where he is?' her aunt puzzled.

'Charles said he is away on leave and cannot make it back at present.' Celia lied easily to her aunt. Where *was* Michael? It was a question she had asked herself many times over the previous days. The most obvious answer was that he had been shut off from Audrey and was serving at his post off shore. He had been relinquished — along with Audrey and her precious Charlotte. The Prices did seem to be very resourceful people with quite powerful standing in society. This allowed them the element of casting their strength far and wide to get things working to their benefit.

'I find that most odd, don't you?' Lady Montague stared at Celia, awaiting her response.

Celia began to flush. 'Oh, I am sorry, Aunty. I was just thinking of poor Audrey and Charlotte.' Again, she lied. She could barely speak Michael's name without gritting her teeth. That he could permit his wife to be left in the asylum was disappointing. As the law stated, a husband could turn his wife over to the institution if it was deemed she was unfit in any manner. Michael had proven to be one such man and it was devastating that he had not advocated for his wife.

'If he could be here, he would. I assure you, Aunty,' Celia lied again. 'He is very far away and cannot be reached, I believe.'

When Celia thought of all the injustices Audrey had endured, she became aware of a growing list of people who had failed her beautiful friend. She had not yet paid her respects to Mrs Price and did not know how she was going to face the woman. She would love to point her finger at Audrey's beloved mother and ask her how she could look at her own image in the mirror with the knowledge she had cast her daughter to the devil.

How could the Colonel allow such a thing to happen? Celia considered him a man of enormous strength and moral integrity — and yet he had allowed such a thing to happen to his daughter. It was confusing to Celia and sincerely heartbreaking.

As Lady Montague continued to lament the recent turn of events, Celia's mind turned to Charles and Doctor Rushby, two men who had obviously been capable of living with the knowledge that they had a young woman of social standing living in the bowels of the asylum like a caged animal. How many other secrets did Charles possess that were set to unravel without the aid of cover-ups and lies?

Bidding her aunt goodbye she returned home exhausted. Celia found herself dwelling once more on the fact she had not seen Charles since the evening of the discovery of Audrey's body. He had returned home only to change and would be gone within minutes on both days. Celia would listen for his footfall as he crept into the house and she would hear the closing of the front door latch. How the sound made her feel so lonely. There was no shortage of beds in the asylum. He was getting his rest without her presence.

Celia opened her eyes and immediately wished to close them once more and find sleep. It was Friday, the day of the funeral. As she dressed she felt her nerves beginning to curl in her stomach. Her hands were shaking slightly as she affixed her hat atop her head with a hatpin. With that task complete, she was standing in front of the full-length mirror pushing a few strands of hair over her ears when she heard the sound of his voice as he stood in the open doorway. 'Can I trust you to avoid causing any distress to the Price family today?'

Celia dropped her hands from her hair and looked at him via the reflection in the mirror. 'I did not hear you come in.'

'I have come to get my funeral cloak and I thought it best if I request some discretion today in case you cannot control that tongue of yours.'

She turned abruptly. 'How callous do you think me?'

'I do not think to know you and how you will hold yourself when it comes to matters such as these,' he said loudly.

'Do you think me so cold? The woman has lost her daughter and is also grieving at the loss of her granddaughter for all to witness at a double funeral. Whilst I have an opinion of her and it is not as impressive as one would hope, I am not that unfeeling a person as to cause her any further discomfort.'

'And that is precisely why we are having this conversation. Your opinion holds such judgement. You feel it is so easy to right the wrongs of this world. It is a clear line for you between a person's morality and their misgivings. You have never had to make a decision as grave as the one made by the Prices and God forbid you never have to. So I beg you, please do not allow your mouth to act upon any thoughts you may have.'

Celia raised her index finger and opened her mouth to speak.

'Not a word, do you hear me?' Charles yelled and walked away. The front door slammed behind him as though heralding exactly what she could expect from him throughout the service. Silence.

An hour later, Celia found herself staring ahead at the altar and noted the mere inch of distance between Charles' elbow and her own. The void between them could have been the entire length of the church and it would have felt entirely the same. The Reverend Vickery entered the church from a side door. Everybody stood. He nodded respectfully toward the Colonel and Mrs Price before turning his back to the congregation to face the slender arches of leadlight that depicted Jesus dying on the cross and St Peter staring upward to heaven in prayer.

The reverend prayed for the Lord to take the two perished souls into his home and keep them safe in his care. They were now free from their suffering. Celia wanted to lean on Charles so he could soak up her pain. He could help her find strength if only he would allow her to place her gloved hand in his. She wished to feel him squeezing her hand in acknowledgement that he could be the solid companion he had vowed to be.

She listened to the preaching and prayer; both spoke of God's will. Had it been God's notion to send Audrey past the brink of sanity? Celia could not understand it. Could God see them and judge them on the lies they had told, the secrets they had kept? He should judge all of them for the truth of their actions.

During the morning tea, Celia made the required effort to give her condolences to Mrs Price. She found it difficult to look at the woman and it did help that Mrs Price was surrounded by a throng of supporters, one of whom was her aunt. This limited Celia to a mere moment to face the woman and tell her how sorry she was for the loss of Audrey and dear Charlotte.

Celia's exhaustion was pressing in on her as she bid everyone a good day and almost cantered to the awaiting carriage. She was taken aback when she saw Charles running toward her. They reached the carriage at the same time, and Charles stood aside to allow Celia to climb inside. Once he had done the same, he slammed the door behind him, and she anticipated the wrath he was about to unleash. The stench of beer wafted past her nostrils as he fell onto the opposing seat. His face looked grim as he stared at her. The moment she made eye contact with him he whispered, 'I could feel your judgement during the service. Is there ever going to be a conclusion to you frowning on everything that is presented to you?'

'You judge me with harshness in blaming me for such a thing. Maybe your guilt sitting before God has you shaking in your shoes. I will admit I do have questions about our mortality and God's will.'

'And there we have it. I just knew you would sit in judgement. You cannot help it.'

'It is nothing new. I have questioned the word of God from the moment I was of an age that I could listen to my father's sermons.'

'I now find it disconcerting that it was never something we discussed previous to our marriage.'

Celia swallowed as the shock of his words settled on her. 'Would you have reconsidered marrying me if I had told you something that represented a challenge for you?'

Charles' gaze did not waiver. 'I think if I had a looked into our future I would have reconsidered my decision.'

Celia looked away from him. She could not maintain his gaze as she willed herself to hold back the tears. The days before they were married were cherished ones to her. She knew Charles was trying to hurt her by saying such things. The memories previous to their marriage were joyous ones. She could recall them so easily. Charles had allowed her to question and push against tradition. Back then he had welcomed her curiosity. How had he forgotten how much he had relished the challenges she presented to him?

The day following the meeting at Miss Mable's Tearoom, Celia was elated when a telegram arrived from her father. In his response it stated simply that his daughter had his blessing to marry Doctor Charles Lawler. With Lady Montague calling on her friends in succession over the course of the afternoon the news swept through the district within hours. It was met with jubilation and would also herald the assured longevity of the superintendent in his position at the asylum. It was common knowledge that a married practitioner was much more settled and likely to remain in their tenure with a wife in residence.

Charles called upon Celia that evening. She was so excited that their news could be shared she almost jumped into his arms when he arrived, but Lady Montague was too close in proximity for her to consider any such contact.

'In anticipation, I met with the Reverend Vickery and he is happy at the prospect of marrying us,' Charles said. 'We need only choose a date and meet with him to discuss the details.' He smiled at her as she placed her hands to her lips to stifle the squeal about to escape.

'I did say we would attend church together this Sunday.'

'That sounds splendid.' Celia clapped her hands together.

Charles arrived early Sunday morning to collect Celia for church. They were met with smiles and waves as they sat together in one of the pews. Celia had been privy to hundreds of sermons over the years, with her father at the pulpit, and knew the messages of faith within the Bible.

When the reverend looked at her and stated the importance of the sanctity of marriage, while emphasising the privacy that should exist within the bonds between a man and a woman, she averted her gaze. Celia began to feel confusion and guilt. She knew she had committed a sin gaining inappropriate information from the magazine Audrey had presented to her.

His stare held fast to her when he delivered the sermon on the filth that was entering society through the written words of charlatans acting out the devil's work. He bowed his head when he spoke of the work of women, trying to lure husbands away from the umbrella of God's care and thereby ruining the purity of love for family. While Celia could not deny the path laden with difficulty for those who were wayward, she could not understand the lack of education bestowed on women. Would it not make sense to give her more control if she was educated and allowed the right to decide what was best for her?

She deeply understood the importance of God's love and the importance of family. After all, she was the daughter of a reverend. But she was no fool. She could read and write and decipher good from evil. Her love for Charles would prove they could forge a solid destiny together. Wanting more than just to be an obedient wife she felt a partnership was more fitting for them. Since offering her assistance at the asylum, she wanted to support Charles in his work and his endeavours. She pined to know what he did as a doctor and surgeon. As his soon-to-be wife, she did not want to sit beside him and be bereft of knowledge pertaining to his working life.

The meeting in Miss Mable's Tearoom had opened a cache of ideas, but now the sermon and the guilt it triggered was making her feel confused. At the conclusion of the mass they were to meet some of Charles' acquaintances and travel to One Tree Hill for a picnic. She hoped to have time with Charles to discuss her good news with him. On the way to church he had mentioned that the grapevine of gossip was ripe with news of Miss Celia Loddon's generosity.

It took such a long time to break from the throng of the congregation as everyone bestowed congratulatory wishes on the couple. Finally, they were alone in a carriage, with Charles at the reins, steering them up into the hills beyond the township. Birds were singing and huge gum trees towered above them, their leaves barely wavering on the breeze.

Celia chatted incessantly about the meeting that had taken place in Miss Mable's Tearoom. Charles smiled at her, as her excitement seemed to grasp at him and pull him along. As the carriage drew to the summit of the hill, Celia stopped talking and stared around at the three-hundred-and-sixty-degree view of the countryside below.

Charles pulled a picnic basket and a large sheet from the duckboard of the carriage and spread it out on the lush grass. He untethered the horses from the carriage, switching their bridles for halters and tethering them to a nearby tree for them to graze on the lush grass.

'Where are your acquaintances? Are they meeting us here?' she asked.

'I may have eluded to that to appease your aunt.'

'Oh,' Celia exclaimed as her heart skittered along.

'It is just you and me. Standing beside her, he took her hand in his and kissed it, allowing his lips to linger on the underside of her palm.

Celia looked up at him and the fire in his gaze cast her mind to the magazine.

'I am glad we have this time alone Charles, as I have so much to tell you.'

'We have time for that later.' He moved behind her, laying his chin on her shoulder and sliding his arms around her waist. 'It is beautiful here and I am so glad to have you alone, my darling,' he whispered in her ear.

The warmth of his breath made her legs weak. 'Yes, I believe it is, and I too am equally glad.' She felt her insides grow instantly warm. This was only the second time he had enfolded her in his touch. Her senses reeled as she closed her eyes and breathed deeply.

There was no doubt the content she had gleaned from the magazine was the plain truth. With Charles possessing her physically in his strong embrace, she suddenly believed the truth of men's virility and the needs women were expected to fulfil.

Deviously, she wanted to test the theory and ever so slightly pushed her lower back outward so that her buttocks pushed gently against the front of his trousers.

She felt him startle but he did not move away.

He hissed the words as he exhaled, 'You intend to play some wicked games before we are married, my darling.' He pushed forward as though to meet her evenly in a game of will.

She was in awe of the hardness she felt at her back and her body began to soften as she leaned into it. It was quite enlightening to feel more in control at this point before marriage rather than to flounder and be surprised. She had seen a picture of how a man really looked when he was disrobed and it was a sight to behold. What a difference a day of improper reading could make to one's promiscuous curiosity.

She could never have believed she would be in this situation: an unmarried woman with a gentleman's hands on her. And she was allowing it!

His hands had drifted to both sides of her waist. Slowly he moved her from side to side. She could hear his breathing sharpen as the movement stirred emotions in her. She would have never believed these feelings to be possible. It was a revelation to physically sense how well a man and woman could fit together.

Considering they were not yet married, their actions were of course improper. But what rendered this impropriety scandalous was the fact they were standing in a public place so boldly showing physical intimacy. Their behaviour was dangerous for her.

Charles' voice broke into her thoughts as she closed her eyes and enjoyed the movement, the rhythm of which relaxed her.

'Please keep this up, my love.' He removed his hands from her waist as she pursued the motion of their play.

Her breath left her body in a whoosh as his hands moved slowly up her waist to stop on her breasts. He caressed them on the outside of her bodice and her nipples sprang forth to push against the fabric of her dress. She allowed her head to drop back onto his shoulder as his hands gently kneaded them and his fingers slowly circled her nipples until she was crying in frustration.

'Please, Charles.'

'What my darling? What do you need?' She could sense the smile upon his lips as he teased her.

'I need you to ... to ... ' She could not say what she wanted. She needed him to stop but having discovered this amazing feeling, she wondered if she could bear for the sensation to end.

Amid the delicious feeling warping through her body she knew she had to break the hold he had on her. If they continued on this path she would be with child before they were married. That would be dire. This thought was the only thing that enabled Celia to pull herself from the dangerous dance she had begun. She turned around and flung her arms around Charles' neck and pushed her body against his, kissing him long and hard.

Finally, he set her away from him and they stared at one another, their breath running ragged from their mouths.

Slowly, Charles dropped to his knee, all the while staring into her eyes. 'I know this is quite comical in this exact moment but I have something for you.' He placed his thumb and forefinger in his vest and pulled out a ring.

Celia gasped and placed her hands to her lips. 'Oh Charles. Is it an opal? It is the most unusual stone I have ever seen.'

'Only the best for my soon-to-be darling wife. That is, if you will marry me.' He laughed.

'Oh, of course. I love you so very much.'

'And I, you.' He kissed her lips softly and placed the band on her finger.

Celia stared down at the glistening stone with its flecks of gold and reddish hues immersed in a bed of blue.

'I knew you were quite taken with Audrey's ring. It has a different hue to hers.'

'I absolutely love it but I did not expect it.' Celia laughed. She was so happy at this moment she could burst. She held her hand out in front of her and moved it this way and that. As the sun caught the colours and bounced them around, they appeared to shimmer and swirl like liquid.

'I will call on Audrey this afternoon to show her.'

'Goodness, I can hear the screams from here.' Charles shook his head.

'Oh Charles, I love it!' she said as she kissed him gently on the lips.

A carriage ambled toward them in the distance.

'We had better find a level of decorum,' Charles said as he grasped her hand and walked her over to the picnic basket.

Celia sat down on the sheet and peered into the picnic basket.

'I cannot believe you did all this. It is so lovely,' she said as she pulled the items from the basket. Celia unwrapped the wax paper and handed Charles a sandwich before grasping another, unwrapping it and taking a bite.

'We are going to be married. I feel as though I am dreaming,' she said.'

'I have a question for you, my love. Where, pray tell did you learn to do such things?'

Celia giggled, her cheeks flushing. 'Let me reveal that Audrey has so kindly shared some information that young wives could do well to prosper from.'

'To the contrary, husbands will prosper from this education,' he laughed heartily.

'Well, yes, now that you put it in that context.'

'Whilst we are on the subject of education ... ' Charles stared at her.

'Yes,' she said, turning her gaze from her hand to him.

'I know your offer of sharing your incredible sewing skills at the asylum is very generous.'

'You are not angry at me, are you?' Celia looked worried.

'Oh no, no! I am not angry with you, my darling. But I do have concerns that you expect you will find yourself in a hospital filled with sick people recovering from colds and the like. The reality is very different. The women housed there are lunatics and imbeciles, incapable of caring for themselves. Their minds are broken, and some of the women are more than dangerous. I will not have you amongst them.'

Deep in thought, Celia bit her lower lip. 'But surely, those who are capable of sewing and needlepoint are not so broken?'

Charles thought for a moment. 'I will see to it that anyone you are to assist is not of too cumbersome a disposition.'

Celia was disappointed that Charles did not see it as being in her best interests to be truly among those who needed the most assistance. But instead of beginning a quarrel, she nodded. Leaning forward, she kissed him gently on the lips and whispered, 'I love you, Doctor Lawler.'

Charles looked around them and noted that they were still alone high on One Tree Hill. He deepened their kiss and once more they found themselves pressed together, rolling the confines of the sheet, ending on the lush grass, losing their breath as they longed to become husband and wife and fully succumb to their love under the sanctity of God's consent.

Chapter 11

The carriage pulled to a halt outside the superintendent's lodge. Celia stepped down and turned around, expecting Charles to be on her heel. Instead, he slammed the carriage door and banged on the roof. 'Driver, Shire Hall Hotel!'

She watched the carriage disappear from view. Her heart thumped in her chest and her head pounded to the same rhythm. She was so tired from the events of the last few days and the funeral had taken the last vestige of her energy. She walked up the steps to the front door. She thought of all that had happened. Celia could not deny she was incensed at Charles' behaviour toward her. On reflection, though, she understood why he was so distressed. He had been dealing with the murder of poor Audrey and the mystery that surrounded this. She knew his disapproval had been building for weeks.

She stopped mid-thought. Actually, his frustration had been building for months. The truth dawned; it had begun with her good intentions when she had volunteered at the asylum. There was a part of her that was sad that her actions had caused Charles such discomfort but she would not change anything that she had involved herself in since her arrival to Ararat. Her naivety had been challenged, however, when she first met the poor souls housed inside. Her initial plan to help them after fire destroyed the sewing room had been little more than a selfish ploy to make Charles proud of her. Also, yes, if she was honest with herself, she had also been intrigued to peek behind the walls of the Ararat Lunatic Asylum.

Venturing inside the institution had been scary at first but in a relatively short period she had grown to love being there, to the extent that she allowed her work to consume more of her thoughts than any plans for her impending marriage. According to social expectations, becoming Charles' wife should have been the totality of her commitment in her new life here. Instead, she had become caught up in the idea of evolving into the kind of saint she felt the women needed.

How her heart was torn apart when she thought of those poor women stuck in that godforsaken place and in such unfair circumstances. Charles had forbidden her to see them but she had always found a way to defy him and wend her way back inside. She could not betray their confidence by disappearing from their lives. After all, she had built trust with them, and felt they had all been treated so unfairly. She could not bear to let them down like those who had vowed to care for them.

While Celia's initial selfish intentions had transformed into empathy for the women housed in the asylum, it had also muddied the thoughts she had for all that she knew of the world. Everything had been turned around on her. The simple life she was taught about was in fact, not. The teachings of her father, the reverend, had her questioning God's will. She crossed her arms over her torso in a bid to stave the pain in her stomach, for although she missed the women intensely she knew she could not set foot inside the walls to help them. Tears once more formed in her eyes as her mind flooded with memories of those dear and unfortunate souls she had inadvertently abandoned.

The afternoon sun brightened the massive expanse of cream coloured walls. Celia placed her hand up to her eyes to shield them from the glare bouncing back at her. She had alighted the carriage at the bottom of the drive and walked the snaking gravel path all the way to the gatehouse. Now that she had passed through the gate, the building seemed to grow before her eyes from a dotted blur behind the trees to a mass of stone that commanded her head to turn from right to left to capture a view of it in its entirety.

She had only been in Ararat a few weeks and was already accustomed to the sight of the massive Italianate building held fast against the horizon. In those short weeks she had gone from being a single lady to engaged, and almost married. She was so excited to begin her volunteer work and see more of Charles, hopefully.

Once she was inside the asylum, with the front door closed, her skin began to feel an immediate chill. Any remnants of the sun that had warmed her back had cruelly gone.

'Why, I've been expecting you, Miss Celia,' Matron announced with warmth, taking Celia's gloves from her. 'And how does the soon-to-be Mrs Lawler feel today?' she asked as she held out her hand for Celia's hat.

'I am feeling very overwhelmed ... with excitement, of course.'

Matron laughed. 'Of course.'

'Is Doctor Lawler in his office?'

'I am certain he is, yes.' Matron looked up the staircase.

'I would like to surprise him before I begin the class.'

Matron looked at her with concern. 'I believe we are struggling in our search for an appropriate place for you to hold your lessons at present, Miss Celia, although Doctor Lawler did tell us to expect you. I am sure he has devised some plan to keep you busy while you are here.'

She pointed toward the staircase. 'His office is two flights directly above us. The door has his name on it.'

Celia stared up at the massive skylight as she ascended the stairs. As suggested by Matron, she easily located Charles' door. She tapped on it and when there was no answer she slowly opened it and found his office empty. After entering the room, she closed the door behind her, leaned back against it and stared at Charles' desk. She then walked across the room, went behind his desk and stared at his chair. It made her smile. She ran her fingers over his leather desk pad, his fountain pen, all the while loving the thought that his hands had touched everything she was now touching. Sitting herself in his chair, she made herself comfortable, but as the minutes ticked by she became rather bored. Perhaps Charles had been held up by ward visits or emergency surgery?

After some minutes had passed, Matron knocked gently on the door. She laughed at the sight of Celia moving swiftly from Charles' chair. 'I am afraid Doctor Lawler has been detained in the hospital ward.'

'I am happy to call on him in the hospital ward. Could you point me in its direction?' Celia asked.

'I cannot do that, Miss Celia. Doctor Lawler would not want you wandering unaccompanied on the asylum grounds.'

'Well, could you take me to him?' Celia sounded hopeful.

'Why yes, I think I could manage that for you. This way.' Matron held the door open as Celia slipped past her.

Celia and Matron retraced the staircase back to the hallway entry, at which point Matron turned in the opposite direction to the administration offices and unlocked a door. Celia stepped through it and waited for Matron to relock it behind them. A corridor now stretched before her. She began to feel apprehensive. The brightness of the day was lost to the inner walls of the wards. Everything was overtaken by darkness. Doors were situated on both sides of the corridor in exact symmetry. Matron was chatting away, and her voice broke through Celia's heightened heart rate as it thudded in her ears.

Celia saw two women sitting on a bench between the doors to the cells. One of the women stood and said, 'Hi, Matron Grace.'

'Hello, Sadie,' Matron said. 'How are you feeling today?'

'Me mum's comin' to get me.'

'I will be sure to let you know when she arrives,' Matron said.

The woman put her hand out to Matron and said, 'Bless you, Matron Grace.'

Matron simply took the woman's hand and nodded her head. 'God bless you, Sadie.'

Celia did not stare but felt her heart rate quicken even more as the air around her began to grow heavy with melding odours. As they walked away from the woman Matron said,

'Poor dear. Her mother has been dead for years and yet she still believes she is coming for her.'

Celia said, 'That is sad indeed. Is your name Grace?'

Matron laughed. 'Yes, she knows that to be true.'

With every step, the stench of urine became more potent. Celia began to breathe through her mouth but the odour manifested as a taste on her tongue so she placed her hand politely over her mouth to let out a small cough. Maintaining a calm façade was important; Celia felt it would be rude to let Matron see how uncomfortable she was.

At the end of the hall Matron pushed the door open. Sunlight and fresh air prompted Celia to let out a huge sigh. As she picked up her skirt and stepped over the threshold, the grounds opened out to her like a storybook. There were lush green lawns and the sun was beating a glow along the gravel pathways, which beckoned her to stroll out from the confines of the building.

Nobody seemed to notice them. Some inmates sat on benches, while others strolled arm-in-arm or wandered aimlessly in circles around veranda posts. Taking in the scene before her, Celia could hear whoops and howls of laughter booming from a room that stood alone. Her gaze was pulled upward to the belltower that rose from the ground a few feet beyond and reached considerably high above the rest of the building.

As Celia stared at the open door and wondered why the festive sound was bursting from within, somebody yelled from back inside the doorway they had just exited. 'Matron!'

Matron turned. A nurse held the door ajar, looking distressed. 'We have a situation in the refractory ward that needs your attention.'

Matron looked at Celia apologetically. 'I am afraid I will have to get you to accompany me back to the administration offices until Doctor Lawler is available.'

'Is the hospital ward nearby?' Celia asked in desperation. She did not want to suffer the stench again quite so soon after her first encounter with it.

Matron looked pained. She pointed toward a large house surrounded by a veranda at the end of the path.

'Could you make your way there with haste?' she asked nervously.

'I will.' Celia nodded in compliance.

As Matron disappeared beyond the door from which they had come, Celia turned her attention from the hospital ward to the room much closer in proximity.

The peeling paint of the open door made the small building look unkempt but the sound escaping the building was intriguing. A line of steam escaped the doorway by means of wrapping itself around the doorjamb like hands trying to grasp their way out.

As she stepped toward the room, away from the cover of the veranda, Celia found it remarkable that nobody was as curious as she as to the cause of the noise coming from the room. Considering the lacklustre atmosphere she had observed in and around the grounds, she wondered why everybody was not clamouring for a look within.

She was drawn to the noise. She just had to see what all the fun was about. As she rounded the doorjamb she witnessed a group of women. Some were bent at the waist holding their skirts so they would not fall from the weakness their laughter was inducing. Others were leaning against the walls while their bodies shook. One was giggling while unsuccessfully trying to fold sheets. The humidity in the room hit Celia in the face. The smell of soda crystals and the steam from the hot water filled her nostrils.

Celia's focus found the subject of their banter. One woman had covered her hands and face in 'dolly blue' and was dancing a jig, swirling and whirling around the coppers in the room. Celia drew in a sharp breath and before her mind could engage completely, she shouted, 'Stop that at once!'

Immediate silence blanketed the room. Shocked by the scene, shocked by her own aggravated tone, she placed her hand to her lips. And now here she was standing rooted to the spot, staring at the woman covered in blue dye with droplets of blue sweat running down her face. The woman's lips were pulled into a thin line and Celia was afraid she would burst into tears. However, second by second a grin began to appear. The woman smiled at Celia and began to laugh all over again and dance around as though nothing had occurred.

Celia looked from woman to woman and noticed that they were no longer watching the dancing whirling woman but were, in fact, staring her down as though she were a cockroach they desired to squash beneath the soles of their shoes.

The reality of where she was standing slammed into Celia, and it took all her willpower not to instantly turn and run from the room. These were not the women of her society, nor were they the hired help. These women were inmates in a lunatic asylum and did not have their faculties in order. She was ashamed at her thoughts. To witness this and then pass judgement had come so naturally to her. But she realised she must not show fear or cowardice. After all, any one of these women could happen to be in her sewing class.

Her thoughts came to an abrupt stop as one of the women stepped forward and demanded, 'Who in hell's name are you?'

Celia opened her mouth but before she could mutter an answer another woman piped up. 'Why, she's the doctor's wife.'

Celia suddenly found her voice and indignantly answered, 'I am not. Not yet.'

'Which damn doctor are you marryin' then?' the same woman spat.

'That would be none of your business.' Celia stared back at the woman with heat blazing between them. The woman's nose was almost touching Celia's but Celia's anger was imminent and the woman could sense it. Celia neither cared for people with bad manners nor those who threw insults.

'Well, as I see it pet, you come in here tellin' us what to do. I want to know who you are. I run this place and you are in it.' She let her gaze range from to the tip of Celia's boots then back up to her face.

'I should not have imposed but when I heard the laughter I had to come and see what the fun was about.'

'Ah, so you figured you would see a lovely tea party with women eating cucumber sandwiches havin' a lovely time?' the woman shot back in a haughty tone. Some of the women laughed.

'I was taken aback with what I saw, yes, and I apologise for reacting as I did.'

'Well, apology not accepted, hey girls?' The woman turned and looked at the others, who were still watching intently.

'Well, I suppose I had better be going then.' Celia turned toward the door.

But the woman's voice followed her. 'You didn't answer my question.'

'Your question?' Celia swung around, looking puzzled.

'Which doctor you marryin'?'

'Doctor Lawler.'

A smile spread on the woman's face. 'The new one, ay?'

'Yes, I believe he is. That is correct.' Celia swallowed and took her leave.

As she took her first steps away from the doorway the sounds of laughter re-erupted. Flushed with embarrassment at being made a laughing stock, Celia walked quickly back to the door leading into the main building once more. Whilst she did not relish the sickening stench awaiting her she bolted along the hallway and rapped on the locked door with the administration area on the other side.

'I will let you back through,' came the voice of a nurse behind her.

'Thank you.' Celia heaved a sigh of relief.

The nurse unlocked the door and allowed Celia to step back through before closing it behind her. Celia looked up the staircase toward the landing above where Charles' office was located. Knowing he was not in there she did not wish to wait for him to discuss things with him at present. She would not reveal that her confidence had misplaced.

How had she expected to waltz into the asylum and have everything present itself to her exactly as she had anticipated? She was neither prepared for the lewd behaviour she had witnessed and nor did she want to appear stupid to the women. She wanted their respect, and she expected them to be grateful for her help. She realised now that having such expectations had been very presumptuous of her, and she was ashamed of her attitude.

A young nurse met her in the administration hall. 'Matron told me to look out for you.'

With her hand on the massive interior doorknob, Celia quickly answered, 'Please let Matron know I decided not to disturb Doctor Lawler after all.' She then threw the door open, stepped past the nurse and pulled the door closed abruptly behind her. She wanted to feel the sun beat down on her head until she was clear of the oppressive feeling of the overbearing darkness inside the building. Pulling her gloves and hat on, she approached the gatehouse, signed out and hurried down the drive. Crossing the train line and the main street, she relived the embarrassment of her intrusion into the laundry.

Calmer now, she pondered the difference between her world and the one inside the walls of the asylum. She had been taken aback at the sight of the women in the laundry but they had proven to be of quite sane mind. They were extremely lewd in their manner of behaviour but it was nothing she had not witnessed before among those in the lower classes. How she wished she too could behave more freely without fear of judgement. Would the world not seem more balanced if people could say exactly what they thought and not measure their responses so carefully? Maybe she could teach these women to be a little less abrasive and a little more ladylike. And perhaps they, in turn, could teach her something. Of that she was sure.

To create any semblance of trust she would need to

befriend them. But Celia was neither part of their world nor did she want to force her way in. The possibility of helping these women in any manner was all she could hope for. Everyone in the laundry had seemed quite sane with the exception of the poor woman covered in dolly blue, while the others laughed as any normal person would in that situation. Celia had not seen the comedy in that moment, but on reflection she could see the amusing side of the situation. Considering the sombre lives the women led, it was no wonder they would laugh so easily at anything likely to provide a moment of light relief.

With each step away from the asylum, Celia desperately wanted to turn back. She knew impressing Charles had been at the forefront of her plan but her intrigue now lay elsewhere. Something had altered today. Initially, she had been curious about gauging the insanity of the women, but if she were to be honest with herself they had not looked insane at all. She would discuss her visit with Charles but she would have to leave out certain details. He would be incensed if he knew she had been wandering about without assistance. Also, she did not want to jeopardise Matron's position.

Her attention wandered to the supposed lack of space at the asylum. Surely within its walls there would have to be an appropriate room in which she could hold her lessons? The place was positively huge. For the remainder of the afternoon while back at her aunt's home, she thought of nothing else but her visit to the asylum and a solution to her problem.

At dinner that night she had an idea. 'Aha!' she yelled across the dining table.

Lady Montague jumped from her seat. 'Good God, Celia! Would you refrain from such outbursts?'

'Sorry, Aunty.' Celia said. The smile she was unable to repress made her look as though she was not sorry at all.

Chapter 12

The following morning Charles arrived at Lady Montague's home to join Celia for breakfast. Celia was sitting at the dining table sipping a cup of tea when he strode toward her. He gathered her free hand in his and held her palm up to the warmth of his lips. Before kissing it tenderly he said, 'Good morning. Did you sleep well, my darling?'

Celia smiled up at him. 'I did.'

'I believe you wish to peruse the guest list for the wedding whilst I am here,' he added as he placed her finger in his mouth and drew it out slowly.

Celia closed her eyes as she absorbed the deliciousness of the act. He attempted to do it once more but Lady Montague had entered the dining room and was now approaching the table from behind him. His mouth made a popping sound as he whipped her finger out rather quickly.

Celia placed her hand to her lips to supress a giggle and also to hide the flush of colour rising up her neck.

'Good morning, Doctor Lawler.' Lady Montague's clipped tone indicated either the strong possibility that she had witnessed their inappropriate exchange, or that she did not approve of the early hour of Charles's visit — or both.

Charles cleared his throat as he turned around and straightened. 'Good morning, Lady Montague.' He then turned his attention back to Celia. 'Ah yes, we do need to finalise the guest list. That is why I am here at this early hour.'

Celia regained her senses. 'And there is something else I wish to discuss with you.'

Her future husband pulled a chair out from the table and sat down. 'What else needs our attention?' he asked as he lifted a piece of toast from the fresh pile that had appeared on the table.

Celia watched his hand as he picked up a butter knife and took a knob from the butter dish before spreading a thick layer across the golden toasted slice of bread.

'I visited the asylum yesterday to begin my classes but Matron suggested there was nowhere to hold them at present.'

'Yes, she told me you waited for me for quite some time. I am sorry I was unavailable to you. The hospital ward demanded my attention for far longer than I had anticipated. That entire place is overcrowded. A situation that is keeping me rather busy. That is also where the problem lies with your classes. Without the sewing room there is no other place you can hold them, I am afraid."

'I did notice the laundry room while I was there.'

'And?' Charles said slowly.

'It is very large and could easily house sewing and needlepoint classes.'

'Definitely not.'

'Oh Charles, why not?'

'Because it is an inappropriate space for a classroom and the women in there are positively scandalous.'

'They seemed harmless enough.'

'Why would you approach that room? Did you talk to them?' Charles did not look pleased.

'I glanced inside for a mere moment. The women were busy doing the laundry and hardly noticed me. I think it would be an ideal space. I noticed the shelving, which would be perfect for storing supplies. And there are tables we could use for the lessons. Everything we need can be found in that one area.'

'That may be so but the overall situation is not so simple. Those women will corrupt your thoughts with filth.'

'The female nurses seem to cope with them, and you have led the charge for women to seek employ at the asylum. I can have one such woman assist me if it would make you more comfortable.'

'It would be far too dangerous to leave you alone with that unruly bunch. Some are fairly unstable. I do not see how it could work or seem appropriate.'

'Please, Charles. Give it a chance and if it does not work then I will seek an alternative space.' She stared at him, imploring him to concede.

'When you look at me with those innocent alluring eyes I fairly cannot resist.'

'Please Charles, please!' Celia fluttered her eyelids.

'Where did you learn such manipulation?' He smiled with mischief. 'I give you my blessing but there will be conditions.'

Lady Montague had stayed silent through the conversation but could no longer hold her opinion. 'I think their impropriety has had an effect already.'

'Oh, Aunty. I am just having some innocent fun.' Celia clutched Charles' hand.

He held up an index finger and looked squarely at Celia. 'And it is a trial only.'

'Of course,' Celia said much too quickly.

'And you are to assist the women with the lowest care needs. I will decide which ones.'

'Of course. Of course.' She nodded her head.

'I have not finished. You are to give up your work once we are married."

'Oh Charles, I would not dream of continuing on once we are wed. After all, I will be far too consumed with my wifely duties by then.' She jumped from her chair and fell across him as she placed her arms around his neck.

'Celia, that will be quite enough. Please take your seat.' Lady Montague's harsh tone brought her to the realisation that she was acting inappropriately.

Charles picked up his slice of toast and smiled at her with it poised at his lips. Celia giggled into her napkin. She could not wait to be his wife. The feeling it evoked in her was shattering her nerves.

Lady Montague excused herself from the breakfast table. 'I must begin to ready myself for today's luncheon,' she stated.

The moment Celia's aunt had departed the dining room, Charles leapt from his seat and closed the door. 'Come here,' he whispered to Celia. He pressed his back against the door and pulled Celia against him. 'Now that we will not be disturbed ...' he whispered in her ear before kissing her gently along the side of her neck.

Celia moaned as the warmth of his lips sent shivers through

her. She leaned against him, placing her hands on his shoulders to steady her stance. His mouth moved up to her ear and she felt the warmth of his tongue flick at her earlobe. She could not bear another moment without his mouth on hers. She grasped his head with her hands and pulled his mouth to meet her lips. She kissed him hard and felt his arms tighten around her. She could hear the door chattering against the doorjamb as his back moved to and fro with the rhythm of their mouths.

Breathless after minutes of kissing, Charles grasped Celia by the shoulders and moved her away. 'I have to get to work,' he said.

'No, not yet. We were having so much fun!' Celia pouted.

'That is what makes me fearful,' Charles said with a grin. 'At this rate I am unable to leave you alone and your aunt will no doubt be bashing on this door in a few minutes, which will cause us no end of trouble.'

Before Celia could answer, Charles gave her a quick kiss on the cheek and ducked out of the door. But before it swung closed behind him, Celia placed her hand out and pulled it fully open just so she could watch him gather his hat and coat from the stand beside the front door. 'I love you,' she whispered.

A few minutes after Charles had departed, Celia tapped at Lady Montague's bedroom door. 'Aunty, could you please deliver me to the asylum on your way?'

Lady Montague opened the door. 'I would much prefer you not set foot inside that place. It is so beneath you, so unladylike,' she said with terseness.

'You heard Charles. He has given me his blessing. At least until we are married.'

'I believe you will have to halt your time there before you are married. You only have a few weeks left until the wedding, which means you have plenty to organise in that time.'

'Then I do not have any time to waste!' Celia clapped her hands once.

'Well then, if you must. Gather your things.' Lady Montague closed the door.

'I will just change my dress. Celia's voice heightened in pitch as she ran to her room, where she began to search her armoire for a gown before deciding that a much less impressive dress would do. She chose a pale cream cotton dress and tugged her boots on. She pushed her hat down, shoved her hands into gloves and ran down the stairs.

Once outside, Celia noticed she was suddenly the object of her aunt's unwelcome scrutiny. For Lady Montague was peering out at her from the open door of the carriage saying, 'Celia, you are not to venture out in public looking like that.' The older woman's mortification was clear by the tone of her voice as she took in Celia's appearance.

'With all due respect, dear Aunty, I do not wish to appear overbearing to the women,' she said as she climbed into the carriage.

'There is no chance of that,' Lady Montague said as her eyes lingered on the front of Celia's dress.

'That is splendid. I need them to trust me,' Celia responded.

Lady Montague's gaze had now arrived at Celia's feet. 'Oh Celia, for goodness sake, tie your laces.'

Celia leant forward and began to pull her bootlaces tightly together.

'Are you not concerned Charles will recant his proposal if he observes you looking like the hired help?'

Celia looked up at her aunt while her hands stayed on task. 'He loves me, Aunty. That wins on all counts.' Celia smiled, knowing her choice of gown would not prompt Charles to modify his opinion of her. She knew she possessed his heart and that it was what lay underneath the gown that mattered to him.

'Oh, my dear.' Lady Montague looked out of the window of the now-moving carriage and waved to an acquaintance. 'He may find you desirable at present but like all men, once he has you on the other side of the chapel door, you will soon realise that counting on love is simply not enough.'

Celia smiled at her aunt. 'I do not believe in such things, Aunty. Here we are. Just set me down here. I will walk.'

Lady Montague pursed her lips in disapproval before saying, 'You will be the death of me.' She banged her hand on the roof of the carriage, effectively instructing the driver to draw to a halt at the base of the asylum's drive.

'Thank you. I shan't be late!' Celia yelled as she ran up the drive toward the gatehouse. Reaching the structure in less than a minute, she addressed the gatekeeper. 'Mr Gibbs, I am here to visit with the women.' The old man grunted as he turned the key in the gate lock.

Hitching her skirt up, Celia ran toward the front door. She did not attempt to look in on Charles but made her way to the laundry immediately, insisting that she knew where it was and that no accompaniment from Matron or an orderly would be necessary.

'But Miss Celia,' Matron countered, 'Doctor Lawler has requested you be accompanied.'

'Oh Matron, I will be fine.' Celia placed her hand on Matron's arm. 'Doctor Lawler is busy and will not check up on me.'

Matron looked at Celia with the same kind of apprehension she had expressed the previous day. 'No, Doctor Lawler has given me orders. Jillian!' she called.

A nurse appeared through one of the office doorways. 'Yes, Matron?' she said.

'Will you accompany Miss Celia to the laundry?'

'Absolutely.' The nurse walked toward Celia and pulled a ring of keys from her apron pocket."

Celia followed her through the door and along the same stench-ridden corridor from the previous day.

'How long have you worked here?' Celia asked.

'A few weeks,' the young woman said.

'Do you like it?'

'Yes, some days.'

Celia looked at Jillian's face. There was something apprehensive about her answer. 'I do hope you have more good days than bad?' she prompted.

'There have not been enough to compare as yet,' Jillian said as she pushed the door open onto the courtyard.

Celia quickened her step as the laundry room loomed. She turned to Jillian. 'Please do not think me impolite but I really do wish to approach the women alone.'

Jillian shook her head. 'Matron said I have to accompany you. I will lose my job if I do not do as I am told.'

'I understand.'

The incessant chatter cut through Celia's conversation with Jillian. She stepped into the laundry room. Once she came into view the talk ceased immediately.

'Hello,' she said quietly as the women looked past her to Jillian, who was standing just beyond her right shoulder.

Again, the acrid smells of ammonia filled her nostrils. She breathed through her mouth, as her lungs felt thick with the steam being produced by the coppers.

'I came to see if the fabric and cottons have been delivered.'

The bold woman from the previous day stepped forward. 'Well, well, well, I dare say it has.' She looked over to the neatly wrapped brown paper packages. 'And now you can be on your way.' She waved a dismissive hand at Celia before turning her back.

'I will not be on my way. I had these things delivered here so I can render some assistance.'

'Please do not talk to Miss Celia with such disrespect,' Jillian snapped.

The bold woman turned toward Jillian before demanding, 'What could she possibly do to help us? Her hands have never seen a hard day's work in their life.'

'I will have you know I am accomplished at needlepoint and all manner of seamstressing detail, and I am not afraid to subject myself to some hard work.' Celia commanded the woman's attention.

The woman stood with each fist firmly placed on her hips. 'Why would ya, if you don't have ta?'

'I have placed myself at your disposal. At least until the new sewing room is rebuilt.'

The woman stared at her and didn't respond. Jillian began to talk but Celia held her hand up, halting her.

Celia said nothing but stared at the bold woman, allowing her to either become accustomed to the proposition or shower more hostility in her direction to push her to leave. She then turned toward Jillian. 'I think my help is unwanted here. I feel I will place myself elsewhere.' She hoped this ploy would show the women that there was now a good chance they would miss out on her assistance, which she could soon enough offer to another group within the asylum. Just as she turned toward the door, a small voice stopped her.

'It is ...'

Celia turned to see the face of an angel before her. Her fine features were that of a scared child, not a woman who had lost her senses.

' ... wanted, I mean,' she finished before shrinking back into the group.

Sensing that this lovely young woman would be her saviour in the current scenario, Celia stepped back into the room. 'Well, I do not see a reason why it would not be.' Celia held her hands out and shrugged. 'I feel I could be more help to you all here than sitting idly by while you patiently await a new sewing room.'

She looked around the space. Her eyes pleaded for somebody else to come forth and support her idea. All eyes were on the bold woman. Everybody was awaiting her response.

Without thinking too long and hard, Celia extended her hand. 'I am Celia Loddon.'

'Soon to be Doctor Lawler's wife,' another woman said before swooning and landing heavily with her elbows on the folding table.

The bold woman looked her up and down once more. 'I s'pose we could do with your help. Name's Agnes.' She took Celia's hand and shook it with intent, and then walked the perimeter of the room introducing each woman. 'This is Daphne, Mary, Susan, Maryann, Sally and this …' she paused for effect as she put her hand on the shoulder of the woman still tinged with remnants of blue dye, 'is Lillian.'

Celia offered her hand to Lillian, who grabbed hold of her fingers and dropped to her knees as though she were greeting Queen Victoria.

'That is not necessary, Lillian.' Celia bent forward and placed her free hand on the woman's shoulder. 'Please, hop up off the floor,' she implored, as the woman stood and began to laugh. Celia looked at Jillian with pleading eyes. She did not want this sort of treatment from the women.

Celia pulled her gloves from her fingers and walked to the stack of packages.

'Would somebody assist me with the bolt of calico?'

Jillian was beside her with every step. Celia looked at her. 'As you can see I am fine. You can leave me now.'

Jillian stood in silence, feeling the weight of the decision.

'I really would like to earn their trust.'

'I will do a quick round of the hospital cottage and return after that.'

Celia placed her hand on Jillian's. 'Thank you.'

The young woman with the angelic face walked over to her once Jillian had left. 'I will help.' They gathered an end each and walked to one of the folding tables.

Two women repositioned a pile of sheets to accommodate the calico.

'Thank you,' Celia said, as the rest of the women resumed their work of folding sheets, filling coppers and wringing sheets through the rollers.

Celia slid the string from the end of the bolt and pulled an edge of the paper away. 'Can you help me unroll it?' she said to the young woman. 'Your name is Maryann. Is that correct?'

'Yes,' the tinge of a smile played on Maryann's lips.

Lillian held up a sheet and pulled it over her head, creating a hood. She whirled past them, laughing loudly.

Maryann laughed for a second then looked at the woman with pity. 'Poor dear, she has been here so long.'

'How long?' Celia whispered.

'Longer than anyone else in here I believe. I think she was one of the first to arrive when the doors opened just over thirty years ago.'

'Is everyone here … ah … I don't quite know how to say it.' Celia looked abashed.

Maryann looked at her expectantly.

'What I think I am trying to state is that the women in here seem so normal.' Celia looked around the room, then back at Maryann. 'I fail to see why you are in here,' she exclaimed.

Maryann's eyes widened. 'Do not let the name of this institution fool you.' Her voice dropped to a whisper. 'There are those in here who need to be, but this place also serves as a drop-off point for the convenience of disgraced families and atrocious husbands. If you must know, Agnes' husband had her taken from their bed in the middle of the night and dropped here under a shroud of darkness.'

Celia drew in a sharp breath. 'You must be mistaken. That would not be allowed.'

Maryann nodded decidedly. 'It is. He hasn't been near the place in twelve months and news came that he had remarried.

Agnes was so angry she lashed out at one of the orderlies and ended up in a confinement cell for an entire month.'

Celia swallowed as she refocussed her attention to smoothing the calico across the folding bench. She felt ill. 'What is a confinement cell?'

Agnes was standing behind her. At the sound of her voice Celia jumped in fright.

'It is a room about the size of this folding bench with no daylight. If you want to send the sane over the edge that's where you put 'em.'

Celia looked at Agnes in shock. She was confused at just what the woman was saying.

'It would seem you had no idea what truly happens in here. Not many do unless they are like us,' Maryann's voice trailed away.

Celia felt her surprise was actually more triggered by Charles' lack of empathy for the women housed in here and the circumstances they were in. He had told her his concern related to the unruly behaviours of these women. Instead, he should have placed his apprehension in the behaviours of the terrible husbands that had those women dumped here in the manner of last night's potato scraps. Instead of fearing that these women would hurt her due to their insanity, he should perhaps be considerably more worried that the harshness of their stories would prompt her to help them in ways that exceeded the ladylike requirements of needlepoint.

'You look pale. Are you feeling unwell?' Maryann's face swam before Celia.

Celia leant against the folding table. 'I am quite well. I think I need some air.'

Maryann grasped her elbow and led her from the laundry room. They sat on a small bench against the outside wall. Within seconds Celia began to feel fresh air wash over her and revitalise her senses. Maryann sat quietly by her side. Celia stared across the courtyard and watched some of the inmates strolling arm-in-arm or sitting on benches beneath the verandas.

'I was cast from my parents' home,' Maryann announced.

Celia turned sharply to Maryann. 'What on earth happened?'

'They said I was promiscuous when I ended up with child.' She looked away from Celia and stared across the courtyard.

Celia's cheeks burned as she realised her immediate reaction had been to place judgement on this sweet young woman. 'Oh,' was all she could utter. She tried to keep her expression passive.

Maryann continued, 'My beau Lee and I were going to run away but instead we were discovered and my parents forced me here, under the pretence that once I had had my child, they would fetch me back. Alas, they did not and now it would seem I am to live all my days here.'

Celia's judgement shifted from this poor young thing to her shameful parents. 'Your family? How could they cast you aside like that?'

Maryann looked forlorn. 'I don't blame my mother and father. They did not know what to do with me after the truth was revealed — and by the truth, I mean my growing waistline. They were right in sending me here. I had caused them shame and they were correct in their assumptions. I have not seen my beloved since he ran from our town in the dark of night. He has neither tried to see me nor to rescue me from here. He said he loved me and truly wanted to be with me forever. I do believe my father has driven him from the district.' Maryann paused, biting her bottom lip. 'It's also likely my father wanted Lee gone because he is of Chinese heritage. I fear there has been foul play on my father's part. Lee would have rescued me from here if he knew my whereabouts.'

'Where would he go?' Celia said with haste.

'I have no idea, nobody does. I have been here almost a year now. I am nearly eighteen. A perfect age to be somebody's wife.'

Celia could not believe what she was hearing. It made her heart beat fast to realise that families would turn their backs on any loved one locked in here.

'Where is your baby?'

Tears formed in Maryann's eyes. 'I do not know. I birthed him in the surgical ward. I did not even see him when he was born.' She sobbed.

Celia decided to halt the conversation. She did not want poor Maryann so upset. She could never imagine her father doing such a thing to her. Worse still, she was soon to be a wife. She shuddered to know that Charles could have her committed if he decided on it and she would have no say in the matter. She looked at Maryann with sadness. How could she judge this girl with such harshness? She knew what it was like to love and had already transgressed further beyond the accepted boundaries of propriety. She knew from her few interludes with Charles how things could escalate if not reined in before the point of no return.

After listening to Maryann's story, Celia spent the

remainder of the afternoon in the company of the women in the laundry room. Each time the bell in the tower tolled, she jumped with fright. The belltower was in such close proximity to the laundry room it vibrated through her to the core. 'Why does it toll so often?' she asked Maryann as she tightened the calico fabric across a tapestry frame.

'It tolls on the hour so the inmates who do not possess their faculties can have some semblance of time. At breakfast, lunch and supper it tolls for a longer period.'

'Miss Celia?'

Celia turned to the open door to see Jillian addressing her. The young nurse looked ragged.

'I am so sorry I did not return sooner. The hospital cottage was understaffed. I could not get away.'

'That is fine. I have had a lovely time with Maryann,' Celia answered.

'It is time for me to escort you back. The laundry room will shut down for the day and the women need to head into their wards for supper.'

Celia looked at the nurse with shock. 'What is the time?'

'The hour is a little after five 'o' clock.'

Celia jumped from her chair. 'Goodness, the time has rushed away from me,' she said as she began to gather the needlepoint thread and pile it in one place.

'Maryann, can you please stack the frames and place them in the corner? I will be back tomorrow to continue our work.'

'Goodnight, Miss Celia!' the women chimed as Celia departed the laundry room.

As she neared the door to enter the ward, Agnes called to her, 'Miss Celia, are you seeing your doctor this evenin'?'

Celia turned back and nodded her head. 'Yes, I think I just may, Agnes.'

'Good hands, that man,' Agnes yelled as laughter erupted from inside the laundry room.

Jillian cleared her throat. Celia frowned. 'What on earth?' she said as she stepped through the doorway and into the dusk.

'They can be quite tawdry,' Jillian said as they walked toward the door to the main building. 'You would be forgiven for not coming back tomorrow.'

'Oh, they are not so bad that I cannot bear them,' Celia said. 'I was surprised that the time had grown wings. They are quite satisfactory company.'

'Today their company was acceptable but it can depend on the day and the hour of the day.'

'What do you mean?' Celia was puzzled.

'Some days all is calm but on others it is like the devil walks among them. A full moon turns everything around and not for the better I may add.'

Celia looked right and left at each open door as they walked the length of the hallway. There were noises and mewing surrounding her.

'Even the hour sees a difference in their behaviour,' Jillian continued. 'This time of the afternoon is tricky. It seems to be the setting sun that riles them.'

'Is that so?' Celia was surprised. There was so much information the medical establishment knew that obviously allowed them to administer treatments to patients in the asylum. She wanted to know more — especially in relation to Agnes' parting comment, which seemed to somehow connect her future husband's hands with a treatment she knew nothing about.

'I do wonder what Agnes meant by her comment.' Celia said more to herself as a statement than a question.

The nurse offered a polite but abrupt reply. 'There are treatments that should not be discussed with ladies of your standing.'

Celia did not want to be looked upon as being superior to anybody in the asylum. While she longed to prompt Jillian for a detailed explanation of the mystery treatment, she did not want to press upon the nurse to satisfy her curiosity. Jillian was looking rather terse at present.

Celia straightened as she neared the front door. 'Never mind, then. I am sure it does not concern me. Goodnight then. Are you here tomorrow?'

'Yes, I am. Goodnight, Miss Celia. I will accompany you again.'

Celia walked to the gatehouse and waited for Mr Gibbs to unlock the gate before walking quickly back to her aunt's home. She should have looked in on Charles on the way but with the late hour and Jillian's haste to show her out, she had simply quite forgotten.

Lady Montague was not impressed at the time upon which Celia walked through her front door.

'Where on earth have you been?'

'I quite lost track of the clock, if I am honest.'

'That place has taken up your entire day. Your time would be best served doing other things.'

'It was a good day, Aunty. I feel quite pleased with my achievement.'

'Dinner will be ready any moment and you will not sit at the table in that dress. Your hair needs a brush pulled through it, and it would not hurt to fasten it into a bun whilst you work there. You will contract nits from those filthy imbeciles.'

Celia rolled her eyes heavenward as she walked upstairs. She threw her dress across her bed and prepared to change into something appropriate for dinner. She washed her face and hands and began to section her hair to create a plait. As her fingers worked to wind the lengths of hair in and around each other, she wondered about the comment Agnes had made. She would find out the very next day just what the woman had meant. She was determined.

At dinner her aunt had discussed the luncheon she had attended that day. 'Mrs Rushby is so impressed at your diligence in getting to the asylum so quickly with supplies. It was all she could talk about over our pea and ham soup.'

'It is no trouble at all. Really, Aunty. I had a most adequate day with the ladies.'

'That is hardly a word you can use with conviction, my dear girl.'

'They are very efficient in needlepoint. They work very hard at what they undertake. I think I will return tomorrow and continue it with them.'

Celia did not mention names or discuss any particular individual with her aunt. She really did feel it was her secret to keep and their identities were not hers to share. If Lady Montague had any inkling of the situation Celia had been part of that day, she would be sure to intervene and have her visits halted.

In fact, Celia feared Charles would do much the same

before the week was up. If he knew of the comment Agnes had made or became aware of the stories the women had shared with her today, he would ban her visits and there would be nothing more she could do. Tomorrow she would seek Jillian out and make her aware she did not want Charles privy to the comment Agnes had made. Charles did not call on her after dinner as she had hoped but as she readied herself for bed her mind was held steadfast on the women and their hopeless circumstance.

Tomorrow she would ask Agnes about the comment. Maybe these women could teach her as much as she was teaching them. Of that she was sure. She was also sure her life would turn out to be vastly different to the lives of those who had found themselves on the wrong side of the ha-ha wall.

How fortunate she was. She had a father who cared for and cherished her and her sister, and now she had the privilege to be marrying a man who would love her forever.

Chapter 17

'Celia!'

She heard her name yelled across the street. Although she did not recognise the voice, she dared not turn to see who it was.

She groaned inwardly. Should she enter in conversation with anyone she knew at the present moment and they were to make mention of the funeral or her husband's predicament at the asylum she feared her features would be unable to conceal the truth.

Maintaining focus on the direction ahead, she hoped she could disappear down a side road or laneway. There was thirty-feet of distance until the next corner presented itself. It would be best if she were to blend with the shoppers milling about.

'Celia! Mrs Lawler!' the voice became louder.

'Darn it,' Celia whispered beneath her breath as she turned.

'Well, strike me down,' the caller exclaimed as she raced directly across the street to get to Celia, nearly colliding with a carriage in the process.

'Look out,' the carriage driver roared.

Ignoring him, the caller scurried the entire length of the

footpath, gasping for breath as she drew nearer. 'I didn't think you would ever hear me, pet.'

'Agnes! It is you?' Celia felt guilt at having ignored, albeit unintentionally, one of the most cherished people she had ever met.

She clutched Agnes to her and held her for the longest time. Feeling tears spring to her eyes, she realised this much needed contact with another living soul was soothing her heart.

'Are you right there, pet?' Agnes spoke in her ear as she felt Celia tighten her embrace.

'I am just fine,' exclaimed Celia as she finally found the strength to release her friend.

'Don't look fine to me.' Agnes held her at arm's length and looked at her face.

'What has happened, pet?'

'Not a thing,' Celia whispered. 'Oh, everything,' she stamped out when Agnes did not look appeased, before adding, 'I do not wish to discuss me. How have you been?'

'God bless my sister, is all I can say.' Agnes clutched Celia's arm and placed it over her own. They began to walk slowly along the footpath.

'I am sorry I have not called on you since your release.'

Agnes flung her hand outwards. 'Oh don't be silly, pet. You have much better things to do than to bother visitin' me. Here's something. Let's get a cup of tea.'

Agnes quickened her step as Miss Mable's Tearoom came into view.

Celia allowed herself to be led. It was so enlightening to have somebody take charge over her, if only for a few minutes.

The morning tea hour had just begun and Miss Mable's Tearoom was bustling.

'Mrs Lawler?' Celia heard a few greetings directed towards her by patrons already seated. She greeted those that she knew, all the while moving behind Agnes. She did not linger or begin a discussion with anybody in the tearoom.

'There is a table free right over 'ere,' Agnes announced.

Celia felt grateful as she fell onto the chair.

'Oh pet, there is not much of you, is there?' Agnes leaned across and squeezed Celia's hand.

'I have lost any appreciation for food at present. It is far too long a story to reveal,' Celia stated quietly.

Agnes kept her hand firmly fastened over Celia's.

'I know what happened up there.'

Celia gasped. 'You do?'

'Of course I do. I may have escaped that horrible place but I still know what happens up there.' It was pointed that Agnes dare not call the asylum by its name.

'How? How did you hear?' Celia wondered how much Agnes had heard. She had to be careful not to reveal too much with regard to Audrey's plight.

'Well, I will not set foot in that place ever again, you know that,' Agnes stated with a slight shudder of her shoulders. 'But I still hear everythin'. It all streams down like sludge after heavy rain.'

'And I cannot blame you for being unable to turn your ear from its harshness,' Celia smiled. 'I am just so sad that I am unable to visit any longer.'

'Why do you choose to go up there?'

'I believe I can do some good. After all, if I had not gone up there in the first place, I would never have met you.' Celia smiled at Agnes.

'I remember that first day when you looked almost ready to wring our necks.' Agnes laughed heartily amid stares from the patrons seated around them. God bless Lillian. She gave us such fun, didn't she?'

'Yes, yes she did.' Celia looked around furtively. 'Remember the colour of her?'

They both laughed.

'God rest her soul,' Celia whispered.

'The least we can be thankful for is that she is in a better place now. Much like that Sally Smith.'

Celia whispered, 'Please do not mention these matters so loudly. Charles is so livid with what has gone on. If he knew gossip was sifting down from the asylum to fall among the townsfolk he would be angered further.'

'Oh, it's more than sifted. It's spread like flour on a baker's bench.'

Celia tried to deflect the topic. 'I am surprised it has held interest with the Price tragedy following so closely.'

Agnes pursed her lips and harrumphed. 'There is interest. You know what this town is like.' Agnes looked assured of her statement.

Celia was caught between sorrow and elation. To know the people of Ararat were making it their sport to whisper such atrocities, with seeming enjoyment. She could only hope the audience included Constable Bryant. Surely, he would have to investigate an incident that would seem to hold some truth, would he not?

Celia sipped her tea. 'I really miss you, Agnes. We had some lovely times.'

Agnes smiled across at Celia. 'I will never forget those

afternoons spent in that laundry with you. You really are a good sport, you are.'

'I had my moments where I wanted to turn tail and run.'

'Thank goodness you didn't. Things got so much better after you arrived. You taught us so much.'

'You taught me, too. Helping with your difficulties and the plights of the other women became my life's ambition, and now everything is in tatters.'

'You do realise your husband needed you more than we did. It was selfish of us to have taken so much of you away from him. He is a good man, your husband.'

Celia began to feel tears fill her eyes. 'It is very gracious of you to say so, Agnes, but I hardly think you took too much of my time.'

'Don't forget Doctor Lawler was paid to put up with us and our ailments. You did it for the sheer joy. It was entirely different for you both.'

'I did not agree with the treatment of the inmates, which is why I had to stand against him. I know it is shameful for a wife to defy her husband. In fact, I do not know what came over me at times. It was the liberties he allowed me that gave me confidence in my endeavour.'

Celia was speaking of things no woman should share with another, but with Agnes in the laundry room, she had gone past counting the many times she had crossed the barrier of subjects considered suitable for discussion among women.

'Some treatments weren't all bad,' Agnes whispered. 'Nice hands, remember?' She began to chuckle while the women at the other tables took turns of shrewdly looking at them with unimpressed expressions.

Celia was in no doubt the talk behind their gloved hands was connected to her and the inappropriate company she was in. A lady of her social standing — a doctor's wife, no less! — should not be seen sharing tea with a lower-class woman. It was like having morning tea with your kitchen hand or the maid; it was most inappropriate.

Celia was beyond caring about the judgement of others. After all, she found it refreshing to speak unhindered to Agnes. This discussion would never take place between herself and any other woman in the tearoom at present. It just would not be acceptable. On the contrary, her conversation with any number of women in the room would normally be polite and pointless. At present their talk would border on trying to obtain information with regard to the gossip around the plight of the Prices as well as Charles' predicament at the asylum. She did not care for that type of company at present. Pointless and shallow people who judged and did not understand the pain of others. Those who attended church and teased women like Agnes. She was fast learning that her sensibilities and patience could not endure people who could not possess compassion.

Celia took a deep breath and for the first time this week she felt some lightness flow within. 'Agnes, I am so glad you called out to me in the street.'

'I was glad to see you, pet. When you turned around you had that worried look I used to see in the early days.'

'What look is that?' Celia asked as she took a sip of tea.

'When we first got ta know ya. 'member when I asked ya about your good doctor 'fore you was married? Remember the good hands comment?'

Agnes had a habit of repeating herself. Celia worried it would eventually see her back in the asylum. Celia looked at Agnes and feigned a laugh she hoped would seem sincere. But as the forced smile dropped from her features, Celia felt her chest rise as she filled her lungs with air. She closed her eyes and let out a slow breath. 'We have fallen a long way past the people we once were, Agnes.'

Celia had been waiting in his office for some time. As the minutes ticked by she became more and more nervous. Eventually, she heard his footfalls on the timber and began counting them … 'One, two, three … ' She pulled air into her lungs as the door whooshed open and he looked surprised for a second.

'Hello darling, I was not expecting you.'

She stood and smoothed her skirt. 'I know you are not expecting me but there is something I need to discuss.'

He looked at her with suspicion. 'This sounds like trouble.'

'Well, it could be but it all depends on how you see it, I suppose.' She stood and walked towards him. Standing closer to him than she normally would, she stared up into his face.

'The women in the laundry alerted me to something.'

'Here we go.' He stepped away from her and walked to his desk. 'What stories now from that crazed lot?'

'Oh, this is no tall tale. It is a true story and I wish to know more.'

'Well, I may not be of much use if it is some lunatic tale or gossip for that matter.' He was rifling through his notes on his desk and she could feel she was fast losing his focus.

Coming around to his desk, she sidled her backside on one

edge and crossed her legs so her ankles were well exposed to his gaze.

His eyes fell away from the desktop to her feet.

'The women seem to delight in their knowledge of something you call pelvic massage.'

He cleared his throat. 'Yes. It is a clinical term to treat a condition of sorts.'

She began moving her legs in a rhythmic motion back and forth as Charles stared at them, hypnotised. She had learnt so much in such a short time that her boldness frightened her.

'It may be a clinical term for you but I have been doing some reading on it and it seems it is fast becoming something more of a ...' she slowed her words as though deep in thought, '... sensual exercise.'

'Ladies of your standing should not be privy to such scribbling. Ah, the magazine. I should have been wise to your newfound education. Couple that with the words of the loose-tongued lower echelons of the inmates and ...'

If there was one thing Celia had learnt about Charles in their short courtship was that he was a virile male who could immediately indulge in the lure of a woman's assets. She was not worried that he would stray once they were married. After all, she would keep him interested with all sorts of new and amazing experiences. With thanks she praised one Audrey Price, now Mrs McGowan, on her unearthing of all things wicked.

Celia pulled her arms closer together to push her breasts out and leaned forward until her fiancé's ear was level with her lips. She whispered, 'It doesn't matter where I read or heard it, does it? It is the practice I want to experience.'

Charles' gaze was firmly locked on her breasts. 'Really, my dear,' he said lazily. 'You wish to be treated for hysteria?'

Celia began to feel her nerve waver. Within moments, he had successfully turned the power to his advantage, making her the prey, rather than the hunter.

'Gone quiet, have we?' he smiled, convinced he had won the battle.

But Celia shimmied her backside along his desk until she was positioned between his legs. 'Do your best doctor.'

He stared down and his gaze traced her face before he swiftly placed his hands beneath her backside and scooped her up with her legs partially wrapped around his waist. He walked across his office to the treatment bed. Her heart was racing as vulnerability overcame her. He was staring down at her with a particular look in his eye, one to which she had become accustomed.

'Relax, my darling, this will not hurt a bit.'

Celia placed her forearm over her eyes to hide her embarrassment before he quickly removed her arm and kissed her boldly. Minutes ticked away as he sensually made love to her mouth with his. Her lips would be swollen and red for the next week at this rate but she did not care.

Next, she could feel cool air moving from her ankles, up her calves and over her knees — until finally her thighs were exposed as he slowly tugged her skirt upward from her waistband. Her petticoats followed and were up to her waist as she began to writhe with want for his touch. Slowly, all the while kissing her fiercely, and with her holding onto his neck and then running her hands in his hair, his breath became deeper and more drawn. Inside her mind she had just begun begging him to touch her when she felt his finger on the soft folds between her legs.

She sighed as the feeling of him circling the area with his fingers and softly pinching the area washed over her. Her body immediately began to rise and fall against his hands as he pulled his face away from her to watch her tip over the edge of sensuality. He could not help but place his finger inside the tight sheath of her womanhood and feel warmth and surrender as he drew it out before sliding it back inside without surrendering any motion.

All the while he watched her, feeling no guilt at taking such liberties with this woman. True, she was not his wife, yet she belonged to him. While she could not be further from the need of this treatment he could not have stopped if he wanted to. Once married, he had no doubt she would unveil to him all her capabilities. She possessed such drive and ferocity that he could not wait to bear witness to all that she would reveal to him inside and out of their marital bed, God help him.

Her breath was leaving and returning to her body in deep smooth blasts. Charles was silently chanting for her to give herself over. He knew the precise moment when the sound that escaped her became an elongated long, low moan. Celia looked up at him as the feeling washed through her and once it subsided she felt more relaxed and absolved than ever before.

'How was that, my dear?' he asked as he ran the back of his hand down the side of her cheek.

'It was delicious.'

'We cannot keep this up.'

'It will not be long until we are married.' She smiled up at him.

He kissed her lovingly as he pulled her skirts down and smoothed them for her.

'You must go now,' he said as he gripped her hands and pulled her up to a sitting position.

'Why?' Celia said. 'I had hoped you would wish me to stay?'

'Oh I do, which is why you must leave. A repeat performance of that will ensue if you remain here with me. And there is only so much willpower I possess.'

'Well, in only two more weeks you can toss that will to the wind.'

'I cannot wait, my love. Once I complete my rounds this afternoon I will come to the house for dinner.'

Celia picked up her coat and bag while Charles held the door open for her.

Almost over the threshold, she stopped and turned. 'The women in the laundry were correct.'

'About?'

'You have good hands.' He could hear her giggling as she made her way to the top of the staircase.

It did get him thinking. If a man could keep his wife clearly satisfied in the bedroom while providing monetary support for their household, surely there would be far fewer cases of hysteria and the plethora of ailments that accompanied it, not to mention far fewer women being brought to the asylum door.

Chapter 14

Charles welcomed the diversion the next two days would bring. He was going to escape this abysmal place, if only momentarily. His much loved life as superintendent and husband were not fulfilling at the moment. Instead, he felt he was suffocating beneath the whole sordid mess of Audrey's murder and being chained to the asylum because of it. Celia's insubordinate behaviour had only added to his discomfort. Having attended the mock funeral had almost unravelled him fully. The secrets he was forced to keep were making his conscience reel.

He hoped to spend the following days in Ballarat meeting with a colleague to discuss outdated treatments. He had read the latest medical journals and was hoping to introduce some of the latest treatments being used in the Americas. He could use a fresh outlook at present and the inmates could do with some much needed pain and behaviour management. His colleague was still working in Ballarat but was not so busy now the goldfields had managed to empty out along with the diggers and miners.

The time away would rejuvenate his sense of order and

clear his thoughts. With this in mind, he walked quickly toward the back of the asylum following the path beside the vegetable garden. All the inmates had completed their work for the day and were now indoors eating supper. He needed to make haste, pack a bag and leave the house before Celia had a moment to waylay him.

Charles had been punishing his wife, arriving home at the latest hour and leaving before dawn, just so she could feel the full force of his anger. He had not placed the factor of time on the sizable lesson he was teaching her. While a few weeks had passed since the incident with Audrey, he was not quite ready to have any conversation with Celia. Instead, he felt sure that ignoring her and leaving her alone would allow him to regain control and assert his authority as a husband. Celia had pushed his patience and he was well past talking sense to her and sick to the death of yelling at her. This was the only strategy he could think of to relegate this nonsense into the past.

After opening the front gate to the house, Charles strode up the path and stopped abruptly. He could see Celia's profile through the window into the sitting room. She was so beautiful. Seconds ticked away as he watched her. Catching himself being caught in her spell, he pulled his shoulders back and spoke to himself, 'Charles, do not give in.' Taking a deep breath, he set his mouth in a grim line and pushed open the front door. Without looking into the sitting room, he walked straight past the open door and into his bedroom.

He pulled his Gladstone bag from the wardrobe and threw it onto the bed. Before he could place the pair of socks he was holding inside it, Celia was in the open doorway. 'Are you moving out of our home?' She sounded panicked.

'No,' he answered without looking away from the open bag.

'Then what are you doing?'

'I have a meeting.'

'A meeting? Where?'

Charles whisked past her with his bag in hand and did not look at her. He pulled his hat from the stand beside the door. As he placed it on his head he looked at her and gave a slight shake of his head. He wanted to illustrate that nothing was forgiven and he was going to remain angry for some time. 'Goodbye, Celia,' he said with determination.

'Charles! Charles!' she yelled after him.

Turning his back to her, knowing she was close to tears, it pained him to see her so upset but she had brought this anger on. She deserved his wrath and in time it would work out harmoniously for each of them. He had been shocked when he turned to look at her and had to school his reaction. She was looking rather frail. At the soonest, when he had forgiven her, the situation would be rectified and he would make sure she was properly looked after.

This thought made his mind swing back to the asylum. He should revisit the hospital cottage to check on two inmates who were of upmost concern. Two women had been admitted in these past days with numerous injuries. He found the situation quite foreboding. They had been clobbered severely, but most perplexing was that both had been found in their locked cells. The nurse on duty had not heard a disturbance through the night.

The type of injuries inflicted on the women coupled with evidence of a tell-tale substance that looked much like dried semen left him in no doubt that an inmate or orderly had gained access to the women's ward. Charles did not sense a connection between the Audrey McGowan murder and these incidents. Rather, he recalled similar scenarios that he had attended when he had first begun his work at the asylum.

So many catastrophes had been occurring in recent days that Charles had no idea which way to jump. His decision to call on the constable had been halted by the Colonel. Furthermore, when he had mentioned to Doctor Rushby that he intended to call the constable to investigate the assaults on the two women, Doctor Rushby had warned him not to, as the constable, being aware of the recent murder of an inmate, would be forced to investigate the Sally Smith case also. Should he get a sniff that something was untoward it would bring down all sorts of difficulty for them.

The talk in town with regard to the funeral had not cancelled the gossip over the death of Sally Smith but he had made a point of seeing Constable Bryant and relaying to him that there was an investigation at the asylum being conducted by the commissioner. Charles could not believe his own ears when the words spilled from his mouth. 'Doctor Rushby has ensured the governing authority has all the appropriate assistance whilst the commissioner conducts an investigation for us up on the hill.'

Constable Bryant had offered his assistance should it be required. That was enough to put at ease any talk of police interference at the asylum whilst he figured out a way to solve all the problems. Should anybody turn over the entire truth of Sally Smith's identity it would be sure to cast all their lives into chaos.

Charles pulled his watch from his waistcoat. 'Damn!' he said out loud as he quickened his pace. The hour was getting late and the train to Ballarat scheduled to depart at 11.05 would pull out of the station without him if he did not hurry. He did not have time to head back to the asylum.

The train was at the station by the time he arrived. Boarding a carriage, he placed his bag in an overhead rack and flipped open the newspaper he had bought from a paperboy.

As the train pulled away from the station he looked out into the darkness and saw his reflection in the window. He looked haggard and in need of a visit to a barber. In the morning after a much-needed slumber, that would be his first call. Even the tiny creases around his eyes revealed very few hours of sleep.

Charles rested his head back on the seat and closed his eyes. As the train slowly rolled out of the station and began to gather speed, he looked sidewards out of the window. To his shock, there was Celia, looking quite breathless as she walked beside the carriage, trying to keep pace with it to no avail. He knew she was yelling his name but the sound was mute above the train's whistle as it blew sharp and long into the night. This alone made him feel the tiniest bit of relief. She had finally relented, yielded at his treatment of her. Upon his return from Ballarat he would sit down with her and finally lay claim to an obedient wife. One of his many problems had been solved. He let out a low breath and felt the tension ebb from him.

Celia stayed on the platform and stared at the tracks long after the train had disappeared from view, admonishing herself over her decision to chase Charles to the station. Only ten minutes earlier, she had found herself running along the gravel road to the station. She had been able to see the train beginning to huff steam as it prepared to leave. Desperate to talk with Charles, she had resolved to board it. She felt compelled to keep him close, so he could not escape her.

Stopping at the ticket office window, she had found it empty. Quickly continuing out to the platform, she had felt immediate disappointment as the train slowly rolled forward. The conductor was already holding the flag aloft at the end of the platform. Hurrying along the platform looking in each of the windows as the train gathered speed, she had caught sight of Charles' profile. She had yelled his name but his eyes had remained closed. 'Charles! Charles!' she had yelled for the second time that evening without receiving a response.

Her husband had looked sideways out of the window and looked startled as the train rolled away from the end of the platform. Able to go no further, she had watched the train disappear around the bend. The last time she had chased Charles to the station had been under similar circumstances. On that occasion, just like this one, she had upset him immensely. Was she destined to defy her husband over and over? It would seem the answer was always the same. Things had been so much simpler before they had married. Perhaps, she wondered cynically, had he been easier to manipulate back then?

From across the dinner table, Charles was enlightening Celia with his travel plans for the following day. Lady Montague had extended an invitation to Charles to join them for supper. He placed his fork down before taking a drink from his wine glass and commanding the ear of his attentive fiancé. 'So, you see, it was decided that travelling to the halfway point of Ballarat would be the most convenient and time-efficient way to meet with the superintendent from Yarra Bend.'

She stared at him wide eyed as he discussed the ideas he would put forth with regard to his new tenure as superintendent of Flint Hill. 'Charles?'

'Yes, my darling?'

'I received word from my father today, and I would so dearly love to discuss some of his wishes with you.'

'Well, that would be splendid. Would you excuse us, Lady Montague?' Charles placed his napkin beside his plate and pushed his chair from the table.

'Why, not at all,' Lady Montague said.

'Dinner was lovely, Aunty.' Celia patted the sides of her lips as her gaze wandered back to Charles. She smiled at him as he in turn stared intently at her.

He pulled her chair gently back from the table, positioned her arm over the crook of his elbow and escorted her to the sitting room. It was dark without the candles alight or a fire to cast a glow into the room. The darkness enveloped Celia as she made herself comfortable on the window seat. She could feel the cold air slicing through the gap in the window at her back. 'Do you recall our first memory of this very place?' she said.

'Why, yes I do. You held me in the very palm of your hand, my lovely.' Charles leaned in and nuzzled her neck.

'Oh Charles, please stop. I cannot think with any clarity when you do such things.' She pushed him away playfully.

'I could not be swayed from your scent and absolute beauty,

my lovely. But if I must be swayed now, I will gaze upon the letter from your father to keep my hands busy.'

'About that.' Celia bit her lip. 'I may have stretched the truth somewhat to get you alone.'

'You cheeky little minx.'

Charles grasped her and pulled her onto his lap and began to kiss her neck.

Celia was fast losing her resolve as he took full advantage of the time he had with her alone in his grasp. It did give her the upper hand for her delivery. 'However, there is something I do need to discuss with you.'

'Yes?' he whispered as he kissed the skin behind her earlobe. Celia was pressing further into him with her eyes closed. The allure of what he was capable of doing to her was becoming too great for her to resist.

She could barely string a sentence together and what should have been an easy delivery of syllables sounded like gasps of random words. As his mouth continued its passage to the top line of her bodice and his tongue softly traced the contour of her breasts, she feared she would not get the words out at all.

'I have ... been ... visiting ... the ... asylum ... on a few ... occasions ... as you know.'

'Yes.'

'And I am ... all too aware ... that once ... we marry ... the appropriateness ... of this ... will diminish.'

'Yes.'

'I really ... feel ... that it is unfair ... that I ... oh, Charles!'

She grasped his head in her hands and pulled his face level with her own, staring at him momentarily before plunging her mouth directly onto his with such force that they clung in a wrestle of lust. Her hands ran through his hair and down his shoulders as she held him fast to her while his hands quickly found their way to her breasts. He gently kneaded them through the fabric of her gown and then lightly rubbed her hardened nipples as they conferred how dearly she wanted him in every way.

It was alarming to her that she could give herself over to him so freely considering they were not married. Only weeks ago she would never have dared dream of such behaviour and now she wondered how anyone, once she had found love, had denied herself of this. As though reading her thoughts, Charles, gripped her shoulders and held her away from him. 'We have to stop this before it travels out of our control.'

Her face was flushed and she wavered in his grasp as though she had just been woken from a daze.

'I love you so much,' she whispered.

'And I you. Can we move the date forward?'

She wrapped her arms around him and held him to her tightly. 'I would love nothing more, except you.'

He laughed. 'So tell me, what is it you wanted to discuss that I waylaid you from?'

'At what point of my tenure did you stop listening?'

'I do not think I heard any of it. Between what sounded like lost syllables, I cannot say I was in any way making sense of our discussion.

Extracting herself from his lap proved more difficult than she had anticipated, and Celia felt the cool air surround her once again as she stared out the window.

'I have become rather fond of my visits to you at work.'

'I know. It seems to bring out a certain seductiveness in you. I welcome many more visits once we are married.'

Celia looked at him and smiled. 'I have every intention of keeping you very busy, Doctor Lawler. And there is one ulterior motive I would like to confess.'

'And what is that?'

'After we marry, I would seek your approval to continue visiting with the women. I could be of such help to you, with your work.'

'Absolutely out of the question.'

'Please Charles, I beg of you. I do not think I can endure the dull expectations of a wife and sit demurely awaiting your arrival home from work each evening.'

'Is that how you feel about marriage and its expectations?' He stared coolly at her.

'It is not that I am not ecstatically happy at the thought of being called your wife, but I feel I have stumbled across something far more important … '

'Really? Is that the truth? Beware, my darling. You are about to stumble headlong into a scenario from which you may not be able to retreat.'

'Please, Charles. I was not about to say marriage was unimportant. I love you more than words can express. That will never change. But I feel so alive and useful when I am in the asylum. As though I can make a difference.'

He stared down at her, disdain lacing his features. Her lungs constricted.

'It unnerves me to hear you speak of making a difference. I could open the world to you once you are called my wife. It is I making a difference to everything you stand for and you have the audacity to feel that you would be put to better use as an advocate for fallen women. Do not forget, my dear, that I am the open door to the asylum you seek. I am the reason you have continued your work behind the façade. You need to make a choice on where your loyalties lie.'

Charles stalked to the door, flung it open and before stepping through turned back to her. 'We will call a halt to the wedding until you have made your decision. In either case, you will not see the inside of the asylum. I am the gatekeeper and I hold the key.' The door closed behind him and Celia was left staring into empty space, with her heart pounding, her mouth dry and the pit of her stomach in the soles of her shoes.

'Why did Charles leave so abruptly?' her aunt had asked when she entered the parlour.

'He decided to gather some paperwork before his trip to Ballarat in the morning.' Celia tried to keep her voice even.

'Very well, then,' her aunt said as she held out some needlepoint work to Celia.

'I am really rather tired, Aunty. I think I will retire.'

'Have a pleasant night's sleep then, my dear.'

Celia could not sleep. Throwing the covers off, she sat up in bed and put her hands over her face. She needed to make amends with Charles, and if this meant her work at the asylum would grind to a halt, so be it. More than anything she wanted to be his wife. As she made her choice, guilt washed over her for the women she had befriended. She had made promises to them that she would now have to break, but there was no moving past the fact that at present Charles was more important to her than anyone else.

The following day, in the clear light of morning, Celia

decided she could not bear to wait the whole day to see him. She had to speak to him and apologise for her abhorrent behaviour. What was she to do? It would be another day still until he would find the time to allow her to speak to him.

She hatched a plan. Dressing in one of her finest frocks, she bundled her shawl in her arms and walked casually into the dining room, where Lady Montague was sitting at the table digesting her breakfast and ordering more tea.

'Did you hear the bell, Aunty?' Celia asked.

'Why, I did not. Who was it?'

'Audrey has sent a note, inviting me to her home today. I have it here.' Celia unfolded the note and handed it to her aunt.

In quite different handwriting to her own, Celia had penned a few simple words, creating a casual invitation for her to join Audrey for lunch at her home. The premise being that she arrive that very morning so the young friends could spend the entire day together. The final line stated that the carriage would arrive to collect her by the eight am.

Celia shovelled a triangle of toast smothered with jam into her mouth, jammed an apple into her shawl and excused herself.

'You have not had a proper breakfast.' Lady Montague looked perplexed.

'I'm quite full after last night's supper. I will run along the drive and meet Audrey's carriage on the road. I am rather excited to see her.'

Lady Montague raised her brows at this but before she could protest Celia kissed her on the cheek and headed for the dining room door. Once outside, she quickly scooped up a bag she had earlier hidden in the garden bed and scurried as fast as her legs would carry her to the driveway's end.

Her tummy churned with anticipation and dread. She had decided she would endure Charles' wrath and would do anything to make amends for her questionable behaviour. She had disrespected his position and he had every right to be angry. He was correct. He was the reason she had been granted entry and the freedom to the inner world of the asylum. And if he wished for her to stay away, then so be it. She would. She would do it for him, out of respect for him and because more than anything she wanted to be his wife.

Celia prayed he would forgive her. If he did not, she did not know what she would do. A failed engagement would lead to a life of no further proposals for her. She could hardly imagine another who would fill Charles' shoes. She began to blush as she reminisced of the stolen kisses and the untethered way he unleashed feelings within her under his touch. She could hardly allow another man to have such a way with her.

Shaking the tumultuous thoughts from her mind, she walked as quickly as she could to the station. With her bag digging into her shoulder, almost out of breath, she managed to purchase a ticket and slink past waiting commuters to the furthest end of the station. From here she could easily see the length of the platform. She spied Charles immediately as he walked onto it with his bag in one hand and a newspaper tucked beneath his arm.

As the train slowly pulled into the station, Celia waited until everybody had boarded then quickly crossed the platform and stepped on board. She had to find Charles as quickly as possible to give her optimum time to gain back his love.

She walked between carriages and showed her ticket to the conductor as she passed him in the dining car. Moving along the narrow corridor, Celia discreetly looked sidewards into the window of each compartment. Finally Charles' profile came into view. He was chatting to somebody seated across from him. With the angle of her approach she could not see who it was.

When Celia entered the compartment, it took Charles a moment to register her presence, and when he did she saw his expression change from surprise to shrewd questioning. He jumped from his seat and opened the door, inviting her inside. Celia halted in her tracks as she recognised the person to whom he was talking and knew she was in a mountain of trouble.

'Why, Mrs Price. How nice to see you,' she said, trying not to give away her nervousness.

'Celia, what on earth are you doing here? Are you with your aunt?' Mrs Price looked to the corridor, expecting to see Lady Montague appear.

'Ah, no. She is not accompanying me. I am here with … '

She looked to Charles with a pleading expression. He smiled back at her, his lips closed in a daring grin.

'I am here with Charles. We are shopping for wedding clothes.'

'Yes, yes we are,' he offered curtly.

'And we are buying a spectacular gift for Lady Montague, therefore she does not know I am travelling to Ballarat today. Do you think you could keep it a secret?'

Mrs Price lips pursed. 'I do not think Lady Montague would approve of your lack of a chaperone. Do you?' She looked none too pleased with Celia, and continued, 'Young women embarking on the threshold of marriage should be very careful where they place themselves. It all seems that the approach of the turn of the century is bringing a boldness that is ungoverned. The Colonel speaks of such things with the military services and I am afraid it is washing over all of our morals. What next? Will women seek participation in the military along with the troops? Will they soon be joining men in the front line of combat? God forbid such things.'

Celia bit her lip. Mrs Price was not helping her cause one iota. She clutched at things to say but nothing seemed fitting. It was glaring to her that Charles held opinions on women and their place and he was at present not very forthcoming with any opinion whatsoever. Celia prepared herself. She would be dealt with severely for lying to her aunt. As frightening as that prospect was, it was no more so than the thought of losing Charles.

Celia offered up a silent prayer for rescue, which was answered as Charles' intervention broke the silence. 'Mrs Price, if I may implore on your goodwill to keep this secret, just this once. For you see, Celia and I are having our portrait taken and we would cherish it as a surprise for Lady Montague and Celia's whole family for our upcoming nuptials.'

Mrs Price looked from Celia to Charles and her features softened when her gaze fell upon the charmed look on Charles' face.

'Well, I suppose we all have our secrets. I am happy to keep yours. But just this once. I do not cherish the burden of a conspiracy.'

In the silence that ensued, Celia found both Charles and

Mrs Price staring at her. The sound of her thudding heart and the chug of the train as it sped past Beaufort Station en route to Ballarat, had her at a loss momentarily.

Finally she blurted, 'How are Audrey and Michael faring on their honeymoon?'

'Audrey sent word through the office in Sorrento on the Peninsula. They are having a lovely time visiting the area and its seaside villages,' Mrs Price said before gathering her bag from the seat.

Planting her hat back atop her head she stood. 'I have decided that I will take a spot of tea in the dining car. It will help me extricate myself from your secret and create my own alibi that I did not see either of you today.'

With the sound of the closing door echoing in the space between them, Celia fell onto the seat and sighed. Charles' smile disappeared from his features. He stood and walked from the suite also, leaving Celia ready to burst into tears. He was not going to listen to her, and her dread of losing him was looming larger each second.

She watched him in the hall. He looked right and left before he re-entered the suite. He snapped the lock on the door and pulled the shutters down, plunging the suite into a hue of subdued light. 'Now it would seem we are quite alone to discuss a solution to our dilemma.'

Celia's hopes soared. 'Charles, I am so dearly sorry to show up but I had to see you and ... '

'Stand up.'

'But I had to speak to you.'

He held his hand out to her. 'Stand up,' he ordered.

'Please Charles, listen to me,' she stammered as she took

his hand and feared he was going to put her over his knee. 'I need to ...'

He gripped her hand abruptly, pulling her up until she fell heavily into his chest.

His mouth found hers and silenced any words that were surging forth. He kissed her hard and forcibly. At first she loved the feel of having him in her grasp but as his ferocity grew she began to fear he was teaching her a lesson she could not back away from.

He pulled his mouth from hers. 'Is this how you want your husband to treat you?'

She took a step back before he gripped the tops of her arms and pulled her to within an inch of his face.

'Do you want to defy your husband and have him treat you like this? Do you?'

Tears began to spring forth. 'Charles, please don't treat me this way. I did not mean to make you angry. Please Charles, please.'

Her sobs struck a chord in his heart as he pulled her roughly to him once more but this time he held her in a crushing embrace. His arms became a protective shield and his hands caressed her back. 'Or is this way you want your husband to treat you? Protect you from the harshness of the world and have you obey and put his needs before everything else?'

She felt warmth flow through her at his words. She knew the truth of them as well as the expectation that she would become an adoring wife. For the love of her husband, she could forsake her newfound passion for the women who relied on her. The dread of selfishness ebbed through her but she pushed it away and wallowed in the security and amazement she felt each time Charles touched her.

Her voice sounded odd from the tears she had cried. 'I will do as you wish. I will stay away from your work and the asylum. I will be your adoring wife. I will wait for you to arrive home and I will love you forever.'

Charles pulled away from her and tilted her chin up and kissed her gently on the lips. For a long moment they stood in the centre of the suite with their mouths gently dancing to the thrum of the train's chorus. Celia decided she did not want to demurely await Charles' flirtations. She threw her arms around his neck and pressed her mouth to his for a deeper kiss. He responded by gripping her waist tighter, and then his hands wandered up to the sides of her breasts.

'I cannot wait any longer,' she whispered.

'Celia, my darling, not here.'

'We will not be disturbed. You have assured that with the locked door. Nobody can enter or see us.'

She pressed her body into his and began to unbutton his vest. Charles stilled her hands. 'Celia, this is very untoward.'

His vest hung open as she began to work the buttons of his shirt down. Charles closed his eyes. 'I beg you to still your hands,' he whispered as though in pain.

Her eyes wandered over his chest as she exposed it inch by inch and when she placed her hands on his bare skin she felt his body shudder. As her hands tentatively crept down to the button of his trousers he held her hand still. She looked up at him and the look he saw in her eyes was the same bold daring he had seen in his office when she had begged him to allow her the release women longed for.

It seemed the impending turn of the century had brought with it a sense of carefree abandon when it came to women and the power sex could yield for them. This information had been delivered via women's literature and the revolution of the printing press. The scratching of the pen across the course of the previous century had now produced copious amounts of written material and newfound information that had allowed desires to be unleashed. Charles had read the medical journals, which had made him aware there was much more to women's inner workings that made them desire more than just the use of their bodies to bear children. He was thankful that at this time in his life he was fortunate to be able to receive and give pleasures of the flesh to this woman.

As he stared transfixed on the beautiful face of his fiancé and weighed the dangers of what they were embarking upon, she released her hand from his grasp and plunged it forth to the buttons of his trousers and in doing so brushed the hard flesh trying to break free.

That moment officially plunged his sense of saving her for marriage into the depths of the flames of hell. His sense of propriety was slashed away. He walked her back toward the window and pushed her against it. Kissing her with fervour, he felt their bodies heave for release with the decision made that they would not turn back. The verdict was unspoken, with heightening pulses and lust surging through them. In his own mind, he realised that the way he had held her feet in such a perverse and sexual manner had led to what was happening now. He had only himself to blame, and had tossed away the promise of what he would show her once they were married.

He spun her away from him and she braced her hands on the base of the window shutter to steady herself. The rocking motion of the train was adding to the bliss as he pushed onto and away from her with the same intensity. In her back she could feel the bulge of him, which would subside, only to press into her again to tease her once more.

His hands deftly began to undo the buttons of her bodice as he pushed her hair aside and kissed her neck. She rolled her head to the side to allow him the full exposure of her skin. Her nipples pushed against her cotton shift and she could feel cool air surrounding her skin as he exposed her slowly. Once her breasts were free he cupped them in his hands, rolling her nipples between his fingers, gently at first then tugging at them slowly. She could hear herself panting, unable to believe the pure ecstasy coursing through her body. Her sins would not be forgiven but she could not turn back now.

Celia pushed her buttocks out to feel his body against hers and managed to steady herself with one hand on the shutter before moving her free hand back and feeling him fully through his trousers. Her hand moved the length of him over and over and it was when she managed to delve beyond the buttons of his trousers to feel the hardness of his warm length she felt a jolt of shock. How was she to go through with this? Suddenly, she was frightened at the thought of such a thing entering her body. He must have felt her fear as her hand stilled.

'If you are afraid, we don't have to do this, my love,' he whispered in her ear.

She turned in his arms and looked up at his face. 'I want this more than you would know.'

He sat down on the seat and pulled her onto his lap. Her exposed breasts caught his attention as he slowly kissed his way down her neck and along her collarbone, eventually finding her nipple. He licked and sucked each in turn and gently kissed the skin of her breasts until she was begging him to make love to her.

Standing her before him, he pushed her dress up, untying her undergarments until they fell to the floor and she was exposed beneath the cover of her dress. He pulled her on top of him once more with her legs spread on either side of his hips, and kissed her tenderly on the mouth.

With their heartbeats thudding to the rhythm of the train, he slowly slipped his fingers inside her where she was soft and moist. He felt himself beginning to lose control with just the touch of her and the promise of what she was going to deliver to him. Pulling his fingers free and angling himself at her opening he slowly rocked her forward and backward until she opened to him.

There was the look of pain on her face. 'Am I hurting you, darling?'

'No, I love you so much. That is what hurts.'

He knew she was lying, if only a little. His selfishness and his need to possess her fully heralded no turning back for either of them.

Charles pushed into her a little more, then some more again, and felt her body relax over him. Holding her hips, he slowly lifted her and then lowered her over himself again. He was losing control and summoned all his will to make this a better experience for her than she could have hoped. Her eyes began to close as she savoured the feel of him inside her and he watched her with intensity. He wanted the look on her face to be branded into his mind forever. The moment they had fit together so perfectly and the sheer love he felt for her had him tumbling along at a rapid pace.

She began to make tiny noises and her moans increased as she built up to the height of ecstasy. A second elapsed and he was pushed over the edge and spilt over inside her. As they clung to one another and tumbled back into the present with the sound of the whistle and the rocking movement of the train they needed to face the actuality of what they had just done, but before they allowed reality to set in they kissed long and deep, trying to retain contact. Neither wanted to let go, for they wanted this moment to be theirs forever.

Beyond the locked, shuttered door they could hear the conductor stating, 'Five minutes until we arrive in Ballarat. Please gather your belongings, if you will.'

Charles extricated himself from Celia and helped her with her undergarments before re-buttoning his trousers, shirt and vest. He placed Celia's shawl tightly around her and huddled her close to his side so she would not be recognised by anybody else from Ararat. 'I think we will wait until the station is clear before disembarking,' Charles said. 'We do not want to make excuses to anybody else we may know.'

Celia stared at him in silence, a melancholy look upon her face.

'Are you all right, my love?'

She nodded. 'I am more than all right and I will not risk losing you for my own selfish virtue again.'

Charles did not comment. If he had responded to her he

would have stated that after what she had delivered to him just moments ago, he would have granted her permission to visit the asylum and do as she pleased. But he said absolutely nothing. The power women held over men was lost to them, he thought, and should they realise the full extent of that power they could rule the world. Instead, they would be kept forevermore in the home, rearing children and the like, keeping their husbands happy. That was their calling, and should men be clever enough to keep that information to themselves, the circumstances of women would remain that way.

After the bustle of train travellers had subsided, Charles continued holding Celia close to his side so that she was somewhat hidden, and stepped from the train and onto the platform. The rain had left the streets sludgy, allowing carriage wheels to churn it up further.

'What a dreadful mess these roads are.' Celia stated pulling her skirts up past her ankles.

Charles smiled in spite of the exposure. His mind wandered back to all he had just experienced and he could have pulled her to him and kissed her again right here in the street. He was contemplating dragging her to the nearest hotel and renting a room just so he could enjoy a repeat performance. The risk of her reputation would be one reason he had to refrain from doing just that. The other would be the tardiness he would show by missing his appointment with the superintendent from Yarra Bend.

The next fortnight was going to untether him. Now that he had been exposed to all she was capable of doing to him, he knew he would find it more difficult to tolerate the anguish of having to wait for her to be his wife. He would not be able to steal the time he required to have her in all the ways he wanted until after they were married, and he realised that he would dare not entertain thoughts of enticing her to the asylum for fear she would take it upon herself to believe she was welcome there at any time.

He did have an important meeting today and feared Celia had not planned what she would do until the return train trip. He smiled. How his thoughts wandered to the day's end and the return trip back to Ararat.

'What will you do whilst you wait for me, my love?'

'I will call in to the dressmaker whilst I am here to look at my gown,' she stated.

'Well then you cannot afford for your petticoats to become too unruly in this sludge. The dressmaker will not have that, will she?' Charles said as he averted her to the undercover storefront veranda.

'I have to make my meeting. I will meet you in precisely two hours for our return trip back, my love,' he whispered in her ear.

'I will meet you back at the station, then.' She looked at him with all the promise and allure that he could hope for.

Celia stood before the mirror and gasped at her reflection. The finest lace delicately cuffed her wrists and waist. Yards of pristine white silk adorned the curves of her body. From the exterior she was the epitome of innocence. Onlookers would view her as a young woman on the precipice of a new life. Only she and Charles knew otherwise. She was surprised she did not feel guilt of being unworthy of white, traditionally worn by the virginal bride. She loved Charles and could see absolutely not a thing wrong with the events that she had allowed to unfold not so many minutes ago.

It was the moment the dressmaker placed the fine tulle over her head to cover her face that she drew a sharp breath. She was to be married and she had committed the highest sin out of wedlock. Would she be punished? Just as quickly as the thought appeared she pushed it away. She loved Charles and he loved her. That would surely be enough in god's eyes to forgive. For those women who fornicated outside of marriage there were consequences to be sure. Poor Maryann had been dealt the cruellest of blows and yet, now Celia could see how easily the choices made, in the name of love could cost.

Celia walked the main street of Ballarat in the time she had left before returning to the station to meet Charles. As he approached her she wanted to run toward him and fall into his embrace. She did not dare, as there were sure to be people they knew returning to the station to catch the train to Ararat.

Once on the train, Celia trilled about the dress fitting and the ornate work that adorned the back of the gown. 'It is just too lovely to be covered over by my veil so I told the dressmaker to gather the veil in a headpiece so it is only long in the front. Oh Charles, it is so beautiful!' she gushed, unable to contain her excitement.

Charles gaze wandered over her features as he smiled at her.

They were seated in the dining car on their return to Ararat. Celia was eating a scone and talking around a mouthful of jam and cream, and Charles watched her mouth with all the attention a wolf gives its prey. He had decided it would be safer to travel back in a public area so they would not allow their passion to run away with them once more. Celia traced the pattern on the plate with the end of her butter knife as

Charles told her about the knowledge he had just gained with regard to new treatments he was going to initiate at the asylum.

'How I wish I could assist you in this new endeavour.' Celia said.

Charles looked none too pleased.

Before he could begin to chastise her she said, 'I promise I will stay true to my word. Once we are married I will be far too busy to attend to the affairs within the walls of the asylum. Far too busy.'

Charles smiled. He did not believe her one ounce.

Chapter 15

Celia pushed the front door open and stared at the empty hallway, not keen to step over the threshold. She was tired of the loneliness of her home and exhausted by the unknown turn her marriage would take. Would Charles forgive her, if ever? If only she had followed him as soon as he had left the lodge. With the exception of a candlestick burning atop the hallstand the hallway was cast in darkness. She still admonished the time it had taken her to gather her thoughts enough to follow Charles to the station. Instead, she had sat in misery far too many minutes before racing from the cottage. If so, she would have found herself bound for Ballarat and into Charles' good graces once more.

Lydia had laid a cloth across the final third of the dining room table before leaving for the evening. On top of it, a silver cloche covered a plate that was keeping Celia's supper warm. She passed it, instead making her way to her room to change into her bedclothes.

As she returned to the dining room she pulled her dressing gown tightly around her and tied it at her waist. This room was so lovely with its decorative border wallpaper creating a line below the cornice. No longer did she admire it the way she had in those first days of their marriage. She and Charles had shared many fabulous meals and colourful conversations in here. Now, she found she was alone, without Charles, without anybody at all.

She lifted the cloche and placed it gently down on the table. Picking up her knife and fork she stared at the food on her plate. She was not hungry. She picked up the plate and walked into the kitchen, and with an overwhelming surge of anger pitched it into the sink from the doorway. Food spattered across the floor and onto the window above the sink. Broken china scattered everywhere. 'Damn it to hell!' she yelled before slapping her hand across her mouth. But it was too late, the blasphemous words had escaped.

It took an hour to clean the huge mess she had created, so the time was past midnight when she crawled into bed, exhausted. At such a late hour she hoped sleep would come easy to her. She closed her eyes but could not drift off. Her thoughts swirled around. Charles was never going to forgive her. He would not speak to her. The look he cast at her from the train window was startled at first but turned grim as she watched on. She needed to make a decision. Perhaps she should return to her father? But no sooner had the scenario entered her thoughts than she quashed it. Such a course of action would confirm the failure of her marriage. She was not prepared to admit her failings as a wife.

Maybe she could write Charles a letter and disappear for a short while. That would give him time to miss her, or to at least allow him to calm down. But where would she go? Ballarat was an option but she quickly decided against that too. It would be considered truculent for her to travel alone. She could stay with her aunt but again she would be opening the business of her failed marriage to all who knew her. She did not want a scandal to evolve, which is what would happen if the townsfolk discovered her living at Lady Montague's home.

Each scenario was no better than the one before. As dawn approached and her mind spun a web of never ending possibilities, there was still no clear decision for her to make. Only one possibility stood out to her. She wanted to stay here, in her home, and to win her husband's trust. She also wanted to retain the trust of the women at the asylum. She could not leave and turn her back on them.

But what a dilemma. Charles had banned her from the asylum and she held no doubt he would never lift the embargo. She had to find a way to gain his trust again and hopefully in time his opinions would swing in her favour. Although she was filled with doubt, she still had hope. As soon as Charles returned from his meeting she would do just that.

As that final thought registered, Celia swung her legs out from beneath the covers. Charles had packed a bag to attend a meeting in Ballarat, which meant she was guaranteed one to two days without him at the asylum. With the help of the women, she would uncover the person who had killed Audrey. The women would be more willing to discuss matters with her than with the doctors, and with Charles away she would have an excellent opportunity to do some sleuthing with little risk of detection.

Celia did not stop to eat breakfast or drink a cup of tea. After dressing quickly, she raced from the house. If it were reported to Charles that she had been seen in the asylum his retribution would be dire, but she reasoned that things could not get any worse. What was she jeopardising? With Charles ignoring her it would seem her marriage was over. But if he discovered she had defied him, at least there was a chance the discovery would force him to communicate with her on some level, even if only to scream at her. The best outcome would occur if she came forth with information, perhaps even the name of the perpetrator. In that case, surely Charles would forgive her.

Celia peeked inside the laundry room and watched the women as they worked. They did not see her. She felt excitement build as she stood quietly just beyond the door. One of the women looked up and squealed. Everybody looked to the woman and then swung their attention to where she was looking. Screams of joy followed as Celia rushed inside and was greeted with hugs and kisses.

'We have missed you so,' Maryann said as she grasped Celia's hands.

'I have missed you, too. How are you all?'

'It has been simply awful without you. We have been locked in our cells far too long. It is for our protection.'

'Well, you all need protecting. Thank goodness something is being done,' Celia said.

'It does not seem to help everybody,' Maryann said.

'Why do you say that?' Celia asked.

'In the past weeks since that poor woman was found hanging in the belltower …'

Celia shuddered as the image flew to her mind.

'… two women have been admitted to the hospital cottage with injuries.'

'What do you mean? Were they from the refractory ward?' Celia looked worried.

'No, they were from the ward on the second floor.' Maryann lowered her voice as though it would soften the harsh reality of the tale. 'They were attacked.'

'What on earth do you mean?'

'They were severely attacked. A woman delivering linens this week told us about it.'

'What did she say?'

'That she heard the distinct voice of a man in the ward and nothing more until one woman was discovered the next morning with severe injuries.'

Celia felt her frustration build. So one woman had been killed and another two attacked. Could this mean there was more than one perpetrator? And a man's voice had been heard? Was he an inmate or a member of the staff? The latter seemed more likely. And right under Charles' supervision! Charles had been at the asylum night and day. What was he doing about this?

Somewhere in the asylum somebody had free reign to commit these violent acts and yet Charles had been unable to garner any information.

That Charles had managed to keep the constable away, when it was obvious he would be privy to gossip around town, was a mystery to Celia. Did Constable Bryant need an official summons or could he gain access to the asylum of his own volition? That thought alone gave her the ammunition she required. While she did not know what Charles was uncovering in the asylum or if he had indeed discovered who had done such a thing to Audrey, she could not bear to imagine that another woman could be likely to suffer the same fate.

While Celia fretted over the possible outcomes of her actions, she decided it was vital for her to make a clear statement about what was happening at the asylum. Her marriage was already in tatters and she would use it to her advantage. Knowing Charles would not welcome a scandal when he was so fragile, she felt she was safe. It was this point alone that forced her to forge ahead, ready to strike at him while he was vulnerable. It would not be easy, but she nonetheless steeled herself for the conversation she would draw him into. This was a side to her she neither thought existed nor would ever have imagined could exist. For her mind to conjure such manipulation was a new concept. It seemed the desperation of her newfound calling was driving her to do something a wife should never consider.

She entered the hospital cottage looking from side to side. Should a doctor be on rounds, it would not do to be caught and sent away before she could unearth any truth. She sought the nurse in attendance and was thankful it was Jillian.

'Do you know anything about this situation?' Celia whispered from the opposite side of the bed that stood between them.

'No. It seems there is a ploy to keep us busy with all the other cases in here at present,' Jillian said in a hushed whisper.

In the bed was a sleeping woman with bruises covering her face and neck. Celia looked down at her. 'What happened to you?' she mused out loud.

The silence stretched around Celia and Jillian as both women stared down at the unmoving figure.

Chapter 15

Celia left the hospital cottage and returned home. For the remainder of the afternoon she thought of nothing else but the danger the women faced in their cells.

While sitting alone in the dining room, she scripted everything she wished to say. Stammering around mouthfuls of mashed potato, she spoke to the walls. She was determined to gain Charles' attention. 'I will not have you railroad me on this,' she said as peas rolled from her fork back onto the plate.

She jumped in her seat as the front door slammed and the familiar sound of Charles' bag thudded onto the floorboards in the hallway. She stared at the open door and waited for him to ignore her and saunter past, so was surprised when he looked into the dining room and said, 'Is there enough for another plate?'

'I thought you were away for a few days at least.'

Charles pulled a seat away from the dining table and sat opposite her. 'It would seem I decided to return home to my wife earlier than planned.'

Celia looked at him momentarily stunned.

'Well, is there enough for another?' he repeated.

Without answering, Celia pushed her chair away from the table and walked into the kitchen, returning with a plate in her hand.

She scooped potatoes from a dish, and then dished out a spoonful of peas and three slices of roast beef from a platter, positioning the food on his plate just the way he liked it. They ate in silence. Celia was quite stunned. She could not believe Charles was eating supper with her after ignoring her for weeks.

'I was so grateful you chased me to the station. It really

proved to me that you are prepared to become an obedient wife.' He grinned at her over his fork.

Celia spoke slowly, 'I am glad that is what you gained from me following you to the train station.' Her voice did not withhold pleasure.

She had made a vow as she watched Charles eat his supper that they would not argue over the events of the past few weeks. This time was precious, and she would have her say when things had settled somewhat. Hearing his words and seeing the smug look on his face made her feel an instant disdain for his shortcomings. Before thinking it through she blurted, 'I went to the asylum today.'

Charles looked up from his plate. 'Really? Why is that?' His mouth set in a thin line as his jaw bunched. 'You do realise that the discussion we had on your visiting, or more to the point, abstaining from your visiting, was intensely serious?'

Celia took a deep breath. 'I understood our discussion, or rather, the statement you thrust at me.'

'Why do I get the feeling there is a statement about to be *thrust* at *me* that I will not relish?'

'I have had some time to think and I respect your decision but it is frightening me no end to know there is a murderer in that place, someone who was able to commit such a heinous crime. And now it seems there are women being brutalised in their cells.'

'This is not your concern.'

'Well, I think it needs to be my concern. Those women are my concern ... '

'They are not,' Charles yelled at the top of his voice.

Celia stayed in her seat in spite of her desire to jump and run. 'Charles, would you please listen to me?'

'I will not,' he yelled.

Celia's voice began to rise. 'If you do not listen to me you will leave me no choice but to officially summon Constable Bryant to investigate the crime that you have decided to ignore.'

Charles looked bewildered and while he was silenced by her threat she quickly continued. 'While I have to be thankful for your decisions on all accounts, I cannot ignore my plight. You banned me from the asylum's door. If you had not placed an embargo on my visits I would not have ventured via the lower level refractory ward where I discovered things you tried to keep hidden. I forced you to entrust me with secrets that few know about and now it seems your hands are tied. It is obvious to me that you have not discussed Audrey's murder with anyone outside the walls of that godforsaken place. The gossip in town is rife with the happenings but nobody is prepared to act. While it pains me to deliver this ultimatum to you, I cannot help the ferocity I feel within to fight for what I feel is right and just.'

Storm clouds seemed to gather in the room as Charles stared at Celia, who finally concluded, 'I have decided that if you do not allow me to continue to visit I will have no choice but to reveal your secret.'

'You stupid, selfish woman.' Charles had risen to his feet and was now bellowing above her.

She remained sitting, looking up at the towering figure that loomed over her.

'I am sorry to make you angry but I have no choice but to

continue my journey. In time, you may come to see me as an asset to your work.'

'You have not thought it through very well at all, my dear wife. If you allow Audrey's identity to be revealed it would have you and I cast from the town, rendering us both useless to all its inhabitants including those you hold dear to your *plight*. Do you think the Colonel and Mrs Price will be able to remain here also? The lives it would ruin would be further reaching than your current plan allows. You do not possess the skill to deal with these women. You are not a doctor. You cannot save the souls of these inmates. To allow you to continue on the path you are on is of risk to both of us. If I were assured you could survive I would toss you in there myself and give you a good dose of humility.'

Celia looked down at her clasped hands on her lap. She was immediately overwhelmed that her supposedly splendid plan had not come to fruition as she had hoped. She was frightened at the prospect of being tossed into the asylum and becoming an inmate, a situation she would never have considered but one she knew her husband had the authority to easily oversee.

'I am sorry to threaten your position, Charles. I just feel an innate desperation to do something to help.'

'I came here this evening hoping to find my wife. Do you understand what I mean by the term?'

'A ninny who cannot think for herself? Someone who rubs your feet when you return from a day of work?'

His eyes narrowed. 'In answer to that statement I must say that yes, that would be rather refreshing. I do not like the course your mind is taking with the distraction of the asylum.

Do you realise you are prepared to sabotage your husband's work to get access to people you do not know? They are perfect strangers. Are you prepared to jeopardise everything I hold dear for their sakes?'

Charles sat down once more and held his head in his hands. 'I am tired. Tired of this. Us.' He flung his hand out. 'I have a murder to contend with, women being beaten in their cells. I now have the government bearing down on me with questions and a ridiculous timeline in which to answer them.'

'Oh Charles,' she whispered as shame washed over her.

'I cannot come home to you with expectations that you will support me as a wife should and instead find myself bearing the barrage of your incomprehensible needs and wants.'

'Charles, I do not wish to put you and your position at risk. I can help. There are so many things I cannot shake from my thoughts. So many questions I need answered. If you share anything with me, I vow I will help. The women trust me. You know this to be true.'

It was her plea that made him take note but he did not relent. 'I do know how hard you have worked, and I acknowledge the passion you bring to your newfound ideals. But I cannot assist you to navigate your demands except to say that you must stay away from my work. It is immoral with your standing as my wife that you continue on the path. It is going to end our union if you continue. I need to be your priority. As your husband I will not stand by and allow you to risk my reputation.'

Celia wanted to weep. She had been so certain her plan would work. It had not entered her mind it could be turned so easily against her.

Charles witnessed her disappointment, and it struck at

something within him. 'I insist that you are to stay away from the asylum, but I will attempt to keep you informed of any events that unfold. That is my final word on the matter.'

Celia stared at him. It was a mere morsel of entry back into Charles' good graces. She would take anything she could gain.

'Have you uncovered anything with regard to Audrey's murder?' she asked.

'No.'

'Nothing?'

'Nothing.'

'Why have you not summoned the constable?'

'You stated you wanted to discuss the women and their present situation. Could we please stay on that discussion?'

'Very well.' Celia bit her lip as her mind spun quickly to find a new avenue of information. 'I was talking with one of the women. It was some time ago.'

'Which one?'

'Maryann.'

Charles looked up to the ceiling.

Celia pushed on. 'Are you aware she was forced to give her child over to an orphanage?'

'Why, yes I am.'

'Well, don't you believe that is quite untoward?'

'The asylum is a facility for lunatics my dear, not a nursery for children.'

'And would it not bode well for a woman's state of mind to have her child remain with her?'

'Each facility has its purpose. Ours is to keep the unhinged away from the general population. The orphanage is to look after children when their parents cannot.'

Celia placed her hands on the table and waited a moment before saying, 'Well, for all it is worth I do not think it is a sensible idea to have these poor little souls all alone in the world never knowing where their family roots lie.'

Charles picked up his knife and fork. 'Well I think it is their saving grace that they never know where they came from, or rather from *whom* they came. It would only halt their ability to find their way through life. Discovering one's bloodline casts the facts in one's mind from which there is rarely an escape.'

'You really are beginning to sound like … ' Celia quickly clamped her mouth closed as Charles' eyes narrowed.

'Oh continue, I implore you,' he dared.

'It's just that … I … do not worry about it.'

'No, I would not hear of it. Please continue.'

Celia squared her shoulders and retained her steady hold on the table. 'I was just going to point out that you are sounding more like Doctor Rushby than a doctor who wants to make a difference.'

'Allow me to enlighten you. The doctor you once met was from a much different world to this one. I have given up tending to physical aliments and gunshot wounds of the sane to deal with those whose minds have been affected by all manner of things that I could not control if I tried. I cannot stop the level of alcohol consumption that affects behaviours you will never understand. I cannot stop men from contracting syphilis from wayward women, for which the only cure is mercury, a substance that causes lesions in the brain large enough to remind one of the craters on the surface of the moon. And there is one attitude in particular that I will not be frowned upon for holding. I will continue to save these poor souls who do not have a choice about the kind of world they are born into. I will not condone nor will I ever feel pity for a woman who has spread her legs before she is betrothed and has been punished by God himself for her sin.'

'Well, it would seem that you would not hold me in very high regard then, would it?'

Charles stared at Celia before tersely saying, 'That is different.'

'Is it?'

'Yes, it is. We were to be married within days of our indiscretion.'

'Would you have me cast inside the walls of the asylum if I had become pregnant after the event?'

'No, I would not. Although I do recall it unfolded after a dispute between us. Can you recall the nature of the disagreement?' His eyes held a challenge.

Celia looked away. She was ashamed at how much resistance she had shown Charles and the length of time over which she had pursued it. 'I was determined to continue my work in the asylum after we were married.'

'So it would seem that even then you would not listen to an answer you were not prepared to hear. And here again we find ourselves fighting with regard to that exact topic.'

Celia's gaze swept back to Charles. They stared at one another, caught between the passions of love they could not deny and the possibility it would not be enough to keep them together.

'Are you serious when you argue that these so called wayward women should have the right to dictate whether or not they are sufficiently fit to care for their bastard children?'

Celia ignored his question as she moved on with her next argument. 'Well, what of the women who had their children within the sanctity of marriage? Will those who find themselves in the facility under your care wake one day to discover their babies stolen from their arms?'

'Of course not. Do not be daft. There have been many cases where the families of inmates are willing to take on an infant and give that child a normal life beyond the asylum walls.'

'Well, I know it to be fact that Mrs Price does not possess Charlotte, so where is she? I realise there was that masquerade of a funeral to do away with Audrey and Charlotte in the one scenario.'

'You are crossing a line I do not think you want to tread beyond, my dear,' Charles responded in a menacing tone.

'Why not? Is the answer to my question too difficult? Where is Charlotte? I know for a fact Michael would be unable to ... '

'Stop this at once!' Cutlery clattered against crockery as Charles slammed an open hand on the table.

'Where is Charlotte? I want to know!' Celia was now shrieking above Charles' booming voice.

'I. Will. Not. Bear. This. In. My. Home.' He stood up, knocking his chair backwards in the process, before stomping into the drawing room.

Celia jumped up and followed him. 'Mrs Price would never have allowed her granddaughter to be shipped off to an orphanage.'

Charles stood with his back to her and was staring at the bookshelf. His hands were curled into tight fists at his sides. Celia feared her own ferocious drive to discover the truth but she could not give up until she knew where Audrey's precious Charlotte was. 'I am that child's godmother and I demand to know where she is, Charles. It is my duty to protect her.'

Charles turned to her. His features were like stone. 'Is it?'

'Why yes, it is.' Celia's voice had become a whisper compared to the shouting that had filled the house until this point.

'Well then, it would seem that you could not protect her when she needed you most.'

'That it most unfair Charles, considering I have been kept from the truth all this time. I had to uncover it for myself with no help from you.'

He bore down on her and grasped her arms so tightly that her breath caught in her chest.

'You want to bear the brunt of the truth. You want to lay blame on me because my professional word of confidentiality does not sit well with you? It has tortured me to be entrusted with locking away a woman who became the rotting carcass of the person we once knew. It has tormented me to keep it from you. I am bound to the Colonel and Mrs Price to keep this quiet to those that we know. I implore you to do the same.'

'They knew all along Audrey was in there and yet there is no sign of their granddaughter. What kind of people are they?' Celia spat.

'It is not what you think.'

'What am I to think, Charles? Audrey disappears from our lives, then she reappears and you are entrusted to keep her hidden from the outside world. Somebody gets a hold of the secret and murders her to make some sickening point. Her daughter is missing and there is no sign of Michael. I just need to know one thing, Charles. Where is Charlotte? If you confirm for me that she is with Michael, I will never raise this matter again.'

Charles released his grip on Celia's arms and dropped his hands to his sides.

'She is of this earth no longer.'

'What?'

'The devil whispered in Audrey's ear and she drowned her.'

Celia fell back a step as Charles grappled in an effort to steady her. 'I … I do not understand.'

He moved her toward the chaise and attempted to help her settle onto it.

'I do not want to lie down, Charles.'

'At least sit down. I have just shocked you to the largest degree.'

Celia's face had turned as white as a sheet. It was only after she had accepted the dose of sherry that he poured for her that the colour began to form back into her cheeks.

Charles sat in silence, holding her hands, alert for any sign of the shock subsiding.

Minutes stretched by. 'Where is Michael?' she said in a quiet voice.

'I do not know. After Charlotte was laid to rest in secret, and Audrey was placed in the asylum I believe the Colonel organised a new post for him. I often wonder where he is now. We were in such close acquaintance with the McGowan family.'

As Charles spoke of the friendship they had shared, Celia reflected on the times they had all spent in one another's company. She frowned as a memory dawned.

Charles looked at her with worry. 'Are you going to be ill?' he asked.

'No. I just recalled something.'

'What?'

'You knew.'

'What on earth are you talking about?'

'After you returned from the hotel with Michael that day. He had told you. You knew what was happening to Audrey.'

Charles realised the moment she was referring to. His features hardened. 'And?'

'You kept the truth of Audrey's condition from me. I specifically asked you about it. I was worried for her and you dismissed it.'

'There was nothing to be done,' he said.

'Darling! Darling! Look at this.' Celia leaned over Charles' shoulder and held the photograph in front of the book he held in his hands. 'It is our first glimpse of Charlotte. Oh! She is such a handsome baby.' She whisked the photograph from Charles' gaze and stared at it more closely.

Unfolding the letter that had accompanied the photograph, she lay on the chaise and began to read. Every few seconds she would stop reading to peruse the picture of her best friend's brand new babe. Charles peered at her over the top of his glasses watching her mouth turn up at the corners as she read the letter.

'Oh, Charles.' Celia clutched the letter to her chest. 'Audrey and Michael wish us to be Charlotte's godparents. Is that not a grand gesture?' She clapped the letter between her hands.

'That is grand indeed,' he said, watching her excited glow.

'She writes that I am to send her a telegram at my earliest

convenience to confirm my receipt of her letter. She asks that I organise Charlotte's dress for the christening.'

Charles could imagine the cogs of her mind already plotting a course of action. He was not disappointed when she said, 'Well then, I will send word to Audrey right away so she knows I am only too happy to do as she asks. She need not worry about the gown at all. I will order it from the dressmaker in Ballarat. After all, that dressmaker did an exquisite job with both our wedding gowns. Yes, that is what I will do.'

Celia looked at Charles but talked to herself as she continued with the discussion. He could hear her voice echo down the hallway of their home as she left the doorway. 'And I will visit the milliner in Beaufort. Her work is exquisite. I will order an elaborate bonnet for Charlotte. Oh, I have so much to do.'

Charles spoke under his breath. 'I trust Audrey will be well aware that you have everything in hand.' He smiled as he turned his attention back to his book.

The christening day was set for the first of the following month. Celia organised a return telegram immediately.

> CHARLES AND I EXCITED STOP WE ACCEPT STOP GOWN IN HAND STOP SEE YOU FIRST OF THE MONTH STOP

Days later, Celia boarded a train with a neatly wrapped package of fabric from the haberdashery store in Ararat. As a surprise, she decided that the same fabric used for Audrey's wedding gown would serve as a lovely detail on her daughter's christening gown. After visiting the milliner in Beaufort to purchase a bonnet from the stock kept in the store, she continued on to Ballarat for her appointment with the seamstress.

Celia fell in love with the most expensive lace the seamstress offered. She decided the lace would finish the gown beautifully if used to cuff the sleeves and border the hem. Satisfied with her decisions, she made a date the following week to collect the finished garment.

Upon her return to Ararat, Celia decided to visit the asylum so she could stop in on the women in the laundry room and also call in on Charles while she was there. She found Charles in his office. Falling into the chair opposite his desk, she let out a huge sigh. 'I am exhausted from my travels today.'

'Why are you here then?' Charles lifted one eyebrow as he looked in her direction.

'I wanted to come and see my adoring husband.'

'And?' he looked at her expectantly.

Celia tugged at the end of her gloves as though to remove some lint. 'I thought I might check in on the laundry room and see if anything is afoot.'

'Is that so?' he said.

She alighted from her chair and walked around his desk. Standing behind his chair, she draped her arms over his shoulders and hugged his back. 'I know we continually battle over the same argument, my darling.' She nuzzled his ear. He closed his eyes and allowed her to use her charm to disarm him.

'I am surprised you came to see me. I am sure you neglect to tell me of all your visits.'

'That is not true. You know each and every time.'

'Liar.' He smiled as she licked his ear and allowed her warm breath to travel down his neck. He gathered her hands and pulled her around to the front of him and settled her on his lap.

'You think that all you have to do is caress me into your good graces and I will allow you to do as you wish.'

'Yes!' she giggled as he kissed her. As his mouth found her throat, he began to trail kisses across her collarbone.

She let out a sigh. 'I know you suggest that I seek other interests to fill my days and I have tried all measure of things. But I must say that calling on the local women and sipping tea, or talking mundane chitchat with those who do not understand or care for my work does not suit ... me,' she finished on a sigh as his lips silenced her.

The following week, Celia delivered the gown and bonnet to Mrs Price at her home.

'We are expecting them all this afternoon.' Mrs Price was flustered at the prospect.

Celia could understand her anxiety. It was the first time her daughter had visited since having her new baby. Mrs Price's delight at the impending visit of her granddaughter was overwhelming and exciting all at once.

'Mrs Price, I am just as excited as you at the thought of seeing Audrey. And to think she is a mother now. It is positively lovely.'

Mrs Price took a moment to grin at Celia. The woman's features always seemed so hard but in that moment Celia could envision the young woman she had once been. The life of a soldier's wife could harden the most sensitive woman. With the worry of sending her husband to battle and the torture of moving from family and friends over and again, it was little wonder such women learnt to develop hard exteriors.

'Please tell Audrey I cannot wait to see her in the morning. The christening has excited me so very much,' Celia said as she stood to leave. 'I am sure you have lots to organise before Audrey arrives. I will see you all tomorrow unless there is anything more I can do to help now.'

'Thank you so much, Celia. I will be sure to let Audrey know. She will be very grateful for the gown for Charlotte. I will leave it wrapped so I can share in the surprise when we see it for the first time together.'

The following morning, Celia dressed in a brand new frock. She had chosen it for the occasion. It was a deep crimson colour that would, once she was holding the darling baby, provide a lovely contrast to the infant's pristine white christening gown.

Celia smoothed her skirt down after alighting the carriage and waited on the roadside outside the church gate. She could hardly contain her excitement. While she and Audrey had written consistently when they were both newly married, the letters had become less frequent when Audrey's pregnancy had progressed. Once Charlotte was born the letters had come only from Celia's direction. Celia did not mind. She realised Audrey would be busy looking after a newborn and had been happy to write to her every few weeks sharing anecdotes and stories of experiences as a doctor's wife who spent her days in an asylum.

She watched the carriage roll down the street toward her. As it drew to a halt, Celia stepped forward. Michael was the first to alight. He held Charlotte safely in the crook of his elbow.

'Hello,' Celia cooed as she looked at the tiny face framed inside the bonnet. The train of the gown swung only a foot from the ground. Celia was delighted with her choice.

'Could you take her please?' Michael held Charlotte out to Celia, who gathered her in her arms and felt her heart swell as she looked into the adorable eyes staring up at her. Michael placed his hand inside the carriage to assist his wife. As Audrey stepped down from the carriage, he placed an arm across her shoulder. Celia beamed as she looked up from Charlotte towards Audrey — but then her smile faltered. Audrey had lost so much weight. She looked far too thin to have birthed a babe only two months prior. Nonetheless, she did not hesitate to greet her friend with anything other than warmth.

'Oh Audrey, she is beautiful!' Celia leaned forward to give Audrey a kiss.

Audrey looked at Celia and smiled. 'Do you think?' she said.

'Oh yes! She is a cherub.'

'Best we get this baby christened and in God's good grace,' Michael said with grim determination as he ushered Audrey up the path to the church door.

Once everyone was gathered inside, Charles joined Celia at the front of the church. The minister trickled water onto Charlotte's forehead. As it ran into her eyes she did not cry or fuss. Celia looked from Charlotte's adorable face to Charles and prayed they too would one day be blessed with a child.

At the conclusion of the service, the women of the parish announced that a delicious lunch had been prepared. All invited guests who had gathered to witness Charlotte's baptism into the Lord's protection were ushered into the hall attached to the rear of the church.

Celia delivered a plate of food to Audrey. 'Here you go,' she said.

'Thank you,' said Audrey but stared down at the food as though it were poison.

'You look tired,' Celia said to Audrey.

'I am,' she sighed.

'I have heard that night time with a new baby is impossible to bear.'

'It is not so bad. I am used to rarely getting much sleep,' Audrey said.

'You have lost a considerable amount of weight. Are you well?'

Audrey shrugged her shoulders. 'I am well enough,' she said woodenly.

Celia was mystified. Audrey did not seem herself at all. Was it motherhood that changed a woman so entirely? She did suppose that having a baby would be an ordeal and had possibly caused havoc with Audrey's sensibilities.

Charles approached. 'I am sorry to interrupt, but I am accompanying Michael and a few others to the Shire Hall Hotel for a drink. I will not be too long.'

'That is fine. I will keep Audrey company and hope to have as many cuddles with Charlotte as I possibly can.'

Audrey looked forlorn. Celia asked her all manner of questions. 'Tell me, what is it like being a soldier's wife?'

'It is lonely at times. I thought that having Charlotte would fill my days with wonder and delight.' Audrey looked across the room at Charlotte housed in her grandmother's arms. 'But it has not.'

Celia looked at her friend. 'What has happened to you, Audrey?'

'I do not know. I feel empty, like I am in a dark hole and I cannot get out.'

'Oh, Audrey. That sounds awful for you. Do you think if you stayed with your mother a while it would ease?'

'No, I cannot. We are leaving in the morning. We have to get back to Michael's post on the Peninsula.'

'That is a shame. I had hoped we could spend some time together in the coming days.'

Audrey did not smile or laugh or talk with Celia as she had when the young women had first met. She seemed distant and so different. Minutes ticked away where there was nothing but silence that stretched between them. Celia was thankful that other friends from the town were approaching and having small discussions. This was easing the discomfort she was feeling as she perused her friend's demeanour.

Charles and Michael re-entered the hall. 'I think it best if I get my wife and child back to the house. It has been a trying day.'

Michael grasped Audrey's elbow and helped her to her feet. Charles looked on and Celia could not ignore the concern that laced his features.

'Let me walk with you, Audrey.' Celia slid her arm over Audrey's and walked with her down the path. As they approached the carriage, Audrey leaned across and whispered in Celia's ear, 'I am so sad.'

'Stay with your mother a little while,' Celia said as she tried to keep the shock from her voice.

'Come then,' Michael said. 'Charlotte needs to be fed and put down for a sleep.'

Before Celia could continue her conversation with Audrey or press for a solution to her friend's problems, the carriage drew away from the kerb.

'I think I will visit with Audrey this evening,' Celia said to Charles as they set off for home.

'She is far too tired. Michael told me she has been unwell and needs her rest.'

'But I may not see her for some time and she is leaving in the morning,' Celia argued.

'Please, Celia. Audrey will not want company this evening. She is a mother now and needs to tend to her child. Please leave it be.'

'I fear she is unable to tend to her child, Charles,' Celia almost implored.

'She is doing all that is required. Please leave it be, my dear.'

As Celia undressed in her bedroom, the excitement of the day was overshadowed by the concern she held for her friend. Audrey was sick. But unlike a flesh wound that you could plainly see, her sickness lay hidden beneath the surface. Something had stolen her happiness. What was it and when had it happened? While they had exchanged letters over time, there was no way of deciphering Audrey's mood between the lines of script. It would seem the birth of her child had dampened her lively spirit.

Celia tapped at Charles' bedroom door.

'Come in,' came the muffled response.

As she pushed the door open, Charles looked up from the pages of a book and grinned in greeting.

'I do cherish your visits, my love.' He whisked the covers back. 'May I invite you to join me?'

'Why yes, you may.' Celia slipped her dressing gown from her shoulders and stood naked before him. She slid into the bed beside him and snuggled close to him as he placed his arm around her shoulder and held her to his side.

'Did you have nice time today?' he asked as he rubbed his hand up and down her arm.

'I did. Thank you.' Charles silenced her with a kiss but she pulled away from him momentarily. 'Charles?'

'Yes,' he whispered as his hand found her breast.

'Did you consider there is anything medically untoward affecting Audrey?'

'No.' He again attempted to silence her with another kiss.

'Did you not think she looked different?'

'Yes, she did. She is a mother now. A little tired. A little weary. Women undergo changes as their lives progress. You should know this.' He kissed her neck and felt her becoming more relaxed and pliable in his arms.

Chapter 16

Downing the entire contents of a whiskey bottle were the only way Michael could find the numbness he sought. Over time, he had consumed more and more to dull his nerves and escape the interminable pain of the loss of his wife and child. The heartbreak that had ensued after he discovered that his precious Charlotte had been taken from him at the hand of his wife changed his opinion of her immensely.

Michael's initial thought after leaving his post at Point Nepean and taking off on foot had been to rescue his wife from the asylum and snatch his daughter from her parents. After his arrival at Ararat, he had stood behind the massive trunk of the very tree where he had garnered his interlude with Audrey so long ago, and from there he had watched the Price home as he waited for a glimpse of Charlotte. He had observed Mrs Price come and go on occasion, and figured Charlotte was in the care of a nanny, but there was not a sign of his baby girl.

Weeks slipped past, and although Michael often saw the Colonel and Mrs Price, he had still not glimpsed a baby. He was confused. Charlotte was not in the asylum. He had done some sleuthing and there were absolutely no infants in the place. There were certainly children there, but no babies or toddlers. He feared she had been handed over to an orphanage to deflect the shame and questions from the townsfolk directed at the Prices. He was at a loss as to where she could be and it was sending him further into the abyss of grief and anger.

Late one afternoon he was scrounging through his billfold in the pursuit of a few shillings for a bottle of sherry when he caught a folded piece of paper between his fingers. There was a name and address on it. He frowned as he tried to piece together just who it was:

Margaret Smythe
24 Lyons Street, Rye

It was weeks later when the truth struck him like lightning. Margaret Smythe was the wet nurse who had accompanied Audrey and Charlotte to Ararat. He had acquired her name and address from the practitioner assisting him at Point Nepean, where she had introduced herself as Maggie. That is why it took him so long to connect the mystery note with her name scribbled on it.

He wrote to the wet nurse seeking information with regard to what she had experienced upon her arrival to Ararat. There came no response. He sent another letter imploring her to at least respond. In this letter he asked that she please share any information with him with regard to his precious wife and daughter. He begged for her to help put his mind at ease so that he could piece together just what had occurred after she had accompanied Audrey and Charlotte to the district. Whilst he could not afford such a gesture he sealed a few pounds inside the envelope in the hope this would prise open her willingness to share information with him. Weeks passed still and he had given up all hope of hearing from Maggie. It could be possible she no longer lived at the address and good luck to the recipient of the few pounds and the great mystery of a letter.

Upon stumbling to his room one evening he opened the door and found a letter on the floor. He ripped the envelope open and watched the pounds flutter to his feet. He was impressed that the possibility of Maggie no longer living at the address had caused the recipient of his letter to return his money. The words within the letter swam before his drunken haze.

To Michael,
After receiving your first letter I was surprised at the questions written within. I decided to delay my response. However, after your second correspondence I have decided it is only fair to respond. I find this letter most difficult to write and after much reflection I feel it only fair to alleviate your pain, albeit I fear that what I have to say will add to it immensely.

Upon our arrival at Ararat, Audrey was spiralling further beyond what you had witnessed at your home in Point Nepean.

The doctors suggested she be taken into their care but the Prices would not hear of it. It is this scenario that I have lived with that has caused me much angst since.

Audrey committed the most atrocious of acts but I believe she was beyond the brink and any comprehension of the realisation of what she was doing could only be attributed to the work of the devil.

I was given many of Audrey's belongings and paid a handsome sum to ensure my silence on the matter. On reflection I have always felt that it was wrong of me to accept this and once I received your letters I felt within my heart that you, the husband of Audrey and father of Charlotte, are owed the truth.

Michael's eyes were skittering over the words faster and faster to end the pain of the words and the unexpected truth. His heart was smashing against his rib cage. He wanted to stop reading. He really did not want to continue as the contents of the letter were sending him into a darker void. Of all the scenarios he had swimming in his mind this tragedy was one that he had not considered.

To alleviate some of my guilt over this unfortunate situation please find your generosity returned.

I give you my heartfelt condolences on the demise of your beautiful baby girl and I will not enter into any further correspondence on the matter with you or anyone else that was privy to the situation.

God Bless You and Good Luck.

Maggie did not sign her name to the letter and he felt that indicated her wish to lay the story to rest and have no trace of her connected with it. Michael struck a match and held the letter between his fingers. As he watched it burn he felt the pain sear his heart. Dropping the letter before the flames burnt his hand, he stomped on it until it was just a charred cluster on the floor. He pawed at the pile until there was a black blemish on the filthy timber floor of his room.

After the arrival of the letter there was no beginning or end to his drunkenness. He was desperate to sleep but the words that would forever be seared into his mind, revealing the truth of what had befallen his baby girl, chased him night and day.

Each time Michael closed his eyes he would see Audrey's face. The horrific image of the lifeless mask staring at him was making him crazed. He jumped at shadows and would swear he could hear her humming that haunting song, which seemed to drift through the hallways of the asylum. While he stared at the ceiling in the dismal room he rented at the hotel, the tune resonated in the darkness and whirled within his thoughts. He let out a snort of disgust. If he failed to pull his wits together, he would find himself locked away in the very place in which he worked.

The evil that filled Audrey's soul had seeped into his, for he had not imagined that she would haunt him forevermore once he had completed his mission of doing away with her. In the beginning he plotted her death as retribution for his own daughter's demise. Then it became more than that. He wanted to punish the doctors in the asylum for their neglect of the inmates. He had created a travesty of such proportion that common opinion now suggested the safety of inmates could be put at risk by any person who worked and lurked in the asylum.

His hopes that Audrey's death would shock and destroy her parents had also turned out to be futile. While he was sure the Colonel and Mrs Price would feel some guilt for placing her in the asylum and losing her in such a sinister way, he would never know their exact reaction. He could only hope that the loss of their daughter and granddaughter had landed a crushing blow to their souls.

The Colonel and Mrs Price had turned their backs on both he and Audrey since she had been committed. Michael knew that according to everyone in the community, he had been posted to Point Nepean with his family. After Audrey and Charlotte were both respectively disposed of under a shroud of secrecy, he was given orders. His father-in-law had made it perfectly clear that he was to disappear and never return, and also to never speak of the events that had led Audrey to her exile.

So disappear he did, becoming the man who bore the same name but now looked ten years older with his full beard, glasses and longer hair — reincarnated into an orderly who wandered the halls and was as forgettable as soggy boiled potato.

'Fuck the lot of 'em,' he said.

If only his plan had not failed in relation to its most important objective. Constable Bryant had not been summoned to the asylum once Audrey's body had been discovered. 'Why? Why? Why?'

He stalked up the hill. Dusk had almost turned to dark as he walked past the gatehouse.

Once inside the front door of the asylum he signed the logbook as was required at the beginning and end of each shift.

His heart quickened. There was a notation for him to meet with Matron before his shift for the evening.

Michael breathed into his enclosed hand and sniffed. The

stench of whiskey on his breath was detectable. This could be the moment he dreaded. If he were seen as being drunk and about to start a shift he could be dismissed immediately. He knew the meeting with Matron had no bearing on Audrey. If there was any risk that he had come under suspicion it was the doctors who would be calling him to their offices, not Matron.

With his nerves bristling, Michael tapped at Matron's door. While he waited for her to respond he pushed his hands through his hair and cupped his beard in a bid to form it into a semblance of neatness. He pushed his glasses higher up onto the bridge of his nose, realising Matron would be able to see the redness within his eyes but hoping the frame of the glasses would hide the bags beneath.

'Enter,' Matron finally said.

Michael slid inside the open door and closed it gently behind him. As he turned to greet her she physically recoiled. Yes, she had seen his eyes and he needed to convince her there was no need for concern. It was imperative he retain his occupation in this place.

'Are you unwell, Michael?' she asked.

'Yes, yes I am.' He placed his hand over his mouth and coughed. 'I have been.'

'Well, that is not good news. Your eyes do look rather unwell.'

'I am on the mend and should be right in a few days, Matron. Now, what is it you wanted to see me about?'

'I have rostered you to a different ward this evening. Doctor Rushby is of the opinion that staff are becoming complacent within the wards and that making a few changes is the best option.'

'That sounds fine to me!' he answered before his mouth could deliver what he really wanted to say. Doctor Rushby and complacency were the reasons why this vile and disgusting place operated as it currently did.

Matron handed him the file with the ward and cell numbers he was to oversee.

'That will be all,' she said, dismissing him.

'Thank you, Matron.' He let out a slow breath as he closed the door to her office and walked from the administration wing.

He walked down the stairs to the lower men's refractory ward. As the wards were identical in every way on each level, he did not have to familiarise himself with a new area. The same key unlocked each door, and as always there was the acrid smell of urine and faeces that filled his nostrils and made his insides roil.

He had become so used to this that it was easy to concentrate on the line of doors before him and gulp in oxygen through his mouth. He had hidden the flask of whiskey he required to see him through his shift in his duffle bag minutes before he had entered the asylum. This also helped dull the stench and sounds that pummelled his senses. He began checking each door by giving each handle a sharp tug to ensure it was locked. Holding his gas lamp to the peephole allowed him a view of the occupant within the cell.

Without warning, a face appeared hard up against one peephole. A man screamed in hysterics. Michael jumped back in fright. He made a mental note to be wary of the occupant of this cell. To quickly learn each inmate by name and vice he needed to be sharp. Nightshift made it far more difficult to get a handle on the inmates. As this was the refractory ward it was to be expected that the worst inmates were housed here, yet after only three doors he had been yelled at and had to step over bodily fluids escaping beneath the door out to the hallway. His anger surged.

'I'll tie ya all to ya fucking beds if you keep this up,' he yelled down the hall. But his shouting was to no avail; it just made the inmates more determined to screech and scurry. None of the men knew his notorious ways yet. He would soon show them how difficult he could be. Most of them had no idea how to behave, but that would not stop him dishing out punishment if they did not do as he expected.

Once he had passed the final cell with its stench wafting beneath its door, he made his way upstairs to a ward with less troubled inmates. These men were placed in sections according to their conduct. The unruliest were kept together in the same proximity and the easier to control were placed in other areas. This type of compartmentalisation served as a reward. If you were well behaved you had a quiet, calm ward. If your behaviour was notorious you were placed with loud, noisy and difficult inmates much like yourself.

As he passed cell number five, the sound of moaning rose up from the surrounding silence. Michael looked heavenward and gave a loud huff. Was there going to be no peace in this godforsaken ward tonight? He let out a huge breath and prepared to deal with the type of mess that always resulted from a bout of gastroenteritis, which was the illness he normally associated with that godawful sound. Pulling his handkerchief from his pocket he held it over his mouth and nose. The damn sickness seemed to come in waves, literally, and oozed within the walls, floors and the very air held within the asylum. Nights were the most difficult, as gaslight left staff vulnerable to the bodily fluids of inmates, thus exposing them to a greater risk of contracting an illness.

He turned the key in the lock and slowly opened the door. He needed to be sure an inmate was not lying in wait to attack. While the inmates in this area seemed quiet enough, he could not be too careful. Patients were capable of inflicting all manner of damage on one another and staff alike.

Grunts and moans could be heard in the darkness as he swung the lantern forward. The light found the bare back of a patient.

'Are you right there?' he asked, swaying the lantern to and fro to capture the broader picture.

The man did not hear him and continued to groan ever louder in the darkness. Michael opened his mouth to speak again but the words fell away unspoken. The man was heaving in the darkness, his face pointed up at the ceiling. With his teeth firmly clenched, the chorded muscles of his neck bulged. Michael was mesmerised by the rhythmic motion of the man thrusting forward and backward, seemingly in perfect union with the motion of light. Initially, Michael suspected the man was having a seizure but upon closer inspection saw he was not alone. In fact, he had someone in his grasp, and that person was the recipient of the plundering thrusts. Michael had been unaware the cell held two inmates, and found this arrangement instantly disagreeable for reasons that were vivid and plain to see.

The sight repulsed him. Undistracted by the drunken haze swimming at the edges of his mind, he flew into action. He tore his belt from the loop of his pants and thrashed the two men over and over until they were left shuddering at either ends of the mattress with their hands protecting their heads.

'You filthy bastards! Get out of it!' he yelled.

Patrick Riley would normally jump to the defence of Thomas Pitts but was so shocked at being brutalised by the orderly's belt that all he could do was cower. The true nature of his relationship with Thomas had been discovered and the consequences would be dire.

'You fucking dogs,' Michael slurred his words into the darkened room. He had dropped the lantern. Light spilled across the floor and up the walls, sliced time and again by the fierce movement of the orderly's arm as it rose and fell over and over.

'Please do not tell anyone,' Patrick implored. 'We will do anything if you do not tell.'

'Bit late for that, i'n't? Michael spat. He was trying to gather his thoughts as they wallowed in the abyss of the whiskey. It made him almost stagger in front of them. He had no concern they would notice.

The fact they were scared out of their minds proved to him that he possessed the upper hand.

'The constable will be hearing about this. You have just signed your own jail terms.' Michael was of sound enough mind to think of voicing a threat he could use to his advantage. While talking, he noticed the man who had not spoken was cowering so cleverly as to almost disappear at the point where the two walls met, and he could not help but feel more disgust at his weakness. This one was whimpering like a child.

He lifted his hand again and smacked the belt across the man's shoulder. 'You weak pig!' he shouted.

'Stop it,' the other man yelled. 'He cannot speak.'

'Is that right?' Michael asked as he snaked the belt back through his hand before yelling at the man's face, 'Are you dumb, boy?'

The man looked away from him, further revealing that he was defeated.

'He cannot hear you, either,' said the other man who was now beside him, much too close for Michael's safety or comfort.

Michael jumped away. His senses were dulled with the effects of the alcohol, and while deep down he knew that neither man posed a threat to him, he was aware of not allowing them to be too close.

He was still cursing them as he bent down and picked up the lantern. He backed toward the cell door. The flickering light cast from the lantern played across his features, making him look skeletal and dangerous. Patrick waited for him to close the cell door before crossing quickly toward Thomas and grasping him and holding him against his chest.

The two men lay awake all night, shuddering in the darkness in the knowledge they would be sent away from the asylum and forced apart into the belly of J Ward.

The arrival of morning, however, brought Patrick hope that he could perhaps find the angry orderly and implore him to take pity on them. Despite his fatigue, he realised this idea was ludicrous at best. Nobody paid any attention to the ravings of the idiots and imbeciles in here. The staff members would no doubt have lost count of the number of times they had heard a patient's rants about not belonging here, to the point where they certainly would not entertain the protests of any particular individual denying the supposedly unspeakable acts for which he or she had been incarcerated.

Patrick had committed the orderly's features to memory and realised that he had seen him before. He had not seen the man in this ward before but there was something familiar about him. Without a doubt the orderly saw it within his jurisdiction to call the authorities. After all, what he and Thomas had been doing was illegal.

Were this place and this cell not confinement enough? Not to mention the locked gates and ha-ha walls that surrounded the entire perimeter of the asylum? The pair was imprisoned behind the door of a cell each night with no freedom to leave the grounds. From the perspective of all the authorities involved, wouldn't J Ward, where the criminally insane were housed, simply represent the exact same version of how they were currently living? Neither he nor Thomas knew anything different.

He stroked the side of his lover's face, lamenting the years that had swallowed up their youth. The companionship they had shared would be stolen from them once the constable was alerted. In the single mile journey from the front door of the asylum to the large gates of J Ward a life of being locked away from one another loomed. Patrick's heart hammered in his chest at just the thought of this possibility. To recall a time they had not been together was to remember a past so very distant to them now.

The small holes in the shutter that covered the window sifted the morning light into their cell. He looked at Thomas who remained recumbent on the bed. With the morning light penetrating the room he had no doubt as to Thomas' pain as the back of his arm covered his eyes. How he loved him. And in this moment he longed for the faded memories to become a reality and cast him back to a childhood that had long since passed. A childhood that had been plagued with shards of darkness and fear until Thomas had arrived.

As a boy, Patrick had passed the massive castle on the hill whenever he travelled along the road below. But there was one particular day when, for the very first time, he got to see it up close. As the sight of the structure began looming larger in the carriage window, a huge grin spread across his face.

His mother, however, did not smile, and nor did she gaze out as he did from the carriage window. Instead, she looked at Patrick, her lips pursed tightly together. He tried to alleviate the concern that shrouded her features. 'It really does look exactly like a castle. Especially up close.'

His sister had described it as such. 'It stands high up on that hill and there are princes and princesses inside,' she had said. 'Mother, may I come with you when you deliver Patrick?'

'You can't come with us today but you can visit him very soon,' their mother had said but she did not smile in that moment either.

Since the day Patrick had opened his eyes and found himself in his teacher's arms, everyone had looked at him with sullen looks upon their faces. He was told he had fallen from his chair onto the floor while reciting timetables. On Patrick's part, he did not remember anything but darkness. After his mother had been called to collect him, she had taken him to the doctor's office. The doctor had asked him questions and checked his heartbeat. The voice his mother had used to whisper to the doctor was so hushed that he could not hear anything she said.

After the school incident, Patrick's teacher and doctor assumed he had suffered a seizure. Soon, these began to happen more and more often. Patrick would wake during the night to find his mother standing over him praying, with the Bible clutched tightly in her hands.

'Why are you praying, Mum? Have I done something sinful?'

'No, Patrick. Go back to sleep. You are just unwell and I am hoping this will help you get better,' she said.

The boy did not understand why his mother was saying such things. He was frightened at this. He was not feeling unwell.

He would awaken with wet pyjamas only to discover he had wet the bed through the night. It was not every night but it certainly happened enough to find him embarrassed at the incident. One week after his seventh birthday, his mother took him to see the doctor again.

'The convulsions have been happening while he sleeps,' she had said.

'Well in that case, Mrs Riley, we assume he has been over-taken by the devil and will need some treatment,' the doctor suggested as he held a stethoscope to Patrick's chest. 'I think a stay in hospital could help.'

Patrick was frightened by the thought of something evil taking over his body. Had he committed a sin to cause such a thing to happen to him? In the doctor's office, he began to sob. 'I do not want to be away from my family,' he said aloud.

'It will only be for a short while so the doctors can help you get better,' his mother said as she grasped both his hands and crouched in front of him.

And now she did exactly the same thing as they stood on

the top step of the entrance and waited for the castle's large front door to open. She smoothed his jacket and licked her handkerchief before wiping round his mouth. 'Everything is going to be just fine,' she said again. Somehow, Patrick began to get the feeling she was trying to reassure herself more than she was trying to reassure him.

The carriage waited as Patrick's mother gripped her son's shoulder, holding him in place. Matron opened the door and led them to her office. It was cold. He sat beside his mother as Matron wrote a lot of things on notepaper. Patrick's mother kissed his forehead and left. He was marched upstairs to the doctor's office and examined thoroughly — from the skin between his toes to the inside of his ears.

'You realise you have the devil's curse on you, boy?' the doctor said.

Patrick looked at him and nodded.

'The devil has inflicted this disease on you, young man, and I am afraid to say that here is where you will stay until we see some improvement, if we see any at all, that is.'

Matron had said the doctor's name was Doctor Rushby, and Patrick never forgot it because he was afraid of the man from the very first instant he saw him. He did not speak at all that day and it was not until night closed in and the bolt on the cell door thudded against the timber that a sound was to pass his lips. It was a sob.

As his fatigue grew and monsters wailed and yelled in the cells around his, he curled into a small ball and imagined he was in his own bed, safe, with his mother and sisters only a few feet away. He awoke drenched in urine. Clutching for his nightshirt, which sat on top of a small stool in the corner of his room, Patrick accidentally pulled the stool over and the bucket beneath it rolled across the floor. Urine spilt onto his mattress and he felt ill knowing it was not his, as it became obvious the previous inmate had left a parting gift.

The draught billowing beneath the door raced along the stone floor gathering as much cold as it could muster before crawling along his body. He would wake each morning with his eyes almost swollen shut from crying in his sleep. Scared, alone and freezing cold, he had only a thin blanket and a dismal straw mattress beneath the decreasing weight of his shuddering body. He dreamed his mother would hear his tears and feel his pain in the darkness, knowing that he needed her to come fetch him.

Months slithered by and Patrick soon became accustomed to the tumultuous seizures that regularly wracked his mind and body. He did not know they had occurred, only that as he regained consciousness he would be tired and usually slumped on the floor. The doctors hardly gave him any attention and they had no treatment to offer for his condition. As the days streamed past, Patrick gave up any hope of seeing his mother or sisters again.

After a month of being left helpless and alone, Patrick began working in the vegetable garden and was eventually given the job of carting the produce to the storage sheds ready for sale in town. Old Jim Sneddon was the caretaker and had been in the place for years and years. Old Jim had a good amount of control over everyone in the vegetable garden and if ever a fight broke out he would fly right in and break it apart with his massive hands. Patrick was in awe of Old Jim and his gnarled knuckles, which protruded from his hands at such odd angles it was hard to believe his fingers worked so well. He ploughed and dug and pushed a wheelbarrow. Patrick often stared at Old Jim's fingers as he worked. He wondered how they had become so odd in shape.

Patrick first saw Thomas on a Wednesday. The lunchtime bell had tolled and he ran through the hall to the dining room, where Thomas was sitting at a table all alone.

'Hello,' Patrick said as passed him but there was no response.

Patrick watched the new boy for a few days. He spoke to nobody and disappeared from the dining room only to sit outside his cell down the hall. That was all he would do every day — simply sit on the floor outside his cell.

After a week had passed, Patrick walked by Thomas and again said hello. Again, Thomas did not answer or even look at Patrick. But Patrick did not give up. Each day he would pass Thomas and call out a greeting.

Soon it became a game, and Patrick would make a funny face as he passed by. Thomas did not react to the noises but began to smile at the sight of Patrick's tongue poking out or his eyelids pulled up with his eyeballs pointed to the sky so the whites of his eyes were the only things exposed.

Patrick stopped in the hall one morning. 'Would you like to come out to the vegetable garden today?' he asked.

Thomas cast his eyes toward Patrick and watched him speak but he did not respond. He stared at Patrick with a blank look upon his face.

'Do you want to come?' Patrick asked and pointed his finger towards the end of the hall. Thomas frowned at him as though he did not understand any of his words.

'Are you an imbecile?' Patrick asked as Thomas continued to frown at him.

'He is mute,' a nurse said as she walked past.

Patrick shrugged. 'I do not understand.'

'He cannot hear you and he cannot speak. He is a deaf mute,' she said. 'Be on your way, then.' The nurse pointed her finger toward the end of the hall. 'You have work to do.'

All day in the vegetable garden Patrick considered how he could communicate with the deaf mute. Was there a way he could encourage him to venture out to the vegetable garden? It would be far better than sitting inside all day. He placed an apple in his pocket and kept it safe until the next morning when, hiding behind the closest corner, he waited for Thomas to take his place in the hall. Once Thomas was there, Patrick rolled the apple toward him. Thomas could not see Patrick and frowned as the apple hit him on the knee. He picked it up and stared at it for the longest time before placing it in his mouth and taking a huge bite. Patrick walked past him and pretended not to notice anything untoward.

The following morning Patrick rolled six grapes down the hall one by one. Some found their target, others rolled to the walls. He watched Thomas laugh to himself as he crawled along, gathering every single one and shoving them into his mouth until his cheeks bulged. Children were not allowed to work in the vineyard and if they were found among the vines they were punished. Patrick had risked being caught gathering grapes for his escapade, but he felt it was worth the risk to see grape juice dripping down the silent boy's chin as he walked past him to reach the door that led outside, pretending not to notice.

Each day Patrick chose a different fruit to tumble into the path of the deaf mute. After he had exhausted the fruits that were available he turned his attention to the vegetables on offer. The funniest one was the carrot that rolled and skittered across the hall. Thomas looked at it with disappointment but nonetheless picked it up, wiped it across his trouser leg and took a bite from it. Patrick could hear him crunching on it as he walked by.

By the time Patrick had utilised every single fruit and vegetable the gardens had to offer, he walked by Thomas with nothing. Thomas looked at Patrick and frowned. Patrick placed his hand out and Thomas grasped it. Patrick pulled him to his feet and the boys walked out to the vegetable garden together. From that time forth they worked and played together every day, and learnt to communicate in their very own unique way.

Their families never came to take them home. They did not visit. The boys realised that they had one another and that was the way it would be from now on.

Patrick never allowed his thoughts to dwell on the lies his mother had told him. She had said everything would be all right. She had told him that the doctors would look after him and that once he was better she would come to fetch him. The fact that he was not better was a side issue. She had not seen him since delivering him to the asylum. That broke his heart more then anything.

The vegetable garden and the work were never ending, but the friends would manage to escape and create havoc with their well-devised games of mischief.

'Patrick! Thomas!' Doctor Rushby could be heard yelling

as the boys both dodged out of sight, laughing so hard their sides hurt.

Patrick had heard Doctor Rushby well enough and Thomas moved with Patrick to hide as though they were one and the same person. Patrick would laugh in spite of the hurtful mumblings of Doctor Rushby, who often stated that he had better things to do than chase young children who were beyond help.

Patrick became a voice for Thomas. He was the brain behind their schemes. Even though Thomas was considered a mute and an imbecile by the authorities, the boys knew better. The authorities were the stupid ones. Just to wile the days away the boys would play tricks on the doctors to prove just how idiotic they were. Patrick would tell tales of fairies he had witnessed in the vegetable garden while the doctors nodded at him with their lips turned up in knowing smiles. Patrick found it incredible that they were convinced he was mad when delivering these whimsical stories.

Patrick sometimes thought of his younger sister, who believed that fairies and goblins did in fact exist, and he knew she was neither crazy nor sick. He also knew he would never see her again and while he did desire life beyond the walls of Ararat Lunatic Asylum, he could not imagine a life away from Thomas.

The day the boys pulled up three rows of carrots and reburied them with their roots sticking up out of the ground cost them time apart. After performing the mischief, the boys had watched from a distance and giggled like the two crazed children they had been labelled as. Inmates had looked perplexed and screamed for the orderlies to correct the confusion. It had been such fun until Doctor Rushby had grabbed each of them by an ear and marched them straight into solitary confinement cells.

Each cell was a foot wide and six feet in length. The walls closed in on either side of Patrick as he slept, and the cell was only long enough for him to take eight steps from the narrow door to the end wall.

Being separated from one another was difficult and the boys would never know exactly how long they were in the cells. With no window to tell daytime and nightfall it was difficult, but Patrick had counted at least thirteen big sleeps, which he figured had occurred at night time. By the time they were released Thomas' cell had been given to a new inmate. The asylum was so crowded that the friends were placed together until another arrangement for a cell could be arranged.

The first night the boys shared that cell, they doubled their blankets and crawled beneath them. Enjoying stretching out for the first time since their upside-down carrot trick, they fell asleep together, Side by side, with their bodies in close contact, they fell asleep easily. A separate cell for Thomas was never discussed so they quietly continued sharing a cell as days turned to months and then years.

Time spun away and suddenly they were young men. The frightened young boys who had entered the asylum were strong and confident in their surrounds. The brotherhood they shared ran deep, rendering them inseparable, and as the fun of childhood games ceased, something entirely different seeped into its place.

The night Thomas was sick and trembling from influenza everything changed. Patrick lay awake all night wiping his brow. As morning broke, along with his fever, the pair found themselves slumped together and exhausted. First, there was a small kiss on the forehead from Thomas as his eyes slowly closed in thanks, expressing the unspoken love they had been nurturing. Thomas then placed his hand on Patrick's cheek and the two men stared at one another for the longest time before landing a kiss on one another's lips. The floodgates opened and the closeness they shared became a passionate exchange of souls that would be both their liberation and their demise.

Chapter 17

'Might be some leftover puddin' if we're lucky, Wally.' Wally Stuckey nodded his head at the head gardener. He had no name for him but he knew his face and was happy enough to follow his orders.

'Is the only time we get puddin', is at Chris'mas time,' the man continued.

Wally clutched the shovel and leaned on it and stared at him. The bell tolled. He thought of church. The bell would toll many times each day. Was it heralding a never-ending series of church services? Wally did not know.

Amid the acres of land that made up the grounds, the vineyard was his favourite place. Row upon row of exactly the same vine allowed him to be at ease, not like in the vegetable garden, where he felt lost and confused.

Wally would toil between the vines and listen to the tolls of the bell ring out across the grounds of the asylum. It was said you could hear the sound in town, which was miles below. Each time it tolled, the staff and workers among the vines reacted. Sometimes they would down tools or move indoors. He would follow along and most times there was a meal in the dining room at the end of the trail. After nightfall he would follow the orderly to his cell and the doors would slam in unison along the hallways as everyone was put to bed.

Some days he was confused and lost track of the tolling of the bell, while on others he could easily count each toll. Those days he would twist his belt round a few inches at a time with every second toll landing on a loop of his trousers. By the time the buckle lay on his right hip it was time for lunch and by the time it reached his left hip he knew that meant the end of a day's work and dinner. Today he did not know how his belt buckle had landed around the back of his trousers.

'Tools down, Wally,' the head gardener said. 'Time for lunch.'

Wally nodded at him.

He followed the others to the dining hall and took a seat. Picking up his fork, he stared down at hands that looked foreign to him. The young man's hands he had once possessed were now gnarled with arthritis. It confused him. The look of the thick knuckles and brittle nails left his thoughts tangled. His gaze moved to the plate in front of him. A pile of shrivelled peas and dried carrots sat to one side and half the plate was covered in potatoes that were grey in colour. A trickle of gravy ran off to one side of the less than appetising fare.

Suddenly, two men began to holler at one another and a fight broke out. Wally stared at them as food flew in all directions and everyone in their immediate surrounds held their plates. The loud slap of skin as fists landed their mark made him flinch. There was no other sound quite like it. He closed his eyes to drown it out but his memories of the mean streets of Ballarat returned.

'You copped a beatin' tonight, boy!' his mate hollered at him. 'An' now we ain't got a penny.'

'I know, but we always have tomorrow to make it up,' he yelled back over the crowd.

Fighting was all he knew. It was his only means of scraping by after the mines had dried up.

Wally had learnt at an early age to survive the streets of Portsmouth in England by running and lying. With no formal education, he had managed to survive by stealing as a youngster, then fighting to keep his place at the top of the chain of command. There were so many families in the same situation as he and his mother, that it became a hierarchy of strong and weak in a cascading pecking order. His mother was a drunkard who entertained the men from the port and made what she could for booze. Wally did not know his father and doubted whether his mother knew who the man was either. He felt he was defined by struggling to defend his honour after being called a bastard from the age of eight, and that he was destined to become a violent, thieving thug who clawed and carved his way through the world every day, just to survive.

One of the sailors who regularly visited his mother would throw Wally a penny to fetch his duffel from the port and drag it up to the house. The following morning, the boy would scurry back to return the duffel to the docks in the hope he would be thrown another penny for his efforts. On one such morning, the old sailor pushed him through the gate that kept the pier off limits to anyone not authorised. The boy's eyes widened as he took in the huge mast that loomed high over his head.

'Up you come,' the old sailor beckoned.

Wally followed the man up the gangway and walked along the decks. For the first time in his life he experienced the pull of something he could not understand. Being on the ship made his body feel alive and his mind begin to fill with dreams. When he found himself back outside the gate as the ship sailed away, he dared not tear his gaze from the sails until the tip of the mast had disappeared below the horizon.

After that day, fully realising his life was in the shithouse, he spent countless hours dreaming of a job on the docks. He was so tired of the life he was caught in and often could not find a glimmer of anything better. Time marched on and his youth ebbed away, wasted, as he ran from the law day after day, living lies and dishing violence.

Returning home in the early hours he found his mother sitting at the kitchen table with an almost empty bottle between herself and yet another sailor.

'Hey boy. You been at the dock?' the stranger slurred.

Wally grunted at the man as he walked past him to his room.

'Heard them's lookin' for workers down there.'

'Wha's that you say?' Wally retraced his steps back to face the man.

'Government's commissionin' war ships. Need workers, they do.'

Wally lay awake all night and at the first sign of daylight he got up in his clothes and ran along the rutted streets to the dock. His heart beat heavy in his chest as he was met with the sight of hundreds of men ahead of him. Their age and experience far outweighed his and for the first time in his life he was afraid. He was terrified that he had not and would never amount to anything, and that fear beat a steady rhythm in his ears.

Leaning on the timber pickets and looking at the slipway where the ribs of a hull were beginning to rise, Wally made a promise to himself that he would be one of the men chosen to build a ship on the other side of the fence. If they could line up for the work, then so could he. Desperation did strange things to men. He decided that the tenacity he had lived with until now on the streets of this godforsaken place would give him the strength he needed to stand here until he was given a job, and that if doing that was what it took to forge a better life, he would do it.

Day after day, he arrived in the darkness just before the dawn and lined up until darkness fell again. So as not to lose track of the days, he stood in the same place each time and etched a line on a picket for every day that he was there. Thirty-six had passed and he was at war with himself. He had come too far to give up but with each day that passed there was no success and he began wondering if he should give up.

One morning, the foreman approached the group and chose the same crew he had chosen every day for the past month. But then something different happened. The man yelled across the heads of the men gathered outside the fence, 'Need six extra today!'

A fight broke out as men rushed and shoved at one another. For the first time in his entire life, Wally did something that surprised even himself. He gripped the lapels of one man and pushed him off another. He stood between two others and pushed them apart yelling, 'This is not the way.'

As the group dispersed the foreman yelled, 'You!'

Wally was startled and stood like a fool before realising the foreman's finger was squarely pointed at him. Accustomed as he was to being ignored, Wally was stunned. The foreman then yelled, 'Last chance!'

Wally shook himself from his reverie and marched toward the open gate. He could neither describe the exultation nor recognise the feeling that responsibility brought out in him. Being given a chance to prove himself was a first. He could only liken it to the old sailor and the duffel bag in his charge. It would earn him an honest wage for his work and that made him feel worthwhile.

Although he was starving, Wally worked his guts out the whole day to prove his strength. Desperation did things to a man, it made him grab for anything he could to survive. At the end of that day's work he had been handed a shilling. He handed it back to the foreman. 'Can I trade it for a meal?'

The foreman looked at him for a moment and not believing the question, as one like that had obviously never been posed to him before, he sneered. 'There's no rum in the officer's mess.'

'I know that. I just want a warm meal and a place to eat in peace.'

It was the first time Wally had completed a decent day's work, and he felt the full worth of the hours wash over him when he swallowed the mutton and boiled potatoes and swiped at his plate with the stale bread and gulped down the ginger punch.

The foreman seated himself well enough away not to talk to him but near enough to keep an eye on him as he downed his own plate of dinner.

Afterwards, he passed behind Wally and said, 'See you tomorrow at the gates, then.'

That was the beginning of a life of exhaustion from hours of hammering and becoming a leading hand on the docks. But Wally would not trade the fatigue he endured for any other feeling. The immense size and sheer weight of the war ships he shaped gave him a sense of pride.

When the rush for gold beckoned in Australia, he answered. Work in the yards was drying up and he could afford the passage so he set out across the Atlantic. Ballarat was mean and the work gruelling. He watched men die in mine collapses. He looked on in awe at the others that were lucky enough to strike it rich only to piss it away on booze and women. It would seem that secondary business was the reaper of the spoils the mines turned out. Shop owners, madams and publicans had the good fortune of having set up in the right town at the right time.

Wally struggled to make a quid on gold but soon found his learned craft of violence afforded him the means to pound his way to a meal and liquor. His face quite often copped a beating and he had lost count of the times he had heard his nose crack when a fist connected with his face. Stews and ale were all he could afford to ingest thanks to the state of his wallet and the broken teeth he possessed. Seldom did he count a wad of notes and most times there was barely a penny.

Wally came to with an orderly holding him down in his seat. 'You all right, Wally?' the man said in a calm tone.

Wally craned his neck to see who had hold of him and why. He was confused.

'I think the excitement rattled ya, mate.'

Wally shrugged. He had no idea what excitement the orderly was talking about. He felt the man's hands fall away as he looked down at his plate, noting the shrivelled peas, dried carrots and grey potatoes. He forked some peas into his mouth and chewed them in a slow, rhythmic motion more attuned to a cow chewing its cud.

The doctors had told him his brain was shrivelling inside his head. What the hell did they know? Some days he remembered things and others he did not know his own name. He was an old man. His body had aged and along with it his mind. What concerned him more than anything were the blackouts.

In the aftermath of these moments someone was usually hurt, or worse, bleeding. Sometimes it was an orderly; other times it was an inmate. On all accounts people got hurt at his hands. He was only made aware of the damage he inflicted when friends told him about the violence he had unleashed. Fist fights and too much boozing in his younger years had ruined his brain, and the hazes that came over him now were beyond his control.

He couldn't relay anything or apologise because some days his tongue did not work and would sit like a lump of coal in his mouth. He communicated with the boy who could not speak. They had their own signs and signals between them and if they ran into any trouble the boy's friend would step in. The two young men had pulled him from trouble on more than one occasion and he himself had stayed with the one that had seizures as they wracked his poor body.

After downing the last mouthful of bread with a big swig of cold tea he followed the crowd, ending up back out in the vineyard. The afternoon sun shone solid on his face as he sweated beneath its heat.

He was tossing rotten grapes onto the soil when he saw Thomas. Yep. That was his name. Just as he raised his hand to wave a greeting, he noticed the young lad look beyond him to an orderly on the approach.

The staff member was shaking his head as Thomas grasped his hands together in silent prayer pleading with the man. But the man looked upon him with contempt and shook his head at Thomas, who had now fallen to his knees in a sign of defeat.

Thomas' friend approached the scene and began a heated discussion with the staff member, who then retreated to the shed. He returned with a thin garden stake and picked up pace as he walked briskly back towards the two men. Thomas' friend was helping him to his feet. It was plain to note Thomas was upset and struggling to gain his footing. His friend was consoling him when the first whip of the stake landed across his back. Both men began to cower together as they were struck over and over by the staff member, who was yelling at them.

He could hear the yelling. He shoved his hands over his ears to block out the screams beginning to rise from the men receiving the whipping. He could not tear his eyes from the huge swipes of the thin timber cane through the air that found their mark across Thomas and the other man's flesh. He dropped his hands from his ears as the bell tolled in the distance. He pulled his belt around the waist of his trousers. The vineyard fell away and the sounds of his youth surrounded him.

He could hear his mother's voice, 'Don't hurt me. Don't hurt me.'

'You fucking whore!' a garbled voice boomed, ripping him from sleep. He jumped from his bed within a second.

His mother cowered in the corner. The man raised his hand and slapped her then clenched his fist.

Young Wally grabbed the first thing to hand and flung it with overarm force. The broomstick took some moments to strike the man due to its length. The impact did not do much more than make the man angry, though, and as he now used it to whack Wally over, over and over until he eventually passed out. When he came to he could hardly move for the pain that had been inflicted on his body. On close inspection, Wally could see the man was lying atop his mother in her bed.

For years Wally had tried to protect her, sometimes winning, other times losing. Each time there was one thing to be guaranteed. Regardless of the outcome, she would still continue her whoring ways. It was all she knew. He could not always protect her but the instinct to fly at the perpetrator never waned.

The brightness of the day hit him as he opened his eyes. He looked at the shovel in his hand. There was a garden stake lying on the ground to his right. He focussed on it. What was that doing there? He felt the cool breeze wash across his skin. Wiping his arm across his face, he looked down at his sleeve. The cotton was zigzagged with a smear of fresh blood. Wally looked down to see hundreds of drops spattered down the front of his shirt and trousers. The tip of the shovel dripped blood onto the soil. Orderlies were running towards him. Yelling, screaming. He dropped the shovel and put his hands over his ears. In the silence that filled his head, he looked around him to see everyone staring at him then down to his feet.

Wally saw Thomas and the other man, his friend. He could not recall his name. They were staring at him in astonishment. He then followed everyone's gaze to his feet and saw the shovel perched on the back of the blade. He stared at it as though it were a foreign object. He shrugged his shoulders as he noted for the first time the heap that lay to the left of him.

With its cleaved skull, the body twitched and shuddered for a few moments as the surrounding sound and movement rose to a pitch. Some of the inmates were moving ever closer to take a look and others were wailing at the grisly sight.

The throng of inmates was soon met by a gathering of staff, who began moving everyone away.

An orderly, having witnessed the scene from afar, raced inside the asylum and up the stairs to the doctors' offices. He pounded the door to Doctor Lawler's office and was just about to resume another round of thumping on it as it opened abruptly.

'God man, what is going on? I thought your fist was going to come through the timber,' Charles said.

The orderly was bent over with his hands placed squarely on his thighs as he tried to draw breath. He cast his hand toward the wall. 'Outside,' he said between breaths. 'Orderly dead.'

Charles closed the door to his office and raced past the exhausted messenger. As he skittered down the staircase he yelled, 'Where?'

'Vineyard,' was all he heard as he picked up his pace and raced out into the sunlight.

He arrived at the vineyard and saw the aftermath of the

macabre scene as he drew nearer. 'Who did this?' he yelled on approach.

An orderly who was the first to have happened upon the scene, pointed at Wally looking confused as he stared down at the corpse.

'Take him to my office,' Charles shouted to the closest orderly. 'Wait with him.'

'Yes, sir,' the orderly said as he grabbed Wally's arm and turned toward the main building.

Charles bent down to look at the lifeless body with brain matter and skull exposed. Blood pooled at his feet, looking like oil as it began soaking into the soil.

'Orderly!' Charles yelled.

'Yes, sir?' at least three orderlies said in unison.

'Remove this mess to the morgue.'

One of the orderlies was in the wrong place at that moment and found himself at the unwanted end of the corpse. He felt his throat begin to constrict as he bent and attempted to grasp the victim under the arms and lift him onto the stretcher that had just been delivered. His breakfast began to make its way up to the outside air as the floppy V- shaped human head moved atop the neck without any control.

'Right there, mate?' another orderly quipped. Smirking, this man had positioned himself at the feet of the corpse.

'Just dandy,' the orderly answered, turning his head to one side before taking a deep breath of air and looking away to give himself a break from the view.

He looked straight ahead as they transported the stretcher and the victim to the morgue a few hundred yards away. He shuddered when he thought of the life of a fellow colleague having just been taken. It could have been any one of them. Leaving the stretcher inside the small receiving room, he stepped out of the tiny space with fervour.

As he walked back to the yard, the merrily dancing vines weighed down with ripe aubergine coloured grapes caught his eye. He stopped where his colleague had fallen. A pair of broken glasses spattered with blood sat a short distance from the stained ground. His heart raced and his legs could barely hold him upright as he remained steadfast and tried to quash his urge to run to the gates of this damned place. If it were easier to find work he would relish the opportunity to leave this very minute.

'You!' Doctor Lawler yelled.

The orderly was shaken from his thoughts. He did not answer but looked at Doctor Lawler with a questioning gaze.

'Did you see what happened here?'

'Yes, yes I did,' he said quietly.

'Make your way to my office. I will join you shortly,' Charles ordered before entering the morgue and staring down at the table. 'What a mess we have here.'

Charles studied the corpse before turning his attention to the ceiling. It sounded like a box of tacks had been thrown on the roof as rain began to create an incessant tune above. Charles walked from the morgue, locking the door behind him before walking out into the drizzle. He stepped past the vineyard and looked down at the blood being watered into the soil. He gathered the broken glasses in his handkerchief, wrapped them securely and clutched them in his hand. Soon there would be no trace of anything that had unfolded today.

The sky looked clear ahead so the shower would be short. He

raced toward the veranda that ran to the main building. Passing the laundry, he noted how quiet it was. The inmates would have been returned to their cells as word spread with regard to the situation in the yard. All was silent with the exception of the beating of raindrops in and around the grounds. He looked at the door that stood ajar leading into the laundry. He hated to admit that he wished to see Celia in that moment. He had loved watching her rush through the doorway to greet him as he walked to and fro between the main wings. He would never again see her excited as she delivered news about the inmates. He had forbidden her from visiting with the women forevermore, an order that would certainly prevent any chance of him seeing her appear. Today was a replica of that day when he had finally, or so he thought, put an end to her meddling.

Charles shook the thermometer with enthusiasm in an attempt to drive the reading down. It was futile. Nonetheless, he placed it in the old woman's mouth and held his stethoscope to her chest. 'It is no surprise your heart is galloping,' he said as he removed the stethoscope's tips from his ears and draped the device back over the back of his neck.

He looked around the room and wiped his arm across his brow. Pulling the thermometer from the patient's mouth, he looked down at the length of tiny lines and numbers and let out a breath. 'I would normally take action by administering some medicinal relief but I believe the climate is playing havoc on us all.' He patted the inmate's arm.

'Nurse,' he called.

A nurse opened the door. 'Yes, doctor,' she said in a harried voice.

'Can we get some windows open in here?' he said in frustration.

'Yes. Right away, doctor.' She rushed to the window and pulled the lever to release the lock before pushing the sash upward.

The temperature in the room remained the same as the heat pushed down on them like a lead apron. No breeze flowed in and around the ward, as was the usual case.

'I will wait for this heat to dissipate and reassess your symptoms then.'

The old lady waved him away with a smile.

After Charles cleared the veranda he stopped to look across to the vineyard. The ground shimmered in the distance and it was no surprise there were no inmates in or among the vines. Charles placed his arm up to wipe his brow, pushing his hat up in the process. He walked toward the main building and felt immediate relief as he stepped inside. The interior of the asylum gave welcome respite. For three days the heat had stretched out, with the temperature hovering at just over 100 degrees Fahrenheit; even so, the interior remained as cool as marble.

The relief the interior offered was short lived, however, as the hairs on Charles' exposed arms lifted. The cold wrapped around everyone and everything within the buildings, and while it offered protection from the elements, it made the winter months pure torture. On clear nights, a thin layer of ice would cling to the inner walls of the cells.

As Charles ascended the stairs to his office, he heard thunder in the distance and gazed out the window to see huge storm clouds spreading across the horizon.

'Thank goodness,' he whispered as he welcomed the cool change the thunderstorm promised.

There was an abrupt knock on his office door. 'Yes?' he called.

An orderly opened the door and leaned inside. 'I have an inmate with a nasty burn, Doctor.'

'Bring him in, then,' Charles said.

The orderly grappled with the inmate, who obviously did not want the attention. 'Get in here,' he said as he dragged the man over the threshold.

'Sit down!' Charles ordered the inmate, who sat down hard on the chair opposite Charles' desk. The man's hand was wrapped in a wad of wet cotton.

'He burnt his arm on the furnace in the pump house.'

Charles frowned. 'Working in the pump house today would be like working within the bounds of hell.' Charles could think of no worse working conditions, and would bet this man had burnt his arm on purpose to escape his work for the remainder of the day. He would not blame him if that were the case.

The man was agitated and squirmed in the chair, while the orderly held his shoulder in a firm grip.

Charles walked over to his medicine cabinet and discovered an empty tin of salve. He opened the door to his office and walked across the landing. He looked over the banister and called for a nurse. A crash of thunder sounded in the distance, drowning out his voice. The inmates would be worked into a frenzy as the storm approached. The nurses and orderlies would be busy attempting to maintain some semblance of peace.

Nobody came rushing to the base of the staircase, as was usually the case. Charles huffed and returned to his office.

'Wait here with the inmate. I will fetch some salve and dressings from the hospital cottage.'

Charles stepped from the building and felt the breeze cooling his skin beneath his clothing. He smelled rain on the way and felt the respite would be welcomed.

The windows of the hospital cottage were thrown open to capture the breeze as it raced across the countryside. He unlocked the storeroom and picked up two tins of salve and two bandages.

As he walked back toward the main building and rain began to fall he yelled out to two inmates who were loitering beneath the airing courts. 'Best you both get back inside!' They looked at him and waved. Mud spattered up onto his trouser legs as big fat raindrops tumbled down, hitting the ground and causing them to splash inches into the air.

Charles quickened his step and could see figures coming out of the laundry room through the curtain of rain. He was certain they would run to the door leading inside the main building or seek the cover of the verandas that skirted the perimeter toward the building. But the figures did not run for cover; instead, they flung their arms out wide and pointed their faces to the sky and danced in circles as the rain plummeted down on them. He strained his eyes to confirm what he was witnessing, before shaking his head in disappointment. These women could not be saved. They were beyond reproach. 'For goodness sake,' he said between gritted teeth when a particular person caught his attention.

He stalked toward the group, yelling as he neared, '... take you inside this instant!'

The women were raising such a ruckus that they did not hear him at first. His voice boomed louder and louder until the squeals and shouts dissipated and the inmates stood still. Their dresses and hair were soaked through. They looked a dismal lot. 'All of you, make your way back to the main building and confine yourselves to your cells! Now!' he yelled. Agnes and Lillian turned toward the laundry room.

'Your cells!' Charles yelled as the women quickly turned tail toward the main building. 'You!' He pointed his finger toward one particular woman he had in his sights. 'You can make your way to my office.'

Celia picked up her skirts and huffed as she passed her husband. 'Killjoy,' she hissed under her breath as she passed his back.

He walked behind her as she raced beyond the door and up the stairs to his office. Her dress clung to her hips as they sashayed with haste and her feet stomped on the treads in anger.

Charles pushed Celia's shoulder and lowered her into the chair outside his office door. 'Wait here,' he barked.

He closed his office door. Five minutes passed before an orderly departed with a dishevelled inmate looking highly agitated.

'Celia!' Charles yelled from the confines of his office, and then, as she came to stand in the doorway, he shouted, 'Shut the door!'

She pushed it closed with her backside and placed her hands on her hips.

'Do not look to me as though I am the one who is misbehaving, my dear,' he said with a menacing smile.

'You had no right to send them to their cells,' she said.

'I did,' he said, before adding, 'and it was all I could do to stop myself from picking you up and throwing you over my shoulder and depositing you on the outer perimeter of the place.'

'I do not see any harm in what we were doing.'

'Is that right?' he said quietly.

'And there was no cause for you to yell at us,' she said indignantly.

'This is a statement delivered from the only one among these fallen women expected to have the capacity to observe the absurdity of the situation.' Charles was standing with both his hands flat on his desk. 'You are the only one among them who is not crazed and unhinged and yet you act as though you are. Just what is it you are trying to prove? Is it a ploy to get your audience's attention or are you falling in with them?'

'I was doing nothing to disprove your theories, surely? Is there a medical phenomenon to prove insanity, should one be caught dancing in the rain?' Celia said with sarcasm.

'It is not normal behaviour.'

'Says you,' she spat.

'It is time you realised I am in charge of the care of every inmate in here and I have granted you access to them. It does not permit you to begin …' and now he yelled the final three words '… behaving like them!'

'How do you define an act as being insane or sane, Charles?' Celia demanded.

'There are clear-cut definitions of what is considered

normal.' Charles shook his head and held his hand up. 'I do not know why I am indulging you with an explanation. It is time I put a stop to this once, and for all time.'

'Charles, you are not serious. There are no defining factors to which we need adhere. The situation is quite simple. It was stifling hot and then the rain came and it was so enticing that we could not help but rejoice in its spirit.'

'You are beginning to sound like those hysterical lot.'

'Charles. I … '

'No more.' He slammed his hand down on the desk.

'But Charles … '

'No! No more. You are never to set foot in the asylum again!'

Celia crossed her arms over her chest.

'Or the grounds.' He pointed his finger at her. 'Or the laundry room, just to be clear.'

Celia looked up at the ceiling. 'This is ridiculous,' she whispered.

'Do not think for a moment that if you get all haughty over my decision I will relent,' Charles said, moving so closely to Celia that he was now looking down at the top of her head.

'You will not intimidate me,' she said as she lifted her chin and looked up.

His eyes wandered down her face to her neck and her torso. He inched closer and felt the heat emanate between them.

'Intimidate you?' he whispered. 'Never,' he said with sarcasm.

He lifted his hand to graze her nipple, which was jutting out beneath the wet fabric of her bodice.

She stilled his hand. 'I have made this part of my life. Just as I have made you the very largest part of my life.'

Charles moved his hand to her shoulder and ran it down the outside of her arm. 'You are going to catch cold if you stay in this wet rag,' he said.

Celia closed her eyes as he disarmed her senses and forced her anger to dissipate. 'They have told me things they will tell no one else,' Celia gasped between breaths.

His hands began to unbutton her bodice and within moments the wet dress fell to the floor with a thud. Her underskirt and chamois followed, pooling at her feet as he lifted her and deposited her on his desk.

Celia drew in a sharp breath. 'I beg you to please let me continue visiting the laundry room.'

He ignored her pleas and continued to kiss her neck and her exposed shoulder. 'So sweet.' Tracing a line down her neck he found the rise of her breast and licked the skin until he had her nipple between his lips.

'Charles.' She chanted his name over and over until finally she fell silent as he made love to her. This woman would be his nemesis and his undoing. The only way he could silence her was to make love to her. Then, once he had made love to her, he would surrender to her demands. It was a scenario he found himself constantly replaying with her. This time he would not give in. He just had to put an end to her visits.

If he continued to bed her she would be with child soon, and that would put a halt to her infiltration of the laundry room. It was so difficult to keep an eye on her whereabouts. Lately, she had been entering through the rear entrance, within very few feet of the superintendent's lodge before making her way to the laundry room, usually via the hospital cottage. He rarely knew when she had been and gone unless he happened upon her. The latest crazed scene in the rain robbed him of the final vestiges of his patience.

Chapter 18

Charles rubbed his eyes. 'Could you please tell me why you were being beaten by the orderly?'

Patrick shrugged. 'Do orderlies need a reason?' he answered with chagrin.

'I would hope they have reason, otherwise there is no point to the violence, is there?' Charles said with sarcasm.

Patrick stared at him and narrowed his eyes.

Charles persisted with his line of questioning. 'You would have me believe that there was no motive behind the whipping Thomas and yourself were enduring?'

Patrick did not break eye contact with Charles. 'No sir, no idea.'

'Well, it would seem that Wally Stuckey will be transferred to J Ward for his actions. And I take it from your lack of response that you and Thomas will not try to hinder or interfere in this transfer, which is designed to spare an inmate from receiving similar treatment at Mr Stuckey's hands.'

Patrick flinched. Charles saw the subtle movement with such clarity. He knew there was a story behind the tragic event and wondered if he should press further or let Patrick simmer over it.

Patrick said nothing. It surprised Charles that he would let Wally take such a fall for whatever truth was lurking behind his silence. To remain mute on this issue when so much was at stake, Charles decided, Patrick must be feeling extremely threatened.

Long after Patrick left his office, Charles pondered the event and persisted in his examination of every angle he could conjure. He was baffled. He held his head in his hands.

His office door was open. 'You right there, Doctor Lawler?' Constable Bryant said as he walked through the doorway.

'Yes, yes.' Charles swept his hand forward. 'Sit, please.'

'Is that the one I am here to fetch?' The constable looked toward the door.

'Orderly, bring him in please,' Charles called.

Wally trudged into the office. After staring at the two men he looked quickly down at the desk between them.

Constable Bryant stood and pointed to his seat. 'Here you go, then. Sit.' He patted the back of the chair.

Wally sat down with a thud as the constable immediately began a line of questioning. Charles tried to keep his mind on proceedings as the attempt to interview Wally ensued. If he had not been so exhausted from the past week's series of unrelenting problems, he would have done the constable a service and not called upon him to engage in such a futile pursuit. Wally had no idea what he had done. Most days, he did not know his name.

It was troubling to Charles that he did not possess the energy to seek the dead man's next of kin, and had therefore summoned Constable Bryant to perform the task. It was highly likely the orderly had family living close by or in town. If the constable handled the situation it would less likely become fodder for gossip in town. To have this story made into a conspiracy by *The Advertiser* would bring unwanted scrutiny to the asylum. He could not possibly deal with a reporter sniffing about on top of everything else. His attempt to let the constable answer any and all questions on his behalf was definitely the most efficient way of handling this particular matter.

'Tell me, Wally,' the constable said. 'Do you recall what happened in the yard today?'

Wally stared from one man to the other and was silent.

Moments passed. Constable Bryant looked at Charles and raised his eyebrows.

'Wally, do you remember anything that happened today? Anything at all?' Charles said in the hope that his voice would prompt a reaction.

Wally walked to the window and stared down at the grounds for the longest time. He pointed out to the clear day and slurred, 'Ship's leavin'.'

Charles watched the old man and felt pity. Wally was so lost in the past it was beyond a doubt that he had emulated an act from long ago on the poor unsuspecting orderly.

The constable looked to Charles. 'I think it is time to make arrangements for a transfer to J Ward, doctor.'

'I think so,' Charles stated with disappointment.

'Ship's leavin' soon,' Wally repeated, talking around a tongue that no longer moved freely.

The constable walked to Wally's side and patted his

shoulder. 'Yep, the ship's leaving soon and the carriage will be here shortly to take you down to the dock.'

'Take him to the administration offices and wait for the constable there,' Charles said to the orderly. Once they were alone, Charles turned to the constable.

'Now we are faced with letting our deceased's family know the news.'

'After the transfer to J Ward is complete, I will seek his residence in town and find his next of kin.'

'I will ask Matron to supply you with the necessary details.'

'Glad to be of assistance.' Constable Bryant shook Charles' hand and left.

Charles crossed the floor to Doctor Rushby's office.

'One moment,' he heard him say. Charles tapped his foot as the minutes ticked away.

Finally, the door swung open and Doctor Rushby ushered an inmate out.

'Goodbye,' the girl giggled, turning to blow a kiss to Charles as she passed.

Charles raised his eyebrows and walked past Doctor Rushby.

'Lively thing, isn't she?' Doctor Rushby stated.

Charles was in no mood to discuss another inmate at present.

'One of the attendants was killed in the vineyard earlier.'

Doctor Rushby threw his hand in Charles' direction. 'I know. I had every intention of seeking you out and discussing it, but I was bogged down with inmates and their ailments, as you could see.'

'There was no need. I summoned Constable Bryant to

execute the inmate's transfer to J Ward and he will inform the deceased's next of kin.'

'Why did you alert the constable?' Doctor Rushby snapped.

Charles was quite taken aback by the tone in his colleague's voice.

'Well, I assumed it was the correct and just thing to do. Do we want the risk of his widow exacerbating our situation here?'

'I have stressed the importance of remaining self-sufficient, Charles. 'A family can always be bribed into silence.'

Charles was confused. 'Clearly, the authorities should be privy to a crime within the walls that resulted in snuffing out the life of someone in our employ. I certainly should have but I did not mention the other situation to the Constable.'

Doctor Rushby gave Charles a disapproving look. 'I consider that someone in our employ is worthy of attention. But the timing could not be worse. If a staff member sees it in their interest to further highlight the McGowan situation we would be up to our ears in it. Why, at Sunbury they are in all sorts of strife with the do-gooders believing they possess knowledge of subjects they do not understand and on which they should not be forming opinions. The place is on the brink of closure due to all sorts of ridiculous claims made in the papers. We can only presume *The Advertiser* and in turn *The Argus* will report our crisis in the short term and we will be made to answer to the governing body for it. It leaves us a paper trail that we neither have time to ponder nor deal with.'

'Whilst we are speaking of the McGowan case, have you turned up any evidence on the perpetrator?'

Doctor Rushby shook his head. 'Nothing.'

'I did have one thought I wanted to float past you.'

Doctor Rushby steepled his fingers and placed them in front of his lips. 'Go on.'

'When I started here, there was a woman badly beaten in the hospital cottage. There seems to have been a few repeats of this scenario over time. Do you think there could be some relation between the two?'

Doctor Rushby considered the question. 'You could be onto something. I will tell you what. I will seek Matron's assistance and have her cross-reference orderlies on duty to see if any corresponding ward duties show up.'

'That sounds … '

Charles was interrupted as a heavy knock resounded behind him.

'Enter!' Doctor Rushby yelled gruffly.

The young woman who had left minutes earlier now returned with another young woman in tow.

Doctor Rushby raced to the open door as Charles stood to leave. 'I have some further work to do here if you would not mind, Doctor Lawler.'

Doctor Rushby ushered Charles from his office with such haste that Charles was left out in the hall looking quite perplexed. As the door was shut abruptly he could not avoid hearing the shrill voice of the girl. 'You wanted me to bring one other.'

Charles was left with a confusion that would not abate. The current scenario echoed an experience he had had on his first day, namely a discussion he had held with Doctor Rushby that had made him question the management of the asylum. Now, he was left with the same discontent. He did not want to believe the course his thoughts were taking but he feared that the situation involving the young women he had just witnessed waltzing into Doctor Rushby's office was most untoward.

As promised, Charles was seated opposite Doctor Rushby at his desk. He had put the man off at the cricket match the previous day and was now ready to discuss his occupation at the asylum.

'Well, now that I am finally here and my tenure has begun, I am really chomping at the bit to make a difference in this place.'

'Have you ever worked in these circumstances before, Charles?' Doctor Rushby leaned back in his chair.

'No, apart from doing the required paperwork to commit patients to the asylum this is my first real chance at dealing with them once they are incarcerated.'

'Patients? That is an interesting word. These people are indeed inmates once here and their sicknesses seem to be of the type we cannot remedy.'

'Well, hopefully in time we can make some headway into how we treat some of their ailments.'

'It would be so much easier if we did not have the interference of the authorities,' Doctor Rushby said. 'J Ward is also part of our jurisdiction, so do not hesitate to arrange the relocation of patients from here to there if you suspect any criminal activity. We have the need to do this when the odd situation arises. Some of the inmates commit crimes of their own volition. Whilst we have tried to create our own town within the walls of the asylum, in order to be totally self-sufficient, it seems the outside world insists on being invited in.'

'There is something I do not understand,' Charles replied. 'If it is a requirement by law that the authorities be called upon when a crime has been committed, why should calling the authorities pose a problem? Calling on their assistance does not affect finances or the work being done here, does it?'

Doctor Rushby shifted in his seat and silence ensued as he searched for the right words. He abruptly stood and walked to a locked cupboard. Pulling a key from his waistcoat, he unlocked the cupboard and pulled out a bottle of brandy. He proceeded to pour two snifters before handing one to Charles and taking a sip from the other.

'Oh Charles, your naivety will abate. This lot in here are not thinking clearly and have all manner of blanketed minds. Why, the last time the police attended it was due to one of the female inmates throwing around accusations of disgusting and lewd conduct directed at her. We had the police in here for weeks sifting through a heap of filth and lies to get to the truth.'

'Which was?'

'Which was that there was nothing at all underhanded going on inside the walls of Ararat Lunatic Asylum.'

Charles had seen all manner of lies and spectacles since becoming a doctor three years ago. One had only to look at the goldfields in Ballarat from whence he had come to see that deceit and thievery were rife.

Doctor Rushby spoke loudly, breaking into Charles' thoughts.

'I see your brow is furrowed and you look confused. I too was once new in the place and thought I could make a difference, but as the days turned to months and now years, I am afraid I have given up the dream of setting most of these poor souls free to return to a normal life. They are a lost cause and if some of the techniques we use do not restore their normal demeanour then there is no hope for them.'

'In your time here, how many of these people have returned to family and normal life, as you call it, Doctor Rushby?'

'Only a handful. Of the nine hundred we have here at present, if we got to attend to half of them in a six-month period it would be miraculous. To evaluate and assess whether they are fit to return to their own kin is almost impossible. The women are a lost cause. If they are able to return to their husbands they are not wanted, and their families feel burdened at the thought of taking them back. Those who are suffering from depressive illnesses do not pose much of a workload here. They are so withdrawn from reality they are almost non-existent. Then there are those who harm themselves or others, but they are kept under fairly tight restraint and the attendants look after them quite nicely. As you are aware, you will be quite engaged with surgical procedures. Our last superintendent left us months ago and it has taken quite a spell to replace him.'

Charles sat forward in his chair. 'I am aware it has been some time since there was a roster of surgery, therefore I wish to begin rescheduling operative rosters to gain an upper hand on any ailments that have been left untreated for too long. Would you supply me with the register of patients who require vital intervention?'

Doctor Rushby harrumphed. 'I can provide you the last scribblings from the superintendent upon his departure but aside from that I am at a loss.'

'What is your responsibility in here, then?' Charles blurted as his astonishment rose.

'I am bogged down with all manner of unyielding problems. There are the masturbators who run rife with their filth in the men's ward, just as there are women who are suffering from hysterics. With the women I have to administer the hands-on approach. Whilst this does the trick, it does in fact take up copious amounts of time.' As he spoke, he unwittingly moved his hand to the front region of his trousers as though having awoken a satisfaction.

Charles shifted and quickly stood and walked to the window. With his glass in hand, he looked out over the township in the distance below. It was a beautiful sight to behold. Patients could stare out over the horizon to assist their mental demeanour, but to see the outside world and be unable to possess tangibility of the life beyond the walls was unfortunate.

Doctor Rushby spoke to Charles' back. 'You will like it here, Charles. Lots of freedom to practice your work and try some new methods, if you so wish.'

Charles looked back at Doctor Rushby. He was well aware of the procedures doctors used to further their knowledge in an attempt to write their own names in the history books, and such research only came about with experimental treatments performed on live patients. Doctor Rushby alluded to this but did not need to spell it out. Doctors were of the same breed, trying to further their knowledge. It was an unspoken rule.

'I am sure my tenure here will have its trials and tribulations,' Charles said. 'However, I do very much look forward to being the superintendent and curing those presenting with operable conditions.'

What Charles really suspected, however, was that the challenge of working with the man who sat before him, would prove considerably more difficult than treating patients.

Chapter 19

A heavy rap at the door caused Celia to jump in fright. Wiping her flour-covered hands across her apron, she rushed down the hall.

'Coming!' she yelled, but the banging continued.

The moment Celia opened the front door, Trinny stumbled across the threshold. Stepping back, Celia ushered the nurse inside, and then quickly slammed the door behind them.

'Whatever is the matter?'

Trinny wrung her hands. Breathless, she was almost doubled over. 'I ran here,' she gasped. 'No one must know I have come.'

'No, of course not.' Celia led Trinny to the sitting room and waited for her to sit down and catch her breath.

'What is the matter? What has happened?'

'I was assigned to the hospital cottage today as the nurse in charge has taken ill. Maryann is in there.'

'Oh no, what happened to her?' It was obvious the situation was dire. Celia knew Trinny had taken a great risk to give her this information.

'Oh Celia, she is in a very bad way and will not talk about her injuries.'

'What injuries?'

'She has bruises to her face and neck and it would seem that she has extensive bruising to her lower region.'

Celia's mind processed the information but she was confused as to how such abuses continued to happen. 'Has anybody had access to her from the men's wards?'

'Not that I am aware of. It would seem that the answer would lie with a member of staff.'

'Oh, and what gives you cause to think this?'

'Maryann was delivered to the nurse in charge of the cottage in the early hours of this morning.'

Celia looked puzzled. 'She is not sharing her cell with anybody.'

'I know.'

'Who checked her into the hospital? Which orderly?'

'The person who checked her in was not an orderly. The person was Doctor Rushby.' Trinny fixed Celia with a knowing gaze.

'Well then, surely Dr Rushby must have stated why he was placing Maryann in the cottage.'

'Dr Rushby reported that he discovered the patient outside her cell whilst he was completing his evening rounds. His decision to place her in her cell was warranted, as there was no observed discolouration on her skin at that time. He decided to check on her later that evening, only to discover she was quite tortured and in need of attention.'

'But I don't understand. Why would she be outside her cell in the first instance? And why, if he did not suspect that she had been injured, would he return later in the evening?'

'Or rather, so early in the morning?' Trinny added. 'If I may be blunt.'

'Oh Trinny, enlighten me please. I implore you.'

'I feel there are sinister behaviours going on.'

'Well that would seem to be the case,' Celia stated in a clipped tone.

Trinny paused slightly before delivering her final pronouncement. 'The reason I raced here is because she has asked for you.'

Celia sucked in her breath. 'I am forbidden to pass the perimeter. Charles has cut me off.'

'I know,' Trinny empathised, 'and I am at pains in beseeching you to come to the asylum, but Maryann is so damaged and frightened. I would not be putting both you and I at risk were the situation not urgent.'

'Oh Trinny, this puts me in a spin.' Celia stood and began to pace the room. 'And she is in the hospital cottage?'

'Yes, and I am due back. I cannot be notably missed.'

'Go then, go!' Celia implored Trinny, grasping the younger woman's trembling hands. 'I will do all I can to get there. Assure Maryann of this.'

Celia held the front door open and watched Trinny until she disappeared beyond the rear gate.

She pressed her fist to her lips and was deep in thought as she returned to the task of making bread for dinner. As punishment for Celia's misdemeanour, Charles had given the housekeeper a leave of absence. In his wisdom he decided that if his wife were to be kept busy, she would be distracted from thoughts of visiting the asylum's laundry room.

Charles was correct in his assumption. Since he had made

the decision, Celia had indeed been occupied with household chores. Leaning against the kitchen counter now, as she kneaded the bread dough, she felt her frustration grow. Beneath her hands, a clever idea sprang forth.

Celia set to making scones. Once they were rising in the oven, she churned fresh butter. Within the hour, her kitchen chores completed for the morning, she had a basket over her elbow and was pulling the door closed behind her. She hurried past rows of carrots and wheelbarrows full of potatoes.

The women's hospital cottage sat independently of the massive wings of the main asylum building, with verandas wrapping around it on all sides. Flowering passionfruit vines adorned the posts, casting wide pools of shade onto the timber deck. Each cottage window had been thrown open to allow a fresh flow of air to aid in the recovery of the inmates.

Trinny opened the front door and ushered Celia inside. 'She is in here,' she said as she pushed open the door to Maryann's hospital room.

Celia stopped mid step as the shock of seeing Maryann's face almost made her weep. The sight was far worse than she could have imagined. 'Hello Maryann, it's Celia. Can I get you anything? A drink? Another blanket?'

Maryann shook her head slowly from side to side. She winced.

'Who did this to you?' Celia's words were fraught with anger.

Maryann remained silent. Celia implored her to answer. 'Please, you must tell me.' But the silence between them stretched further. Staring at Maryann's bruised face and swollen mouth, Celia noticed that the woman's attempts to simply swallow or lick her injured lips looked torturous. One eye was swollen closed and her jawline was so mottled with colour merging from dark blue through to black that it was impossible to observe the hue of her normal skin. Maryann's throat showed distinct lined marks where fingers had grasped her in an extreme act of violence, clearly in an attempt to choke the life from her.

'Maryann, I am here now so please tell me who did this. If you will tell me, I promise I can help you.'

Celia jumped as the door opened behind her. She turned to see Trinny's pained face.

'Doctor Rushby is coming.'

Celia squeezed Maryann's hand and bent over her. She whispered close into her ear. 'I will return.'

Trinny held the door open as Celia squeezed past her and gave her a quick kiss on the cheek. 'Thank you,' Celia whispered, before quickly disappearing through the rear door of the cottage. After tiptoeing down the rear steps and tracing a direct line to the rear door of the main building, she leaned against the wall. Once she was safely out of sight she peeked around the corner to see Doctor Rushby disappear inside the hospital cottage. She held tight to the basket and tried to catch her breath as she pressed her back against the wall. She did not have to wait long until her worst fears were confirmed. Only a moment after Doctor Rushby entered the cottage, Celia heard a heart wrenching cry that was distinctly Maryann's.

'This has to be addressed,' Celia said matter-of-factly to herself as she flung the door open and entered the main building. Anger propelled her forth. She stomped up the stairs and knocked with more force than would be considered appropriate.

She heard Charles' annoyed response. 'Enter.'

Once inside, Celia closed the door and leaned against it for a moment to gather her thoughts and strength.

Charles glared at her. 'What in hell's name are you doing here?'

'I came to give you these.' Celia plopped the basket on his desk. 'And I may have been intercepted at the hospital cottage.'

'That is absurd, Celia, and you know why. Did we not discuss at length your visits here? I ordered you to steer clear, and ... '

'I did not promise. You told me that is what you expected.'

The delivery of baked goods was not softening their exchange. Charles looked fit to explode.

'I promise you, my intention was to come directly here,' Celia explained, 'but I was waylaid by a request to visit with one of the women in the hospital cottage.'

'And who summoned you?'

Celia dared not divulge the identify of her informant, knowing that to do so would cost Trinny her employ.

'It was an orderly. I do not know his name.'

Charles flung his hand aside. 'And how are all the unwell women today?' His sarcasm mocked her.

'One of the women in there has been absolutely battered to within an inch of her life.'

'Yes, I know, my dear. I am the superintendent.'

'I think there is cause to believe it was a staff member who inflicted the injuries.'

Charles threw his hands above his head and clasped his

hands together as he prayed to the power above. 'Pray tell we have a sleuth among us. Who is the dastardly staff member who would dare traumatise a fair maiden?'

'You should take this seriously, Charles. After all, this is not the first time that ...'

'What makes you think you are in a position to make this preposterous accusation?'

'That does not matter. All I know is Doctor Rushby has been named as ...'

Charles slammed both hands down on the desk in front of him and rose so abruptly that Celia stepped back to give her some space from her husband's imposing figure looming above her. 'How many times do we need to traverse this discussion?'

Celia was not shocked by Charles' anger.

'How many times?' he repeated. 'I'm asking you! Too many ... This is what I am continuously discussing with you, but to no avail. You are lawless unto yourself. I am a trusted and respected doctor who cannot have his wife standing up on her soapbox fighting the cause for every crazed harlot who sits within these walls.'

Celia turned toward the door.

'Sit down!' he bellowed. 'You are to not to leave.'

In the time it would take to strike a match Charles had quashed her anger by replacing it with his own.

Later Celia would have time to ponder the moment but for now she welcomed the simple fact that Charles was not tossing her out of his office and sending her home. She sat down on the chair and faced Charles.

'What is it going to take for you to leave this damned place and transform back into the woman I married?'

As suddenly as Celia's calm demeanour arrived, it began to slip. In a quiet voice, between gritted teeth, she said, 'I will not retreat nor turn my back on the women in here even if you so choose to. It is your duty as a *respected* doctor to do everything in your power to assist these inmates to get well and yet, you are choosing to neglect that responsibility, on the grounds that you believe they are, and forever will be, crazed and unworthy of your protection.'

Charles' face became impassive. Something shifted and she was not sure whether she should be afraid of him or give herself a pat on the back for softening his tone somewhat. Had she struck a chord with her words, or was her point finally breaking through his antiquated ideals?

Charles rounded the desk and crowded in on her. 'You are forgetting your place, my darling.' His eyes twinkled and his smile remained hard to read. 'You want to fight me for these women? I admire that for the sake of strangers you are willing to challenge your husband and risk your standing in society. When I think of it, it is what I do also. But what you forget is that, unlike you, I went to medical school and earned my standing. You, my dear, earned yours by marrying me, so do not underestimate my strength and standing in the world, and do not forget the fact that I am a man and have control over you and what you can, and cannot, do. Do you hear me?'

His voice was a harsh whisper in her ear. And although she felt stung by his words, they did not hinder her resolve. If there was one thing she had learned prior to marriage it was the power a woman could yield over a man. A manipulative plan arose in her mind, and despite her self-doubt she felt determined to see it through, knowing that it presented her with the best chance of securing help for the abused women of the asylum.

'You may be my husband and a man nonetheless, but I can control you in ways you cannot resist.' Celia grabbed his vest lapels, pulled him to her and kissed his mouth. Flooded by a powerful determination — as if she were on a sinking ship being torn from her husband, and this was the last time they would ever touch — she refused to let go.

Charles tried to pull back from her hold but she deepened the kiss and stood slowly controlling him until he was grasping at her shoulders, pulling her to him. Keeping her in a tight embrace, he walked her backwards to the bed and lifted her onto it. Within moments he was ferreting under her skirts and petticoats in frenzied indignation. She spread her legs wide and bent her knees so she could clamp his hips with her thighs. The sound he made in her ear as he unfastened and pulled his trousers down spoke of his lust for her. Celia was so intent on measuring up to him that she grasped his manhood and slid her hands along, massaging it. He clutched at her hand and guided himself to her opening. He thrust into her so hard that they both cried out with pleasure. With each plunge into her he chanted, 'I Am Your Husband. Do You Hear Me?'

Celia's hands raced over his shoulders and chest, scraping at the fabric of his shirt and vest. She wanted to feel his skin beneath her hands. Well aware she was using her body as a ploy to control him, she nonetheless loved his touch and the disarming power he held over her when they made love.

One long thrust sent fire through both their bodies and when it subsided he withdrew from her body and rested his hands on both sides of the mattress, keeping her trapped. His head dropped forward and for a moment she thought she might hear an apology. She quietly pulled her skirts down, buttoned her dress and whisked her pantaloons into her purse before looking at him. His gaze was difficult to read. There was no hint of remorse or forgiveness in his eyes.

'I realise you are angry with me and I acknowledge that I am your wife, and a woman, and that my social standing has risen since marrying you, but I need you to know I was destined to meet you, to end up here, in this place. I am wasted unless I help others and you are my muse in enabling me to do that. Please allow me to make your job easier by letting me in and not blocking my help.'

He stared into her face as though he were searching for the correct words. 'Well, then you leave me no choice but to grant this wish of yours.'

Celia was elated. She had finally made Charles realise her worth. He was going to comply with her demands.

'Come with me.' He held the door open and waited for her to pass through. He walked behind her as she alighted the staircase down to the administration office.

'This way.' He allowed her to walk ahead of him to the refractory ward. Celia turned to him with astonishment.

'Are you allowing me to visit the refractory ward?'

'There is somebody I would like you to meet.' He stopped at the door of cell six.

'Is there a new inmate in Audrey's old cell?' Celia asked as she passed through the door.

But the door slammed behind her. 'You want to be closer to the women. You are now among them, my dear. Enjoy.'

Charles fastened the padlock, turned on his heel and walked off towards the staircase.

'Charles! Charles! Open this door!'

Charles could hear Celia yelling. Closing his eyes, he fought the urge to release her. His wife, he had decided, needed a lesson in humility. As he made his way back up the stairs and into his office, he felt as though his heart were pounding against his ribcage. He stood at his desk with his fists curled hard against the wooden surface.

There was a knock at the door. His head shot up. He would not be at all surprised if Celia had already coaxed a nurse to release her from the cell. As much as it would pain him, before she could utter another insolent word he would personally march her back down to the refractory ward and throw her back inside cell six.

He pulled the door open aggressively, expecting to see his wife's beautiful face steeped in fury. Instead, he was shocked to see an injured man before him.

'What on earth happened to you?' he said in disbelief.

'That damned woman in the hospital cottage. She lost her mind when I tried to examine her injuries.'

Charles stood to one side and allowed Doctor Rushby to enter.

'Please, sit down. Let me clean your face and put a dressing over that.'

Doctor Rushby removed the handkerchief he had been holding over his eye. Charles winced at the bloodshot mess. 'Goodness, I hope your eyesight is not affected.'

'I cannot see anything at the moment but I hope in due course my eye will become useful again.'

'I hope so, too.' Charles wiped alcohol around Doctor Rushby's eye socket. Deep gashes lined the man's cheek and Charles wondered how the injury had come to express itself across such a large canvas.

'How on earth did she manage to do this much damage to your face?'

'Get too close to these inmates and they will claw their way through you. She may have thought I was somebody else. You know how few scruples these people possess.'

Charles' hand stopped in mid motion. Doctor Rushby was considering him, albeit through one eye.

'Well, did you reach a conclusion about how she was injured in the first place?' Charles said.

'I had not begun to inquire about her injuries before she stuck a hair pin in my eye and proceeded to drag it down my face.'

Charles grunted. 'What in God's name was she thinking?' He knew the inmate in question and she had definitely not shown this sort of violence at all before.

'There. All done. Now Mrs Rushby will not scream blue murder quite so much, we hope.'

'Yes, well thank you, Charles,' Doctor Rushby said as he straightened himself in the chair. 'There is one more thing I wanted to discuss with you and it is of a sensitive nature.'

'By all means.' Charles steeled himself.

'Around an hour ago, I witnessed Mrs Lawler heading away from the hospital cottage.'

Charles gulped. 'I can assure you my wife has been dealt with and will not be seen within these walls again.'

Doctor Rushby waved his finger at Charles. 'You see, this

matter is of great concern to me, Charles. I have had this discussion with you on more than one occasion, and yet she always seems to claw her way back.'

'I realise this has been a problem in the past and ...'

Just as Charles was about to tell Doctor Rushby that Celia was tucked away in one of the lower refractory cells, Doctor Rushby cut him off mid-sentence, saving him from divulging more information than was necessary — something that would later turn out to be a blessing.

'These female inmates were more pliable before your wife found her way in here,' the injured man complained, 'and began to put all sorts of ridiculous ideas in their heads. This wound ...' he pointed to his eye, '... would never have happened previously. I believe your Celia is giving these women a nonsensical feeling of power, and as a result they are lashing out at us. We are their protectors and we should be treated accordingly. If the refractory ward tragedy did not highlight the dangers of her interference, then what will? She is defying you, Charles. Take charge. A bit of physical manoeuvring may do the trick.'

Doctor Rushby stood and walked to the door. He was almost over the threshold when he turned back, 'One more thing, Charles ...'

Charles tried to school his features as he reeled from the shock of Doctor Rushby's statements. 'Yes?' he said too loudly.

'Please refrain from visiting that woman in the hospital cottage. It would do for you to keep your distance. She may try to do away with you also and we would not want that.'

Charles realised Doctor Rushby had attempted to make light of his final order in jest, but the joke had fallen flat. 'Thank you, Simon. I will pay heed to your concern. And be assured, Celia will be dealt with properly this time.' He cleared his throat.

'Very good, Charles. Very good.'

Doctor Rushby disappeared, and Charles stared at the empty space left behind. There, in the silence of his office, he felt the utmost contempt for both his wife and his colleague.

Celia had caused a stain on his reputation. Due to her escapades, he had lost the respect of his peers. His present anger at her cemented his resolve to ensure her imprisonment in the refractory ward lasted for at least a few days.

Charles harboured many concerns at present. He had been given an unpleasant insight into Doctor Rushby's attitude. This was inconvenient, as more than once Celia had mentioned her concerns about the man's cruel nature. And while Charles knew the women in the laundry room could cause all sorts of trouble with their immoral ways, he believed they would confide in Celia. These women were not violent, which is why they were given the freedom to work in the laundry. The injured inmate in the hospital cottage was one of those women. Charles had read the report on her injuries and the events that had ostensibly led her to the hospital overnight.

Charles was torn between his concerns for Celia's safety while she was locked in one of the refractory cells and his conviction that he could not release her while she was being so indignant and defiant. What if something sinister was to befall Celia while she was down there? He thought of her, alone, in that horrible cell. He was all too aware how horrific conditions were. After all, he had visited the stench-laden place on many occasions. Keeping her under lock and key, however, seemed the only way to allow him the time to investigate his concerns free of her interference.

He would alert Matron to the short-term guest in the refractory ward. The door to cell six would be kept tightly shut and the nurse in charge would be ordered to keep a close eye on the cell but not to meddle.

As much as he feared for his wife, he knew she could fight. Verbal wars with her could prove hazardous, but would she be able to protect herself from the physical advances of a man? Charles thought himself a keen observer of the weaker sex. He knew them to be gentle with their offspring, yielding in the bedroom and keenly ambitious to fight for their rights. He had seen the ugliness of the goldfields and the unruly behaviour it brought out in desperate people. Men and women had to fight for survival in difficult circumstances.

He thought of the woman in the hospital ward. Charles had not treated her for any particular ailment since he began his work here. She seemed to be in good health overall. The only thing he would suspect could be that she was entering a phase of hysterics, which would explain why she was exhibiting violent tendencies but it would seem a sudden turn of events. And that theory was at loggerheads with her present situation. She had been injured in the worst possible way. It could be of no wonder that she acted like an unbroken thoroughbred if she was snuck upon.

Charles had observed similar scenarios over the course of his career and people rarely surprised him these days. The goldfields had opened his eyes wide to human behaviour like nothing else he had experienced. 'Hell hath no fury like a woman scorned.' There were no truer words. A woman who is fighting for her survival at the hands of a man can be lethal. Especially if the man is attempting to take something to which he is not entitled. This brought to his mind a number of scenarios. One in particular came forth. It was closely aligned with the present events he was facing.

'I want that fuckin' wench put in shackles.' The dishevelled miner, still numb from the drink, was on a rampage for justice.

'Hold still,' Charles said, frustrated. He had considered administering some medication that would subdue his patient but thought better of it. He needed the man lucid so he could establish the location of his head wound. There was blood matting his hair and the smell emanating from him made it difficult to hover above him. It wafted off him as he moved this way and that. His filthy clothes carried the acrid smell of the gases from the mines. This melded with other unpleasant aromas, such as whiskey fumes and the stench of stale tobacco. It was enough to warrant a handkerchief tied across one's mouth.

'I want the constable called to arrest that bitch.' The man bellowed and yelped as Charles found the area he had been searching for.

'Got it. Now if you will sit still I can clean the wound and suture it.'

Charles took to the wound with a pad of gauze and a good amount of alcohol. The sting did nothing to quieten the unruly miner.

'What did she hit you with?' Charles asked, noting that although the clean gash was easy enough to stitch up its depth was of great concern. Charles prised the wound apart with two pairs of tweezers and saw a hairline fracture where the length of the object had slammed into the man's skull.

'A fire poker. The bitch went crazy!'

'Looks as though she landed it with a mighty blow,' Charles said as he looked down at the wound and prepared to cut some of the filthy hair around it. 'Why did she hit you?'

'There was no reason,' the miner said in a more subdued tone.

Charles knew the man's sudden sheepishness suggested a lie was afoot. 'No reason?' he questioned. 'She just took to your skull with a fire poker?'

'Well, she got mad because I decided not to pay her.'

'Ah, I see. So there was a reason for her to want to smash you over the noggin?'

'She didn't perform like I asked so I told her she not gettin' a pittance from me.'

'And you see that as no reason for her to want to seek retribution in the form of violence against you?' Charles looked down at the miner with contempt. Yes, the type of woman capable of causing this type of damage to a man was surely immoral, but the acts she and her ilk were expected to administer to these men were lewd. The miners were filthy, unkempt beasts. They were lucky to wash on a weekly basis and the stench of their breath and their bodies would be enough to make any woman want to turn away. These women were desperate to keep a roof atop their heads and the only living they knew was to become slaves to the sexual appetite of the men who paid them for their bodies. The ill treatment they endured was abysmal.

'All done. Now, keep it dry for a week and then come back in and I will give it further care.'

'Thanks, Doc. I'm headed right to the constable.' The miner lumbered out of the surgery.

Charles let out a heavy a sigh. He knew the woman would be arrested and felt this would be a disservice to her. It was obvious she had been fighting for self-preservation.

He was familiar with the plight of the women who worked in the hotels, inns and pubs. They were trying to make a dollar. Hell, he even visited them himself on occasion — which is why there was one thing he did know. The woman in question would not have taken to the miner with the fire poker if he had paid what he had owed her. Goodness only knew what she had endured under or atop that man. If there was something he knew about the weaker sex it was this: they were never weak when it came to retaliating against someone who was violent or threatened their livelihood or God forbid their survival.

Chapter 20

'Charles! Charles!' she screamed until she could yell no more. Her voice was hoarse. She pulled her pantaloons from her purse and pulled them on. As she sat in the corner she curled up to gain warmth. She wept at the deplorable condition of this place. Experiencing this punishment dished out by Charles would only spur her on to gain better conditions for the women in here. She was no stranger to this ward. It was only weeks ago she had discovered its most damning secret.

Celia had been sneaking around the asylum all morning. Earlier that day, Charles had again instructed her to refrain from frequenting the place — but here she was, drawn once more to the laundry room. She found that she was moving furtively around like a petulant child playing hide-and-go-seek. It would seem that all the women including the nurses were siding with her and wanted her to visit as often as possible. She was thankful that as payment for her supportive ear they would hide her and give her fair warning if a doctor was in the vicinity.

Celia's mission that morning was to find Maryann, so she soon made her way to the kitchen, where Maryann was rostered. Her recent good behaviour had earnt her a spell from the laundry. Celia knew Maryann wanted to see her. The woman had given a note to Trinny — and Trinny, following the usual custom, had placed it beneath the stone on the stoop outside the superintendent's lodge for Celia to find.

As Celia stepped into the kitchen, the smell of soup hit her nostrils. 'Something smells delicious in here,' she announced, attracting Maryann's attention.

'You came!' Maryann threw her arms around Celia.

'Of course I came. You said you needed me.' Celia held Maryann close to her. 'Now, what can I *attempt* to assist you with?'

'My request is rather silly,' Maryann said.

'Tell me what it is and I will be the judge of its importance.'

'I have been thinking about my baby. I just cannot stop wondering where he is and if he is all right.'

Celia tried to chase the worry from her features. 'Oh Maryann, I am sure he is being well cared for.' But even as the words tumbled from her mouth she doubted their truth.

'Do you think so?' Maryann gripped Celia's hand.

'Yes, yes I do.'

'Is there any way you can find out where he was sent? Which orphanage? I just need to know.' Staring at Celia, Maryann looked hopeful.

Celia gave the situation some thought. 'I could make some inquiries,' she said. 'But for now I must go.' Celia kissed Maryann's cheek. 'I will pop back to see you very soon,' she assured her before leaving the kitchen. After looking both ways to check there were no doctors in the vicinity, she rushed along the covered veranda toward the rear of the main building.

One of the kitchen hands passed Celia on her way toward the kitchen. 'Your husband is on rounds,' the young woman spoke in a hushed tone without halting.

Celia was grateful for the warning. 'Thank you,' she whispered back. How fortunate she was to have lookouts on the prowl, helping to ensure she retained a regular presence in the place.

Jillian was on duty in the administration office. Celia closed the door and leaned against it. 'I cannot stay long.'

'What are you doing here?' Jillian hissed. 'Doctor Lawler is on rounds.'

'I know. That is why I need to be quick. Are there any records of the babies born in here?'

'I believe there should be but I would have to do some checking,' Jillian said. 'Why?'

'Maryann wants to know. She is worried and I believe she deserves some answers, if only in the form of reassurance that the child is alive and well.'

'All records are kept in the first room at the very base of the stairs in the refractory ward.'

Celia gave Jillian a nervous smile. 'Will I need a key?'

'Are you going there now?' Jillian shrieked.

'I do not know how long it will be before I am able to visit next, so I think now is a better time than not at all.

Jillian walked towards the door, opened it and peered out into the hall. 'You had better hurry and get out of here before Doctor Lawler catches you.' She pushed a key into Celia's hand. 'This opens every lock down there.'

Celia placed her hand on Jillian's arm. 'I will never tell Charles of any assistance offered by my friends in here. Rest assured you will not be punished for my wrongdoings.' Walking quickly to the foyer, Celia disappeared down the stairs.

The temperature dropped considerably as Celia stepped off the last tread. It was dark and damp in the lower bowels of the asylum. The refractory ward had been the only place she had not visited since her introduction to the institution, and as a result she was intensely curious about the condition of the ward and its inmates. Each of her requests for access had been steadfastly refused, and she now knew why — in no uncertain terms.

The place was confounding. It was horrendously cold and contained a smell that permeated her mouth and nose. 'Do not bring up your breakfast, Celia,' she said as the stench caused her to retch. The hall ahead of her housed kerosene lanterns that cast yellow shards of light at intervals along the bluestone corridor. Celia sensed this would be her only opportunity to look beyond, into the belly of the asylum, where the most unhinged inmates were held.

Although aware she was here to search the records room, Celia found herself drawn to the doors lining the corridor, from behind which she could hear mournful and incessant cries. Standing on tiptoe beside the nearest door, she opened the peephole and looked into a cell. Its inhabitant sat in the corner, where she was rocking back and forth, chewing on her fingers. Blood dripped down the poor soul's arm, and the floor beneath her was a blackened ring of darkness. Celia realised the darkness was entirely comprised of dried blood, obviously the result of the days and days of being neglected.

Celia gulped as her stomach once again threatened to heave up its contents. Door after door did not go unchecked as she looked in on each inmate through the peepholes. One inmate in particular held her perplexed.

Celia stared at this inhabitant for the longest time. Matted hair covered most of the woman's features. Celia felt that she knew the face but could not instantly place where she had seen it. From her position at the peephole, she flinched as the acrid smell of dank urine and filth assaulted her nostrils. Every instinct she possessed made her want to flee, yet she could not move from this spot.

The woman was sitting idly on the floor, her gaze dormant behind vacant eyes. Celia could not shake the feeling that she had met this inmate before — and as she continued staring, this feeling intensified. Was it one of the women from the laundry? And if so, why had she not heard about her?

In the dim light, Celia could make out that the edges of the woman's smock were indistinguishable from her skin. In the way a vine covers a wall, the smock seemed to have grown over the woman's body to encase her in a tight new skin of greying filth that clearly not even a bath could remove.

Celia gasped as recognition dawned. 'Audrey?' she whispered. The woman showed no sign of having heard her name, or any awareness that there was another human nearby.

'Audrey, it is you?'

Celia clutched the skeleton key in her hand. She would be in dire trouble if she were found down here; Charles would punish her beyond words. But as she looked at her lost and forlorn friend, abandoned down here in this filthy hovel, this thought fell away just as quickly as it had arisen.

The sound of the bolt giving way resonated down the corridor. Celia looked both ways before entering the cell. Kneeling before Audrey, she saw beyond the matted hair and filthy skin. Audrey's eyes, once so vibrant and happy, were now flat and dormant. Celia's breath caught in her throat.

'I will help you. I promise,' she whispered.

Not wasting a moment, Celia left the cell and walked to the end of the corridor. Finding only a bucket filled with dirty water, she carried it back to her friend with the water sloshing and careening from side to side. Grappling in her sleeve for her handkerchief, she dipped the fine fabric into the water, wrung it out and clumsily pulled it out as flat as she could to allow the clean up to begin. As soon as she touched Audrey's cheek, the woman sprang to life. Without warning, she flung Celia away from her, hollering and ranting like she had been thrown into acid. Celia was knocked onto her backside and now sat with her mouth agape.

Someone grasped Celia by the arm and wrenched her to her feet.

Strong arms pulled her from the cell and she felt the cold corridor wall against her back as she was pushed against it. Charles' fingers bit into her shoulder as he held her to the spot. His gaze bore into her. 'What in hell's name do you think are you doing?' he seethed.

'That is Audrey.' Celia pointed to the cell.

'It is not.' He snarled as he took hold of the top of her arm and hurtled her down the corridor at speed.

'You are hurting me!' Celia tried to wrest her arm from his grasp, but in a vice-like grip he held her fast.

He marched her all the way up the refractory ward stairs

and the two flights of stairs to his office and threw her down onto a chair. He then proceeded to yell at her like never before. 'Listen to me! You have no business in here. When are you going to heed my warnings? I would throw you in here myself if I was not so desperate to banish you from my place of work. God Almighty Celia, why are you beyond listening?'

Celia stared at Charles, allowing his rant to taper off. 'What is Audrey doing down there?' she said quietly.

Charles placed both hands on the arms of the chair and leaned down until his face was close to hers. 'I told you; that woman is not Audrey! I want you to forget you ever set foot in that ward, and I will say this for the last time: I want you to cease visiting anyone who has anything to do with the inner sanctum of this place. In case it has escaped your notice, you are a doctor's wife. All this behaviour is beneath you, not to mention grossly improper.'

Celia's voice remained calm. 'Even so, if that woman is not Audrey, I do not see the harm in helping her or bathing her, nor do I understand why such actions, ministered with kindness, could be so abhorrent to you.'

'It is just not the right practice in these circumstances. What if she had assaulted you, or killed you, for goodness sake? I agreed for you to visit the laundry room when help was required before we were married. Then you managed to weasel your way back inside the asylum long after we were betrothed. And here we are repeating the same circle of conversation. I kept my word but you have abandoned our agreement over and again.'

Celia's eyes narrowed. 'I know it is her. I will not be told otherwise.'

Charles took a sharp intake of breath, and Celia imagined she saw his eyes glisten like those of a bird coveting his prey. 'Well then,' he finally said, 'if you insist on arguing the point, so be it. Either way, you are never again to engage with the inmates in here. In fact, from this point, you are forbidden from acknowledging or recognising them in any way whatsoever.'

Celia ignored his statement. 'How am I to avoid the recognition of someone who was a treasured friend?'

'Do not trifle with me, Celia.'

'I want to help. I cannot sit idly by, watching these people shrouded in their own stench, and not feel a need to help them.'

'Yet you will have no choice moving forth now, will you?'

Celia nodded slowly. She knew she had been bested, for the moment at least, and realised she would have to give Charles time before she could negotiate the resumption of her visits.

'Do the Colonel and Mrs Price know Audrey is in here?' After she had asked the question she knew the answer. 'Did Michael sanction this injustice? Why is my dearest friend here in the first place?' Celia could not resist an urge to learn the truth.

Charles dropped his head forward. 'Audrey is battling demons you will never understand, and I have no doubt your little intervention today has done nothing but send her into further turmoil.'

Celia was in doubt of this but she dared not argue that particular point with Charles. It would be futile.

'I will call for an orderly to accompany you home. It is time you left.'

'As you wish, my dear.' Her words were light. She stood up and smoothed her skirt.

Charles held his hand out and motioned her forward with his fingers.

'Why are you doing that?' she asked.

'The key,' he said.

She reached into her bag and handed it across to him.

'I suppose it is pointless to ask you who supplied you with it.'

Celia did not answer but instead turned toward the door. After the morning's activities, she was feeling rather fatigued, and felt that she would prefer to smooth things over with Charles rather than be at war with him. She felt ill over what had transpired today but could not be at all sorry that she had discovered Audrey. There was a small part of her that wished she could undo the image of Audrey and her dismal condition but now that she knew her whereabouts she felt she could possibly help her in some way. Beyond the edges of her morality she knew it was not her business to pry into an inmate's history and ailments, but she simply had to know what had happened to her friend and how she had ended up in here. It was quite simply shocking.

The truth would find its way to her, and if she delved gently into the situation and discovered the problem at its heart, she felt sure she would have the potential to help.

She had so many questions. How could the Colonel and Mrs Price allow Audrey to be locked away like this? What had happened to their dear Audrey? But her most pressing question above all this was where were Michael and Charlotte?

Chapter 21

Matron scrawled the address onto a card. She held it out to Constable Bryant. 'This is all I have on his record as being his place of residence.'

'Thank you, Matron,' he said as he took the piece of paper from her and looked at the information.

Michael Shaw
Shire Hall Hotel
Barkly Street

For the first time she realised how little she knew about the staff who worked at Flint Hill. The only conversations she ever had with them related to practical concerns like the performance of ward duties and the administering of treatments.

'That place is a disgraceful hovel. How anybody could lay straight in that hotel is beyond imagination,' Matron said.

'I suspect anyone that resides there will have no next of kin,' he said. 'Regardless, I have been charged with unearthing any information pertaining to the victim.'

'Good day then, Matron.' He tipped his hat.

Upon his arrival at the Shire Hall Hotel, the constable appreciated the reprieve from the heat of the day.

'After a beer, Ken?' the publican asked.

'No thanks, Wes,' the constable responded. 'Just need the master key. Need to check out one of the rooms.

'Which one, then?'

Constable Bryant looked down at the card in his hand. 'Ah, Michael Shaw.'

'Weird one, that one,' Wes said.

'How so?'

'Kept to 'imself. Had something to hide. Not surprised you are lookin' through his room. Ain't seen 'im in a while.'

'He's dead.'

'That right? Any of the girls involved?'

'No, one of the lunatics from the hill did him in.

'That right?' If there was one thing about publicans, they knew all the goings on around town and beyond. They never said much but listened intently.

There was also an unspoken agreement between the publican and the law. The police indulged in free samples of the flesh of the women who provided entertainment in the hotel, and in return for these pleasures turned a blind professional eye to various happenings.

The room recently inhabited by Michael Shaw was no larger than eight foot by six, and was full of filth and rubbish. There were dozens of bottles and newspapers strewn across every space. The bed sheets were filthy and grey, and the dinner plate on the floor was so laden with mould that the constable could not imagine what it had once held. Clothes originally piled high in one corner sprawled halfway across the floor.

As the stench of an unkempt man reached his nostrils, Ken began to breathe in and out steadily through his mouth.

Gathering the newspapers, he began to pile them on the bed in an attempt to clear some space. Doubtful that he would find any clues leading to the man's next of kin, he nonetheless continued his search through the cesspit of a room, using his foot to sweep bottles and newspapers against one wall on the flimsy chance he would discover something useful in the process.

One of the girls stopped at the open door. 'What ya doin'?' she asked as she raised her arm and ran it up the length of the doorjamb.

'Get in here and make yourself useful,' Ken replied.

'What'll ya give me?' she countered.

'A "get-out-of-lock-up-free" next time I am ordered to meet my quota for wayward women.' He grinned at her although the smile did not meet his eyes.

The girl walked into the room.

'What do you know about the man who stays here?' Ken asked as he bent to pick up several whiskey bottles, which he then tossed out into the hall.

'He was miserable. Never said much. Never indulged the girls, if you know what I mean.' She looked him over.

He did not return her gaze but gestured toward the pile of clothing.

'Go through the pockets of every piece,' he barked.

'I will not touch that wretched pile of clothing.'

'Pay you a pound if you do.'

The girl was already crossing the room. She huffed in disgust as she began to ram her hand into every pocket. One after another, she tossed each shirt aside, even hurling a pair of pants over his head. Finally, she yelled. 'Ha!' Ken turned to face her and saw she was holding up a ring. 'Can I keep it?'

He snatched the ring from her grasp. 'No. Keep looking.' Pushing it into his pocket, he threw the last of the bottles out into the hall.

There were now two piles of clothing: one diminishing, and one growing. Suddenly, the girl exclaimed, 'Well, lookey here.' Draping a jacket across her shoulders, she sashayed before him. 'It would seem we have ourselves an army man!'

'Let me see that.' The constable whisked the jacket from her grasp and held it up before him. He stared at the insignia and narrowed his eyes.

Pulling the ring from his waistcoat he perused it once more. Looking back at the jacket he tried to connect the items. He had seen this ring somewhere before. Where? His memory served him well. It was Mrs Lawler's ring. This man was a thief.

'Once you 'ave finished over there, best be on your way.'

The girl tossed another shirt onto the growing pile of worthless clothing.

'Can I be done? Give me my pound.' She looked close to gagging from the stench.

Ken was standing up after his search beneath the bed uncovered nothing. 'Yes. All done here.'

They exited the room. He turned back to lock the door before handing the girl a pound. Pulling her to him, he whispered harshly in her ear, 'I will make your assistance today worth your while next time I am looking for a special delight.'

He released her and smacked her on the rear. She squealed.

Matron greeted him at the front door of the asylum, where they both eschewed pleasantries. 'I would like to speak to Doctor Lawler, if I could,' he said directly.

'Certainly, Constable Bryant.'

Matron ushered him up the staircase to Charles' office.

'Do you have anything for me, Constable?' Charles looked grim.

'I have discovered something I think may belong to your wife.'

Charles ground his teeth together to prevent himself from yelling, 'Where has she inserted herself now?' He dared not allow such an outburst with his present company.

'I have not yet discovered the identity of the deceased, but I did uncover this.' He pulled the ring from his waistcoat and held it up.

Charles took the ring from him.

'It is very similar to my wife's ring but to my knowledge she has not lost or misplaced it.'

'It seems very strange that an orderly would be in possession of such a thing,' the constable surmised.

Charles rubbed his chin. His mind was spiralling through the scenario as it was presented to him. A staff member was dead. Audrey was dead.

'The room the deceased had rented at the Shire Hall Hotel was no better than a pig's sty. Clothing, whiskey bottles and litter everywhere. Beneath the pile of clothing was an army uniform. Can you believe it? So disrespectful to his rank if you ask me. For someone to turn their back on that means they have something to hide.'

'An army uniform?'

'Why yes, quite a high ranking insignia adorned it, I may add.'

A thought slammed into Charles' mind. He looked at the ring once more. There was only one other ring that looked like that. 'I need to seek further information pertaining to this,' he announced, holding up the ring and turning it this way and that between his fingers.

'Absolutely. Do you have an idea of his next of kin?'

Charles shook his head slowly. 'Not at this moment. Let me not waste any more of your time today, Constable. I will inform you of any further developments as soon as they come to hand.'

Constable Bryant walked to the door. 'Excellent. Well then, are you able to keep him in the mortuary until tomorrow?'

Charles nodded. 'That will not be a problem. If I cannot uncover any family connections we may have to bury him beyond the wall with the other unclaimed souls.'

Ken looked relieved that his work would be made easier for lack of family ties. 'I will leave it in your hands then. Thank you, Doctor Lawler.'

Charles saw him to the top of the staircase. 'Goodbye then.' Charles could not get back into his office quick enough. He closed the door behind him, and leaned back against it. He could not believe that the deceased orderly was Michael. This was truly a calamity and such a ridiculously far-fetched situation that he needed a moment to put the pieces together. Could the mystery of Audrey McGowan's murder be explained? But if it were in fact Michael, who the clues pointed toward at present, it was just such an unnerving scenario. It played havoc with his mind. He needed to find the answer and deal with it regardless of the outcome.

Charles' knuckles beat three steady knocks on the door.

'Is the Colonel home?' he asked the housemaid.

The maid stepped away from the door and ushered him inside. 'May I take your hat and coat, sir?'

'No, I will only require a minute of his time.'

'Charles!' The Colonel's voice boomed from his study. 'I thought it was you. Come in, sit down.'

Charles closed the door and stood with both hands clutching the brim of his hat. 'I will stand if that suits.'

'What is it, Charles? You look like the devil has taken hold.' The Colonel studied him with concern.

Charles held the ring forward. The Colonel took it and Charles watched his demeanour alter. 'Where did you get this?'

'It was discovered in a room at the Shire Hall Hotel. I believe it was in the possession of an asylum staff member, now deceased.'

'I do not understand, Charles. How did this man get Audrey's engagement ring, or at least what would appear to be her ring?' The Colonel walked to the door, opened it and called, 'Eleanor!'

Within moments, Mrs Price was on the threshold, looking flushed.

'Yes, Colonel? Oh hello, Doctor Lawler.'

'Mrs Price.' Charles looked grim.

'Look at this, my dear. Give me your thoughts.' The Colonel extended the ring to her. As her focus fell on the glistening hues of golden blue and turquoise, she gasped.

'Where did you get this?'

'Is it Audrey's?' the Colonel enquired.

'I could not be entirely sure, although I dare say the markings on the stone are not dissimilar to my recollection. I do not recall seeing it on her finger when she returned with Charlotte. If it were on her finger I would have been sure to remove it before … ' Her voice trailed off.

'I understand,' Charles interjected. He wanted to change the course of the conversation to stave off the pain of the Price's decision to release Audrey to the asylum.

'I have a grim theory for you but I am not entirely sure Mrs Price will want to hear it.'

Mrs Price looked from her husband to Charles. 'I am quite capable of bearing the brunt of difficult truths.'

'As you wish.' The Colonel opened his hand, imploring Charles to continue.

'There was a tragedy at the asylum. An inmate murdered an orderly, who had this ring in his possession. Constable Bryant attempted to unearth his next of kin and in turn came across this at his place of residence.'

'The Shire Hall Hotel?' the Colonel offered.

Charles nodded. 'It would seem that is where this was discovered.' He pointed to the ring. 'I would not have thought the discovery too untoward,' he continued, 'until Constable Bryant mentioned something else.'

The Colonel and Mrs Price stared at Charles as seconds stretched by. Bracing himself for grim news, the Colonel suddenly seemed overwhelmed. 'Well, out with it,' he demanded.

'Amid the mess in the orderly's room, Constable Bryant uncovered a uniform. The jacket was adorned with insignia which I believe to be … '

'Who was this man?' Mrs Price looked fit to fly apart.

'His name was Michael.'

Silence ensued.

'Oh dear Lord.' Mrs Price mashed her fist to her lips.

'Do you know the last whereabouts of Michael McGowan?' Charles asked the Colonel.

'He disappeared the day of his repost from Point Nepean. I will admit I did not attempt to uncover his whereabouts.'

Charles ran the brim of his hat through his fingers.

'Would you not know if it was Michael?' Mrs Price whispered. 'Audrey's Michael? How could you not recognise him? After all, he was in your employ.'

'Well, I would feel a fool if I did not. After all, we became much more than mere acquaintances upon my return to the district, but no, I did not note any resemblance to Michael and if I had, I would not be here now,' Charles reasoned. 'I can only assume the grief of losing his wife and child took a toll on him. His appearance was rather dishevelled and haggard to say the least.'

'Where is this corpse?' the Colonel demanded, refusing to mention Michael by name.

'He is in the morgue at the asylum. I am afraid the body will be difficult to identify.'

'And why is that?'

'I would rather spare Mrs Price the details.'

'I need you to take me to him.' The Colonel rose from his seat.

Charles thought for a moment. 'Meet me at the superintendent's lodge. We will enter the asylum from there. The lodge is closer to the rear gate and the morgue and there will be little chance of anyone paying us any notice.'

'Is Mrs Lawler at home at present?' Mrs Price asked. 'Can she be spared this information, for all our sakes?'

'Absolutely,' Charles said assuredly. 'She is otherwise engaged this evening.'

Bidding farewell to Mrs Price, Charles walked back to the asylum. His thoughts spun in all directions. Mrs Price's question as to how he had failed to recognise somebody who had once been a good friend bothered him. Celia's present whereabouts and just what he was going to do about her frustrated him. The occupant in the hospital cottage and her evident injuries angered him. When in God's name would he be allowed to see his way clear of all this drama?

As dusk closed in, the Colonel tapped at the door of the superintendent's lodge. Charles led the way to the rear gate of the asylum where he pulled his watch from his waistcoat pocket. 'Only a few minutes until the final toll, then we will be unhindered in our endeavour.'

In the distance, the din of the asylum's bell sounded. It was time for all inmates to head indoors for supper. The work day was complete. Charles and the Colonel waited a few seconds, then entered the asylum grounds and slowed their pace to allow the inmates ahead of them to gain some distance. Amid the clatter of tools and the rush to fill their bellies with supper, the inmates were steadfast in their endeavour to return to the main building. Nobody took any notice of the two men headed to the door of the morgue.

Charles took a key from his waistcoat and unlocked the padlock. He held the door open for the Colonel, entering close behind him and feeling along the wall for the kerosene lantern. Once the lantern was throwing a blaze of orange light across the receiving room, he ushered the Colonel into the autopsy area, where the smell of sickly sweet death warped itself up and into his nostrils. The confined nine-by-nine-foot windowless space swamped his senses. His work as a doctor did not make him immune to the heaviness death cast across one's soul.

The glow from the lantern fell across the single pedestal table. The corpse was still fully clothed. Rising from the collar was a head that now fanned out in two large slabs of flesh already void of blood. The flesh had discoloured to a sickly grey. The blood that had dripped over the lip of the table and onto the floor was now dry and looked like the floor of a wine cellar where a barrel of port had been spilled.

The Colonel set about unbuttoning the man's shirt. To Charles' observation it would seem that after the things to which the Colonel had been exposed, the macabre sight before him — of a carved skull within torn flesh and an unrecognisable face — failed to rattle him.

'There it is,' he announced as he pointed to a circle of puckered skin, roughly the size of a penny, 'a gunshot wound he received when he first served in the regiment. I read the documentation on his file when he first came to the district. Beyond a doubt, Charles, this is Michael.'

Charles placed his hand to his forehead and wiped away a film of sweat. 'How did I fail to recognise him?'

'Look at him. Who would think this was the same man we knew from previous years? Which leads me to ask: Should we consider that he is the perpetrator who lured Audrey to her demise?'

'I think we must,' Charles said decisively. 'That conclusion would enable us to lay to rest the disturbing mystery surrounding Audrey's murder.'

The Colonel drew in a deep breath. 'At the very least, it begs to be said that the man was obviously as mad as everyone housed in this place.'

'I think this event demands we carry out a thorough check on all staff members in our current employ,' Charles said. 'This is grave.'

The Colonel placed his hand on Charles' shoulder. 'You could not have known it was Michael. He managed to disguise the truth with his appearance. And he did that quite well, obviously.'

As Charles and the Colonel walked to the rear gate, Charles unlocked it and stepped through. As he locked it once more, the Colonel turned to him. 'Thank you for keeping this whole situation closely guarded.'

'I am glad to serve you, although I wish the circumstances had never eventuated. I do hope Mrs Price finds some peace after the grim news I delivered today.'

'Charles, Mrs Price will be just fine. She has less to worry about since Audrey ... Well, you know.'

Charles gave a curt nod. He could not find words to express how he was feeling. He hoped Mrs Price would find some measure of consolation after the loss of her daughter. He wished to convey his remorse at not having protected Audrey from her crazed husband. It would seem his opinion on the tragic death of Audrey was in vast contrast to the relief her death had brought to her parents.

The Colonel and Charles parted ways at the gate of the superintendent's lodge. 'I appreciate your discretion, Charles.

You know I do,' he stated as he clasped Charles' hand and shook it.

Arriving home, Charles opened the front door and welcomed the silence that enveloped him. He uncapped a whiskey bottle and gulped from it. He did not possess the energy to fetch a snifter as he allowed his body to sag onto the lounge. His mind was bogged down by fatigue. He could neither find the energy nor inclination to face his office tonight, or his wife in the refractory ward.

Guilt began to weigh on him as he considered Celia. How would she be feeling at present? She would be as ropable as an unbroken horse when he released her. And whether he did so tonight or tomorrow, her reaction would undoubtedly be the same. In sickness and health, 'til death do us part. No truer words could he heed tonight as he took massive swigs from the bottle. When it was almost empty, his drunken haze began to yield a blur of moments and memories forged with his inflexible wife. She had challenged him at every turn.

Since the first touch in the carriage when his hands caressed those slender feet, he was lost in immediate love for her. The boldness she had shown in the weeks leading to their wedding day had bewitched him. The influence of the women in her midst within the asylum had certainly assisted in unleashing the brazen woman that she was destined to become.

Charles smiled at the memory of the moments spent in his office taking liberties of which he had no right. The memory of a particular train journey had proven fruitful also. It had opened a plethora of delicious excitement working well in his favour.

However, she had stood up to him on many occasions,

and the main point of contention was always her insistence on visiting the women in the asylum to help them. Charles found this aspect of her behaviour so vexing. She seemed willing to risk her life and her marriage for those she felt did not possess the strength to fight for themselves. His emotion swung like a pendulum. He realised Celia was pained by the loss of Audrey. It was cruel of him to force her to bear witness to the horrific sight of Audrey in the bell tower but she had incensed him to the extent that he could not stop his fierce want to punish her that day. His anger should not have clouded his judgement. Celia was his cherished wife and yet he had exposed her to something that he would never allow any other woman to witness. Now, tears welled up as the shame of his actions ebbed into his conscience.

He pushed them aside and took another large swallow of whiskey. 'She needs to be taught a lesson, goddammit,' he said as he wiped his mouth with the back of his shirtsleeve. As the alcohol filled his gut and dulled his mind, images of Michael and Audrey seeped into his thoughts. They had married only three weeks prior to he and Celia's own wedding. Those memories were supposed to be collectively treasured as their lives moved forward. Now, he found himself caught amid the torture of how Audrey and Michael's lives had turned out. He should be rejoicing at the good fortune that had been endowed on him; instead, he was punishing his wife in the worst way.

On the periphery of his thoughts was the subject of the unfinished investigation into the violence befalling the women in their cells. He was concerned for Celia's welfare but had given Matron specific instruction regarding her guest in the refractory cell. Surely Matron would see to Celia's protection by keeping the cell door shut tight until she was told otherwise. He desperately hoped his wife would be less incensed and more remorseful after a spell in the depths of the asylum.

He would pull Celia from her place of misery tomorrow and seek her assurance that she would not interfere anymore. Although Charles felt such thoughts were futile, as Celia had made and broken promises on many occasions, he clung to the belief that his wife's time in the cell would eventually have him win their battle of will. He allowed her to manipulate him in the bedroom and could never stay angry with her. He felt ashamed that he had taken advantage of her good nature by tricking her into the predicament in which she found herself.

He should release her tonight. He stood up and immediately felt the room spin. He was drunk. Too drunk to stand up. While he had every intention of releasing her there was no chance he could physically make the journey back into the asylum. Falling back onto the lounge, his head lolled on the headrest. His present state dragged him down. 'Forgive me, Celia,' he whispered. The dancing flame cast from the logs in the hearth created a flutter of gold and red behind his closed eyelids.

Hues of gold, green and red mottled the countryside. Charles thought about Celia as he admired the brilliant autumnal landscape through which his carriage was passing. He was wishing the morning away. In just over one hour she would officially be his wife. The carriage pulled to a halt outside the church. A throng of parishioners greeted him as he stepped down onto the roadside.

He waited for Celia at the end of the aisle. The minutes ticked away and the longer he waited, the more his nerves bristled. It was surprising to him. He did not foresee his levels of anxious anticipation besting him in church. All he had foreseen was the evening ahead, to the point where he had not fully anticipated the day's nuptials and everything that would come before his plan to enjoy the splendour of making love to his wife.

The organist began to play. As Celia made her entrance, Charles stared at the minister. It took all his strength not to turn to watch her walking toward him but tradition dictated that the groom did not look at the bride until she was by his side. It was only when the minister had asked her father if he would hand his daughter across to the man standing beside her that he looked at her. She looked exquisite in the white gown. If he were not privy to the truth he would swear she was the most virginal woman he had ever seen.

The service was short and succinct. He languished in the word of the good Lord, the words responsible for the very readings and rituals that were making this woman his possession. He intended to make her his, in every way possible. Her mind, body and soul belonged to him now, and he would ensure she was a devoted and subservient wife.

With his gloves clutched in one hand and his other hand resting on the back of the chair, he looked over her shoulder as she signed the wedding register. His thumb rubbed across the base of her neck. The anticipation of the night that stretched before them had her breathing deeply. He watched the rise and fall of her chest and could not wait to run his tongue across her flesh. Over the course of the wedding breakfast he whispered in her ear the promises of love he would bestow upon her.

Boarding the train in the afternoon allowed them time to reminisce about their transgression from weeks earlier en route to Ballarat. Their first night as husband and wife was spent in the luxurious Royal Hotel. Celia delighted in the company of her husband. He showered her with love and buried himself inside her, taking over her senses and teaching her the true enjoyment of lovemaking. It was in this moment she began to use her prowess to plant ideas in his mind.

'Charles, I do love you so very much,' she whispered, sated, as she laid her head on his chest, 'and now that I am Mrs Charles Lawler.' She giggled.

'Yes you are.' He ran his fingers gently over her back.

'I was hoping I could work in the asylum just until ... '

'Absolutely not, we have spoken of this and you agreed that once you became Mrs Charles Lawler, you would quit that foolish notion.'

'But Mrs Rushby has eluded to requiring more volunteers.'

'Let others put their hands up. I will not have my ... '

His words were lost as she began to kiss his chest moving downward until her mouth slid over him. He groaned languidly and allowed her to increase the ferocity and pressure of her task, never slowing or faltering until he fully succumbed to her.

Wiping her mouth and resting her head on his chest once more she said, 'Please, just think about it.'

He whispered, 'I will give it some thought, my love.'

She knew he was under her spell. She knew how to gain his attention and manipulate him to the largest degree.

Chapter 22

'Jillian!' Matron called from her office.

'Yes, Matron,' Jillian answered as she signed the staff log.

'Could you come here, please?'

Jillian stood at the door, expecting Matron to be in the company of one of the doctors. Instead, Matron was alone, peering over her glasses at Jillian.

'Come in. Close the door, please,' Matron ordered.

Jillian stepped into the room, her hands trembling as she gently closed the door behind her. She was relieved Matron was alone. If she were in the company of one of the doctors, she feared she would have to answer some tricky line of questioning. She had been assisting Celia with her plight and while it was fulfilling to know she had the interests of the women in hand, it was not without risk. Had somebody witnessed her leaving a note beneath the rock at the rear entrance to the asylum, it would mean instant dismissal. Out of need and desperation, it was the only way to communicate with Celia. Her mind raced with the possibilities. Had her discussions with another nurse, or worse still, an inmate, been overheard?

It was only yesterday that she had aired her opinion regarding the lack of empathy and treatment in the facility. She had been speaking out loud to Trinny, and could have easily been prey to eavesdroppers. Jillian found she was firmly caught between the desperate need to earn her living and the oath she had taken as a nurse. She was ashamed to admit that she did not possess the strength of mind that Celia displayed. The doctors would say it was Celia's negative influence that had begun to send decay through the place that would seek to undo their work. But in Jillian's opinion, Celia had simply exposed the ways in which the doctors could better advocate for the treatment of the inmates.

Jillian could hear the blood thumping loudly in her ears as she turned to face Matron.

'I am not proud of what I am about to ask of you,' Matron said.

'What is that, Matron?'

'It is with regret that I present orders that you ignore the inmate in cell number six this evening,' Matron said quietly.

'I see,' Jillian said.

'Before you pose the next question forming in your mind, do not ask it. Just ignore the cell and keep it firmly in your sights but keep it locked. Can you do that?'

'Yes, Matron.'

'That will be all.'

As Jillian's foot left the last stair tread, cold air spiralled straight up her leg and crawled beneath her skirt. She should have neglected the purchase of the new cotton stockings advertised in the latest women's magazines. The woollen ones she had loathed over the years now seemed a more practical option to stave against the freezing conditions within the asylum.

Jillian passed cell six. She knew there was a distinct reason for Matron's orders, but she could not ignore the overwhelming feeling that the connection to this cell had something to do with Sally Smith. The cell had remained empty since that fateful Sunday, and now its inhabitant was to be left in seclusion and ignored. Why?

From inside the cell, Celia heard the footfalls of the nurse on duty. 'Help, help!' she yelled.

Silence ensued as the sound disappeared. Celia began to feel tears form. While she had vowed that her anger would not see her fall into hysterics, the darkness and freezing cold biting into her skin, not to mention her incredulity that Charles had placed her in this dismal place began to unravel her resolve. The way he had tricked her into accompanying him down to the refractory ward was wicked. His intent had been evil, and yet, she had believed that he had been willing to allow her to witness the inner workings of the ward. She had been foolish and naïve to believe that he would relent and allow her to assist in any way. After all, this ward was a disgrace. She should have known that he had something else in store for her but she had trusted him. She knew he would not leave her here for long, or so she hoped.

But whatever the outcome, there could be no means to salvage anything they had once had between them. Celia had thought she had known the man she married, but that man would never have placed her in here, and nor would he have kept others here under these conditions. She felt such despair that she would never again call herself Mrs Charles Lawler.

Minutes ticked by. Celia stared at the door. The solid panel that stood between hell and freedom held her captive. She ran her hand along the brick wall. Droplets ran in rivulets down to the floor as her fingertips disturbed the moisture that covered it with a perfect sheen. She began to shiver. Her teeth chattered and there was no end to it. Her body was wracked with a deep cold that sunk right through to her core.

She moved from the wall and began to crawl toward the door. Surely the cold would not be as bone chilling if she distanced herself from the walls. Cold air squirreled beneath the door and ran across her skin. There was no reprieve and she was so tired. Her limbs gave in as she lay down at the base of the door.

She closed her eyes and counted the seconds. As her mind began to drift and sleep beckoned, she heard footsteps once more.

'Please, I need to be released!' she yelled. 'You have to let me out of here!'

Silence.

In desperation, she began to scream out names. Her voice was a drawl as she strained to keep her mouth below the door. She called out as many nurses' names as her mind could muster.

She closed one eye and strained to see beneath the door. She could see the toes of two shoes. 'Please, if that is you Trinny, I need you to open this door.'

The feet moved back two steps. It was the cotton stockings that alerted Celia to the nurse's identity. 'Jillian, I know it is you,' she whispered.

Jillian's confusion cleared in an instant. She now knew

precisely the reason Matron had ordered her to ignore whoever was on the other side of the door. But then she felt ill as a more complicated predicament clouded her mind. Matron had ordered her not to open the cell door, but now that she knew Celia was the woman inside the cell, how could she knowingly leave her in that predicament? Had Doctor Lawler ordered Celia's entrapment? Yes. That was the only way Matron would allow it.

Jillian realised Matron was going to skin her alive when she knew her orders had been ignored, but the friendship she had forged with Celia and the oath she had taken as a nurse propelled her forward. She pushed the key into the lock and slid the bolt across. She swung the door open.

'What are you doing in here, Celia?'

'Thank goodness you answered my call, Jillian,' Celia said as she skittered away from the door. Her teeth chattered as she spoke. Her lips were dry, and her voice was gravelly. It was no revelation to Jillian that her friend was suffering from dehydration.

'I'll fetch you some water.' Jillian clambered back through the door and returned minutes later with a jug of water and a tin cup. She gathered a blanket from over her arm and draped it across Celia's shoulders. The blanket was threadbare but to Celia it felt like a summer's day wrapping her up in its arms.

Celia gulped, before finally catching her breath. She grimaced at the discomfort the water created in her sore, dry throat. 'It would seem my husband followed through with his threat to throw me in here.' Celia's strength had suddenly returned and anger had taken hold.

Contemplating Charles' treatment of her, she no longer

feared him casting her from his life. She felt she would be fit to leave him once she found release from this cell.

'I cannot believe he put you down here.' Jillian sounded pained.

'I know, Jillian. I know. I need you to get word to Trinny. Tell her I am being detained in here. Tell her to comfort Maryann until I can find a way to get to her.'

'What happened to that unfortunate creature?'

'She was beaten. I did not have time to retrieve further truth from her before I had to take flight from that despicable Doctor Rushby. It would seem that both the doctor and superintendent have forgotten their place at present.'

Jillian sat beside Celia, hugging her with vigour to try to warm her more fervently.

'I am so ashamed that I know more than I care to admit. I wish I could be more like you. Brave and bold. Instead, I have hidden behind a secret that I dare not share.'

'Oh Jillian, I have heard just about all there is to know. I cast no judgement on any soul in here and that extends to the nurses.' Celia put her hand over Jillian's. 'It would seem I have let my bravery and boldness steer me into a place I cannot escape. If it will unburden you, let your secret out once and for all.'

Jillian tightened the pressure around Celia's shoulder and hugged her more tightly within her embrace as she began her story.

It's a Long Way to Tipperary looped in Jillian's mind as she did her rounds. Edna had been singing it long into the night. It was becoming increasingly obvious the poor dear was headed for the refractory ward for the next stage of her abysmal life. Her lewd behaviour had reached the point where action was required. Like a piece of sinew stuck between her teeth, the song bothered her and there seemed no escape from the lilting tune that fixed tight inside her brain. Edna had smeared faecal matter all over herself and it was a nurse's job to clean her up in the hope that she did not repeat it after another bowel movement.

Jillian was in the throng of a double shift, and she found herself yawning repeatedly. As she walked the line of cells and checked on each inmate, the words continued to tumble from her mouth. 'It's a long way to Tipperary.' The tune was wearing thin. 'Arrrggghhh!' she growled.

As Jillian neared the end of the corridor a long overdue ease washed over her. The ward, finally, was quiet. Exhausted from hours spent working coupled with the cleaning she had endured, she could not help but lay her head on her desk, if only for a few minutes.

To her own disgust, she did, in fact, fall asleep. While she did not know how long she slumbered, a strange sound stirred her awake. She fought to open her eyes with the knowledge that an inmate might be in need of assistance or be unwell, and within moments, the stifled sound of someone who was clearly in distress forced her to act. If it were screams or moans of pain she doubted she would have reacted so abruptly. But the sound was startling.

Walking along the length of the corridor she listened with intent at each cell door. It puzzled her to hear the voice of a man. She quickly pulled the key from her pocket and was surprised that the padlock was missing and the bolt was in the unlatched position. She slowly pulled the door open. The darkness in the room obscured her vision for a moment and with a whoosh, before she could step across the threshold, the door was abruptly pulled from her grasp and slammed closed. With the momentum of the door being hurtled forward she fell against the edge of it. Moments passed as she rubbed her arm and pulled at the door once more. She could hear the shuffle of feet and rustling of clothing before the door swung open abruptly and Doctor Rushby stood before her.

He walked forward, almost knocking her off her feet. With his face as close as any man would get only to his wife, he whispered in a low and dangerous voice. 'Get back to your station and seek slumber once more.'

She was rooted to the spot and could only manage to nod.

'Well?' he bellowed.

As though he had slapped her into action she skipped to attention and turned back toward the nurses' station.

As he walked past the station on his way out of the ward the menacing tone in his voice frightened her. 'If there is any mention of this I will see to it you never work here again. I will discredit your name and your competence. Do you understand?'

'Yes, sir,' Jillian whispered.

She waited until long after Doctor Rushby had retreated, until she was sure he would not return, before rushing back to the cell to check on its inhabitant. She whispered into the darkness before entering the cell. The young woman was shaking. She had pressed herself into the corner of the cell as though trying to blend into the darkened space. She was clearly distressed at what had been inflicted on her. A terrible sound escaped the young woman's lips as though she feared Doctor Rushby had returned to continue what was clearly torture for her.

'It is me,' Jillian whispered.

She crouched down and could see the blood beginning to dry on her face. Her lip was swollen and her eye was starting to swell. Jillian used a wet cloth to wipe the blood from the young woman's face. 'Oh Sarah, what has he done to you?' Jillian implored.

'This is not the first time,' she said.

'I promise you. I will do something to help you,' Jillian said. Even as the words tumbled from her mouth she knew that they were futile. 'I will be back,' she said before leaving the cell. All the while her despair at being unable to protect the women in this place weighed on her. She would wait for the moment to present itself when she could bring the truth of Doctor Rushby's character forward.

She returned to the cell with a clean nightgown. As the young woman lifted her arms and Jillian removed her nightgown the red marks on the tops of her legs were prominent.

'Oh God save us.' She sounded pained. As a nurse she had never felt quite so ill at the sight that presented itself.

'Thank you,' Sarah said as Jillian placed her into bed and pulled the sheet up.

'Try to get some sleep,' she said as she felt the fatigue that she was experiencing minutes before had been replaced with a sick feeling of dread.

For days afterwards, Jillian would feel tortured by the memory of Sarah's injuries, as well as by the knowledge that Doctor Rushby was such a callous and cruel man. She wondered what course of action to take, thinking of a variety of scenarios and continuously turning each one over in her mind. One scenario involved marching straight to the new superintendent's office and demanding that he listen to her story. Selfishly, she knew she would lose her employ if she embarked on this and she would certainly not be believed. Should a visit to the constable be considered? Alerting him to the barbaric treatment of the asylum's female inmates would be so low on his priority of things to investigate. To be truthful, he would not respect the perceptions of a nurse.

In the end, she resigned herself to taking no action other than simply continuing with her work, the only consolation being her hope that there would one day come a time when she could reveal the truth.

Months passed and to the best of Jillian's knowledge there seemed to be no repeat scenarios. She would check on Sarah more often than was necessary. One evening on her rounds the cell was empty. Upon looking up the record book, she had hoped to find that the young woman had been released; instead, she discovered that she had been moved to the hospital cottage.

An overwhelming fear that Doctor Rushby was continuing with his abhorrent behaviour had Jillian racing to the hospital cottage to look in on the young woman. Bursting in on the nurse on duty, she demanded to know where Sarah Ashby was.

'She is recovering from surgery,' the nurse told her.

Jillian secretly prayed that the injuries inflicted on her would be discovered, prompting everything to unravel for Doctor Rushby.

'Doctor Rushby just performed a hysterectomy on the

young woman as she had endured significant problems of the female vice,' the nurse said. Reading from surgical notes she continued, 'The patient appeared to have intense swelling of her abdominal area that could only be attributed to her ovaries and uterus bearing signs of intense disease.'

Jillian's heart dropped to her shoes and still she remained silent. She would get nowhere pointing a finger at a respected doctor. She realised that a foetus would have been evidence of the man's crime, and that he had in all likelihood just cast that foetus into the waste — along with any chance Sarah would ever have of becoming a mother.

As Jillian returned to the ward and resumed her duties, she wept quietly. She had allowed young Sarah Ashby and many others to be abused by a system that protected the outside world from the people within, but could not protect those caught within from the ones who swore to protect them.

Celia clasped Jillian's hand. 'Oh Jillian, you poor, poor thing. What a burden this has placed on you. Whatever happened to Sarah? Is she still here?'

Jillian shook her head. 'She was transferred to Kew Cottages after her recovery. It seemed, and this came as no surprise, that she would become violent each time a doctor attempted to tend to her.'

Celia shook her head in despair. 'I vow that when I get out of here I will make it my life's work to protect those incarcerated here. I am so incensed with the men who govern this place. One in particular who is going to get far more than he would ever dare imagine.'

'I cannot release you,' Jillian said as she wrung her hands.

'Oh, do not fret. I will wait here and relish my release. I have so very much to enlighten my husband with when that moment presents itself,' she said. 'You best get back to your rounds. I do not wish to jeopardise your work.'

Jillian pulled the cell door open. 'I will bring you something to eat.'

'Thank you, Jillian. I am grateful. And could you please get word to Trinny? Ask her to relieve Maryann of any concerns. I will assist her as soon as I am able.'

Chapter 23

Maryann looked around the hospital room. She then stared out the window, focussing on a passionfruit vine that was winding its way up the veranda post. Any attempt to forget what she had endured was futile. Bees buzzed around the flowers. How she wished she had wings so she could fly far, far away from here. Although she was recovering to some extent, her body still ached, serving as a reminder of what had been done to her.

What was going to happen when she was returned to her cell? No doubt that violent man would visit her again? She hiccupped as a sob escaped from her. He had forced himself upon her. The image of him on top of her, heaving and huffing while tearing at her nightgown, would haunt her until she died. She threw her head from side to side to shake the memory away. It would seem that she had endured the worst thing any man could inflict on a defenceless woman. He had slapped her and beat her until she was so weak that he could easily lie on top of her and thrust himself between her legs. With no concern for her cries of pain and fear, he had taken only minutes to have his way but it felt like an eternity to her.

Maryann had woken in the hospital cottage with no recollection of how she had been delivered there. As the days passed, disturbing images raced through her mind. She recalled her attacker turning towards the cell door afterwards, preparing to leave. He was looking down, buttoning his trousers.

From her bed in the hospital cottage, Maryann recalled that it was at that point that she had lunged from the bed and jumped on the man's back. Her fists had hardly connected with his shoulders and head before he had heaved his body to and fro, easily throwing her off. Her decision to fight him had only made him seek to hurt her further. She had felt his weight atop her once more. She had screamed, 'Get off me!'

'Shut up!' he had yelled into her face as he grasped her head between his hands and began to bang it on the floor. She had screamed in pain until she could no longer hear her voice as it faded away, and she had lost all awareness. But now, days later, as these snippets of memory flooded her mind, she realised who had caused her injuries.

It was Doctor Rushby. It confused her that somebody who had taken an oath to cure the sick could inflict such violence. He was such a cruel man. It was not God's will for a person to seek to hurt another. She had been brought up in a religious household and this was the word of the Lord. Her outburst of violence toward him was at odds with her beliefs. She had more questions than answers to all that she had been taught as a child regarding religion. How God had allowed her to end up in this place would placate her til the end of her days. Her feelings for her one true love Lee were real. He had never hurt her, yet her family, as a result of her love for him, had discarded her. Even her one indiscretion that resulted in her birthing a bastard did not make sense to her. Why could she not love a Chinese miner from the goldfields? The bible stated that love came in all forms and now, she found herself at the mercy of a despicable man who had assured her that she would die at his hands as soon as she was alone.

Trinny had delivered a message from Celia, whispering in Maryann's ear while bathing her wounds. 'She has been waylaid and will call upon you to assist you as soon as possible.'

And now, a different voice made her suck in a deep breath. 'Hello, my dear.'

Doctor Rushby closed the door and leaned against it. The menace in his slow steady steps made her feel ill at ease. He walked to her bed. She scooted backwards, pulling her knees to her chest. As fear overtook her, she began to cry.

He leaned in and gently grabbed a strand of hair in his fingertips. One of his eyes was covered with a bandage and his smile curved with the promise that she would be punished. 'So pretty, so, so pretty.'

Maryann could not speak and dared not scream but sobbed and wished him away.

He spoke loud enough for anyone within the hospital cottage to hear. 'I think it is high time we got you back to your ward, Maryann.'

While his tone gave no inkling of anything untoward, his proximity to her demonstrated that he would make it his purpose to revisit her. She could not survive his intentions and she had so much to fight for. She clung to the hope she would someday leave this place and find her little boy. Even though she now questioned her faith in anything holy, she nonetheless found that she prayed for her baby every day.

There was a large chance he was still in the orphanage. Who would want to adopt a child who possessed an Asian appearance? Add to the balance that boys were not as sought after as sweet baby girls. She could not allow her life to end in here, not without ever knowing what had become of her little boy.

Doctor Rushby leaned in once more and pushed the words through his lips. 'I will make you pay for almost blinding me, you little witch. You will comply when I am between your legs and if you do not I will strangle you until you take your last breath. Do you hear me?'

He stood upright and moved swiftly toward the door. Opening it, he looked out to the hall and in his brash voice he said, 'Yes, I think you are doing quite well, young lady.' Then he was gone.

Maryann held her breath. Her lungs constricted. She had to flee. She had to get out of here.

Without further thought, she flung the covers aside and lunged from the bed.

Throwing the window sash open she threw one leg out, then the other and ran around the return veranda. She jumped over the rail and dropped onto the garden bed below. She was set on a course to the only person who could assist her. If Celia could not come to her aid she would seek her out. The fate awaiting her inside a ward that should be her safe haven posed too large a danger for her.

The superintendent's lodge was beyond the wall. She would have to find a way out. Sheer desperation prompted her to face such an impossible task. She could feel the moist earth seeping between her toes as she ran a haphazard line between the rows of staked vegetables.

Inmates stared at her. Some pointed, and one even yelled as he blocked her path. She screamed and dodged his outstretched arm. A familiar face swam before her. She blinked numerous times. They stared at one another before she whispered, 'Lee?'

He pulled her into his grasp and held her to him.

Her arms wrapped around his waist and she felt immense confusion that she had found him, right at this very moment, and in here.

'Help me. You have to help me.' She sobbed into his shirt.

Lee pulled her further into the centre of several rows of corn. They would be severely punished if they were caught together.

He rubbed her back until she had calmed somewhat. 'Maryann, how did you come to be here?'

'I came from the hospital ward and I was attacked and I need to see the doctor's wife.' She was making no sense. She had been placed in here because she was showing signs of lunacy.

He closed his eyes as sadness overcame him. He had given up all hope he would ever see her again. Yet, she had stumbled right into his arms. He knew the hopelessness of their plight would fall upon deaf ears, yet he could not deny he was stunned that she was here, with him, once more. However, it was too late. She had become an imbecile. It pained him to hear her talking nonsense. The fact she was racing through the rows of vegies with no shoes on was proof enough that she had become unhinged.

Maryann pushed against Lee. 'You did not come for me. Why did you not come for me? You said you would.'

'Your father saw to it that I ended up in here, never to be heard or seen from again.'

She closed her eyes and began to weep. 'They took our baby away.'

His pain was evident as he looked to the heavens. 'I did not know,' he whispered.

She sobbed and fell against him. 'They took our baby boy. He is ... He is gone. He is gone forever.'

'What do you think you are doing?' An orderly ripped Maryann away from Lee's grasp. She began to scream. Panicked, she tried to kick and claw her way free. Lee moved forward as the orderly yelled, 'Step back! Stay back!'

Lee drew to a halt. He had been treated as a threat when he had stepped off the boat onto Australian shores and his right to be treated as a human had diminished even further when he had been dumped at the door of Ararat Lunatic Asylum.

Bundled out of his bed, a sack thrown over his head, his feet and hands bound tightly, Lee had not known which way was up until his body hit timber. The shudder of the wagon's flat-bed confirmed he was being transported elsewhere. He was assured that death was prominent but fear of being tortured loomed large. The goldfields attracted all kinds, but a man was treated most poorly if he looked different and spoke 'in tongues'.

The men spoke in harsh whispers and Lee was fairly sure he did not recognise any individual voices. But as the wagon rolled along and the noise of the insects increased in volume, so did the voices. At this point he recognised one pitch in particular, thus revealing the reason he was here. Mister Harper owned the mercantile and was among the group that had stolen him from his bed. His body was already being jostled around with the momentum of the wagon, and his hips and back had endured the torture of being hogtied, but he knew things were going to become far worse.

He counted the voices as they delivered their anger and insults. He was used to ridicule. It did not concern him. But tonight would be his last on Earth, and that made him sad. The wagon rounded bend after bend and he began to black out, mostly from fatigue and pain. The man in the flatbed with him slapped, kicked and insulted him, but this voice was definitely unfamiliar.

'Careful, Charlie,' someone else finally said. 'We don' want him too banged up before we're finished with him. Bloody slant-eye bastard. Think they can come and take our land, our gold and now they dare touch our daughters.'

If he could speak to Mister Harper and tell him the truth, he could make him understand that he loved Maryann.

'Mister Harper, you must understand. I … ' his voice was muffled through the hessian and the dust he breathed in made him feel sick, but he had to try to talk to the man.

'Oh, I do. You put your filthy hands on my daughter and filled her head with rubbish. She thinks she loves you. She thinks you are going to marry her. How could that be?'

'I love her. I do.'

'I will not stand by and let my daughter bear a bastard child with slanty eyes and yellow skin. Your filthy vile act of indecency with my daughter has cost my family and now you will pay for it, as will she.'

Jostled uncomfortably on the flatbed of the wagon, Lee had no answer. He had indeed taken liberties with Maryann, and while he had performed only in the name of love, he knew it had been very wrong of him to have acted as he had. Awaiting his fate, he thought of his beloved's face and her skin and how she felt in his arms and knew he would never see her again. For that he was sorry and he knew that no matter how much he loved her it would never be enough and their love would never be accepted. His only hope — that she would escape this situation less scathed than he — seemed futile.

Lee closed his eyes and sent a silent apology to Maryann. Unless she was aware of tonight's events, as well as privy to the plans her father had in store for him, she would think he had abandoned her. Surely if she had known of her father's intentions, she would have sent a warning to him to flee.

He had promised he would take her away, marry her and give her a happy life. But as he had tried to gather together enough money to aid their escape, things had conspired against them.

Her family, his background, his lack of wealth and now it seemed their time had run out. The secret had been uncovered and he was going to leave her in this life; their only hope of a reunion would be if she joined him in the next. Her father had intimated they would both be punished. Knowing Mr Harper, he wondered what Maryann's fate would be. He did not consider for a moment that the man would kill her. Just what would he do with her now that she was a tainted woman?

The wagon bed tilted upward as the wheels hit a steady rise. Lee could not see a thing and could only guess he was being transported up One Tree Hill to be disposed of in the lake or buried beneath a stand of trees. The incline persisted for so long, he began to feel giddy.

The sound of the crunch of gravel beneath the wheels dissipated until all he could hear were the chirping of the crickets. Someone picked him up and tossed him onto the hard ground. He endured a few swift kicks to his back and head while he waited for the world to fall dark and for God to take him.

He heard a knocker drop loudly against a door before the scurry of feet and the chatter of the wagon could be heard moving away and into the night. He was puzzled. Left to live and dumped on somebody's doorstep? How could this be? He fell backwards over the threshold as the door was opened. His body stretched across the cold doorstep and the hard floor within.

Two sets of hands were upon him, untying him and lifting him to his feet. They whisked the sack from his head. Staring up at two men dressed in white, Lee realised he had been dispensed to the Ararat Lunatic Asylum.

'No, no, no!' he began to say as they dragged him roughshod away from the open door and further into the building. He tried in vain to pull his arms free of their hold, finding himself prisoner for the second time tonight. He was petrified. Everyone knew of this dreaded place and what became of those who entered it, never to be heard of again. Now, he found himself on the wrong side of the fortress front door and ha-ha walls of the place on the hill.

The burly orderlies dragged his beaten and weary body up stairs, through hallways and then down stairs once more, ignoring his pleas for release. With his body pinned between them, the thugs would not relinquish him, nor respond to his words.

They pulled Lee to a halt in front of a narrow wooden door. One of the men yanked a key from his pocket and then turned it in the padlock. Sliding the bolt along before pulling the door open he said, 'Enjoy your new home.' Both men shoved him into the cell before slamming the door closed. The bolt slid back into place and landed with a thud that reverberated through Lee's chest.

Clutching around in the darkness, Lee knocked over a bucket with foul smelling liquid in it. He discovered it was excrement and bodily fluids from the previous inhabitant. Gasping air into his mouth, he dared not subject his nostrils to the stench for a second time. He grappled with the canvas blanket on the floor and draped it around his body. It gave him no warmth, only protection from the moisture dripping off the ceiling and running down the walls.

Days passed. He measured the weeks by the removal and return of the bucket. He received one meal a day. His body ached from constant contact with the hard floor, and cold seeped into his bones through the draft that ran under the door and found him regardless of where he sat.

He despaired for Maryann now that their relationship had been discovered. Their plans to run away and marry had been thwarted. She would think he had abandoned her. He hoped but highly doubted her parents had forgiven her the transgression. Her father knew Lee was locked away and was no longer a threat to Maryann's virtue; this fact was the only positive among the many negatives that comprised his present situation.

Countless were the hours Lee spent pondering the idea of making a noose from his canvas blanket. He used his teeth to try to tear a strip of the canvas away, but it frayed in tiny threads. It would never work. Just when he thought he could not bear another minute, an orderly came to the cell. 'Get out!' he yelled while holding the door wide open.

Lee tried to move as quickly as he could but his body was sore from the relentless days of cold and discomfort. He moved like a decrepit old man. He followed the orderly down a corridor, up a flight of stairs and down another corridor before a door was opened before him. 'After a month in that cell this should feel like heaven,' the orderly said as he walked out into the courtyard with Lee following close behind him. Lee placed his hand up to shield his eyes from the daylight. The wind blew across the yard but he did not care. He walked across mud and dirt but it did not bother him at all. The orderly showed him to the vegetable patch. 'This will be your new line of work,' he said. 'A bit of a change from diggin' for gold but you will get the hang of it.'

The orderly's snigger was not lost on Lee but he did not reveal that the aroma of the fresh fruit was heaven after smelling the vial odours from the cell and ward he had been locked in for weeks. He dropped to his knees and plunged his fingers into the earth. It squelched between his fingers and felt wonderful to the touch.

The days became bliss and the nights bearable. He began to cherish his time among those suffering with severe afflictions, and these folk became his friends. After all, they did not treat him differently because of the colour of his skin or because of the way he spoke. The orderlies and doctors continued to throw abuse at him due to his ancestry but that was not unusual to him. He remained thankful that he was still alive but held no hope that he would ever see his Maryann again. If tending to the vegetable garden was to be his occupation from now on, that was the best outcome for him. If this place was to remain his home until his dying day that would be very sad, but there was really nothing he could do about it.

Maryann fought the orderly until she could no longer stand unaided. He delivered her back to the hospital ward. Trinny raced to her bedside. 'What in God's name were you thinking?' she demanded. 'Do not move. I will fetch some water to bathe you.'

When Trinny returned with a basin of water and a wet cloth, Maryann was staring at the wall in front of her in dismay. 'I found him. I found him. He is here. I found him,' she declared over and over.

'Who?' Trinny asked, perplexed.

'My Lee. I found him.'

'Who?'

'He was stolen from me and now I know the truth.' She was smiling in spite of her injuries and fear of the future.

'I thought he had left me but he has been here the whole time.'

Chapter 24

Charles awoke with his nose and lips mashed hard against the arm of the chaise. As the stench from its fabric filled his nostrils he whipped his head back quickly, but the smell followed him even as he rolled over and landed on all fours on the hard floor. He realised that the stench was his own breath; rotten from the liquor he had downed the night before. After lying in a ridiculous position for the few hours of sleep he had managed to muster, his joints felt jagged. His head felt heavy as he dropped it from side to side to free the stiffness vexing his neck.

He would go to Celia first thing. She had been kept prisoner long enough in the refractory cell. Once he had explained himself to her and gained her understanding, he would call on Constable Bryant and garner his support on how to proceed.

As Charles splashed water on his face and brushed his teeth, blanching at the foul-tasting baking soda, he changed his mind with regard to the day's agenda. Although he had only just hatched a plan to release Celia at first light, he decided she was best left tucked away in the refractory ward for a while longer. He could not deal with her sharp tongue and interference while he navigated the disposal of one Michael McGowan's body from the morgue and worked out how to deal with his fellow doctor's behaviour. The release of his wife would force him to share information with her and God forbid her reaction to knowing she had been correct in her assumptions all along.

Rinsing his mouth with fresh water, Charles concluded that Celia could jeopardise his mission if she were to share certain information with the asylum's staff or inmates — information that could be passed onto Doctor Rushby, an action that would unravel everything before the noose was tied. He knew that she had her spies within the place and had tried to feign that what she learnt from her network of informers had no impact on his work. On that note, Doctor Rushby could have his own inmates and staff assisting him with his untoward treatment of the vulnerable.

Celia was going to be as angry as a cornered possum however the day's events unfolded. Deciding to postpone the moment of her release would have no bearing on the tide of anger that was going to rain down on him, so he may as well buy himself precious time to concentrate on the tasks at hand.

He looked at the hour. It was still early. His stomach roiled at the thought of breakfast as he made his way to the administration offices in the main building. He headed down the stairs to the refractory ward and gave cell number six a fleeting glance before locking himself inside the records storage room. For hours he pulled file after file from the alphabetised drawers. Comparing records and reports between particular years was tedious but he needed proof before he called upon Constable Bryant. His eyes stung and the dust made his nose itch like nothing else but he remained steadfast in his pursuit of what he required to cement proof of his suspicion.

Visiting the hospital cottage on the premise that he was doing rounds, Charles held a private audience with Maryann Harper. She had been frightened upon his arrival but soon helped him with his inquiry. The poor girl could have been killed at the man's hands. He was ashamed that he had not taken heed of his wife's warnings on many occasions, but nonetheless he made Maryann swear to keep their conversation private. She had agreed before adding that she would cherish a visit from Celia as soon as she could make it.

Charles felt ill at ease calling himself a doctor at present. Now that he was on the road to uncovering each facet of Doctor Rushby's deceit, he became more and more angry with himself for allowing such behaviour to continue. While he himself could not be held accountable for his ignorance over any of the doctor's wrongdoings before his time here, he was gravely disappointed he had not allowed himself to acknowledge the extent of the man's recklessness in recent months. It was now blatantly obvious to Charles that Doctor Rushby held his own agenda and used his position to intimidate staff and inmates, including Charles himself on more than one occasion.

Charles left the asylum and called back in at home for a short while. He washed his face and hands and looked at his tired appearance in the bathroom mirror. He still had to release Celia and the hour was getting on. He tore a piece of bread from the loaf left uneaten on the counter, dipped it into the adjacent tub of lard and strode from the house, eating his meagre meal along the way into town. He could dally no longer. He had to cover distance quickly to allow himself enough time to discuss the matter with Constable Bryant. He had so much to do and the day was racing away from him.

Arriving back at the asylum after his meeting with Constable Bryant, Charles tapped lightly at the door of Doctor Rushby's office.

'Yes?' came the short reply.

Charles entered the room.

'Hello, Charles. What brings you here? I thought you were headed to Ballarat again this week.'

Charles approached the edge of Doctor Rushby's desk. 'I was supposed to travel but decided to postpone my journey until next week. How is the eye?'

'Still sore but it looks worse than it is.' Doctor Rushby dabbed beneath his reddened eye with the pads of his fingers. 'Please, sit, sit. Surely the concerned look on your face is not for my tortured eye?' he said.

'I wanted to get your opinion on some information I have garnered,' Charles said as he sat across from Doctor Rushby and passed the file across the desk.

'Absolutely. I will be happy to assist.'

Doctor Rushby opened the file and looked at the first sheet of paper. His demeanour did not alter. He flipped the file closed and just as quickly reopened it again, flipping to the next section as though skimming through the pages of a book. He kept his gaze fixed on the next sheet of paper as it revealed a different name. He looked at the date. 'I do not understand.'

'Continue your perusal,' Charles implored. 'The pattern will become apparent in the next few moments.'

The next sheet revealed yet another name and subsequent information that began to reveal a much larger picture.

Doctor Rushby's eyes slowly lifted from the file to Charles. 'Would you please explain the meaning of this?'

'To the contrary. You can explain it to me.' Charles' heart beat a heavy thrum in his ears.

Doctor Rushby cleared his throat. 'Each of these cases has an explanation. There are all manner of unsavoury characters in here. For goodness sake, Charles. Look around you. Are you so naïve to think that the conditions in here warrant a normal response to these cases?' He slammed the file closed and slapped the back of his fingers against the cardboard cover.

An awkward silence ensued, during which Charles allowed his superior the opportunity to conjure for himself a truth to dig him free of the information set before him.

'What are you suggesting with this?' Doctor Rushby said through gritted teeth and once more slapped his hand against the file.

'I think you know exactly what this suggests, Simon.' Charles nodded toward the file. I have a question for you.' Charles paused as though trying to seek the correct words. 'I will not seek nor sugar-coat the words to make you feel at ease. I will just say it! What gave you the right to abuse your position? These people have been placed in here under our protection from an intolerable life beyond these walls, and ... '

'That is where you are wrong, Charles,' Doctor Rushby interjected. 'These *people*, as you so adoringly call them, are placed in here to protect those on the outside from their idiocy and imbecility. We are placed in the position of seeing to it that they do not burden the lives of the townsfolk below, and this gives us the right to do what is required from our professional standpoint, to do as we see fit.'

Charles seized the moment to reveal a vital piece of his findings from his morning's sleuthing. 'Doctor Harcroft strayed from his position to the extent that he is now in gaol for his misdemeanours.'

Doctor Rushby's mouth snapped shut.

'You trained under Doctor Harcroft,' Charles continued, 'and it seems he taught you well. After all, his teaching has led you all the way to where you find yourself right now.'

Staring up at the two towers in the distance he felt excitement rise within. Finally, medical school was complete and he was now a training doctor. Simon Rushby Junior was about to enter the Ararat Lunatic Asylum. A perfect dumping point for training doctors, as once they were qualified it was the last place a practicing practitioner wanted to be permanently placed. He had not quite earned his title as Doctor but was fondly called 'young Simon' by his peers.

The first time he had encountered a patient of his own, albeit an inmate, she had been frightened of him. He had had to check her over to make sure her injuries did not extend beyond her ankles or hands. She had been chased by the police and had been caught only when her dress had snagged in a bramble of blueberries. The constable wanted to have her charged for stealing but she was so distraught and acting so crazed that the police officer decided to bring her straight to the asylum. A nurse managed to get the girl to undress. Once she had on a loose nightgown and the covers pulled up to her chin, he visited the girl in the hospital cottage and tried to find out some information.

'What is your name?' he prompted. She did not look at him

nor did she answer his question. He quickly deduced that she was in the correct facility. Being deaf and a mute certainly rendered her an imbecile.

For the days that followed he would call on her in the hospital cottage and she would ignore anyone in the vicinity. He gave her a chalkboard and a piece of chalk and implored her to write something for him. Still, there was no communication from her. There were no desperate pleas from worried family members who had lost a beloved daughter, so she was released from the hospital cottage and placed in a ward. Because she was mute and thus considered an imbecile, she would be kept here at the discretion of the doctors who considered her care their responsibility.

As he was new to the asylum and eager to learn everything he could, much of his time was spent running between the hospital cottage, the wards and the offices of his peers. With their age and experience, the surgeons and superintendent — those who knew the inner workings of the institution — could propel him from being someone who blended into the whitewash painted on the building to an esteemed doctor of considerable significance and reputation.

He looked up to Doctor Harcroft the most. This man had been the superintendent of the asylum for twelve years and was succinct enough in his judgement and decision-making prowess to keep the place running like a finely tuned clock.

Today, Simon Rushby Junior was particularly in awe of his mentor's efficiency. How did he manage his time so astutely? Even though young Simon had been at work for five hours, he had still not managed to catch up with his ward rounds. Instead, he had been waylaid attending to a new inmate.

This hysterical woman had been left at the door of the asylum with sores and filth covering her body. From the moment she had been in a nurse's charge she set about picking and scratching at her skin until blood oozed from the intensity of her gouging. Her fingernails dug deep crevasses along her arms and legs, and she was almost bald as she continued to twist her hair around her finger and tug on it until it would tear free from her scalp. Her wounds were infected and oozing puss and he did not believe that she could be left with dressings on them; it was clear she would simply tear off any coverings and thereby undo all his efforts.

With the assistance of a nurse, he strapped her arms and legs to the bed rails to stop her from further injuring herself. How her vulnerability changed his demeanour. She struggled and winced and moved this way and that while they restrained her. He almost slapped her face when she spat at him but he found his own restraint within. He would not put up with it a second time though. If she fought him tomorrow he would see her punished. He was a doctor and he was helping her. Could she not see this?

Late that day, after he had completed his ward rounds, he was surprised that the young deaf mute was on his mind. She intrigued him. He wanted to find some time to work with her, to see if he could not garner her name or age at the very least. If he visited her many times, he would gain her trust.

It was late and all the inmates had been put to bed for the night. He unlocked the door to enter her cell and caught Doctor Harcroft in the throes of holding her face down on the mattress while pounding into her with such violence. The sound of the older doctor's flesh slapping against the woman's backside as he pushed into her with vigour had the younger doctor staring in shock at the scene. He thought she was moaning but could not be sure, as the straw mattress muffled the sound.

It was only after staring for minutes on end, unable to move his gaze from the scene before him, that he realised that the sounds she was making were cries of hysterics. He stepped into the cell to rouse Doctor Harcroft's notice. His strategy worked. The man stopped mid stroke and turned around. Showing no concern for his behaviour, however, he continued to hold the inmate's face hard into the mattress. As though there was nobody else in the cell, he turned back to his task and continued on with his rhythmic hammering into her, until he let out a curse and held her fast for a few seconds then pulled himself free from her body.

He pulled up his trousers and began to button them before stopping and looking up at his witness. 'Well, do not just stand there boy, step up and take a turn.'

Young Simon looked perplexed and stood rooted to the spot. He stared at the young girl, who had scooted back into the corner of the cell aghast with fear.

Doctor Harcroft was also looking at the girl, 'Do not tell a soul', he said as he placed a finger to his lips. Chuckling to himself he walked to the door of the cell and switched his gaze to the junior doctor before saying. 'You will get the hang of it, young Simon.' He adjusted his trousers before pulling the door open and walking out into the corridor.

With the door closed, young Simon approached the mattress and knelt beside the weeping inmate. He wiped her hair from her face. Tears and mucus made his hands sticky.

He also felt something else. He was aroused beyond resolve by what he had witnessed. He loathed watching her being ravished but at the same time it unleashed something in him. He pushed her back onto the mattress and pulled her nightdress up. He gave no more thought to his actions as he pulled his trousers down his legs while she pushed at him and tried to escape. He pushed her down and lay on top of her. Placing his hand over her mouth, he looked into her eyes. 'Shhhhhhhh,' he whispered quietly, as though she were a baby being laid down to sleep. The soothing sound of his breath as it escaped his body made her relax a little. 'Shhhhhhh,' he whispered once more before settling himself inside her and feeling her screams reverberate against his hand.

The gentle movement between their hips soon gave way to something in him that made him feel immense control. He felt such power. After finding release he pulled free and for a fleeting moment looked down at the shuddering young woman. He felt a glimmer of guilt. He was a doctor. He was supposed to protect and care for these inmates in his charge but the things he had been taught in medical school had somewhat made the body a mere chunk of flesh. He held no passion for the notion that the heart had control over love and that this new view of romance between a man and a woman that was bandied around was in actual fact a reality. Women's bodies were for the sole use of reproduction. They were second-class citizens and the ones in here were at the bottom of the heap. She could not talk, was deaf and dumb. After all, Doctor Harcroft had called it correctly. Who was she going to tell? Better still, how would she divulge her tale?

The following morning, Simon Rushby Junior joined Doctor

Harcroft on rounds. As they discussed the various ailments and cures of the inmates they checked upon, Doctor Harcroft said, 'So, young Simon, how are you settling in?' He smiled at him in a way that barely disguised the secret to which he eluded.

'Quite well, Doctor Harcroft. Quite well, thank you.'

Doctor Harcroft clapped the younger man on the back. ''That's the way, chap. You are going to fit right in here.'

Charles watched Doctor Rushby slip back into their conversation as quickly as he had snaked away. It was a clever way to intimidate and retain control over anybody who dared question his resolve.

'You see, Simon?' Charles said, finally deciding to strip the man of his honorific. After all, during discussions Doctor Rushby had always referred to he himself as Charles. This had occurred to him from their first meeting. He should have put an end to the discomfort he felt for the man right from that moment. Being new to the position and having very little experience with the laws of institutionalisation, however, he had adopted the respectful approach of deferring to those who were teaching him from their own professional experience within the asylum.

'I have watched your professionalism slip ever since I arrived. You have manipulated your position in here on many occasions and I am sorry that I did not try to put an end to it sooner,' Charles said.

The disrespectful tone of the sentiment was not lost on Doctor Rushby. His face began to turn red and his neck bulged, forcing his collar to tighten. 'You fucking dare to come in here and accuse me of my failings as a doctor!'

Charles watched Simon's anger build as the man pointed his finger at Charles and said, 'You cannot control the inmates in here just as I cannot. The hell of it is, is that you have little control over anything, Charles. Your wife defies you. The staff members do as they please behind your back and you take no notice. And it is the same situation with the inmates.'

Simon drew himself up from his desk to create a sense of drama as he spoke. 'The inmates, these fucking lunatics and imbeciles in here, have no logical function in the world — and yet you allow them privilege with your devil-may-care attitude. It is up to us to yield our power over them in any way we see fit. I could see from the first that you were not up to it and nor were the others before you. That is why I have to make a stand to show my strength when they get out of hand. I am a doctor to be respected. I can do as I wish and nobody stands in the way of that. Not you, not the staff, and definitely not these crazy bastards in here who have been punished by God for their sins. Do you hear me, Charles?' he yelled. Spittle flew from his lips as he banged his fist on the desk again and again. He picked up the file and flung it across the room where it hit the opposite wall and burst open, sending a flurry of pages cascading to the floor.

As Charles watched the tirade his composure did not alter. 'You see, Simon, that is where you are entirely wrong. The qualities you perceive as weaknesses, I see as vulnerabilities. You prey on those who cannot advocate for themselves.'

'You cannot prove a thing!' Doctor Rushby yelled.

'Wrong again, Simon. The proof has been revealed to me and I intend on gathering every shred of evidence to ensure you pay for your sins.'

Doctor Rushby's face began to drain of blood and grow pale. 'You will never prove anything. Never!'

'Would you believe that I know that you have been receiving payments to lock people away in here at your discretion?' Charles could see the surprise in Doctor Rushby's eyes as the truth dawned on the man.

'I know,' Charles continued. 'That came as a surprise to me, too. Even I did not expect that additional element of corruption to lengthen the list of charges that will be brought against you, but there we have it. Surprise!' Although Charles grinned he was not happy. He realised he had added that last statement in an attempt to help him hold his nerve, which was fast beginning to slip as the meeting began drawing to an end.

'I will fucking have your head for this.' Doctor Rushby thumped both hands on the desk.

'I doubt that. Evidence of your evil acts will show up in more places than we will care to count, but in the meantime it is your present reaction that speaks most strongly of your guilt.' With that, Charles turned toward the door and pulled it open. He had to get out of the office. He had to release Celia right away.

'I believe that is where you come in,' he said to the person in the hall.

Constable Bryant passed Charles on the threshold and entered the office.

Charles ran down the staircase to the refractory ward and fumbled with the key in the padlock.

The hour was late. As he searched in the darkness he questioned whether Celia would still be in the cell. A crumpled heap lay on the floor and he knew in that moment he had made a grave error of judgement.

He dropped to his knees and scooped her up in his arms. She came to life and began to scream.

'It is me! It is me!' He thought the sound of his voice would appease her.

'Take your hands off me!' she yelled.

She remained in his arms until he had cleared the cell door. Once out in the hall where the shard of light from the kerosene lantern assisted his vision, he placed her down, as the look of disdain she cast upon him forced him to do nothing else.

'Get your hands off me,' she whispered as she slowly turned and limped with fatigue toward the stairs.

He placed his hand on her shoulder and said, 'I will shower you with apology in due course. I had to see to things without you meddling.'

'Do not. Do not.' She pushed away from him and continued to look pained as she ambled to the base of the stairs.

He caught her as she began to lever herself up onto the first tread. 'Please, my love. Let me ... let me help you.'

Celia pushed away from him. 'Leave me alone.'

He stopped to allow her some distance until her anger had cooled somewhat. She was almost at the top of the stairs when he decided it was a safe enough distance. He placed one foot on the tread and looked up. She had stopped on the top step when her body began to waiver. Time slowed as she began to tumble downward. He rushed up the steps and fell forward to capture her as the gap eventually closed between them. She was so feeble that her attempt to escape from him had thrust her off balance.

'Celia. Oh my god,' he said, horrified as he caught her lifeless body in his hands. Convinced she was dead, he yelled her name and the sound reverberated in the confines of the refractory ward. He held her body to him and gasped for air as though his life was ending. Feeling the smallest breath escape from her lips, he scooped her up in his arms and ran like a man crazed. It was easy to carry her frail figure up the many stairs but he found it difficult to gain momentum with the narrow opening closing in on them. The many stairs down which she had tumbled seemed endless but he finally made it to the top. He ran through the hallways and believed they too would never end. Shards of light from the lanterns flickered by in increments as he passed door after door and could see no end to them.

As the door loomed before him, like a threat that would keep him enclosed, he shoved at it with all his might. He looked down at her frail body in his grasp. 'Please stay with me, Celia.'

He lunged up the steps to the door of the hospital ward and yelled for a nurse.

The front door opened. 'Doctor Lawler?' came the questioning voice.

'Clear an operating room for me.'

The nurse looked perplexed.

'Now!' he yelled.

The nurse scurried ahead of him and opened the door to one of the rooms where procedures were performed. Charles placed Celia down on the bed in the centre of the room and began to undo her clothing.

'Get her shoes off,' he ordered.

The nurse was unlacing her boots and pulling them from her feet.

'And her pantaloons?' she asked.

'Everything. I need to see what damage she has sustained.'

He held Celia's chin in his grasp and looked into her face.

He put his ear close to her mouth and could still feel the faintest breath escape her blue lips.

'Thank goodness,' he said, looking heavenward.

Once his wife's clothing had been removed he checked her arms and legs and her chest to see if any compounded bones were visible.

'Celia, can you hear me?'

She did not respond.

'Please Celia, you need to open your eyes,' Charles implored.

He looked down her body and was immediately ashamed at her present physical condition. She was filthy and he noted how much weight she had lost. How could he have let this happen? How had he treated her in such a way?

Her arm was broken so he placed it in a cast. As he straightened the bone, she groaned in pain. It was a sound he should not have relished but he was relieved she could at least announce her pain. It surprised him that the rest of her body had survived the battering. He could hardly conceive that he had been cause of her injuries. 'Unforgivable!' he said aloud.

Charles stayed with Celia for the rest of the night, finally falling asleep in the chair beside her bed. His patient did not stir but her breathing returned to normal as dawn snuck through the windowpane.

A nurse continued to check on Celia throughout the night, and her presence now caused Charles to wake also. He was exhausted by the fitful sleep he had endured but he did not care. He was thankful for the diligence the nurse showed.

'Would you like a cup of tea?' she asked as she carried a tray into the room.

'Thank you,' Charles said, taking the saucer that held a lukewarm cup of tea and also a slither of bread.

Sipping the tea, he looked over the rim of the cup. Returning it to the tray he turned back toward the bed and jumped in shock. Celia's eyes were open. They seemed vacant and she was staring at the ceiling. Her lips were closed so tightly and were so pale that they resembled a thin line. He fell to his knees beside the bed and grasped her hand. 'Oh, my darling. I am glad you are awake. How do you feel?'

She turned her face away.

'I know I have upset you immeasurably. I hope that in time you will forgive me. I will do anything to make amends. Anything.'

Celia did not look at Charles, instead her gaze remained fixed on the window. The silence that stretched between them proved to Charles that only distance would assist him in being forgiven. 'I will leave you to rest and recover.' Charles walked from the room.

Celia dared not turn her attention to him at all. The sooner she recovered from her injuries, the sooner she could flee this place to never return. The injuries could have been avoided had she not been thrown into the refractory ward. The worst of it was that the person who had vowed to protect her had been her gaoler and warden.

She would not allow her thoughts to ponder her diminished marriage. The fear previous to her imprisonment that she would be cast from his life had always been a concern. Now, however, she was in no doubt she could not live another day with this man.

There would be no return to the home they shared. Instead, she would heal and begin to put ideas in motion as to how to ensure these women were protected from these incompetent doctors and their immoral care.

She would lobby the government if she had to. She would travel to Melbourne and visit Parliament herself. She would bleat so loudly that someone would eventually listen. She would not rest until she was heard, but she would have to do her yelling very far away from here.

Chapter 25

Celia blinked a few times to clear the sleep from her eyes. She lifted her head and looked to her right and then to her left. She felt momentarily startled to see Maryann sitting in a chair looking down at the tapestry in her hands.

'Hello,' Celia was happy to see Maryann, yet her voice was laced with confusion. She winced at the pain racing across her skin. 'Where am I?'

Maryann left the chair and clasped Celia's hand. 'Thank goodness you are finally awake. We have all been so worried.'

Celia closed her eyes and shook her head. 'Ow, everything is so sore. Even my eyelids.' She attempted a smile, which looked more like a grimace.

Maryann bent her face closer to Celia's ear and whispered. 'Trinny told us what Doctor Lawler did to you. Even Matron is treating him with contempt at present.'

'He will get what he deserves,' Celia said in jest. She did not want to enter into any conversation that placed Charles front and centre, so continued, 'I do not want to talk about my husband. I want to talk about you.' While it pained Celia to physically speak, she was glad Maryann had recovered. Her eyes moved to Maryann's neck. 'Your bruises are fading.'

'Yes, I am hardly sore except for a small ache in my back,' Maryann said.

Celia ignored her aching limbs and gathered Maryann to her, hugging her in a protective embrace. 'I do not know how, but I vow I will not leave you to the vices of that man any longer.'

'Which man?' Maryann looked puzzled.

'Why, that horrid Doctor Rushby, of course. He was the reason you ended up in here.'

Celia stopped short of stating that her husband was also the reason she herself had ended up in here.

'Doctor Lawler came to see me yesterday,' Maryann said. 'He asked me all manner of things.' She lowered her voice again. 'He made me promise I would not tell a soul about anything we discussed.'

'Why?' Celia looked shocked. 'I would assume he came to see you as your doctor to ensure you were healing well.'

'Well, yes, but no. He asked me about the attack I had endured. Well, in actual fact he told me what had happened before I had a chance to tell him. I did not know how he knew so much but it gave me a confidence I otherwise would not normally possess. Doctor Lawler assured me I did not have to be frightened any longer. That made me feel it was going to turn out well.' Maryann paused, her brow furrowing. 'In fact, I thought you might have told him what had befallen me and that is why he came to see me.'

Now it was Celia's turn to look puzzled. 'Well, I did try to discuss it with him as soon as I left you but my information was not met with his approval.'

'I feel so awful. Is that why he put you in that godawful refractory ward?' Maryann looked pained.

'No, do not worry yourself about any of that. All we need to concern ourselves with is the danger that horrible man poses to you while he is here.'

Maryann shook her head. 'No, I feel that things will change. There was something about Doctor Lawler's visit that made me feel he was going to make things right.'

Celia bit her lip. 'I do hope you are correct in your assumption.' She felt some ease with this new information and she hoped that Charles was going to make the necessary changes to ensure a safer place for the inmates. She would not allow this turn of events to soften her feelings for her husband at present. After all, it was time enough that the inmates become a priority for the doctors in here. That should have been a normal occurrence, not the exception.

'Oh my goodness. I almost forgot to tell you the best part of all.' Maryann grasped Celia's forearm.

'There is more?' Celia looked surprised.

'My prayers have been answered, as well as all the questions that I had pondered for so long' Maryann looked up at the ceiling and clutched her hands to her chest. 'I was so panicked by Doctor Rushby's visit. He frightened me so much so that I ran from here to search for you. I set out for your house and discovered something shocking and amazing all at once.'

'Really?' Celia looked desperate.

'I found Lee. I found him. He has been in here for the longest time.'

Celia placed her fingers to her lips. 'No!' she whispered.

'My father had him put in here.'

'Allow me a guess as to whom had his hand in that,' Celia said with distaste.

Maryann stared at Celia. 'It gives me hope, Celia. It really does. I do not know how everything will turn out but I have faith.'

'Oh Maryann, I am so happy you have discovered Lee and even more thankful that you now know the truth. I do feel it gives us more difficulty to ponder but maybe we can use this to our advantage also.' Celia narrowed her eyes and imagined Charles' reaction to this new unfolding story.

'I told Doctor Lawler of this news also.'

'You did not?' Celia was proud of Maryann for divulging what would be deemed a shameful secret.

'What did he say?' she asked.

'He was silent for a while. Then he said he would look into it after everything was settled.'

Noticing her softening attitude toward her husband, Celia admonished herself. She pushed the thought away. It was too late for her marriage but it may not be too late for Maryann and Lee.

A tear ran down Maryann's cheek. Celia stroked her hair. 'Please do not cry. Everything has turned out well. Charles knows of your plight. He will be sure to help you. You will see.'

'It still does not alter the fact that my father's interference cost me my baby. I would have a family. Lee was going to run away with me and we were to be married and our baby would be with us now. My father took all that away from me, Celia. Why do parents cherish their children when they are young and cast their happiness aside when it does not fit with their wishes?'

Maryann's father had not looked at her since the truth of her condition had presented itself. Her mother had observed her daughter's thickening waistline and plumped-up breasts, and since Maryann had confirmed that she was with child neither of her parents had spoken a word to her except to ask whom the father was. Her mother looked as though she would be ill after hearing the truth and her father had slapped her face. Her mother called her into the kitchen and would not look at her when she said, 'You are going to go away, have your baby and then return to us when all this is behind you.'

'You cannot send me away. Lee is going to marry me and we will be a family.'

It was only when Maryann had showed defiance that her mother had leant in close to her face with her lips hardly moving as she pushed the words forth. 'Do not be so ridiculous. You cannot marry his kind. He is not one of us. We will be ridiculed beyond reproach. Your father is respected in this town and this news would ruin his reputation. It would do untold damage to his business.'

'But I love him!' she cried.

'You should be more concerned of your love for your parents. There is to be no further discussion on the matter. Do you hear? Not one more word.'

'Father?' Maryann waited until the shop was devoid of customers.

He did not look at nor answer her.

'Could I ask you to please listen to what I have to say?'

'I have nothing but contempt for you.' He looked at her with such hatred that she was shocked at first. 'If it were up to me I would send you away for good. If your mother had not made me see sense I would kill the man that you allowed to fuck you like a whore.'

She was sobbing mercilessly by the time her father had delivered a tirade of insults.

'Anyhow, do you think he was going to marry you? He fled town when he found you were with child. He left you here with us to clean up this mess, so before you start to beg for forgiveness consider your mother and me, you selfish girl.'

Maryann felt her father's hatred with every word. The disgrace she would bring upon them should this news get out, was frightening. Now, her hopes that Lee would save her before she was removed to have his baby were dashed.

Even as her luggage was being placed in the carriage, she still did not want to believe that Lee had left town and abandoned her. She thought about running away but where would she go? Would her search for Lee end with him confirming he had fled because he did not intend on making her his wife?

Before climbing into the carriage she pushed open the door to the mercantile. She should say goodbye to her father. It was the just thing to do. After all, her actions had caused such problems for her parents. The bell tingled above the door. Thinking it was a customer, her father looked up from the ledger he was perusing. Upon seeing her, he immediately lowered his eyes. Maryann simply walked back outside.

As the carriage rolled through the main street to the quiet outskirts of town, she hung her head low.

The building came into view as nothing more than a creamy blemish protruding from the hill in the distance. Maryann felt her lungs tighten as she came to the realisation she had not breathed for some time. Her mother continued to look sidewards from the wagon.

Her mother was right. Her father would lose friends and customers if news broke of her pregnancy. Her parents could not bear the burden of it. She had not given any consideration to them while she was caught up in the love she felt for Lee. All she could think about was the future he promised her. It would not be fair for her family to have to bear the scorn and ridicule of having a daughter who had tumbled with a Chinese miner. On top of all this, her short list of prospects would evaporate along with her self-respect if she were not given a chance to begin over once her pregnancy had been dealt with.

She did not know much about the place she was being delivered to except the horrific stories that flew around town. Maryann had asked how long she would be kept but her mother had stopped short of announcing a specific answer. She did not look at Maryann when she said, 'Once the problem has been taken care of.'

Maryann was ill prepared in these matters and stopped herself from asking further questions. Secretly, she hoped that Lee was spying on her from afar and would gallantly ambush the carriage once it had reached the outskirts of town. Her beloved would carry her away to their much-talked-about life beyond this place, and they would live happily ever after. But it was not to be. The gatekeeper allowed the carriage through the gate and with it closing behind them all she could do was watch the expansive building grow larger before her eyes. Her longed-for rescue would be more believable between the pages of a picture book set on an exotic hillside in a large city.

It made Maryann's heart heavy to know that her baby, made from so much love, was going to be given to somebody else. Maybe Lee would find her and steal her from this place with their unborn child before it was ripped from her.

The carriage pulled to a halt at the massive front door.

'Breathe dear,' her mother said in a huff. 'If you are determined to be a sour sack at least let the air in and out of your lungs.'

Maryann stepped down from the carriage and looked up at the huge building as its arches frowned down at her.

'Carl, I shan't be long. Please wait.' Her mother's words set her teeth on edge. While she knew she would be left here, the truth dawned and sat heavy upon her shoulders.

As quiet engulfed her, she became truly fearful. Meanwhile, her mother was not wasting a moment as she lifted her hand to the knocker and abruptly let it drop.

The woman who opened the door introduced herself as the Matron, and she listened as Maryann's mother spoke in a low voice. Maryann looked around the entry hall and the quiet that hung within was haunting.

Her mother showed no emotion as she pecked her daughter on the cheek and turned abruptly away. Matron closed the door behind her and turned to Maryann. Placing her arm across the young woman's shoulders, she walked her gently towards the stairs. 'Come along. I will see to it that you settle in. Doctor Rushby will see you tomorrow.'

Maryann thought of Lee every day until their baby was born. Then she thought of her tiny baby boy each day since. A piece of her heart would be missing forevermore. She had often asked the nurses if there was word from her mother or father. Most times they did not comment. Weeks after her baby had been taken from her she ceased asking or expecting to ever see her home or her parents again.

During the months she had spent in the asylum, while the changes to her body had occurred, something else had unfurled. She had found family of a different kind. Her fellow inmates did not judge her harshly but to the contrary, they loved and supported her. While each of their stories differed, there was one thing they shared. Abandoned by those who loved them, they found themselves bound together by the common thread of sisterhood.

Celia did not have the answer, as she had never faced adversity as Maryann had. The role of parents was to nurture their child, love them unconditionally. What her parents had permitted to happen to their beloved daughter was appalling. Momentarily, it made her consider the tug of war she and Charles had endured. What sort of parents would they have made? Their continuous tug of war on matters pertaining to those that she cared for had seen them in conflict often. Who was right? It was looking more likely that she was. If Charles' discussions with Maryann were anything to go by, her relentless arguments with him had proven as much.

It seemed such a waste, that it had taken so much death and violence in here to force change. Her marriage had also fallen victim to the issues she had argued over. That would always hang over her as the price she would pay. Her dreams of having her own children to nurture with the man she dearly loved were lost to her now also.

At nightfall Maryann kissed Celia on the cheek and left

her to rest. Celia was hesitant to admit she was disappointed Charles had not called on her throughout the day. She was so angry with him but a small part of her still found her heart pined for him. She tried to repress this feeling more than any other, as she knew she had to leave Charles and her life with him behind.

Celia was very tired and had fallen asleep soon after Maryann's departure.

'Wake up, Celia, wake up,' came a hushed whisper.

Celia was wrenched from sleep and pulled the blanket to her chin.

'It is only me.' Jillian laid her hand on Celia's arm.

'What, what's happened?' Celia was instantly alert.

'Doctor Rushby has been arrested.'

Celia drew in a deep breath. 'Really?'

'The constable …' Her words were cut off by a deep voice.

'Nurse?'

Jillian looked at the door. Celia did not. She would not give him an ounce of credit for his hand in the removal of Doctor Rushby, even if it were evident that he had made the pivotal move.

Jillian ran past him. 'My apologies, Doctor Lawler.'

He did not acknowledge her but kept his gaze trained on Celia. She could feel his eyes penetrate the space between them.

'I apologise for calling on you so late yesterday.'

She had not seen him the whole day before but she dared not point that out. She could not bear for him to even read one iota into anything she said. Her anger was still bristling and she wanted him to realise that anything he had to say was of no consequence to her.

Sensing that he was not going to get a response from her he said, 'You were fast asleep when I called on you last evening. The hour was late. How are you feeling this evening?'

'I am still very sore and very unwell, because of you.' Her voice was firm.

'Yes, I know, and I am very sorry to hear it. You will never understand the pain my actions have caused me, and I pray that all will be right between us in time.'

Celia did not say anything to allow Charles to believe he would ever be forgiven. She would not relent where he was concerned.

'Let me begin to make amends by sharing some of the changes I have begun to make.'

'I fear it is too late for that but I will cherish the information if it benefits anyone in here.' Celia glared at her husband, her disdain for him plain on her features.

'As was communicated to you before my arrival, Doctor Rushby is, in fact, gone.'

Celia stared at him, unmoved.

'He was taken away by the constable and there is no doubt in my mind he will not be seen free of leg irons any time soon.'

'What will happen if he lies his way clear of any ill doing? Will he darken the doors of Beechworth or, God forbid, Yarra Bend?' Celia folded her arms across her chest.

'That is doubtful.' Charles pulled a newspaper from beneath his arm and handed it to her. Celia unfolded that day's edition of *The Ararat Advertiser* and her eyes widened as she read the headline. DOCTOR ARRESTED OVER LUNATIC ATTACKS!

The article reported the arrest of one of Ararat Lunatic

Asylum's esteemed doctors, before announcing his impending trial. Doctor Simon Rushby had been accused of atrocities against the inmates including assault and battery. The article intimated that a trial and sentencing would be rapid as the victims of his crimes were of unsound mind and their testimonies would be difficult to believe.

Celia looked up from the newspaper at Charles. The smile dropped from his lips, as the reaction he had anticipated receiving from her was not forthcoming.

'This article will serve as a thorn in my side,' she said. 'How dare this report send a further message to the masses that all the inmates in this place are ridiculous? What further untruths must these people endure? My Lord, this makes me cross.'

Charles looked up at the ceiling. 'What do you intend to do about it? Whose ear will you bend who is high enough to see the truth reported?'

'I intend to march to Parliament in Melbourne to bang on the door and demand better care for all inmates in asylums. I will not leave until somebody takes notice.'

'Be careful, my dear. If you seem unhinged, they may just see to it that you are transferred here to be placed under my care.'

Celia's eyes narrowed. 'That would not be the first time.' she said.

Charles winced. Celia enjoyed the discomfort she had caused him.

'I would rather jump from a moving train than be placed in your care in here.'

'I am remorseful for my actions and just as sorry to hear that you loathe me so much, my darling.'

'I am leaving you as soon as I am able,' she snapped.

Charles let out a sigh. 'Well, I admit I do deserve to lose you. It pains me to hear you say it. If only you could allow me time to explain my view. That has always been something you have never found easy to do.'

Celia considered this for a moment. 'If you could have proven me wrong all the times I tried to alert you to my misgivings I would have admitted defeat but ...'

'You never let me gain evidence, always wanting me to act upon hearsay from the inmates in here. Pardon me for not going in guns drawn to remove distinguished practitioners from their posts immediately upon my arrival.' Charles held his hands up in a sign of sarcastic surrender.

Celia clamped her lips together. His statement did have some merit, and for a moment she considered how hastily she had thrust her demands on him.

'Well then,' Charles continued, 'now we know, as we have evidence, and the lives of those in here will be safer without him.'

'That only resolves one of the many problems you have,' she accused.

'I realise I have numerous situations to improve but I assure you I will turn over every stone and create better conditions in here.'

'What about Audrey? We know Doctor Rushby was not the culprit? After all, he was at the Christmas party. Does that mystery still remain?'

Charles cleared his throat. 'It is a mystery no longer. That is another thing that has come to light but I do not wish to discuss it.'

'Well, that is no surprise,' Celia shot back.

Charles grasped a chair and placed it closer to the side of the bed. He dropped down onto it and rested his forearms on his knees.

'Very well, but I did not wish to burden you with the sordid details at present.'

'Tell me,' she ground out. 'Do not leave me to scrounge the truth behind your back.'

Charles stared at her for the longest time and shook his head.

'I discovered that the person who murdered Audrey was … Michael.'

Celia blinked in astonishment.

'Well, that is a first. No biting dialogue for me?' Charles inwardly cringed at his feeble attempt to inject some light-heartedness into the moment. It was a selfish ploy but his fear that she was lost to him compelled him to seize any chance at making amends.

'Michael infiltrated the asylum as a chameleon.'

'How could you not have realised it was him?'

'He disguised himself so cleverly that even though I crossed his path on occasion …' Charles ceased talking.

Celia watched his expression and wondered at his sudden perplexed gaze.

'I spoke to him the day of Audrey's disappearance,' he said in a low tone.

'And still you did not recognise him?' Celia questioned Charles again. She was most confused by this confounding event. 'So how did you eventually uncover the truth?'

'That is a rather sordid subject. You see …' Charles shifted in his chair and leaned closer. 'He was murdered by an inmate and we made the discovery of his identity when Constable Bryant attempted to locate his next of kin. The Colonel visited the morgue with me and also confirmed his identity.'

Celia could not disguise her feelings. 'I am in a state of shock. I do not know quite what to say.'

Charles looked grim. He touched Celia's forehead and then her cheek. 'I feared this would all prove too much for you. You do feel very warm. I hope you will not swoon from overexcitement.'

'I will be fine. I need some rest.' Celia was in danger of falling beneath his spell if he did not remove his hand from her face. It took all her energy not to turn her cheek into his palm and soak up his remorse.

Charles allowed his hand to linger far longer than was necessary to check his wife's temperature. He reluctantly removed his hand away, stood and walked to the door.

'I hope that what I am about to say will change your opinion of me, because I know I have lost your trust, but I promise you, never again will I allow the ill treatment of any inmate whose care is entrusted to this asylum.'

As Charles closed the door Celia whispered into the silence, 'you are right. I do not trust your word, just as I do not trust myself to remain here while I still feel so much love for you.'

Chapter 26

Charles visited each day to check Celia's wounds. 'You are healing very well,' he said.

Celia would never look him in the eye but rather would stiffen at his slightest touch. She feared her resolve would waiver if she allowed him to continue to stay in such close proximity. It made her sad but she would continue to deny the fact that their marriage could be salvaged.

An entire week had passed. Charles had visited her each day and returned most evenings. It was becoming so comfortable for him to touch her whilst checking her wounds that she could feel herself warming to him.

Before leaving this evening he placed his hand gently beneath her fingers and turned her hand over. 'The colour in your hand is looking quite good. I was considering replacing the cast but I think I may leave it for the moment. In a day or two you should be fine to return home so I will give it some consideration between now and then.' He smiled down at her and Celia found herself staring at him. For seconds they said nothing but stared at one another. She could feel herself slipping beneath his charm. Celia felt a surge of panic.

'Do you feel you are well enough to consider coming home?' He said as he slowly bent forward and kissed her forehead.

Celia sucked in a breath.

'Please forgive me,' he whispered in her ear. His breath was warm on her jawline. She closed her eyes and was being swept along. Admonishing herself for allowing him to slip so quickly back into her good graces she had to jar herself back into the present. He had moved away and was almost at the door of the room.

'If you give us time, upon your return home, you will see that I am willing to be everything you expected from me from the beginning. Goodnight my love.' He walked through the door and closed it. Celia squeezed her eyes shut and staved the tears that threatened to spring forth.

'Celia!' His voice boomed through the house. He slammed the front door. The silence that fell around him was frightening.

For the past two days, since discussing Celia's return to the lodge, Charles had managed to clear his schedule. He had left earlier that morning to accompany Celia home. He wanted to ensure she was settled and comfortable under his care. His plan had gone awry when he had arrived at the hospital cottage to find her missing.

'Where is she?' he yelled at the nurse on duty.

'I cannot say, Doctor Lawler.' She held her arms away from her sides.

'You cannot say because she has you on her side.' He pointed a finger at her. The nurse shrugged and looked perplexed. 'No sir, I have just started my rounds. I have not yet visited her room.'

'Well, she is not in there. It is obvious she has disappeared. You should be in a panic.' He did not wait to hear her response, but instead, slammed the door on his way out of the hospital cottage.

The familiar scent of the peppercorn tree just beyond the stairs of the hospital cottage hit his senses. He did not expect her to be at their home but he prayed he might catch her trying to gather some of her belongings. God forbid, if he had to begin to search the asylum he may never find her.

'Celia!' he bellowed. He dropped his head. She was gone. His chest hurt as he struggled to breathe. He yelled her name over and over.

Racing into her dressing room he flung the wardrobe doors open. 'Dammit!' he yelled as he pulled empty drawers from the bureau. He had missed her.

He ran from the room, down the hall, out of the front door and jumped from the veranda to the path below. His lungs were heaving as he bolted down the road into town and the train station. He was thankful the superintendent's lodge was much closer to the train station, being the last and furthest building beyond the rear of the asylum.

He could see steam brimming from the funnel as he neared the station.

'Do not dare pull out, do not dare pull out,' he chanted as he ran past the ticket office.

'Oy, oy,' the man behind the glass yelled.

'I will pay on return,' he hollered over his shoulder.

Looking to the very front of the train, he studied every closed door as the sound of the engine intimated that it was seconds away from pulling out and away. As his gaze swung to the end of the train, he saw the conductor holding onto the rail on the outside of the train while waving his flag to herald its departure.

It was the only door that remained open and would secure him a leap of hope.

'You cannot board the moving train, sir.'

In sheer desperation Charles yelled, 'There is an escapee from the asylum aboard. It is imperative you allow me to board.'

The conductor looked ready to resist dropping the flag and halt the train altogether but Charles did not want to bear responsibility for something so dire.

'No, do not stop the train. Just let me board. I do not want to frighten her.'

'Very well then, sir,' the conductor stepped aside and Charles slid past him.

Charles placed his hands on his knees for a few moments in order to catch his breath. He then began to walk the length of the dining car.

'Why hello, Doctor Lawler,' one of the commuters began to stand. 'Would you like to join us?' he placed his hand on Charles' shoulder and gestured toward the empty seat beside him.

'Thank you so much but I am on a mission of the utmost importance and cannot be waylaid at present. My apologies.' Charles tried not to run from the dining suite but his stride was prompt.

Taking discreet sidelong glances inside the suites, he could not hide his frustration. The compartments that had the shutters down made him curious but he decided to double back if he had no luck with those suites into which he had a clear view.

He was almost at the engine and was beginning to dread the possibility of backtracking when he whispered to himself. 'Eureka.' She was sharing a suite with three young women. Upon seeing her, his heart thudded hard against his ribs. He knew he had a battle of wills with which to contend, but he would not let her go without a fight.

The conductor was following on his heels. 'Could you see to it I am left alone with her? She may not be very pliant.'

The conductor looked inside the suite and perused the individuals for a time.

'That is your wife,' he announced slowly.

'Yes, and I would appreciate your discretion with this matter. I do realise your professionalism will shine through on this occasion.' Charles placed his hand on the conductor's shoulder. Flattery would assure his privacy would be respected.

'Absolutely, sir,' the conductor said as he opened the door and sought the occupants' tickets.

'Ladies, would you accompany me to another suite? I have been given instructions that this one is unavailable at present.'

The women began gathering their belongings, Celia included, until the conductor placed an even hand on her arm and said in a pleasant voice, 'Except you, my dear.'

'I do not understand,' she said, looking beyond the conductor's shoulder and noticing Charles.

Her hand moved to her lips in shock. 'Conductor, there has been a mistake. I wish to … '

'Thank you, ladies. She will be quite all right.' Charles

waited for them to pass, then swiftly closed the door and gently pulled the shutters down.

'Do not bother,' she said as she fell back onto the seat and sat upright with her hands balled into fists on her lap.

'I cannot lose you.' As the words fell from his lips he realised he had jeopardised the wellbeing of this beautiful creature he had sworn to protect. 'Celia, my darling, you must believe me when I swear to you I will never, and I mean never, risk you again.'

'It does not alter the fact that you did, in fact.'

'You gave me little choice with your despicable behaviour.'

'You never sought to stop me from my *behaviour* while I was attending to my wifely duties.'

Charles stared at Celia and began to feel defeated. Then truth dawned. He was not only struggling against his wife's low opinion of him, he was also battling against his own shame — and Celia could not help but turn the knife in his heart and hurt him further.

'My fear of losing you before we were betrothed was something I found almost impossible to bear,' she said. 'I recall our interlude in the same circumstances in which we find ourselves at present. It would have spelt the end of my days if I could not have become your wife. Now I find I can no longer trust you, Charles. A husband who can throw his wife into that dismal place is a man I vow I will fight against until my dying day.'

Charles pushed one hand through his hair. 'I am aware of my shortcomings. Can I ever win back that trust I have so visibly broken? I will do whatever it takes.'

Like a volcano erupting, everything she had kept quiet until now came spilling forth, with anger she could no longer hold back. 'It is too late for you and I to salvage any remnant of our marriage. You left me to suffer in conditions I would not see fit for an animal and yet you will allow others to be treated thus.'

'The refractory ward has been scrubbed clean and that process will continue once a week moving forth.'

She looked at him warily. 'The food is inadequate for the inmates. The produce being grown in your very own vegetable garden is being sold to create further funds for the landscaping. There is no end to it.'

'That will be rectified.'

'What about the women who have been left by their uncaring husbands and families?'

'That I cannot see an end to until the government alters its legislation, if ever. Please Celia, I am a doctor, not a politician.'

Celia shook her head. 'There is nothing to be done except join Parliament.'

Charles grinned. 'Oh my darling Celia, you have all the bravado of a man and yet you are so tied to your gender. That is a problem for you I am afraid, but safer for the rest of us.'

'When women get the vote, you will see. We will change things and then everything will be as it ought.'

Charles shook his head. 'Why not return with me? I will begin proceedings to appoint you as an advocate for the women.'

'No!' she yelled a little too loudly. 'I am interested in changing things for every institution and I cannot do that while I am stuck in that house with you.'

'You have firsthand experience with Ararat Asylum. Why not begin there and then move forth, once we have changed things for the better?' Charles moved closer to Celia and attempted to take her hand.

She did not move it aside or flinch. 'I will not return to you, Charles. I am too damaged from your wrath.'

He knew any chance for her to return was fast unravelling for him. He was a man used to getting his way and believed his chance was warranted if he could regain her trust. To do this he needed her back in their home once more.

'Can I pose a proposition to you, then?'

'Quite possibly not,' she snapped, feeling he was wearing through her tough demeanour.

'If you return with me and uphold the premise that we are still husband and wife.'

'No!' she squeaked.

'I will not expect anything more from you than your presence in our home. I make a solemn promise to keep the premise all is well with us, while giving you all the privilege I should have granted you, long before now. Please Celia, this will mean more to you than your heart could imagine. I came to the hospital cottage to deliver you back to our home so you could properly heal and then resume work alongside me, but you had disappeared.'

She pulled her hand from his grasp and folded her arms across her chest. The cumbersome plaster did nothing but make her look awkward. She stared him down nonetheless. 'I do not think it possible to return to our home, or to you.' The train began to slow, and she looked out the window. 'Please make your way back without me. I wish to continue to the safety of my father and sister. Please respect this and leave me now.' Her voice was barely audible.

Charles stared at her in defeat. 'As you wish. I want to leave you with no doubt that I love you and will cherish you forever. If my word counts for anything, please, believe this to be true.' He leaned into her and kissed her cheek before whispering in her ear. 'Just think on all that I offer. I am truly remorseful for my actions. If nothing else will sway you, your return to the women is necessary, although they need you far less than I.'

Celia could not acknowledge that his voice was making her swoon. She kept her gaze steadfast at the platform as the train stopped.

Minutes later, as the train pulled away from Beaufort en route to Ballarat, Celia felt shrouded in loneliness. She squared her shoulders and anticipated life without Charles.

Chapter 27

'She is here, she is here!' Cassandra yelled as she wrung her hands in anticipation of the wagon drawing to a stop.

The young woman shrieked as she hugged Celia to her.

'You are so thin and what happened to your arm?' her sister looked shocked.

'I tripped on a step and placed my arm out to break my fall and it did break in fact.' Celia held up her arm and attempted to smile to lighten the scenario.

'My goodness Celia, you do look quite gaunt. What is the matter?' her father asked.

Celia looked at her father and noticed how much older he looked since she had seen him. 'Aside from this,' she held her arm up a little, 'a fever and some tummy ailment have rendered me a might unwell. That is all.'

'I thought you may have a large pregnant belly the next time I saw you,' Cassandra said.

'No, not yet.' Celia felt her stomach tighten at the thought. It would never become a reality now. 'I just need some much longed-for coastal sunshine and fresh air to clear my chest and I will be better in no time.' Her family believed the lie and ceased their commentary on her physical appearance.

While discussing her life with her sister, she was careful not to mention her visit becoming a more permanent arrangement. She did not know why she could not discuss the truth of all that had happened to her. Was it shame over the failure of her marriage, or rather that she was treating the option of a return to Charles and the asylum as an open proposition?

Late in the afternoon after unpacking her things and talking to Cassandra about all manner of life in Ararat, Celia found solace in the one place she could be alone. This place had held her in its embrace since childhood. How she wished for the innocence of the mind she had possessed again. In the front row of the chapel she stared up at the polished timber cross and questioned its significance.

'Forgiveness.' Her father's voice startled her.

'Oh father, I am so lost,' she whispered with her gaze still fixed on the pulpit.

He joined her in the pew and gathered her hand in his. She looked down at her father's hand and squeezed it.

'You are lost because you have blurred the line of friend, wife and worshipper.'

'I fear you may be right. I have said things that I am ashamed of. I am heavy with the burden of all the truths I fought so hard to uncover. My husband tried to protect me as he vowed he would. He warned me of the things I would be exposed to and I did not listen. And now, I feel such anger toward him. It has been an unfair education, I fear.'

'It is never too late to beg forgiveness for your misgivings.'

'Is it sinful of me to hope he is suffering the burden of me missing from his life? I hope he is reliving and regretting the things that happened between us.'

'My darling girl. You must return to him to ease your tumultuous emotion over these matters. To remain here and have this burden exist day after day will send you to the brink of despair. Marriage is never easy. God tells us this and the Devil tests our resolve.'

'Oh Father, I fear you are right and I know forgiveness is an act of strength. I am feeling far too weak to contemplate it at present.'

'You may not find the strength you require but I assure you, in time, it will find you.' He pointed up at the cross. 'It does not possess all the answers but its silence will allow you to ponder every facet of life's path.' He kissed her on the cheek and patted her shoulder as he left her to contemplate.

As silence enveloped her, and the vortex of emotion threatened to drown her resolve, she stood up and yelled into the massive space above her.

'Why do you make people suffer so?' Over and over she yelled questions. She demanded answers from the one being that held her faith but kept her confused with his silence. When her throat hurt and her nerves were raw she was forced to stop the incessant screeching and the final question was delivered in the smallest voice. 'Why did you make me love him?'

A week passed and Celia was feeling life begin to ebb through her veins once more. She had taken to strolling along the beach each day to assist her thoughts.

Now, her sister raced toward her with a letter grasped in

her hand. 'This is for you,' she stated and peered over her shoulder as Celia opened it.

Celia frowned at the envelope, which had been forwarded from the superintendent's lodge, her home, to her father's address. She did not recognise the sender's handwriting, but her heart fluttered when she saw the amendment to the address written in Charles' neat cursive script. She opened the envelope carefully and began reading.

Dearest Celia,
It is with heavy heart I write to you and I do pray you are keeping well. Whilst I would like to believe my husband is innocent I cannot defend the accusations against him. I made the decision to write you rather than visit, as it is far too difficult at present. I have the utmost respect for you and would like to commend you for your unwavering support of your husband.

Should I have paid more attention to the plight of those unfortunate folk and placed myself in the asylum just as you have I may have been more accessible to my husband and in turn protected others from the accusations stacked against him. I hope to always have you as a trusted confidant and if I could impose, please do not enter into any discussion with regard to my husband's name and tarnished reputation.

I am living away from the district. It is for the best for all I believe. I wish you and Charles well.

Yours truly Mrs S Rushby

Celia took the letter with her when she retired for the

evening. She stared at it and pondered the pain of Mrs Rushby's words. How she felt for the poor woman. Celia was under no illusion her silence was being implored.

She could not sleep, as all the angles of the impending decision weighed on her. It would be very easy for her to return and forget all that had gone before. Doctor Rushby was gone. The grim situation regarding Audrey and Michael was also laid to rest. The danger had passed for the women and Charles would see to it that they were better cared for.

To tell her father and sister her marriage had failed, thus forcing her to live the rest of her days here as a spinster seemed unfathomable. Could she forgive Charles? Or worse still, what if she ended her days with him in their home, living a larger lie? They would play up to the pretence that they were husband and wife, but it would all be a covert shroud. Hour after hour, she lay awake as thoughts whirled around.

Celia propelled herself upright. Her initial response was panic. She was on a hard floor. Darkness surrounded her on all sides. Her fear was short lived when she realised she had rolled from the bed. It would seem unusual that she would not awaken after such a tumble. Perhaps her fatigue from laying awake most of the night had caused her to fall into the deepest sleep, soon causing her to slide from beneath the covers onto the floor?

She stood up, only to feel her body rebel against the movement. Her back was stiff and her legs and feet ached from the immediate strain. She looked at the hearth to see the fire barely aglow. With only dim light to assist her, she did not rejoice that she was back home in her old bedroom. Her sister was asleep in the bed on the opposing wall so she was careful not to awaken her. She stepped across the floor, all too aware of each board that would creak or groan beneath the pressure. Looking from the window out over the land she could see dawn brimming on the horizon. She longed for the fresh air only the bay could deliver. She wanted it to tear at her soul, to uncover and reveal answers to her tumultuous questions.

Celia dressed quickly and flung a shawl across her shoulders before stepping quietly from the house and hitching the horse to the wagon. When the water came into view, she felt immediate respite. There was something peaceful about it. Whether it stirred memories from long ago that gave her a sense of belonging, or the fact that water really did hold magical healing powers. She wished she knew the answer. There were many theories and much talk of it in recent time in the newspapers and magazines. She could understand the principles behind it.

The chill of the early morn touched her skin through the open weave of her shawl. It felt much different to the early morning feel of summer in Ararat where the warmth sat over the countryside and held it flat.

After tying the wagon to a nearby tree, Celia pulled her shoes from her feet. She had not bothered with stockings, gloves or a hat. Her cast had allowed her to omit gloves from her hands in the past days, and she relished this. The cold breeze skimmed across the water's surface and up onto the sand. Standing at the edge of the water, Celia looked to the horizon. Daylight had won the battle against the dawn and the grey waterline turned to a hue of white as it met the sky in a perfect line.

Water lapped over her feet as she felt her body come alive. Taking a step forward, she felt the water pool around her ankles and she could not stop. She trudged slowly and assuredly into the water until it lapped over her knees.

She closed her eyes and fell forward as the cold water enveloped her entire body, her mind reeling at the sensation. She thought of her mother and wondered what she would say to her if she knew how her life had turned out.

'Celia! Watch me, watch me.' Her younger sister took a small running canter and turned sharp on her heel before propelling herself over in a cartwheel. Her skirts fell up over her head and her bloomers were exposed.

'Cassandra!' their mother shrieked. 'Do you not possess any decorum?'

'There is nobody here to see.' Her sister twirled around and around with her eyes closed.

'We never know who is watching. There are vantage points all the way along where one can see and not be seen.' Her mother scanned the trees lining the beach and then tucked her arm inside Celia's. 'Are you worried about school?'

'A little,' Celia said.

'Do not be afraid of anything you do not know. Embrace it. Learn from it. After all, that is what school is for. We do not expect to attend a classroom and know everything.'

Celia looked down at her bare feet and noted the connection between the sand, water and the freedom of not wearing stockings. It was so liberating.

Winter had began to take hold of the bay and the meagre shadows cast by the dying light of the day showed the fragile outline of the lace hem of her dress. The breeze captured her hair and washed across her skin and under her skirt.

She looked at her mother. 'Do you question the life that has befallen you?'

Her mother frowned. 'Befallen me? Why, you make it sound as though I were dropped into the rectory and held prisoner for my shortcomings.'

Celia fixed her eyes on the horizon. The perfect flat line that contrasted between the black of the sea and the grey sky that sat perfectly atop it never ceased to amaze her.

'I adore the life I have with your father,' her mother added.

'Do you believe that God decides everything that happens to us?'

'My dear, you are in a dilemma at present. Is it all those pamphlets you are reading that are weaving thoughts into that fragile mind of yours?'

Celia did not think her mother knew of the pamphlets that had been swapped between the young women during Sunday school. It was a covert operation with copies of the Bible housing indecent information passed around without their teacher's knowledge.

'I did not believe you knew of such things,' Celia said as her cheeks turned crimson.

'I was informed by Mrs Carruthers, but I decided that it could do no harm to your sensibilities.'

'Mrs Carruthers knows?'

'Of course she does. And seeking advisement, she decided to bring it to my attention instead of telling your father.'

Celia was taken aback. 'Did you tell him?' she sounded aghast.

'No, I did not.' Her mother said.

'Why not?' she asked confused. She always thought her

father to be in the confidence of her mother in every issue that involved the church and, more specifically, their daughters.

'I know it is said that these teachings that are not from the Bible are the Devil's words, sent to corrupt our minds with his evil, but there is some real energy to some of the essays.' Her mother placed her hands on either side of her daughter's face and looked into her eyes. 'I realise there is something in you. Something that makes you see every facet of the world as it should be. I know that these differing opinions are not the work of the Devil. To the contrary, they are the words of those who want to open up minds and delve deeper into what we have before us.'

As though a burden had been lifted from her, Celia blurted, 'Oh mother, these pamphlets have taught me so many wonderful things and made me see that there is so much more to life than I thought possible.'

'You will do amazing things,' her mother said as she released Celia from her grasp, leaving her to look down at her feet once more and the hem of her dress furling around her legs.

'Come on!' Cassandra said as she raced up and grabbed Celia by the arm. The girls ran toward the water's edge.

'You will both catch your cold if you pursue this further!' their mother yelled after them.

'Come on, Celia. Let us be brave together,' Cassandra said.

'We cannot just run into the water. It is the depth of winter,' Celia said.

Cassandra held Celia's hand firmly. 'Whatever strength you possess I want you to transfer some to me.' She looked up at her sister with hopeful eyes.

Celia considered the conversation that had unfolded over

recent minutes. Her mother had told her there was something special in her that would make a difference in this world, and her sister was still looking up at her with intense longing and trust in her eyes. Celia suddenly knew that the water and this moment would be her baptism into something larger than anything she could currently imagine.

She did not think of the consequences of her action but gripped her sister's hand and yelled, 'On the count of three! One ... two ...three.' They both fell onto the water before it quickly absorbed them in its depths. The freezing water became a cocoon as it wrapped itself around them. They stayed beneath its embrace connected by hands for what seemed like the longest time before breaking the surface.

'Oh my!' Cassandra yelled. 'It is freezing!'

'Goodness me, it is,' Celia said, shuddering as she stood up and felt the cold wind biting into her flesh and cementing her dress to her body. It made her feel like she was wrapped in ice.

They ran from the water, their arms across one another's shoulders, teeth chattering.

'You two are going to catch your death ... '

Celia did not hear her mother's stern words as they continued to cascade over the sound of her chattering teeth.

'Who does not possess any modesty now?' Cassandra whispered as her teeth chattered. 'Father will be so cross with us when we arrive.'

'He may not see us if we are secretive. I believe he will be in the chapel practicing his sermon. He may not see us at all,' Celia whispered back.

'If you two think your father will not hear of this you are mistaken.'

Celia looked at her mother. 'You know what he will say? He will chastise you for allowing us to run into the water, Mother.' Celia laughed.

'Are you attempting to blackmail my position?' her mother asked more in surprise than anything else.

'Oh Mother, there is no harm. We are brave young women baptising ourselves in one of God's creations. The water gives us a new awakening every time we immerse ourselves in it. Is that not correct?' Celia smirked.

Her mother sighed. 'You will be the death of me,' she said as she placed herself between the girls and spread her shawl around them all. She leaned into Celia and whispered. 'Do not show such wit until after you are married, my dear. You will send suitors running in fright.'

Celia barrelled through the water with her skirt weighing her down and draping itself around her legs. She tripped over and stayed on all fours and sobbed. She felt weak and was so distraught at the mess she had made of her life that she did not think she could stand again. Salt stung her eyes and tears fell onto the sand as she bowed her head and felt defeat overtake her. 'Mother!' she screamed, beckoning any nuance or a sign from her to make sense of her present pain.

Her throat was sore from yelling her mother's name over and over. Finally, with little energy to spare and the cold covering her skin, she said, 'Help me. Help me through this.' Whether it was to God himself, her mother, her father or Charles, she did not know. She needed somebody, anybody to give her the strength or a sign that she would survive the life she had forged.

She willed herself to stand and took slow steps toward the wagon. The cast on her arm was soaking wet and gritty against her skin. The plaster was heavy and cumbersome. She really had not given it any thought before plunging it and the rest of her being into the water. The blanket that was left on the buckboard was a blessing. After wrapping it around herself, she let the horse meander his way back home. She pulled the wagon to a halt and was unhitching the animal when Cassandra came outside.

'If father sees you like this he will have a conniption.'

Celia smiled. 'I know. Although I *am* a grown woman and can decide on my own silliness as I see fit.'

'Do not think for a moment he will not have something to say on your present dishevelment. Each time I do something that does not fit in with propriety he concerns himself with our lack of a mother figure as to the reasoning behind it.'

'I know,' Celia sighed. 'I have been hearing the same line since she left us.'

Cassandra looked at Celia and smirked. 'He will not see you if you dash inside now. He is in the chapel practicing his sermon.'

Celia climbed the staircase with the suctioning fabric of her dress clinging to her legs.

'I have missed you so very much,' Cassandra said as she used a pail to fill the bath.

Celia was steadily peeling the bodice of her dress down past her waist.

'I have missed you too, but I must say, since being married and so busy it did dull the ache somewhat. Now that I am back it has magnified so many memories for me.' As Celia said the words she knew she was fast losing the battle to stay here and forget the life she shared with Charles. Selfishly, it seemed more a life created where she was the central person and he had taken a close second to her wants and needs. She began to feel shame.

Cassandra's voice broke through her thoughts. 'How she would laugh if she saw you now. Soaked through to the skin. Do you need me to throw your petticoat out just like she used to after we ruined them in the sea?' Cassandra laughed.

'Oh Celia, she would be so happy if she saw you now. Married to a doctor and living an amazing life.'

Cassandra left Celia to bathe in solitude. Celia felt needles race across her flesh as the heat of the water scalded her backside and every inch of her that lowered into the tub. She sighed. 'I know what I must do,' she whispered to the tendrils of steam rising from the water. For the first time in days she felt relaxed as her mind cleared and her bones began to warm through.

Chapter 28

'Hello,' she said from the doorway of his office.

Charles looked up from his notes. The intensity of his concentration melted away. He rose slowly from his seat as though she would flee if he startled her.

'Come in, please, sit down,' he implored.

'I left my case downstairs. I came to see you first.'

'I am glad, so glad.' He looked at her in earnest. His eyes softened and his mouth turned up at the corners as his melancholy lifted. 'How is your arm?'

She held it up. 'Heavy,' she said and was glad that he could acknowledge something that spoke volumes of all that had gone before. 'I got the cast wet. It feels terrible now.'

'Is that why you returned? To have the plaster replaced?' he said in jest. Beneath his humour was the hope that he was wrong.

Celia placed her arm in her lap and looked at him, all the while considering that while he looked fatigued he still looked so lovely. Knowing he would catch her off guard when she laid eyes upon him, she had scripted everything she would say. The entire train journey consisted of her mumbling to herself so that her words would be delivered thus.

'No. Not entirely.' She smiled for a moment then quickly resumed her serious expression. 'I have had time to contemplate your offer and it is the reason for my return.'

'And the offer still stands.'

'I have decided to do you the favour of moving back to our home and upholding the pretence of everything continuing as it was, with the exception of some occurrences.'

'I appreciate that very much and have intimated that you were only visiting your family and would be returning in the short term. I will admit I prayed that it would turn out as I hoped.'

She raised an eyebrow. 'Were you so sure of this?'

'No, I was quite in doubt. As I said, I hoped it would come to fruition if I willed it to be so.'

'Well, your wish to have us keep up the pretence of our union has come true. And my wish to return to my work here has been forged, so on all accounts we both win.' She stood abruptly. 'I best be getting to the house to unpack my things.'

Disappointment washed over his features. 'Do not rush. I will get an orderly to deliver your belongings. You should not delay visiting those in here who have missed you dearly these last weeks.'

Celia was not used to him being so pliant. She was startled at his response.

'Very well, I think it would be lovely to surprise them.'

She was at the door to his office when he said, 'Celia.'

She turned toward him.

'I will tend to the plaster when I return home this evening. It will be my pleasure to remove it and replaster it should it be required. I am glad you have returned.'

Celia smiled at him and closed the door. Keeping her hand

firmly on the handle she placed her back against the timber and whispered. 'I feel I am in trouble already.'

Familiar noise erupted from the laundry room as she approached the door. She stood on the threshold with the heat hitting her in the face until the occupants noticed her. The intensity of the screams that hit her almost burst her eardrums.

'Celia!' the women yelled over and over, running over and holding her in their tight embrace.

'Careful of her arm,' she heard one of the women announce.'

Maryann shoved them aside and fell into her. 'I am so glad you have returned.'

'And I have every intention of staying,' Celia announced with tears in her eyes.

'Were you the reason that bastard was arrested?' one of the women yelled across the room.

'I do not wish for us to speak of such things. We have a more useful purpose with which to fill our time,' Celia said, clutching Maryann's hand. 'I have so many ventures in mind for us.'

The women could hardly contain their excitement and bubbled with anecdotes of all that had gone on during Celia's absence. Celia listened with enthusiasm and laughed at their humorous stories. She had not laughed in such a long time that when the sound escaped her lips it was foreign to her ears.

As the chatter ceased, Celia awkwardly attempted to fold sheets. 'How are you feeling?' she asked Maryann in a lowered voice.

'I am not nearly as frightened as I once was, thanks to your husband.'

Celia felt herself waver in her resolve to keep Charles shut out of her heart. He was a good man and had finally seen his way clear to make things right for the women.

'But I have no way of seeing Lee again,' Maryann continued. 'It pains me immensely to know he is within feet of my existence and yet a wall literally divides us.'

'Do not give up, my lovely. I have some thoughts and ideas I hope to put into action. Please stay hopeful for all our sakes.'

Celia began to feel a headache coming on. The immense journey in the pummelling heat had taken its toll and she suddenly looked forward to her return to her home. She wished to unpack and settle back into life in the superintendent's lodge, even though she knew she would be slightly estranged from the traditions of her former life there.

After bidding the women goodbye, Celia began the walk to the rear gate. She could not resist poking her head into the hospital cottage, and this is where she found Trinny in the middle of her rounds.

Trinny held Celia so tight that Celia felt her ribs creak. 'It is so good to see you again and have you back among us.' Trinny sounded elated.

'It is good to be back but I do need to get to the house and lie down. My head is forcing me to seek some solitude.'

'I will not waylay you a moment longer. I have no doubt Doctor Lawler is excited at the prospect of having his wife back home also.'

'I think so,' Celia said, 'Although he is still going to have to do some apologising until he is fully forgiven.'

'I suspect he is willing to do whatever it takes to get back into your good graces. Matron is still cross with him for his decision involving the refractory ward and yourself.'

'Poor Matron. She really is at the mercy of the orders she is given. Please tell her I do understand she was not in any way at fault where I was concerned. I will call on her and alleviate her guilt over the matter.'

'You are so gracious, Celia. I am sure she will appreciate your understanding.'

'I must go. I will see you on the morrow.'

Celia looked awkward as she fought fabric and timber to hang her dresses. Holding her already hung dresses aside with the lump of plaster covering her arm, she was using her free hand to reach up and cast the hooks of the remaining hangers over the railing.

Charles watched his wife for the longest time, resisting the urge to rush forward to assist her. He felt as though his eyes were deceiving him. He had given up hope she would return.

'How was your afternoon?' His voice was gravelly.

She jumped away from the wardrobe. 'You frightened me. I did not hear you return.'

'The house was so quiet I considered you were still ruminating with your charges.'

'I had to excuse myself to have a lie down. I was so very tired from the trip.'

'Did you manage to rest?'

'Yes, yes I did.' She ran her free hand down the front of her skirt.

She walked past him to the sitting room and fell down onto an armchair. She lifted her arm up only to let it fall heavily on the armrest.

'Can I get you anything?'

'A hacksaw.' She smiled.

Charles looked at her and wondered how long it had been since he had witnessed a jovial look on her face. It disappeared as quickly as it appeared as the reason of its prevalence hung between them. 'I think I will reset that plaster tomorrow if you can wait. It does look very emaciated after its plunge into your bath.

'Um, it was into the bay.' Her face flushed.

'I would like to hear how that came about. Let me make you a cup of tea.' Charles disappeared into the kitchen.

'That would be nice.' Celia closed her eyes.

Charles returned minutes later carrying a tray with a teapot and two cups rattling atop saucers. He poured a cup for each of them, placed one beside her and held his in his hand. He sat opposite her. 'So tell me about the plunge into the bay.'

'It was just silliness really. I was having a moment of recollection and the water drew me in and under. It gave me clarity.' The words hung between them.

'Well I am glad you had time to ponder and I hope that those moments of clarity brought you back to me, I mean to our home. Speaking of clarity, I have something I need to tell you.'

Celia's eyebrow lifted.

'I contacted the orphanage in Sunbury. It seems they are still in possession of the baby Maryann birthed.'

Celia looked over the rim of her teacup. 'And you summoned this information because ... '

'I was curious after hearing Maryann's story of how she came to be in the asylum. My request for information regarding a child that was delivered from Ararat Lunatic Asylum only days after his birth was as simple as chasing documentation. The reason he is still available for adoption has everything to do with his being male and slant eyed, as laid out to me in their response.'

'Why do people not look beyond a person's outer layer to truly see that we are all the same? As a doctor you know the truth of this,' Celia said in frustration.

Charles shook his head. 'You amaze me. You look beyond all that has gone before. You see people for exactly who they are.'

'Careful, doctor. You could be in for one reprisal.' Again, she smiled.

Charles stared at her and took a deep breath. 'I am in awe of your strength and your ability to never take no for an answer.'

'Well it would seem "no" will be the answer from the orphanage when you state your case that both mother and father reside in the asylum. Surely legislation would not allow the child to remain in their care until one of them is released, if ever.'

Charles looked at her and waited a few moments. 'That is where I have further news for you.'

Celia looked at him with anticipation.

'I have exhausted a search through the records and there are none regarding Lee's arrival at the asylum, therefore I see no use in persisting with his care. I am organising to have him released.'

'Oh,' Celia squeaked and placed her cup down gently before jumping to her feet. 'Thank you!' She closed the distance between them and leaned down to fling her arms around his neck, hugging him tightly. Using the precious moment to savour her touch, he closed his arms around her.

Several heartbeats later, he released her slowly, as though he had committed a misdemeanour. 'I am afraid I may break you if I squeeze you any tighter. Really Celia, what have I done to you?'

'It is not entirely your doing, Charles. I am to blame for the diminishing diet I had undertaken before your decision and its further impact.' She sat once more and reached for her teacup.

'You are being far too gracious on my account.'

He slid from his seat and dropped to his knees. Placing his forehead on her knees, he said, 'I do not think I will ever be able to forgive myself. In your absence, I have had time to ponder my actions. Selfishly, I am elated you have returned of your own volition, however I fear your presence here will be short lived, as I cannot bear to look at your frail disposition and … this.' Charles grasped his wife's arm and lifted it. Holding onto it with both hands he continued to take its weight in order for her to have some reprieve. He was agonising over the condition she was in. Gently placing the cast back into her lap he shook his head. She stared at him as he remained kneeling before her. His hands rested gently atop her cast. 'I cannot bear it.'

'Are you sending me away?' she whispered anxiously.

'Of course not. I would not dream of sending you away but currently we are at a stalemate. I love you so very much and was tortured when you fled. Now that you have returned I have plummeted further into hell. Respecting your decision to live here under the pretence of husband and wife is all I could hope for, as I do not deserve to possess your body, as a husband should. That is something I can endure just to have you here with me. But to witness the physical pain I bestowed upon you. It is killing me.'

She ran her hands through his hair. She wanted to grasp his face, kiss his pain away and allow him to take her in his arms and love her. She ached as she watched his despair, but was still at war with her own emotions and his treatment of her. He was sharing his thoughts and feelings in raw ferocity and she was glad of it. His revelation about the whereabouts of Maryann and Lee's child, as well as the work he was undertaking to free Lee, were to be celebrated. She needed time to reassess her own relationship with her husband but for the moment she required much needed rest to regain her strength.

'This tension will ease after some time has passed,' she said. 'I think we both need some respite. It has been an exciting day.'

Charles sat back on his haunches and gathered her hands while pulling her to her feet. 'I think some rest and recovery is a great idea. I look forward to seeing you in the morning.'

'I have decided I will call on my aunt in the morning and then Mrs Price after that,' she said.

Charles was almost at her bedroom door. 'I fear Mrs Price is not very well at present. Do not burden her with anecdotes of Audrey's death. I implore you.'

'Please be assured, Charles, that I am calling on her to see how she is. I promise I will not cause any undue concern.'

'And for the first time I can honestly say I believe you.' He stared at her lovingly. 'Now, do you require any assistance to ready yourself for bed?'

She teased him with a smile. 'I think I can manage quite well, Doctor Lawler.'

She crossed the threshold and slowly closed the door, all the while watching him through the slither.

Chapter 29

'Mrs Price, are you there?'

Celia placed her ear against the dense timber door. There could be nothing heard beyond.

It would not be unusual for Mrs Price to not be at home. However, a maid should be present. To receive no response seemed most unusual. Celia rounded the front steps and walked to the rear of the house. The back door stood ajar.

Celia looked at the sheets snapping in the wind on the clothesline behind her, believing there could be a maid in the laundry that stood separate from the house.

'Hello, is anybody there?' she yelled toward the laundry. She waited. Nothing.

Celia pushed the back door open and took a step inside the house. Craning her neck to look beyond the rear entryway, she could hear no sound coming from the kitchen.

'Mrs Price, are you there?'

'Who's there!' came the unmistakable voice of Eleanor Price.

Celia quickly walked the rest of the way inside and spoke to the walls. 'Ah, it is Celia Lawler. I came to call on you. To see how you are.'

Eleanor Price hobbled into the opening of the doorway. Looking lost inside her nightgown with her grey hair dangling in slim tendrils down the fronts of her shoulders, she appeared to bear no resemblance at all to her former self.

'What do you want?'

'As I said, I came to see how you are.'

'Surprised you came to see me. Nobody bothers,' the older woman stated in anger.

Celia could understand why nobody dared call on her. Mrs Price seemed filled with such hatred and wrath. This would be expected from a woman who had lost her daughter and granddaughter, although Eleanor's friends would only make so many visits before her surly demeanour ran them off. She could understand why Eleanor Price was home alone and clearly in need of attention.

'Why are you not being attended to, Mrs Price? Where is your housemaid?'

'She was useless. I sent her away.' Mrs Price stumbled and fell against the doorjamb, only to catch herself with a free hand at the last moment.

Celia threw herself forward to support the woman and grasped her before she toppled over.

'Here, let me get you to bed.' Celia placed her arm beneath Mrs Price, hoping to get a hold of her waist. Instead, her fingers fell on the thin lines of a rib cage. Now that she was in much closer proximity, the smell of alcohol wafted into her nostrils.

'I will see to it you are put to bed, then I will fetch Charles.'

'That husband of yours is a saint.' Mrs Price pointed a finger in Celia's face as she fell back onto the pillows.

Celia felt her heart clutch in her chest. She was caught

between two thoughts. Her husband was truly a caring man but had made some bewildering decisions when it came to his very own wife.

'Yes, Mrs Price, he can be rather extraordinary,' Celia said amid the acrid smell of spirits emanating from the woman.

'Will you be all right if I run to get Charles?' Celia asked.

'How can you bear that place?' she spat. 'It's the devil's doing that it even exists. All those broken folk there ending their days.'

She looked away from Celia and stared into space. 'I can still see her face.'

'I know it has been difficult for you.' Celia held the woman's hand.

'That poor child,' she said, her voice wavering as she began to cry.

'Audrey was so unwell, Mrs Price. It is difficult to really know what she was thinking when Charlotte … '

Mrs Price ripped her hand from Celia's grasp. 'I was not talking about the baby. I was talking about my beautiful Audrey. My child is gone.' She began to sob mercilessly. 'I nearly lost her once before. This time I could not save her … '

'I cannot do this any longer,' she screamed at the midwife.

'Yes you can, Mrs Price. Not long to go now,' the midwife answered in a soothing voice.

The young woman had been labouring for hours and was exhausted. Her body shuddered as the onslaught of each contraction held her within its convulsive tightened grip for a minute at a time. She could barely recover from the last when the next would occur.

'Try not to push yet, Mrs Price. Doctor is on his way,' the midwife added.

Not pushing while her body demanded it was proving more difficult by the moment.

'Hello, Mrs Price.' Her doctor sounded jolly as he entered the hospital room. He was just in time to see the crown of her baby's head forcing itself out of the mother's body. He only had to assist the baby's shoulders to the smallest degree and out slid a baby girl.

It was a full two days until her husband sauntered through the door of the hospital room. He walked to the bed and kissed her on the forehead. 'You look well,' he said.

She smoothed the sheet across her lap as she sat with her back straight against plumped pillows.

'Have you seen the baby yet?' she asked him.

'Yes, the nurse held her up for me to see,' he said.

'Audrey Eliza. After your mother,' she gushed. 'The nurse will bring her in shortly for a feed. Are you able to stay so you can hold our daughter?'

Her husband looked at his hands. 'I am full of dust and grit from the ride here. I would rather not touch such a pure and clean creature.' The new father had been away for the longest time and had been given leave from his post to visit his wife and new child.

'Doctor says you have been doing rather well with the child,' he said.

'Yes, I seem to be getting used to her. The nurses bring her to me so I can feed her. They have been looking after her in the nursery the rest of the time.'

'I have spoken to the doctor about your discharge. We need to leave for Point Nepean in two days.'

'Is that necessary?' Eleanor became instantly distressed. 'I do not think I will be ready to leave.'

'Nonsense,' he waved a hand at her. 'If I am to further my ranking we will leave in two days and that is final. My plan to head the command at the highest level will not be waylaid by our baby. You had better get used to moving around with a family, as that is what we will be doing.'

Her mouth clamped shut and she did not say another word. He had planned to outrank everyone in his midst and he was not prepared to give her any leniency.

The following day she was discharged from the hospital with her new baby, arrived at the temporary home that had been set up near the base and assisted the housemaid to pack up all their belongings. Her husband had hired a nurse to accompany them and help her with their baby until they had settled at Point Nepean.

The travel was arduous. Audrey was unsettled and would not feed the whole journey. The nurse accompanying them tried to assist her by reading the bible aloud. She said it would assist mother and baby to find some peace. After all, they had their own suite in the train. Her husband was spending most of his time in the smoking car. This suited her, as the idea of him bursting in and seeing her exposed flesh made her feel revolting.

She looked down at her daughter's tiny face and wondered how long it would be until she began to cry from fatigue and an empty belly.

After their arrival at Point Nepean the nurse swiftly assisted her with the transfer from the carriage into their new home, then disappeared just as quickly. Eleanor wanted to beg the woman to stay. She could not bear to be left alone with this unhappy, crying babe. However, she kept her mouth tightly shut and did not say a word.

Days later, when things should have settled, there was no improvement. Audrey would not feed and was losing weight. The doctor at the base called on her at the request of her husband.

'It would seem your baby has a bad bout of colic,' he said.

'What am I to do?' Mrs Price asked with concern.

'Gripe water will do the trick, and after you have fed her, keep her sitting up whilst she burps — although breastfed babes do not need too much coaxing. I will call on you in a day or two.'

The next two days proved more difficult than Eleanor had imagined. Audrey was excreting everything from both ends of her tiny body. Eleanor had not slept and was suffering anxiety each time Audrey cried.

By the morning of the third day since the doctor's visit, Audrey had stopped crying and her tiny body was limp. She was cool to the touch, and Eleanor knew she was on the verge of losing her baby. She wrapped the fragile child in a shawl and ran from the cottage. In relation to providing care and love for her daughter, she felt so alone. Her husband was away for days at a time in the fortified area of the point and would not return until tonight at least. By that time their baby would be in Heaven. Eleanor needed to take things in hand and get her baby the help she so desperately needed. The doctor's lodgings were not too far from her cottage. She ran to his door and rapped numerous times. Fearing he was not at home, she began to sob and yell through her tears.

'Please help me. Is there anyone home?'

The door opened suddenly, and there stood the dishevelled doctor with a half-buttoned shirt and roughly pulled-on trousers with their suspenders dangling round his hips.

'Come in. Come in,' he ordered. 'It is far too cold to be out there.'

'She is so sick, Doctor.'

The doctor checked Audrey over and looked grim when he turned back to Eleanor. 'I think it best we summon your husband.'

Eleanor was already crying and his words only increased her sadness. 'No, please do not tell me I will lose her,' she implored.

'I am afraid she is suffering from gastroenteritis and she is much too young and fragile to survive it.'

'Please help her. Please.' She clutched his sleeve.

'We will attempt to hydrate her but our efforts could be futile.'

The doctor sent word to Lieutenant Price to summon him with haste from the fortification site five miles away to the end of the point.

Within the hour, the baby's father was barrelling through the door of the doctor's cottage.

'What is going on?' he asked in anger.

'She is dying,' came Eleanor's reply.

'Is there nothing to be done?' he asked the doctor with vigour.

'We are attempting to hydrate her but I fear it will not do her any good,' the doctor said.

'She is so cold,' Eleanor said as she cradled her baby in her arms and tipped a tiny glass beaker to the tiny lips.

'I want to place her in a warm bath,' she said.

'That will not prove worthwhile,' the doctor said.

'It can not do any harm,' the young mother snapped. 'If I am to lose her I want her to feel warm and cared for until her last breath.'

'Very well,' the doctor said as he left the room before returning with a washbowl.

'I am boiling the kettle over the fire. It will not be too long. We will make the water as comfortable a temperature as possible and place her in.'

An hour later the baby lay in the warmth of the small washbowl. Her skin looked a nicer shade of pink and she began to look lively as she kicked her feet against the edge of the basin.

Over the next hour, Eleanor continually topped up the cooling water with warm water. She also regularly tipped a tiny beaker of cool water to her baby's lips. By the early hours of the morning, things seemed to turn fully for tiny Audrey. It would seem that her mother's persistence had triumphed. Over the months that followed, each time Audrey kicked her feet in a warm bath, her mother was reminded of the day that the water had saved her baby girl.

Returning from her reverie over the healing properties of the water that had saved Audrey, Mrs Price lamented the fact that the same could not be said of Charlotte. The water, after all, had not spared Audrey from giving birth to the Devil's spawn in the form of her own child.

'The water. That is what took her, you know,' Mrs Price said aloud, quite forgetting she was not alone.

Celia was confused but did not want to question Mrs Price considering the older woman's agitated state of mind.

'I know, I know, the water did have an affect,' Celia agreed.

Mrs Price's eyes began to close. She fought against sleep and tried to open them but to no avail. Within seconds she was snoring.

Celia waited a few minutes before backing out of the room. She closed the door behind her and walked briskly to town. Hailing a carriage, she ordered the driver to deliver her to the asylum, hoping Charles would be within easy reach upon her arrival.

She found him in the hospital cottage suturing the finger of Daphne, a kitchen hand.

Celia tapped at the door and apologised for disturbing him.

'Come in,' he said with the same look of longing he felt each time he saw her.

'I am happy to wait until you have concluded.'

'Not at all, I can continue whilst you are here. Besides, Daphne would love to have you assist me. Wouldn't you, Daphne?' Charles clasped the woman's shoulder.

Daphne laughed and looked at Celia. 'Help, Miss Celia, help him,' she giggled.

'Of course, Daphne. What have you done to yourself?'

'It was the silly knife's fault.' Daphne shrugged and shook her head and laughed heartily.

'Well, hopefully you will be as good as new so you can make bread with me soon. You promised you would give me another lesson.'

'Yes, Miss Celia. I will be as good as new soon, soon, soon.'

Celia took hold of the woman's other hand and held it tight while Charles completed his task.

Catching him staring at her between the needle and its negotiations, Celia stared back at her husband with a dead-pan gaze.

His eyes softened each time he looked at her. 'Thank you, Mrs Lawler. I believe you have made this ordeal more bearable for our patient.' He placed his hand on Daphne's shoulder. 'All done, Daphne. I'll check on your wound in a few days. In the meantime, keep it dry.'

'Thank you, thank you,' Daphne heralded as she backed away from them.

Charles turned his attention to Celia. 'Now, let me get that cast off that arm. For I assume that is what's prompted this visit so early in the day? I intended to do it last evening, but forgot, after all. Seeing you made me unravel somewhat.'

Ignoring the remark, she said, 'You are so good to the women in here.'

'Oh it is all part of the oath. Here, sit.'

Celia sat in the chair Daphne had vacated. Charles moved his chair close to her and bracketed her legs with his whilst taking to the plaster with a huge pair of secateurs. The crunching sound of the plaster being prised apart was unnerving at best, but she adored the cool air cascading over her skin as it was freed from the grip of the heavy manacle.

'I think it is more than that. You really do care and they respond to that. Trust me, unkind people cannot make others feel at ease. Sincerity is key.' She found she could easily stare at him as he concentrated on the task at hand.

'It means a lot to me to hear you say such things. It fills me with hope I can be forgiven, if just a little.' He glanced up at her.

'And calling her a "patient" sounds more caring than the word "inmate", which is such a horrid word. Makes them sound like prisoners in here, which they are not. They have not broken the law.'

'There, all done.' He said as he gently turned her hand over. You have lost some size on that arm but it will return once you strengthen it again.

'Do you need to reset it?' How she hoped it was not the case.

He moved it this way and that. 'Bend your wrist.'

She moved it slowly.

'Does it hurt?' He looked almost pained.

'No, it feels quite stiff but I feel it is well mended.' She stood and gently smoothed her skirt. 'Now, I have just come from the Price's home. It seems Eleanor is more ill than you know, although one would lay the blame for this in the bottom of a sherry bottle.'

'Oh,' he raised his eyebrows. 'I can call on her this evening after I finish here.'

'Well, I did say I would fetch you. She did not fight me on the topic but sung your praises as all do.' She smiled at him.

'You flatter me, Mrs Lawler.' They stared at one another across the surgery until Celia smoothed her skirt.

'I think I will call on her on my way into town. I left her asleep and alone. I am unaware when and if the Colonel or anyone is expected. I will assure her you will call on her this evening.'

Charles walked toward her and held the door open as she

set her hat on her head. As she passed him, she stopped. She looked up at him and studied him. He seemed to be holding his breath. His blue eyes still amazed her and she was propelled back to the presence of the man she had fallen in love with more than two years ago. 'Thank you for relieving my arm,' she said.

'You are most welcome, my love.' She could not help what she did next. Standing on tiptoe, she brushed her lips across his mouth and without turning back walked briskly away.

Celia felt her husband's eyes burning into her back and she could fathom a guess he was smiling in spite of himself. She was warming to him once more and she had just given him some hope. Something he could hold onto.

It was well after dark when Charles arrived at their residence. Celia was serving the dinner that had been prepared and left in the stove.

'Thank you, my dear,' Charles sat down and looked from the plate to Celia.

'How was Mrs Price?' Celia asked immediately.

'Very pickled, I am afraid to say.' Charles looked defeated. 'It was very difficult to capture any sense from her. The Colonel seems to have given up on her. He has taken to travelling at every opportunity. I am afraid if she is left alone much longer she will end up in the one place she resents.'

Celia did not respond in the way she once would have. 'So be it, the alcohol will push her over the edge to death or institutionalisation. There may be nothing else for it.'

'You are becoming insensitive to all of this. I am unsure whether to worry or celebrate it?' Charles said around a mouthful of food.

'I have crossed over to a full understanding of what is fated and what is self-inflicted.'

Charles stared at her with feigned surprise. 'Much to your consternation at this time, I have to tell you that I fall further in love with you every moment. Whilst I cannot fathom the depth of your intelligence, you have grasped my heart and will forever hold it in the palm of your hand.'

'Why do you question the depth of my intelligence? Is it so foreign to you that a female can use her own wit to decipher further intrigue?'

'Celia, please do not jump on the only nuance of the statement I have made that could conjure any negativity. I am stating that you have connected with me more widely and fully than any other female has or ever could. This connection is so unfamiliar to me, you must give me the benefit of the novelty of the idea that a woman can hold such foresight and intelligence. I do not mean this to be negative but to the contrary, it is something of such beauty.'

Celia opened her mouth. Charles stopped her. 'Please. Wait. I have been patient with you these past days and it is driving me to the brink, to be perfectly honest. I love that you challenge me. I love that you chose me when I least expected you to enter my life. I loathe that I mistreated you and mistrusted your judgement. I do not think I will ever truly forgive myself for what I did to you. And if I had lost you I would have joined you in Heaven mere moments after your heart ceased beating.'

'It does flatter me to hear that you could not continue to live if I had not, but I will not cease learning everything I possibly can to educate myself and in turn create a better life for others.'

'I will make mistakes and I will occasionally question your insights but I want you to know one thing. You can continue to punish me but I will never risk losing you again. That I can promise.'

'Thank you. I believe you and I am beginning to trust you once more,' Celia said before continuing to eat in silence.

She was tired. After the meal she excused herself and headed for her bedroom.

'Do you need help retiring?' Charles said in earnest.

'I am fine,' she said quietly.

Celia untied her hair and pulled her nightgown over her head. She caught her image in the mirror and stared back at the woman she had become. Her childhood was gone, the youthful innocence she arrived with had drained away and in its place a woman stared back at her. She was different now. In the few short years since she had walked away from being a minister's daughter straight into the arms of the dashing young doctor, she had found her destiny. The life she had forged had toughened her, educated her and made her see far beyond anything she knew could exist.

She could not stave off the crashing of emotion that fell upon her. She was meant to have found the path she travelled. If not for Charles, she would never have discovered her capabilities. If not for him, she would never have found the poise to question or push against convention. He was the reason she sought to gain access to the asylum in the first instance.

Convention had made him react in the way he only knew. But now, he was making every effort to regain her trust, and to create a clear path for her work and her vision.

She dashed from the room and did not hesitate, did not

tap at the door but plunged headlong over the threshold. Charles was sitting up in bed; the lamplight cast a shadow over his features. He held a journal in one hand and whipped his glasses from his face with the other. She crossed the room and fell onto him as his arms enveloped her and his breath left him in a whoosh.

'I love you,' she whispered. 'It is all because of you I have become this.'

'A force to be reckoned with?' he chuckled and rolled her onto her back.

He pushed the hair from her face and stared down at her.

'Thank you for coming back to me.' His tone was so heartfelt she pulled his face down and kissed him deeply.

He peeled her nightgown over her head and ran his hands over her skin. 'I will never let you go.'

'You will not have to.'

He held her in his arms and for hours he made love to her.

She did not return to her bed that night. They slept entangled together.

The next morning, Celia and Charles woke to familiar noises ringing out from the kitchen. The aroma of breakfast was wafting through the residence. Departing the bedroom, they moved to the dining room, where they sat smiling at one another across the breakfast table.

'I am going to call on Mrs Price this morning before I arrive for my scheduled surgeries.' Charles let out a sigh.

'I will call on her, if you wish. After all, you look a mite tired this morning.' Celia stared at her husband, hiding her smile behind the rim of her teacup.

'No, I am not all that tired. Just absolutely sated, you could say.' He raised one eyebrow. 'And I would be at your mercy if you would call on her. It would spare me the time of doing the full circle from here into town and back again.' He pushed his chair from the table and kissed her lips. The kitchen maid was pouring Celia a second cup of tea. Leaving it only half full, she made a hasty retreat from the dining room.

Chapter 30

Celia pushed the unlatched door open. 'Mrs Price, are you awake?'

There was no answer. Assuming Mrs Price could still be in bed, Celia walked inside and dropped her coat and gloves onto the kitchen table. She tapped gently at the bedroom door and in a soft voice so as not to startle Eleanor said, 'It is Celia Lawler. Mrs Price, are you … '

Mrs Price's bed was empty and in a state of disarray. Celia walked back through the house and checked every room. There was not a sign of her.

She began to panic. Where could Mrs Price be at such an early hour? It was difficult to pinpoint a starting place for a search.

Celia decided to check the laundry room, although she had no idea why. The yard was clear of any tell-tale sign of her whereabouts. Celia walked back inside and opened the front door. She walked out onto the veranda and craned her neck to peer up and down the street.

She breathed a sigh of relief as a carriage rolled to a stop at the front gate. She moved towards it. 'Mrs Price.'

Eleanor Price peered from the window. 'Who is that?'

'It is Celia Lawler. Is everything all right, Mrs Price?' Celia was quite shocked at the dishevelled appearance of the older woman. 'I came to check on you. Did you take the medicine Charles left you yesterday evening?'

Ignoring the question, Mrs Price announced, 'He told me that you are working in that cess pit up on the hill.'

Celia was quite confounded. It would seem Eleanor Price had no recollection of their discussion from the previous day. She continued unhindered. 'Do you not hold any decency? The whole town is talking, and your aunt, God help her. She can barely show her face in church these days.'

'Well, I am sorry to hear that,' Celia said, realising she was apologising more for her husband's sake than her own. Charles would be scorned at having no control over his wife's actions and for that she felt remorse. Her aunt had revealed the attitudes of the townsfolk and she herself knew how her work was being received. It was untoward for a woman to undertake the responsibilities she had — although personally, she felt she did not need to apologise for her actions. If the truth were to be revealed, Celia had her suspicions as to the gossipmonger leading the talk that shamed her aunt.

Celia stepped closer to the carriage. She placed both hands on the open window and leaned closer. As Mrs Price also leaned closer and spoke into her face, Celia could smell the pungent odour of alcohol. 'You, you are risking yourself in that filthy demon-infested place. The Devil had taken her over, you know? That is why we put her there. It will take you over too before long.'

Mrs Price's harsh words were alcohol fuelled but they held

such menace. Celia worried that Mrs Price's illness was leading her into hysterics. If she could not calm Eleanor herself, she realised she might have to drag Charles back here after all.

Celia whispered so as not to have any information befall the driver's ear. 'Mrs Price, I realise it was a difficult decision to place Audrey in there but you were left with little choice. What Michael did was a tragedy. Had anyone been suspicious of what was to eventuate I am sure they would have tried to prevent it.'

'Tragedy? He did us all a favour, ridding my departed daughter of that Devil's illness. God rest her soul.'

Celia stood aghast at Mrs Price's loud response. The driver could hear her every word. However, she did understand the anguish Mrs Price must be feeling with the loss of her granddaughter at the hands of her own daughter.

'I feel we should discuss this matter inside the house.' Celia declared.

Mrs Price placed her fist to her mouth. 'Michael was not the reason she is gone from us. If it were not for that baby, we would have never lost her in the first.'

Realising the older woman was not about to depart the carriage, Celia grasped the handle of the carriage door and climbed aboard. She sat beside Mrs Price and placed her arm across her shoulder.

'You must not think such a thing. That innocent child could not be responsible for your deep loss. I realise nothing I could say can bring that poor little babe back, nor your Audrey.'

Mrs Price looked at Celia as though she had never laid eyes on her before.

'I thought Audrey would get better.'

'It was not to be.'

'I tried to bring Audrey back to me but it did not work.'

'Mrs Price, I think I need to get you into the house and back to your bed.' Celia grasped Eleanor's hands and backed out of the carriage.

The carriage tilted as their weight dispersed and Eleanor began to topple as her feet hit the gravel. She waved Celia away from her. 'I do not need to go back to bed. I need another drink.'

'With respect, Mrs Price. It is still only breakfast time.'

As Celia helped Mrs Price down the walk and helped her traverse the front steps she did not notice the bottle held beneath Mrs Price's arm and covered by her shawl. As they entered the darkened hallway, Mrs Price stopped and stared ahead.

'I really do think you should get some rest,' Celia said from behind her.

'It happened right there.' Mrs Price pointed her index finger in front of her.

'What was that?' Celia quizzed.

'I drowned her. The bath was right in there on the kitchen table.'

Surely, grief had rendered Mrs Price quite mad.

'Audrey nearly strangled the life from me when she saw what I had done.'

Mrs Price dropped to the floor. The forgotten bottle finally released from beneath her arm smashed as they both hit the floor. Celia reached forward to catch her but was too late as her form collapsed and she let out an anguished cry.

'Leave me, leave me,' she yelled as Celia attempted to help

her back onto her feet. Mrs Price sobbed and pounded the floor with her fist. 'I thought I could bring my Audrey back. If I could rid her of that Devil child she and Michael had spawned I was sure she would come back to me.' She looked up at Celia who had stood up in shock and taken a step away.

Mrs Price pointed her finger at Celia. 'And now I know he had the Devil in him too. She was with babe before they were married. God punished them. Then Michael killed her. He killed my Audrey.' Celia watched her pick up a piece of glass. Mrs Price wrenched the broken glass back and forth up her arm with such aggression that it sounded like fabric tearing.

'Oh my goodness, Mrs Price. No!' Celia grasped the woman's hand but was too late to stop the deep gashes she had created in her flesh.

Celia ran out into the street yelling for help. The carriage they had departed minutes earlier was standing alone without its driver.

'Driver! Driver!' she yelled. Within moments Mr Smythe from across the street came racing down his driveway.

'Where is the driver?' she huffed.

'I have no clue,' he said. 'What has happened?'

Celia's mind was spinning. She did not want anyone to know of Mrs Price's present state but there was no way around it. 'Oh, Mr Smythe. I need you to assist Mrs Price. She is in need of medical attention. Can you go inside and help her?' she implored.

'Of course. Of course,' Mr Smythe said as he rushed up the path.

The high step was proving difficult as Celia made numerous attempts to climb aboard. Finally, she landed in the driver's seat of the carriage, kicked the brake off and slapped the reins so hard the crack sounded like bone breaking. The horse took off so fast she feared the carriage would topple at the first corner.

Deciding that travelling via the main gatehouse would take far too long, Celia took the back road to the asylum. When she reached the rear gate she jumped from the carriage and unlatched it before swinging it open as swiftly as her strength would allow.

Clambering back up into the driver's seat, she rode the carriage over the rutted tracks between the vegetable gardens before throwing the reins to a curious inmate who had wandered toward her. 'Please look after this and do not move!' she ordered.

She pulled her skirts up and ran. She yelled and yelled for Charles as she passed every building and doorway. Inmates turned to stare at her and the orderlies shook their heads, indicating that they did not know where Charles was.

She recalled her husband was performing surgeries today. She bolted inside and ran to the surgical room housed at the end of the first floor hallway.

She burst through the door as Charles, with a nurse in attendance, lifted an instrument over the body of an inmate.

'Celia, what on earth?' he stared at her.

'I am so sorry … ' Celia looked from the nurse to Charles, '…to barge in on you.'

'What has happened? Are you all right?' Charles searched her features.

'Come, come with me,' was all Celia could manage. She was breathless.

'I just need to finish up. I will be a minute or two. What in the blazes is going on?'

'Mrs Price, it is Mrs Price.'

'Nurse, I will leave you to clean over the wound and bandage it. I will call back here as soon as I return.' He was wiping his hands on a piece of hospital linen. 'I will alert an orderly to summon Matron to assist you,' he called as he strode from the room with Celia.

Charles followed his wife to the carriage as she stumbled over her words while trying to run once more.

The horse was frothing at the bit as it raced back to the Price home. Once it drew to the curb with Charles and Celia at the helm, the driver, who was standing on the roadside, grabbed the reins and hurled abuse at Celia.

'I will have you arrested for this.'

'I apologise for my haste but it was an emergency, you see.'

Charles grasped Celia's elbow and gently propelled her toward the house. As he did so he called over his shoulder to the disgruntled carriage driver. 'I can assure you I will sort this out in due course but cannot right now.'

Mr Smythe stood from his kneeling position beside Mrs Price. He looked relieved as he saw Charles approach and quickly stood back, allowing him space to kneel beside her. Mr Smythe shook his head as though the situation were a hopeless one. The dark crimson patch that ebbed through the cloth that Mr Smythe had attempted to tie around her arm had done nothing to stave the blood. It pooled beneath her body as a stark indication that she had been drained of life.

'There is nothing to be done,' Charles said as he looked up at Celia. 'I am sorry you had to bear witness to this.'

He stood up and placed his hands on her elbows. Celia's arms were crossed over her stomach in a ploy to hold herself together. She shook her head. 'No, do not apologise. I am so saddened that her life is over but I am thankful the truth has absolved Audrey.'

Charles looked to his wife. 'What makes you say that?'

'I will explain later,' she said as she averted her eyes to Mr Smythe as he made his way from the room.

'I think it best if you leave this scene and return home now.' Charles said.

Celia nodded her head in earnest. 'I think I must be kept busy. I feel I am best placed to offer assistance back at the asylum. That way I can await your return.'

Without argument Charles said, 'Well, then that is where I will see you once I have completed my task here.'

Charles accompanied Celia from the house and watched with concern as she departed on foot. His wife walked with a rigidness that spelt out to him that she was trying to keep a hold of her nerves. He needed to get this situation in hand as quickly as he could to allow him a hasty return to the asylum to tend to his wife's needs. The importance of this was not lost to him.

Mr Smythe was standing on the veranda. 'Thank you for your assistance today,' Charles said as he placed his hand on the man's shoulder. 'It would be splendid if you could race into town and call upon the undertaker and Constable Bryant in turn.'

Hours later, Charles locked the front door of the Price home and watched the undertaker pull away from the kerb. The constable said, 'I will send a telegram to the base where the Colonel visits at present and alert him to this tragedy.'

Charles shook his head. 'Three generations snuffed out in such a short time. I just cannot fathom it.'

'The Colonel and Mrs Price buried their daughter and granddaughter only weeks ago,' the constable said as he was reminded of the family's turmoil.

'Indeed.' Charles did not care to elaborate. The less said the better. 'I will ride with you into town then take to the road by foot back to the asylum.'

'I will take you back to the hill, Doctor Lawler. I can save you some time,' Constable Bryant said.

'That would be such a help,' Charles replied.

As Constable Bryant directed the horse and wagon through town, he and Charles talked with regard to J Ward and the criminality of inmates housed inside. It was a common topic that they both possessed extensive information about.

'You have done more than your duty calls for. Just leave me at the gatehouse and I will walk the rest of the way,' Charles said.

'Only too happy to help, Doctor Lawler. 'Next time you are in town we can have a drink in the Shire Hall Hotel.'

Charles shook the constable's hand and walked past the gatehouse and up the driveway. Entering the asylum, he immediately began to search for Celia.

'She is in Matron's office,' Trinny said when he arrived at the hospital cottage.

Charles went directly there and found his wife sitting opposite Matron. She was sipping a glass of sweet sherry and looked entirely wrung out.

'Doctor Lawler, I hope you do not mind but I decided to retrieve Mrs Lawler from the laundry room until your return. She has told me of the events of the day and with all due respect, I feel her place should be at home until she has recovered. After all, her arm and health are not fully restored.' Matron held her shoulders square and her pose dared Charles to trifle with her current demeanour.

'As you wish, Matron.' Charles nodded. 'I will see to it she is accompanied there and looked after until my return this evening.' He looked at Celia. 'I apologise that I cannot stay with you myself. I have to complete my scheduled surgeries.'

'That is quite all right,' Celia said.

Charles looked at Matron. 'Could you see to it one of the nurses accompanies her?'

'I will see to it myself, Doctor Lawler.' The grim line on Matron's lips softened, as she knew she would not have to argue her point.

Matron deposited Celia into bed and set a tray of food beside her. She placed a pillow beneath her arm. 'This still requires looking after,' she said as she gently touched Celia's arm. Looking down at her, she added, 'I should have never let him … '

'It is all in the past now and I have forgiven him fully. You need do the same. He is remorseful for his decision but if you must know I have come to the full realisation that everything that has befallen us has happened for good reason.'

Matron patted her hand. 'I am only glad you have survived recent events, and that once that arm has healed and you put some weight on that frame of yours there will no further reminders of all that has happened.'

Hours later, when Charles returned home, Matron wasted no time bidding him goodnight rather curtly before heading out into the dark. She was still cross with him for having treated his wife so dismally. Whispering to herself, she said, 'Grace, you know the pain a doctor can take away, and you rue the agony he can inflict.'

Matron allowed her anger to stave off the tears that always threatened. She had learnt over time and was well aware that while the respect of a doctor could be earned in the time it takes to strike a match, that same reputation could be lost in the split second it takes for a whisper to blow the flame from the head ...

'My, you are a young one, aren't you?' the Matron of the New Norfolk Asylum exclaimed. She looked at the woman she would mentor, all the while wondering if this mere slip of a thing would last the week.

Grace looked like a tiny mouse draped in a heavily starched uniform, which moved in opposing direction to the rhythm of her gait.

'So, you did your training at The Royal Hobart Hospital?'

'Yes, Matron,' the young woman said as she cantered beside the older woman.

'Very good. That is where I trained. Now, once you have settled into your quarters I will introduce you to the doctors. There are three on staff and the superintendent lives on the grounds. The superintendent oversees all medical decisions, surgeries and staffing.'

Matron opened a door to a tiny room and stepped inside. There was a bed, a bedside table and a gentleman's wardrobe in the corner with a washstand containing a bowl with a pitcher beside it. 'Have you undertaken any work in an asylum until now?' she asked her new charge.

'No, this is my first experience in an institution,' the younger woman remarked as she placed her suitcase on the floor.

'The New Norfolk Lunatic Asylum is the only one of its kind in Van Diemen's Land. I am sure you will become familiar with its workings. After you unpack your belongings I will show you around the entire facility and explain to you the expectations of your work. The superintendent is aware of your arrival and will meet with you at three o' clock sharp. I will be back in fifteen minutes,' Matron said as she pulled the door closed.

Grace waited a few seconds to hear Matron's footfalls fade to silence before she sighed and sat down heavily on the edge of the mattress. The bedframe creaked and the lumps that made up the uneven mattress pushed against her buttocks. She looked around the room. It would do nicely. She hung three dresses in the wardrobe and had to push her full weight against the door to close it after she had forced her winter coat inside. She pulled the pins from her hair and felt the tension in her forehead ease. Scrounging in her bag, she found her hairbrush and scraped it through her hair. It caught on a number of knots so she pulled at the brush until her hair was smooth and she could tie it into a thick ponytail before winding it into a fresh bun and fixing it with pins once more.

Matron knocked on her door exactly fifteen minutes later.

The halls and wards were easy to traverse. Grace committed them to memory immediately as the scale of the building was less than half the size of the hospital she had trained at.

Matron knocked on the superintendent's office door at precisely three pm and led her inside.

'Doctor Martin, this is our new nurse, Grace.'

Doctor Martin looked at her expectantly. 'Well, hello. Matron, thank you. That will be all.'

The sound of the door closing thundered in her ears. She did not expect him to be young … and handsome. He stared at her as the seconds ticked away. 'So,' his voice came at her rather loudly and she jolted. 'I am sorry. Did I startle you?'

'Uh, no,' she lied. 'I have travelled all day and I fear I am rather tired.'

'Well, I do hope you manage to get some rest whilst you are here in our employ. The hours can be arduous and the inmates do not always comply with our agendas.' He looked down at the pages on his desk. 'I can see that you are well qualified after your tenure at Royal Hobart. It is a splendid hospital. Tell me, did you work with Doctor Walshe?'

'Yes, I did. He is a dedicated doctor and gave so much time to the nurses.' She could not hold eye contact with him and found that she kept darting glances from his desktop to his face. He stared at her with such ferocity as she answered his questions and his gaze wandered down to her mouth as she spoke. It was most uncomfortable. She could not keep her mind on a particular path. He pulled a leaf of pages from his desk drawer and held it in his hand. This is the latest report on the asylum. He handed it across the desk to her. She looked at the title page. *Hospitals for the Insane: Report of the Inspector of Lunatic Asylums for the Year Ended Dec 31 1844.*

Doctor Martin pointed across the desk at the pages. 'I would like it if you would read it. It will familiarise you with the practices we are implementing moving forth and allow you to make comparative notes during your time here. I have made extensive inroads into the care of our inmates. Our success will be measured against the numbers from this year's report and the next.'

Grace cast her eyes down to the pages. Doctor Martin rounded the desk and leaned in so he could peruse them as well. He licked his finger and pushed it against the corner of the page and flipped it, then another and another until a table with lines of figures covered the page. 'There.' He pointed down to the fine black print. 'This number list is what I want to focus on in the coming months. All staff will work united to see this number diminish.'

'I see,' Grace said quietly. He was standing so close to her shoulder she could feel his chest pushing into her. The warmth of his breath cascaded across her cheek. She could not make out any of the numbers or the lines of description depicting the differences between them all. She could not concentrate with him hovering above and across her. Looking up from the page, she was startled when the intensity of his eyes hovered over her face. He stood, and stepped away from her. 'So, I think you should take that report with you and read it. Return it to me when you have finished it and we can discuss any questions you may have.'

Grace delivered the report to him the following day.

'Take a seat,' he said as she entered his office with the report held firmly in her grasp.

'I read it, all of it, and I have some ideas,' Grace said as she pulled a note from her uniform pocket.

'I am stunned. I did not expect you to have pored over it in one evening. You stated you were rather tired.'

'I was rather spent but I thought it best to begin my work here as quickly as possible.'

'Well, that is most impressive, I must say,' he said as he placed his elbows on his desk.

Grace opened the report and found the page she sought. 'Well, it states here that there were a large number of Phthisis cases in the last year. I compared that with the previous eighteen years, also in the table on page six.'

Before she could lift her eyes from the pages he was at her shoulder once more but this time he pulled a chair from the corner of the room and proceeded to sit beside her.

'The print is so tiny. I think it best if I sit here so I can see precisely what you have seen.' He looked down at the page.

'As I was saying … ' She cleared her throat and wished for the heat creeping up her face to abate. 'The cases of … '

'Consumption.' He finished the sentence for her.

'Yes.' Grace cleared her throat once more. 'In my work at the hospital over the past three years … '

'My word, you are very young to have been at this work for three years already. How old are you?'

'I am almost twenty,' she said as she placed her finger on the number she wished to point out for him. 'If we confine inmates with the symptoms earlier we can confine the disease. It is far more contagious than first thought. That would decrease the number of cases and in time, hopefully diminish them all together.'

He was silent for a time. Grace looked sidewards at him.

'I am considering the space we would need to make available but it is a good point you make.' He placed his hand on her shoulder.

The first days of her work at the asylum left her exhausted. Nights bled into daylight hours and the quality of the rest she found in her room provided no respite from the fatigue she was feeling.

A separate infectious ward had been set up in the hospital wing of the asylum and Matron had showed great pleasure as her newest trainee nurse demonstrated such promise to the superintendent.

Grace found herself seeking out Doctor Martin around the wards. Depending on the time of day, she would greet him with a 'good morning' or a 'have a pleasant evening'.

It was late in the afternoon one day when he passed her in the hallway and said, 'Nurse? Would you care to join me on the hospital ward round?'

'Yes, yes I would enjoy that,' she said as she turned and joined him in the direction in which he was walking.

'I am so refreshed to have you working with us. You will prove to be a competent nurse after your tenure here. It is a shame you will not make a career of it.'

Her heart dropped. 'I am sorry Doctor, have I done something wrong?'

'To the contrary, I think you are doing a fabulous job but I fear you will be courted and married before you have a chance to reach your potential.'

Grace looked at him, confused. He winked at her and continued to the end of the passage.

She stood on the opposing side of the bed as Doctor Martin checked the inmate's pulse. The older woman looked across to her and said, 'Very pretty.'

Doctor Martin placed his stethoscope to the woman's heart and listened.

The young nurse looked from the inmate to Doctor Martin and his gaze held hers. Quickly looking away, she then questioned whether her imagination was set upon something that was not there.

Slowly shifting her gaze back toward him, her question was answered. His eyes continued to penetrate the distance between them.

Grace had had experience with men and their expectations of women, having combatted unwanted attentions from hospital patients. In this instance, however, she did not want Doctor Martin's attention to cease. He was a lovely looking man and she could only dream of having such a man fall in love with her.

It would never do. Nurses and doctors were at opposing ends of the social scale; she had never heard of a doctor marrying a nurse. But now she had to admit that ever since meeting this doctor she found she had tried to please him every which way — from her range of greetings to her ideas about to how to run the asylum more efficiently.

The pair walked from the hospital ward in silence for a time before he stopped. As though he had just had a revelation, he rubbed his chin. 'Could you come to my office later to discuss further ideas for the inmates and their care?'

'Yes, of course, doctor, of course.'

'I believe you will be a valuable asset to me. I may never let you leave.' His words were flirtatious and the true meaning of them was not lost on her. His eyes teased her in a way Grace could not misread. She wanted him to know his attraction was not one-sided.

'Oh, I doubt that, Doctor Martin. On the contrary, I may never want to leave if you continue to shower me with good words and kindness.' She cast her eyes up to his and blushed. 'But, I do have ward rounds. I fear the hour will be late by the time I complete them.'

'I am here every hour of the day and night. Visit my office and if I cannot be found there I will be in my quarters.'

'Very well. I look forward to it,' she said.

'As do I,' he said as he touched her cheek with his index finger.

She was in love with him. He was married and she had only found this out when a lovely young woman with three beautiful children by her side stopped in for a visit.

'This is Mrs Martin,' Matron had said as she made introductions.

Grace gulped visibly. Doctor Martin had a wife? Well, of course he had a wife. No handsome man who had such a social standing and bold disposition as his would still be a bachelor, after all. How could she have been so silly and fallen beneath his spell? He had never mentioned that he had a family residing in Hobart while he worked at the asylum in New Norfolk.

The fatigue Grace was feeling now seemed entirely due to the stress of finding out Doctor Martin was married. She worried that her life of being a nurse would hold nothing more for her now that she had given her virginity so willingly. When her monthly flow did not appear her shame and remorse at her situation became dire. If it were not for Matron showing her such understanding at her predicament she did not know what she would have done. Doctor Martin had organised a transfer for her back to the Royal Hobart Hospital before Matron intervened and put her on duties in the maternity ward and nursery in the grounds beside the asylum.

Doctor Martin had shown her no respect since the news of her pregnancy became known. Thankfully, nobody asked who the father was; the question would have highlighted the disrespect everybody felt for her but dared not show outwardly. Matron demanded her nurses be treated with respect and politeness at all times and this rule protected her from the hurtful talk that was being conducted behind staff members' hands.

Labour started as tiny pains in her abdomen on a Wednesday afternoon and increased like a tide ebbing in and out of a rocky coastline. Each contraction felt like hands scraping her from the inside and tearing their way out of her body. Her baby was born at two am. Matron insisted she be left alone with Grace. The tiny baby made hardly a whimper when she entered the cold hospital ward. Matron allowed her to hold her baby for a moment before she gently took her from Grace and wrapped her in a cotton blanket and placed her in the nursery. The following day Matron organised for the adoptive parents to collect their new baby girl.

Grace watched from the terrace of the hospital ward as a nurse passed her baby into the waiting arms of her new mother through the open door of a carriage. 'She is a beautiful baby,' Matron said as she placed her arm across Grace's shoulder.

'I know,' Grace whispered. 'And she will have a wonderful life. A life I cannot give her.' She watched the carriage pull away.

'I think it best I seek a transfer away from here, Matron. I need to make a brand new start.'

'I respect that, however I will miss you,' Matron said as she squeezed Grace's shoulder. 'I do think you need a few weeks to heal after giving birth but after that time I will refer you to whichever hospital you would like to work at.'

'I have already thought about it, and I would like to travel to the mainland to seek work at one of the hospitals there.'

'That would assure you the disconnection of Doctor Martin.'

'Yes, I believe it would.'

The carriage was almost beyond the front gates. 'Goodbye, Erin,' Grace said and buried her face in Matron's bosom as she sobbed for the loss of her self-respect and the child she would never know.

Looking over her shoulder as she continued to walk away from the superintendent's cottage, Matron could see through the lace curtain of the bedroom as the kerosene lamp cast light inside. Charles' mouth was moving. She smiled at the situation and how well it had turned out. She realised she could somewhat slowly move past her disappointment of Charles' treatment of his wife.

Had Matron not ended up at the New Norfolk Asylum as a young nurse, her life could have been so different. If it were not for her mentor taking pity on her, she would never have survived the birth and relinquishment of her only child. And although the memory of that time in her life had dulled somewhat, she would never forget the power doctors wielded as they forged their careers, nor her sorrow over the lives they often left in tatters along the way.

Chapter 31

Celia watched Charles from the doorway of her bedroom and raced towards him, falling into his arms as he turned to her after locking the door.

'Oh my darling, what a horrid day you have endured.' Charles ran his hands up and down her spine to comfort her.

'I cannot believe the unrelenting tragedy that keeps befalling the Price family.'

'The Colonel has been alerted and is on his way home. He will arrive shortly. I have offered him our assistance.'

He walked Celia back to her bedroom and deposited her back into bed. 'Do you require something to calm your nerves?'

'You, I need you. I need only you.' Her fear that she was still suffering shock eased after he lay down beside her and held her close.

'I have spent the entire afternoon reliving the scene I witnessed this morning. The words I heard tumbling from Eleanor Price's lips will haunt me forever but I am thankful I learnt the truth. I am sorry she took her life amid the pain and shame she felt.'

'It was such a drastic incident. How could she be so tortured to slash her wrist like that?'

'I believe she was,' Celia said quietly. 'She told me that, confessed to me, that it was not Audrey who killed darling Charlotte, it was she herself.'

'You are not making sense, my darling. I think the shock of today has unsettled you.'

'No, Charles,' Celia said with impatience. 'Whilst today has been arduous, I speak the truth of all that happened. She, Mrs Price, held Charlotte under that water. It was not Audrey.'

Charles placed his hand up to Celia's forehead.

'I am fine, Charles.' She gently moved his hand away. 'Mrs Price believed that if she extinguished Charlotte's life, it would deliver Audrey back to her. The Audrey she once knew.'

'That is grim. I will undertake the task of letting the Colonel know of this upon his arrival.'

Celia stared up at him in earnest and replied, 'I think the lie needs to be uncovered and Audrey unburdened. The truth will give her the respect she deserves. God rest her soul.'

Charles closed his eyes for a beat and slowly nodded his head. 'That is the least we can do for that poor girl's legacy.'

'I love you,' Celia whispered as she kissed him.

'I wish I did not have to leave you,' he said as he placed his lips on her forehead and allowed them to linger. Whispering against her soft skin he said. 'I must meet the Colonel at the station.'

'Now?' she said in surprise.

'He is arriving on the last train.'

Celia slipped into sleep minutes after Charles' departure

but was awoken by the movement of the mattress hours later as he slid into her bed. She knew the hour was late as sleep pulled her back down amid the salacious feel of the warmth of his body against her back. He draped his arm over her hip and flattened his hand on her stomach.

In the morning Celia accompanied Charles to the asylum. As they strolled from the back gate toward the main building, Celia angled numerous questions at him. 'Was the Colonel really inconsolable?'

'Yes, Celia. I told you. He was quite distraught at seeing her body at the undertaker's parlour.'

'Distraught or inconsolable? They are vastly different words, my darling. Is he distraught that he has to deal with the situation at hand, or inconsolable that his wife is dead ... or worse, guilty of murder?'

'That mind of yours frightens me. The man's daughter, granddaughter and wife are all gone, and tragically, I may add. I can only appease you by saying he is dealing with every emotion after being presented with the painful truth.'

Celia relished Charles' calm demeanour. He was not angry with her for speaking her mind, which was usually the end result of their conversations. He now understood and respected the angles from which she looked at every scenario.

'I can understand that,' Celia said.

'Doctor Lawler!' Old Jim yelled from the vines.

Charles walked in the direction of the man. 'We need your help,' he said as Charles drew nearer. 'In here.' He pointed to the shed.

'Stay there,' Charles yelled over his shoulder at Celia, who was following close behind him.

Charles disappeared inside. He did not need an explanation as to what he was required to do. There was an inmate convulsing on the dirt floor. Charles dropped to one knee and grabbed the man's shoulders, attempting to turn him onto his side.

'He has bin like this for near on fifteen minutes,' Old Jim said.

'What can I do?' Celia said as she crouched beside Charles.

'I should have known you would not heed my instruction.' Charles did not break his concentrated stare on the inmate. 'Go to the hospital cottage and fetch me some Potassium Bromide,' he said. 'We have to break the hold this seizure has on the poor chap.'

Celia said, 'What do I have to ask for?' Charles looked at her and was perplexed at how shaken she seemed by the scene before her.

'Sodium Bromide.' Charles squeezed his eyes shut and shook his head. 'No, I mean Potassium Bromide. You are causing me concern, Celia.'

'I am all right, truly I am,' she said as she touched his arm and rushed from the shed.

She returned minutes later with a cup of milky coloured liquid, which was splashing over the sides. 'The nurse said I should only need a small amount so I raced here as fast as I could. I do hope I have not spilled too much along the way.'

'It will be sufficient,' Charles said as he held his hand out.

Celia handed the cup to him and was relieved that the young man was now sitting up with the wall at his back.

Charles held the cup up to the man's lips and allowed him to have a small sip. 'That will do. It should have an effect shortly.'

For the first time since entering the dark and damp shed, Celia saw another inmate in the vicinity. He looked frightened beyond reproach.

'Are you all right?' she asked. The young inmate did not answer her but stared directly at the recovering young man.

'He's mute, Mrs Lawler,' Old Jim said.

'Oh,' she replied. 'Can anybody communicate with him?'

'He can.' Old Jim hitched his chin at the man sitting against the wall.

'If he is one of the only people that communicate with him, there is no wonder he is looking on with grave concern.'

Charles looked at Celia. 'I will have an orderly get you to the hospital cottage. I think you need some rest.' Charles placed his hand on the inmate's shoulder. 'I would like to observe your seizures further and see if we can establish a pattern.'

''There is no need,' the inmate said.

'I believe there is.'

The inmate looked toward his distressed friend. Celia swung her gaze between both men.

'Your friend will be able to visit with you,' she said.

Charles let out a breath and looked to Celia.

She did not acknowledge his gaze.

'Old Jim, wait with Patrick until the orderly comes. If the seizures start again, get Thomas here to run and fetch me. I will be in my office.'

'Yes, Doctor,' Old Jim said.

Charles gently gathered Celia by the arm and walked with her back out into the morning light.

'I am trying my best to be patient with you, my love, but you will defy me every step of the way.'

Celia smiled. 'You know me so very well. May I ask the age of the young man you just assisted?'

'Patrick Riley? He is in his early twenties.'

Celia clamped her lips together and looked into the distance. She was deep in thought. Charles noticed the intensity of her stare but before he could ask her to divulge just what was going around in her mind she kissed him on the cheek and walked toward the laundry room.

Celia joined Charles in his office an hour later. She was smiling after having called in to the laundry room to see her cherished women, who had rejoiced at her return and chatted animatedly about Maryann's good fortune at finding her lost love.

Someone had delivered a pot of tea to Charles' office, so Celia poured herself a cup. 'I have been thinking about something,' she announced.

Charles placed his hands up to his temples and rested his elbows heavily on his desk. 'God save me.'

'Those young men in that shed today.'

'Yes.'

'How long have they been in here?'

'Since boyhood. I looked over their files extensively as they were caught up in the incident that claimed Michael.'

'Have they been educated?'

'You know the answer, so why pose the question?'

'Just checking.' She smiled.

'A school should be available to the young folk in here. No, make that all inmates in here. I see no reason why they should not have the opportunity to be educated just like any other person. Their ailments do not make them stupid.'

'Celia, I have a vast amount of work to undertake because of you. Please allow me to deal with one task at one time before jumping to the next hair-raising scheme.'

'My apologies, but there is so much I would like to do and I feel time is rushing past.' Celia placed her teacup on the desk before gathering one for Charles and walking around to where he was seated.

'I love you,' she said as she placed the cup down. Charles looked up at her and she bent down to kiss him with such adoration he could not help but gather her in his arms, pull her onto his lap and kiss her until they were disturbed by an orderly knocking at the door.

Chapter 32

The white headstone bore the name of mother and child. Celia felt tears begin to well in her eyes. Her show of emotion was acceptable, given the circumstances. The townsfolk had turned out in their best funeral clothing to pay their respects to Eleanor Price. The large deep hole looked gnarled along its edges from the earth that had been dug from inside. The size of the heaving crowd of townsfolk coming forth to pay their respects was sobering. People looked down at the coffin that sat atop timbers in readiness to be lowered.

Through the gap between the edges of the coffin and the plot, encased in clay on all sides, was another coffin, which looked macabre. Celia closed her eyes and felt the tears being squeezed from her eyelids. She knew that everyone around her believed that inside that coffin already deep below the surface was the remains of mother and child, but it pained her to know that the tiny coffin holding Charlotte was deeper still.

Charles had told her that the undertaker had been paid a handsome sum to maintain the pretence that baby Charlotte and her mother were together in death. Celia felt so pained that Charlotte and Audrey were in fact not together. It was such a sad situation.

She watched the Colonel bid his wife goodbye and wondered where he would find the strength to live a life where there was nothing left of his legacy.

After the coffin had been lowered into the grave and the crowd had moved en masse to the church hall, Celia insisted on helping with the tea service. This manoeuvre helped stave off any questions being asked of her and it kept her from sitting in the nearest chair and nodding off to sleep. She was so tired. The refreshments began to run low as the immense crowd gathered to pay their respects, while also making it their business to not require supper that evening. The crowd finally began to thin out by late afternoon.

Celia did not think she could remain on her feet one moment longer. Her arm ached from overuse. She was really struggling to give it the rest it required to heal but was so thankful the weight of the cast was no longer dragging it down. Several women surrounded her in a tight circle and were chatting incessantly about her trip to see her family and her welcome return to the district. Just as one woman asked her if she had heard any news of Mrs Rushby, Charles appeared at her side. 'Ladies, could I be so bold as to whisk my wife away? I think I need to get her home for some much needed rest.'

'Of course, of course,' they all nodded in unison.

'Thank you,' Celia sighed as Charles deposited her into a carriage.

'The Colonel is drowning his sorrows at the Shire Hall Hotel. I promised I would meet him for a drink before retiring home.'

'That is quite all right,' Celia stated. 'I am so very tired. I will be asleep as soon as my head feels the feathers, I am afraid.'

'May I wake you?'

She held his face between her hands and kissed him.

'I will take that as confirmation.'

'Thank you, driver,' Charles said as he jumped from the carriage step and watched the vehicle draw away.

Charles crossed the street to the Shire Hall Hotel and once inside ordered a whiskey.

'Charles, over here.' The Colonel pulled a chair out as Charles approached the table.

'You know John, Bill and Reg.'

Charles shook the men's hands in turn. 'I believe I do.'

In the days leading up to the funeral, Charles had invested in numerous conversations with the Colonel. They had discussed all angles of his wife's demise and what could only be inconceivable events at her hand that had led to the death of their granddaughter and in turn, to their daughter's estrangement.

It was not discussed at present among the group of men, but Charles seemed to be under the watchful eye of them as they downed their spirits hand over fist. He found himself bombarded with questions on the events of Doctor Rushby's removal from his post at the asylum and his instalment in new quarters in a holding cell in the gaol in Melbourne.

Charles imagined that these men's wives had sent them on this errand to gather as much gossip as they could muster.

'So Charles, how much information does your wife gain from those crazed fools you have locked away up there?' one of the men asked.

'Well, it has been a revelation to be quite frank with you. She has succeeded in discovering some of the women's relations, people who had no inclination that their loved ones were locked away.'

'Really?' Reg said, looking much too animated for Charles' liking. As the smoke from the Colonel's pipe curled between them, Charles carefully applied bait to his hook. He knew this man was Maryann's father. The poor young woman had been left in the asylum and in turn, injured by the infamous Doctor Rushby. Judgement must have appeared on Charles' face with such obviousness that Reg stared at him shrewdly.

'I know what you are thinking, Doc, but you would never understand.'

'I believe that I may not truly understand, but that does not mean you have not done anything untoward.'

'If you intend undoing any of the work Doctor Rushby was so stoic in creating, think again.'

Charles stared around the table and realised that there was a hidden agenda in his being invited here.

'I did not intend to pry into the workings of the asylum before my tenure began. After all, I can only establish and work within the government's agenda.'

'If not for the government allowing every foreigner onto our soil, we would never be in this predicament,' another of the men said.

Reg leaned forward and stared Charles down. 'Doctor Rushby would turn a blind eye for a quid. Let's hope you know when to do the same.'

It was a bold look that passed between them. Charles held Reg Harper's threatening stare. 'I have taken an oath, gentlemen, and I intend to keep it. Should I believe that there is cause to seek the constable's counsel, I will undertake it. Do not threaten me and do not question my wife's unwavering support of the women who are in my care. It is truly a revelation that, unhindered, she could care for strangers. It is more than can be said for the familiarity of family and a love that cannot stretch beyond judgement.'

Charles looked at the Colonel. 'I apologise for such harsh words but I must preclude you from this conversation and the attitude I have just expressed.' He and the Colonel shared a knowing look between them before Charles stood, tipped his hat and departed the hotel.

He did not mention his conversation to Celia as he climbed into her bed and wrapped his arms around her.

'I fear I am exhausted but cannot sleep,' she said into the darkness.

'Here, let me help you.' Rolling her onto her back and pulling her nightgown up to her hips he settled between her legs and entered her. Slowly and with gentle motion he made love to her. Within moments she closed her eyes and purred her undying love for him. He held her in his grasp and felt her slip silently into the depths of slumber.

Chapter 33

'He is far too heavy for you to carry. Why did you not think to organise a baby carriage for him?'

'I know, Aunty. I should have been better prepared but time ran short.' Celia held the chubby little hand in hers and squeezed the plump flesh. 'The letter Charles received must have been waylaid in the post. It was dated weeks ago. I worried that this little one would be moved if I waited one more day.'

'I doubt that. Nobody wants the boys,' Lady Montague stated.

'Well, this sweet little boy is definitely wanted. There is not a doubt about it.' She smiled down at the toddler who tried to escape her lap. Celia grappled with him. 'You were easier at the start of our journey when you were asleep,' she said to the squirming little boy.

'I will go to the dining car and get him something to eat and perhaps a cup of milk. That should settle him for the rest of the journey,' Lady Montague said as she stood to leave the suite.

'Thank you, Aunty. That would be splendid.'

The hour was late when their train pulled in to the station at Ararat. Celia was surprised at the protraction of time it took to depart the train and station with a young child in tow.

'Could I ask that you drop me at the asylum on your way? I do not want to wait another moment to reunite this little one with his mother.'

'Very well,' Lady Montague said as she ordered the driver to deliver them to the asylum.

From the top of the drive, Celia waved goodbye to her aunt, who stared up at the façade and visibly shuddered. 'I cannot believe you enter that place of your own accord,' she said beneath her breath as she waved.

Celia held the toddler on her hip and swayed gently from side to side. Matron opened the front door to the asylum and a broad smile spread across her mouth.

'Say hello to Matron,' Celia said to the little boy.

He looked at Matron and a smile formed on his cherubic lips.

'Well hello, little one,' Matron said as her arms automatically reached forth.

'Thank goodness,' Celia said as she handed him across and shook her arms by her sides. 'He is heavy.'

'He is one heavy little chap. Yes you are.' Matron touched his chubby cheek.

'He is an absolutely delightful little thing,' Celia said.

'Yes, I believe he is.' But as Matron looked at him, her smile slipped slightly.

'Is everything all right, Matron?' Celia was shaking her coat from her shoulders.

'Yes, yes. I am fine.'

'May I fetch her?' Celia asked with trepidation. 'I know the hour is late.'

'Absolutely. We shall not delay a moment longer.'

Celia borrowed Matron's key and raced her way through the ward. She unlocked the door.

'Who is it?' Maryann yelled in terror.

'It is only me,' Celia said in a quiet voice.

'Oh Celia, you gave me such a fright.'

'I am so sorry, my lovely. Are you still jumping at every sound?'

Maryann was pushing her hair out of her eyes. 'I am afraid so. I believe it will take some time for the memories to fade.'

Celia clasped Maryann's hand and pulled her out into the corridor. 'I have somebody who would like to meet you.'

The light from the kerosene lantern splashed across Maryann's features. 'Is Lee here?' She began to giggle. 'Ah, but of course I have already met him. Who could it be, then?' she said as she walked beside Celia and looked at her. 'Give me a clue?'

'It is a surprise. You will see,' Celia said.

Maryann wept when she saw her not so little baby in Matron's arms.

'Oh, my precious little boy!' Maryann grasped him and held him close to her. The toddler placed his hands up to her chest and pushed. He looked at her face and frowned. 'Oh, I cannot believe I am holding you in my arms.'

'He recognises your voice,' Matron said.

Celia let the tears run down her own cheeks unhindered.

'How can I ever thank you, Celia? How?' Maryann said as she clutched her child to her.

'This is thank you enough. I am so glad we could return

him to his mother and hopefully, in time, he will know both his parents.'

'Oh, that would be so wonderful,' Maryann said.

'I cannot take much of the credit, I am afraid,' Celia said, as she thought of Charles' unrelenting work to have the baby returned.

Maryann was crooning to her son, who was watching her in astounded silence.

Celia thought better than to present the details of Charles' efforts to uncover the truth for Maryann and Lee to reunite.

Matron looked at the little boy. 'I think it is time to get the little fella off to bed.'

Maryann clutched him to her chest. 'Where will you take him?'

'I do not think it acceptable that he be placed in the ward cell with you.'

'Please do not take him, Matron. I do not think I could survive till morning. What if something was to happen to him?' Maryann was becoming hysterical.

Matron placed her hand on Maryann's arm. 'I was going to suggest a room in the hospital cottage for you and your little one tonight. Just until we can organise better lodging for the two of you.'

'Oh, thank you, Matron.' Maryann jiggled the toddler in her arms.

Celia and Matron accompanied Maryann to the hospital cottage and assisted her to settle into a room with her beautiful boy.

'I will walk you home, Mrs Lawler,' Matron said. 'You look exhausted.'

'I am rather tired,' Celia said, 'and with good reason.'

Matron smiled. 'I thought as much.'

Matron walked through the grounds of the asylum and looked up into the night sky. 'You have done something wonderful Mrs Lawler.'

'Oh, I think Charles is the underpin to all this.'

'My little girl was adopted the moment she was born,' Matron said.

'Oh, I did not know,' Celia said.

'No, nobody does except the matron that looked after me back in Van Diemen's Land at that time.'

'How difficult for you.' Celia placed her hand on Matron's arm as they continued to walk toward the back gates of the asylum.

'I believe she had a good life. That is all I can believe and hold onto,' Matron said.

'She would be well into her middle fiftieth years now,' Matron said matter-of-factly.

Celia kissed Matron on the cheek. 'You are a wonderful woman and a mother and nobody can take that fact away from you.'

'Thank you, Mrs Lawler. You are so gracious and always know quite what needs to be said,' Matron said with the shimmer of tears forming in her eyes.

Celia squeezed her hand. 'It is true. Goodnight Matron and thank you for being truly precious to us.'

'Goodnight, Mrs Lawler.' Matron leaned into Celia. 'And congratulations on the wonderful impending arrival.'

'I am home,' Celia announced as she unlocked the front door.

Charles met her in the hall. 'I was almost ready to come in search of you.'

'It has been a long day but a most fruitful one.'

'Sit down, then. I will get you a cup of tea,' Charles said before disappearing into the kitchen.

Celia was smiling as Charles deposited the tray and poured her a cup of tea.

'I believe the day went well then,' he said.

'Oh yes.' She rolled the back of her head against the couch. 'Maryann has her beautiful little boy back in her arms. I am so satisfied and so proud of you. Without your lobbying we would have been unable to secure him and return him to where he rightfully belongs.' She smiled at him.

'Well, I will attempt to score even higher points from you,' he said.

'Really?' she questioned. 'Please, do tell.'

'Well then, I organised for Lee to be brought up to my office and I listened with intent to the tale he had to tell. As confirmation would have it, there were no asylum records with regard to the young miner. This confirmed Maryann's story and in turn Lee's. He had been stolen from his bed in the middle of the night and become a hostage of the asylum. As there are no records on the young man, I do not need to seek the necessary signatures to secure his release. So instead, I escorted him to the front door of the asylum, opened it and ushered him out.'

Celia placed her teacup on the saucer before placing it on the side table. She knelt in front of her husband. 'I love you more and more as each moment passes,' she said as she kissed him.

As she sat back and placed each of her hands on top of his thighs and stared up at him, he said, 'I realise that having Maryann in the asylum with the baby is not the ideal scenario, so I hope in the time it could take to acquire her release Lee may be able to take the child.'

'I do not think she will cope all that well without him but if he is with his father it may make the situation more bearable.

'I have been trying to secure the signatures required for her release but her parents will not hear of it. I will try as early as tomorrow to put a plan into action,' he said with severe concentration covering his features.

'If I did not know any better I feel I have created a mirror image of myself in you.' Celia laughed. She began to stand and gathered Charles' hands. Pulling him up from the chair she said, 'Let us retire for the evening.'

'You climb into bed. I will join you in a few moments,' he said before kissing her soundly on the lips amid a promise he would take her gratitude and sate himself with it.

The following morning Celia remained in bed long after Charles had left for the day. She was feeling so tired from the events of the day before and had morning sickness. The housemaid set down for her a tray with a cup of tea and a piece of toast slathered with strawberry jam. Celia scraped most of the jam off before taking measly bites of the toast until her stomach stopped roiling. She would tell Charles in the next day or two, after things had been settled with Maryann and Lee.

Charles made a trip into town before heading to the asylum. He did not want Maryann to wait one moment longer to begin the life she truly deserved.

The bell above the door tinkled as he walked into the mercantile. 'Hello, Reg,' he said as the man looked up from the counter.

Reg Harper did not acknowledge Charles with a greeting. Their last discussion after Mrs Price's funeral had not ended in a gentlemanly fashion.

Charles placed his hand across the counter. He waited seconds until Reg slowly extended his own hand and clasped it firmly.

'I have come to discuss a situation that requires rectifying.'

'And that would be?' Reg said as he straightened the boxes on the counter.

'It is unfortunate that I feel this visit necessary, but I must implore your signature and that of your wife's to secure the release of your daughter from my care.'

'Absolutely not,' was the man's immediate response.

'And why not?' Charles leaned his forearms on the counter with his hat held in both hands.

'Because I will not ever be rid of her. After the shame she brought to us, there will never be another man within a hundred miles of this place that does not know her history.'

'I am sorry to hear that, Reg,' Charles said as he peered through the glass-topped counter at the boxes of packed tobacco. Looking up at the older man, he fixed his gaze on him. 'I will tell you what I will do for you. In return for those signatures, I will not expose that you kidnapped a miner from his bed and disposed of him at the asylum. How does that sound?'

Reg Harper's face turned red and he walked around the counter and stepped close into Charles' immediate space. 'Who in Hell's name do you think you are?'

'I know who I am but do you know what kind of man you are!' Charles stared the man down.

'You cannot prove a thing.'

'Oh, but I can. You see, I have set the man in question free and he has assured me he will happily speak to Constable Bryant.'

Charles saw the man's gaze falter and knew he was closer to achieving Maryann's release.

'I think you owe it to your daughter to give her a chance at the life you robbed from her. If you sign for her release, I promise to make unavailable the information that the constable would relish.'

Only minutes later, as Charles departed the mercantile tucking the requisite paperwork into his jacket pocket, he was satisfied. He did not bid Mr and Mrs Harper a good day on his way out.

Whilst it would have been ideal for Maryann to run from the asylum that very day, Charles and Matron had discussed at length the best way to traverse the present situation. A room in the hospital cottage was turned into a comfortable bedroom for Maryann and James and Lee had visited Maryann each Sunday where they would attend the church service together, with their little boy James bounding around the ballroom. It created such a light atmosphere during mass.

Quite quickly, Lee found work at a farm on the town's outskirts. He was saving every penny and was weeks away from securing acreage to build a life and a home for his family. Eventually, a date was set for Maryann and Lee to begin the life they had planned on years earlier. There were no invitations sent. Everyone who needed to be there to witness this day was already in place.

The day was overcast but there was happiness bristling among the women in the laundry room. Celia had been busy all morning with preparations for the day.

The ballroom was transformed into a scene of billowing white silk draped along the pews. Bunches of flowers had been tied to the silk, and the bright coloured roses threw the ballroom into a kaleidoscope of sweet smelling life.

The chaplain welcomed the guests as the bride and groom stood before him to pronounce their undying love.

Celia was Maryann's attendant, and Lee's brother was the best man.

Maryann and Lee's little boy was the cutest pageboy anyone had ever seen. To have a child among the congregation really made for a joyful union and celebration.

After dark, Maryann and Lee's open wagon rolled down the drive and away from the asylum. With their child tucked inside a blanket, sleeping like an angel on the flat bed, they began their new life, albeit a few years later than they had planned.

The following day was Sunday and the weather was fine. Charles surprised Celia with a carriage ride to One Tree Hill. The lawn was crowded with picnickers, but Charles still managed to lay claim with a blanket the exact spot where he had presented Celia with an engagement ring two years earlier.

'This is a lovely surprise,' Celia said as she sat with her legs directly in front of her and leaned back on her elbows. She pointed her face up to the sun, closed her eyes and breathed in the scent of the wattle trees.

Charles dragged her feet up onto his lap and took her shoes off. She hummed with pleasure.

'I love to see you happy,' he said as he gently ran his hands along the arch of one foot and then across and over the top to her ankle.

Celia closed her eyes and sighed at the immense pleasure he was relaying to her. 'Do you remember the first time we found ourselves in this situation?' she said.

Charles laughed. 'You were such an innocent young thing. Little did I know the challenge you would present.'

'Would you have run a mile had you known what was in store for you?' Celia opened her eyes and smiled at him.

'I did not have a choice in the matter. I loved you from the moment we were introduced at your aunt's party.'

Celia thought on it a moment. 'I think I loved you the moment I saw you across the room, before we were introduced.'

'Must you always best me with your answer?' He ran his hands up her calves.

'Well yes, Doctor Lawler, I believe I must.' She leaned forward and grasped his shirtfront and spoke close to his mouth.

'We are having a baby,' she whispered.

His eyes widened before he drew her to his chest.

'Oh my darling, that is wonderful news!'

Celia laughed. 'How do you like that for a surprise?'

'It is no surprise. I knew you would bear me a child sooner or later. But what will this mean?' he said with a smirk on his lips. 'Will it finally force you to hang up your saviour's hat and return my inmates back to me fully?'

'Not at all.' Celia looked aghast. 'Prior to our baby entering this world, I possess plenty of time to action my new idea.'

Charles let out an exaggerated sigh. 'And pray tell, what is it?'

'The school I wish to set up.'

'What!' Charles bellowed.

Celia noticed that Charles had startled a few nearby picnic groups, and found it difficult to suppress a smile. 'I talked to you about it a few weeks back,' she simply replied. 'All those young inmates — well, actually, all of them, regardless of their ages — should be offered the fruits of knowledge.'

'Celia, really?' He was perplexed.

'Just because somebody has an ailment does not mean they are beyond educating. Why, there as so many young men in the place who could benefit from some education. Some of them have been locked away since childhood and they are not stupid. Just like those two young men in the shed.'

Charles looked puzzled.

'Remember, the poor fellow having the seizure and his distressed friend. They could be taught a trade or to read at the very least. Even the deaf and mute inmates could learn sign language. Everyone should learn it. The staff could do with the basics of it so they could communicate with them also.'

'I think you are unaware of the limited capacity some of these folk have.'

'That is my point, Charles. They are being limited because nobody is giving them the benefit of trying to teach them. I insist that those two young men are capable of learning.'

'I am aware of Thomas and Patrick's capacity despite their shortcomings. But Celia, truly, do you realise what it will take to employ a teacher?'

'We will seek volunteers. That is what happens at other

facilities. I have read about the industrial school they had in Sunbury many years ago, which used the premise that young men could be taught a trade to create a fulfilled life.'

'Those boys were not imbeciles or lunatics. They were orphaned,' Charles said.

'At the very least let me attempt it? It will not waste my time and it will work. I just know it will.'

'You will give it some of your time but not all. You will have to garner some rest in the next few months.'

'I realise my energy levels will dictate my parameters. And I will adhere to them, I promise.' Celia placed her hand on her belly. 'And I intend to spend less time at the asylum once our baby is born. I promise it will take up less of my time.'

Charles flung his hands up. 'Hallelujah! Finally, I have gained an insight into your inner workings.'

'And what is that?'

'If I yield to all your whims, you reduce the ferocity of your exploits.'

'Well done, Doctor Lawler.' Celia giggled.

'Now allow me to feel elation at our impending arrival.'

'As you wish, Doctor Lawler.' Celia grasped his hand and placed it over her abdomen. 'This is going to be so joyous.'

'Yes, yes it is. I would have it no other way.'

Celia whispered, 'I am so lucky to have found you, Doctor Lawler.' She kissed him so soundly that they were quite unaware they had an audience of shocked onlookers and nor did they care.

Lightning Source UK Ltd.
Milton Keynes UK
UKHW010630061120
372920UK00001B/128

9 780648 880707